THE BUSINESS AND PROFESSIONAL COMMUNICATOR

WILLIAM W. NEHER

Butler University

▼

DAVID H. WAITE

Butler University

Allyn and Bacon

| BOSTON | ▼ | LONDON | ▼ | TORONTO |
| SYDNEY | ▼ | TOKYO | ▼ | SINGAPORE |

Series Editor: Steve Hull
Series Editorial Assistant: Brenda Conaway
Composition Buyer: Linda Cox
Manufacturing Buyer: Louise Richardson
Editorial-Production Administrator: Elaine Ober
Text Designer: Helane Manditch-Prottas
Editorial Production Service: Helane Manditch-Prottas
Cover Administrator: Linda Dickinson

A Division of Simon & Schuster
160 Gould Street
Needham Heights, MA 02194

Library of Congress Cataloging-in-Publication Data

Neher, William W.
 The business and professional communicator : theory and
applications / William W. Neher, David H. Waite.
  p.   cm.
 Includes bibliographical references and index.
 ISBN 0-205-13994-9 (pbk.)
 1. Business communication. 2. Communication in organizations.
3. Business communication—Problems, exercises, etc.
4. Communication in organizations—Problems, exercises, etc.
I. Waite, David Hawkes, 1944–   . II. Title.
HF5718.N35 1992
651.7—dc20   92-18899
                                                  CIP

Printed in the United States of America

10 9 8 7 6 5 4 3 2   95

BRIEF CONTENTS

CONTENTS

Communication is essential to success in many fields—in business, government, education, and other professions. When executives or recruiters are asked to name the skills or abilities that are necessary to their enterprises, they invariably emphasize the communication skills.

Let us first consider entry-level skills. The career development and planning office at a large state university asked over seven hundred corporate recruiters what they sought in college graduates. The responses indicated that the most critical attributes included skills in written communication, oral communication, decision-making, positive attitudes toward the "work ethic," good judgment and maturity, well-developed work habits, and interpersonal skills.[1]

Surveys of business leaders have long emphasized the importance of effective communication in continuing success on the job. Such surveys report that skills most often mentioned include the following:[2]

listening
written communication
oral reporting
motivating and persuading
interpersonal skills
interviewing
small group (team) problem-solving

In one study, four-hundred and fifty directors of corporate training were asked to identify specific communication skills that seemed most needed in their organizations. Their responses referred to management-employee relations, problem-solving, decision-making, leadership, and listening.[3] These findings were supported by a study conducted by the authors of this book in which we surveyed training directors in a metropolitan area. These surveys all point to the critical importance of several types of communication in professional lives and in the functioning of today's organizations. And, they emphasize a further point that we wish to underline here: communication skills are necessary in a variety of settings.

Of course giving speeches and making presentations require good communication skills. But, effective interviewing, training, mentoring, problem solving, bargaining and negotiating, team leadership, and team participation all place a premium on one's ability to interact and communicate effectively with others. These activities are usually carried out in face-to-face situations, but increasingly they may be enacted through electronic or computer-mediated means. In any event, they are situations that demand sensitivity to the dynamics of human communication.

Many large organizations have recently initiated programs aimed at developing new communication strategies to improve their overall competitive position. These efforts involve managers spending more time in the field with employees, explaining, persuading, reassuring, and listening. Management recognizes that effective decision making is enhanced by increased face-to-face dialogue throughout the organization.

PLAN OF THE BOOK

You will see that many of the topics covered in this book are responses to these considerations and needs. Our approach reflects some important developments that we feel will affect students in the coming decades. We believe that students will find themselves working increasingly in multicultural and international environments. As we move through the 1990s and into the next century, workplaces will exhibit greater ethnic, gender, and cultural diversity than in the past. Communication is an activity especially affected by rules, norms, and nuances which are themselves highly dependent upon social and cultural factors. We believe that any text intended to prepare students for careers in this likely future must take account of these factors. As a result of this concern, we cover several topics often not found in similar texts. These include discussions of dealing with sexual harassment; the use of mentoring as training and for increasing access for women and minorities to management positions; and problems of adapting communication systems and settings for physically challenged individuals.

We give attention to the increasingly global nature of business and the professions and the demands such an environment places on our abilities to communicate. Other real-world factors affecting communication in businesses and the professions include legal and regulatory environments and the growing use of new communication technologies that will affect how interpersonal communication is carried out in business and professional organizations.

Our main focus will be on communication involving primarily oral discourse (written communication will not be directly covered). The book is divided into four sections as follows:

Part I is an opening section that introduces the theoretical principles covering business and professional communication. While the first chapter treats communication as a message-creating, message-sending, and message-receiving process, we believe that there are important insights to be gained from applying a transactional view of communication, especially when considering the complexities of face-to-face, interpersonal communication.

Following a general introduction to the nature of human communication, the second chapter reviews significant theories that bear upon communication within organizations—the environment for most business and professional communication. We then consider the skills involved in listening to emphasize, from the start, the importance of this sometimes neglected aspect of effective communication. We finish the opening part of the book with a chapter concerning intercultural communication in an increasingly diverse and global environment.

Part II deals with settings of face-to-face communication and highlights the importance of interpersonal and small group communication. We begin with a consideration of dyadic communication (communication involving two people) in work settings. We then take up the related topic of nonverbal communication as it affects this and other relevant communication settings. The following chapters move toward applications of these and earlier theoretical chapters in interviewing, group problem solving, and group leadership.

Part III considers public communication settings—those occasions when more formal presentations or speeches are required. Such settings are not limited to public, platform speeches. A member of a work team may be required to report findings to another group or to upper management. There are often occasions for briefings, lectures, training sessions, sales presentations, and so on, that involve many of the same principles. In general, these settings differ from interviewing or group communication in that the emphasis is on one speaker addressing many listeners simultaneously. These situations tend to be more formal and more structured than the dyadic or group settings. We conclude this section with a chapter dealing with mediated communication—touching on both presentational media (that media used as part of a formal presentation) and interactive media (that media used to facilitate interaction among participants, such as E-mail and other forms of computer-mediated communication).

Part IV deals with some more specific applications of communication skills in business and professional settings. We first present principles for dealing with conflict in constructive manners; the related skills of bargaining, negotiating, and mediating are the subjects of the following chapter. The final chapter concerns skills of communication training and helping others with their communication needs, as in speech writing. Recall that surveys of needed communication skills tended to indicate the felt need for help with applied communication skills of this sort.

Theory to Application

As we move through the chapters we tend to move from theoretical background toward more applied settings, in which theory provides the basis for suggested solutions to communication problems and needs. We believe that many communication situations are problem-solving situations. The problem involves coming up with the best technique, skill, or message to meet some need. Our intention throughout the book is to provide you with a systematic approach for solving such communication problems.

Learning Aids

Each chapter begins with a set of main *chapter objectives*, indicating concepts, principles, and skills to be learned. Highlights and summaries at the end of main sections and of each chapter review and reinforce the main ideas. At the end of each chapter we also include a set of exercises intended to direct you in skill-building activities. There are lists of recommended readings at the end of each chapter that can be used to begin further research in relevant topics and areas discussed in the chapter. We have also included several checklists and sample forms that you can use in preparing for different kinds of communication activities. These preparation aids include a checklist for preparing for an employment interview, a checklist for an agenda for a group meeting, a sample form for completing an audience analysis for a business presentation, and several others.

There are in addition special boxed features throughout the chapters providing examples and illustrations of the communication skills being discussed. You will also find *Problem-Solution Boxes* in each chapter which direct your attention to practical communication problems people often face in business and professional organizations. Each chapter also features a *Diversity in the Workplace Box*, which highlights communication issues resulting from the growing multicultural and international nature of modern organizations.

ACKNOWLEDGEMENTS

For their patience and encouragement, we would like to thank Nancy and Virginia, our wives. We appreciate the guidance and help of Steve Hull of Allyn and Bacon, whose enthusiasm kept us on track. We are also grateful for the editorial and production assistance of Helane M. Prottas of Graphic Design & Production, Elaine Ober of Allyn and Bacon, and copyeditor Carmen Wheatcroft. Judy Chapman provided much needed typing assistance. We also thank Professor Mark Uchida of the College of Business Administration at Butler University for bringing us into regular contact with undergraduate and graduate students in business administration. Finally, we wish to thank the reviewers of the manuscript whose suggestions and helpful criticism were extremely useful throughout this process: Pat Brett, Emory University; Ann Cunningham, Bergen Community College; Lawrence W. Hugenberg, Youngstown State University; Lee Polk, Baylor University; Paul Scovell, Salisbury State University; Gary M. Shulman, Miami University.

Ancillary Materials Available to Instructors

- Instructor's Edition
- Test Bank

- Computerized Test Bank
- CNN Video Communication Case Studies

Endnotes

1. The school was Michigan State University, see "Making an Impression," *National Business Employment Weekly: The College Edition*, Spring 1989, pp. 30–31.
2. For example, an early summary of such studies includes Vincent DiSalvo, David C. Larsen, William J. Seiler, "Communication Skills Needed by Persons in Business Organizations," *Central States Speech Journal*, 29:3 (1978), 163.
3. Janis Meister, and N. L. Reinsch, "Communication Training in Manufacturing Firms," *Communication Education*, 27:3 (1978), 235–244.

Basic Principles for Business and Professional Communication

This part presents an overview of theories and concepts basic to an understanding of speech communication in contemporary business and professional organizations. The first chapter provides an introduction to the process and elements of communication. We take a problem-solving approach in presenting a useful way to analyze what goes on when people communicate with each other. At times, for certain communication situations, a linear model of communication as described in the first half of the chapter is useful, while for other situations a transactional perspective on communication is suggested.

The second chapter summarizes theories and principles from organizational communication. We show how the major theories of organizational communication can be applied to typical communication problems in organizations. The next two chapters emphasize the importance of listening and of intercultural considerations in all kinds of communication contexts in the businesses and professions. The information about the elements of communication, the transactional nature of interpersonal communication, the principles from relevant organizational theories, the importance of listening skills, and the multicultural nature of the business and professional life provide a foundation for the skills and techniques developed in later chapters.

PART 1

Analyzing Communication

1

CHAPTER

After studying this chapter, you should be able to:

1. Identify and explain typical breakdowns in communication.

2. Describe the elements in the communication process.

3. Recognize that communication is not a one-way process.

4. Explain the transactional nature of human communication.

5. Understand principles for improving communication.

Overview

The subject of this text is communication. We will look at this most human of activities from many points of view, all relevant at one time or another to the communication settings you may find in your business or professional life. This first chapter introduces a way of thinking about communication in general. Each subsequent chapter builds on this introductory view of communication. By the end of the book, we hope that you will have a more detailed and insightful view of this subject.

We begin by thinking about practical problems that are also communication problems. Each problem emphasizes a different element or step in the overall process of human communication. After describing the problems, we will lay out the elements of communication as they are related to each type of problem. This approach will lead to principles that point toward solutions to specific problems. We conclude the chapter with a discussion of the transactional nature of communication.

THE PROCESS OF COMMUNICATION

Let's begin by considering different kinds of communication problems. Each type of problem occurs at a particular stage in the process of communication.

▶ **Typical Problems in Communication**

Type 1.   Sometimes you have to get the message across very precisely. For example, when a physician communicates with a pharmacist about a prescription, the exact message is important. In addition, the pharmacist must be able to communicate to the patient exactly when and how the medication should be taken. Some patients may have difficulty in following these prescriptions precisely, especially when they are using many different kinds of medications. Similarly, an accountant dealing with a client, perhaps in doing the firm's corporate taxes for a year, must ensure that communication of data is exact. A misunderstanding or miscommunication could result in fines and other penalties for both the accountant and the firm.

Type 2.   A second kind of communication problem is represented by the old story of the boy who cried "Wolf" once too often. The lack of credibility may not be the communicator's fault, however. For example, a young attorney may have difficulty getting a client to accept some advice or direction simply because of the client's bias about the attorney's age or perceived inexperience. Women who have been ordained as clergy report a similar problem with some members of their congregations, who may not yet feel comfortable with women as ministers or priests. Similarly, women moving into corporate executive and management positions may experience this type of prejudice.

Type 3.   The selection of the words or symbols we use to communicate our ideas can be a source of error. An airline tragedy occurred in the New York City area

▶ *The exact message is important when a physician communicates with a patient or pharmacist.*

when a passenger jet from the South American country of Colombia ran out of fuel while waiting for permission to land. Investigators reportedly discovered that the pilots had failed to use the specific words *fuel emergency*, which would have alerted air traffic controllers to the urgency of their situation. In this case, failure to use the proper or expected words led to disaster.

Type 4.   In surveying my desk, I notice that it is piled high with memos and notes, all containing messages of varying importance. My computer electronic mail (E-mail) flasher indicates that several incoming messages are waiting for me. Given time constraints, some of these messages will be shunted aside and perhaps never answered. The earlier air traffic control example again provides more serious examples of this kind of problem. On at least one occasion, a large airliner was inadvertently directed to land on a runway on which a small commuter plane was waiting for clearance for take-off. The resulting accident appears to have been due to an overloaded and overworked air traffic controller.

Type 5.   In the Midwest, Spring often brings tornado watches and warnings. Being able to interpret the difference between "watch" (conditions are ripe for a tornado to form) and "warning" (a tornado has actually been sighted in the area) can have life-or-death consequences. Consider this related communication problem: A high school student looks down when talking instead of looking directly at his teacher. As a result of the student's behavior, the teacher suspects that the boy is lying. Or, take the international business problem that occurs when the Japanese customer says to the American supplier that it will be necessary to consult the home office, when in fact the deal is already off. In these cases, interpretation of certain messages is important.

▶ *A messy desk represents overloaded channels of communication.*

Type 6.   A business executive named George runs into a different kind of communication problem. George is pleased to see that his boss agrees with his presentation of a solution to a tricky problem facing the firm: The boss nodded, after all, when George made each of his points. Imagine George's surprise later when the boss turned down his proposal. "But I thought you were agreeing with me during the presentation," George appeals. It turns out that the boss had meant to indicate that she was following the presentation and that by nodding she meant to show that she understood what he was saying but not necessarily agreeing with it. A related problem occurs when a conflict escalates from a minor disagreement to a major confrontation, as in the following dialogue:

Smith: "I'm afraid that, despite the attractiveness of some of your options, we will have to decline the offer."
Jones: "Not again. You never like anything that we present."
Smith: "That's not true, although I must admit that your presentations could be neater and better organized."
Jones: "So that's it. You think that we're sloppy."
Smith: "I wouldn't have said that—but now that you mention it . . ."

Type 7.   Let's return to intercultural communication to illustrate another type of communication problem. After the long flight to Narita Airport, the American marketing manager takes the opportunity at a dinner held in his honor to launch immediately into an explanation of the deal he hopes to negotiate. His hosts are offended and eventually decline to participate in the deal. We need not go as far as Japan for examples of problems such as this sort. Professionals occasionally find that they must deal with communications that are inappropriate to the time and place. Physicians are pulled aside at parties by people seeking a quick and free diagnosis of a physical complaint. Lawyers are similarly approached for free legal advice at dinners or social events.

Before suggesting solutions to these kinds of problems, we need to have a basic understanding of how we view communication. A preliminary description of the nature of human communication follows.

▶ Elements in the Communication Process

To analyze these problems, we must consider some of the characteristics of this process of communication.

Human communication is never direct. For example, we cannot simply pluck ideas from our heads and insert them directly into someone else's. This sort of thing may happen in science fiction, where occasionally "beings from other planets" have mind-reading capabilities. One famous character from the "Star Trek" television series had the ability to perform a "Vulcan mind-meld," which allowed him to make direct contact with the thoughts of another person through physical contact. Being merely human, we lack this ability, and it may be just as well. Surely there are times when you would prefer that your exact thoughts could not be read by your boss, your parents, or your significant other.

Clearly, before we can get an idea from our heads to yours, several intermediate steps must be taken. For example, that thought or image must be translated into words that you can understand (which could mean translating from one language to another). Our words may or may not be a precise formulation of what we have in mind. Then, we have to select a medium by which to send to you the words we have decided to use: We can use speech if we are all in the same room, or we can write you a note, send you a computer mail message, or call you on the phone. We then need to consider whether or not you receive the message, interpret the words in the way that we hoped for, and so on (see the steps illustrated in Figure 1-1). Because human communication is indirect, the risk of breakdowns or misunderstanding seems great.

This idea can be further clarified by drawing upon one of the major perspectives for studying communication, that is, information theory. In the preface, we indicated that there are several different ways to view communication, depending upon the point of view or the aspect of communication that one wishes to emphasize. The information theory perspective, which focuses attention on the step-by-step nature of the communication process, is most useful in explaining the transformations that the message undergoes as it moves from an idea in our heads to a thought in yours.

The central image of this perspective for analyzing communication was developed by an engineer, Claude Shannon, and a mathematician, Warren Weaver, who worked after World War II on developing ways to improve the transmission of messages over telephone lines.[1] Their linear model of communication directed attention to certain aspects of communication: the need for a channel to carry a message encoded in certain symbols. The two developers were hoping to prevent interference in the physical channel, such as static, from distorting the clarity of the encoded message, so that the signal received at one end of the line was nearly identical with the signal that had started out at the other end. While their model of communication was intended to be applied to physical or mechanical commu-

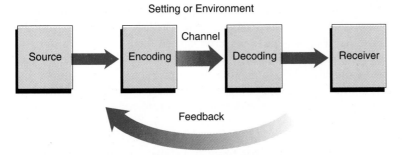

▶ **Figure 1-1** *A model of the elements and relationships in communication. Margo (source) wants to call in an order for 500 mats. She picks up the phone (channel) and calls Tim at Central Supply (receiver). Margo says, "I want to order 500 mats. That's number 5-04 in the catalog (encoding)." Tim hears (decoding), "500 rats." and says, "Rats? I'm confused. Do you mean mats? Number 5-04 is mats (feedback)."*

nication systems, certain of their ideas can be adapted to help us clarify the kinds of problems that were presented in the first part of this chapter.

The following elements of communication are suggested by thinking about communication from this linear perspective.

1. *Fidelity.* The main goal in communication is to ensure that a message gets from one person to another with the highest possible "fidelity." (Fidelity comes from the Latin word *fides*, meaning "faith.") For the purposes of this discussion, consider fidelity as illustrated by a stereo system. Such sound systems are still called "hi-fi," which stands for "high-fidelity" because the purpose of the system is to reproduce as faithfully as possible the sound of the original music. From this perspective, we can say that the goal of communication is fidelity.

2. *Source.* Communication begins with a source, which is usually a person who has some idea, intention, thought, that the source wishes to share with another person. The nature or identity of the source—that is, who says whatever—may be significant in determining how well the communication works. When the ancient Greeks developed some of the earliest systematic theories about communication, they used the term *ethos* to refer to the character of the speaker as perceived by the listeners. Contemporary theorists use the term *source credibility* to refer to the same concept. In addition, sources of messages may differ in their abilities and inclinations to send messages, and such differences may affect the communication process.

3. *Message, encoding.* A defining characteristic of communication is the use of a message to convey thoughts, images, feelings, and intentions. A message is built from a set of signs or symbols, which have a shared meaning among several people. Signs include anything that can be used to stand for something else, such as holding up three fingers to stand for the number "three." Symbols are special kinds of signs in that there is an arbitrary relationship between the symbol and what it stands for. For example, "door" is the symbol for an entrance to a room in English, but the symbol is "*la porte*" in French. English speakers act on the assumption that all other English-speakers have agreed to use the word *door* in that way. Often, in face-to-face communication, some messages are coded in symbols, such as words in speech, while some messages are in signs, such as nonverbal cues that indicate how one is to interpret the spoken message. The act of formulating the message, choosing which signs or symbols to use, is referred to as "encoding," or putting the message into a code.

Beyond this lexical level (the level of meaning of signs and symbols), the message can be encoded with certain structures and styles. For example, how the message is organized—what point is made first, what last, and so on—can determine its effect. Second, the use of humor can be a stylistic factor that could change the meaning of the encoded message as well.

4. *Channel.* Once encoded, the message must be physically transmitted by some means, in order to get it from person A to person B. The physical medium used for this is the channel of communication. In face-to-face situations, the channel can be the sound waves for conveying the words of speech or light waves for transmitting the sights of one's nonverbal signs. Other channels include computer-mediated systems, telephone lines, radio waves, and cables. The concern with channels is their capacity and freedom from interference or noise. Capacity refers to how many signs or symbols it can convey per unit of time. A "noisy" channel is one that is subject to lots of interference, such as when you are trying to converse with someone at a loud party.

5. *Receiver, Decoding.* Communication does not occur until another person receives and tries to make sense out of the message that has been sent. Someone must become aware of the existence of the message, recognize it as such, and decipher or decode the signs and symbols that constitute it. Imagine that all of us are carrying around a dictionary (or probably several dictionaries) in our heads. When we hear or see a symbol that we understand to be a word, we mentally look up the meaning of that word in our mental dictionaries. Because the learning of these meanings has been as indirect as the rest of human communication, there is little likelihood that we all have identical, or even similar, dictionaries, even for our native language. For example, I learned the meaning for the word *ranch* at a different time and place and under different circumstances than you. As a result, our definitions are probably slightly different for this word. Words that refer to more abstract thoughts, such as *value*, or *religion*, are probably even more differentiated in each personal dictionary. Decoding, therefore, is the process of assigning meaning to the behavior and speech of others.

6. *Feedback.* To this point, the description of the communication process suggests that it is a linear, one-way process. Certainly, the Shannon-Weaver model suggests that conclusion because that was the point of view that concerned them. Cybernetics theorists, especially Norbert Wiener, added to their model the notion of feedback: that is, that messages come to the source to indicate how well the process is going. The introduction of feedback at this point serves as a reminder that communication is transactional, which means that the parties involved in the process mutually influence each other simultaneously during their interaction. For example, when a speaker gives a speech to an audience, it may look as if she is doing all the acting or behaving in this situation; but, in fact, her audience is sending messages to her while she is speaking although she may not perceive or interpret these messages correctly. In the give and take of conversation or an interview, the mutual acting-on-each-other is even more evident. Subtly or overtly, the one person adjusts to the feedback of the other. The feedback may be sent intentionally or unintentionally and may be definite in meaning or ambiguous. Nonetheless, it is always present.

7. *Setting.* Communication always occurs in a setting or context. The setting determines what is expected and what is appropriate in regard to the messages and interpretations that can occur. The setting interacts with the other elements of the communication process to determine the kinds of interpretations that can be made.

For example, in an emergency situation, fidelity may be much more important than in a nonemergency. The meaning of certain words can be changed by the setting. (For example, the word *passing* can mean one thing in the setting of a bridge game and something else in a school setting.) Some messages are considered appropriate in some settings but inappropriate in others.

In his many works on intercultural communication, the anthropologist Edward T. Hall points to differences between what he calls "high-context" and "low-context" cultures.[2] In high-context cultures, the setting in which communication occurs carries a great deal of the import or meaning of the encoded message. American culture tends to be more low-context, meaning that we attend more to the encoded message itself and less to the time, place, or manner—in other words, the setting—in comparison with some other cultures.

The importance of setting, therefore, may differ from one national or cultural group to another. In addition to national cultures, there are also co-cultures within the United States. By a coculture, we mean a group that is identifiable, sharing certain traits in common that *can* be used to set them apart (for example, members of an ethnic minority, such as Hispanic Americans, Asian Americans, or African Americans). Sometimes, people with physical restrictions, such as those who are wheel-chair bound, hearing impaired, or visually impaired can be considered as cocultures, in that their communications may differ as a result of their group identification.

We can clearly see the difficulty in human communication now: At each one of these points in the process of communication, meaning can be, and often is, lost.

▶ **Analysis of Communication Problems**

Now we can return to an analysis of each of the seven types of problems with which we began; each problem correlates with an element in the communication model that we have developed previously.

1. *Fidelity*. First, at the point where the intended message is encoded, we often fail to encode our message in the most effective way. There are many different ways to express the same ideas, each with a slightly different nuance. Although we probably do most of our thinking in words, we modify those words when we attempt to encode a message. We may think that we need to use a certain vocabulary or style in order to translate the message in our minds into the conventions of ordinary speech. Sometimes we are frustrated by the feeling that we could have said something better, and we fall back on a hopeful phrase, "You know what I mean." At the point of the first transformation, therefore, we may fail to encode the message in the most accurate way; some meaning may be lost right at the start.

In the situation of the physician prescribing medication to a patient, fidelity is of particular importance. The same is true of the accountant working on the corporate income taxes. While fidelity is always a goal of intentional communication, we do need to make ourselves aware of situations in which it is crucial. The Finnish theorist, Osmo Wiio, has offered a set of hypotheses about communication, beginning with the notion that communication between people never succeeds.[3] His purpose in setting forth this rather pessimistic pronouncement is to remind us that, if we blithely assume high fidelity in our communications with others, we will probably be sadly disappointed. As with Murphy's Law, "If something can go wrong, it will," so with much of our communication. To assume that if "I said it, so you must have understood it" is dangerous, as we have explained in regard to the various points at which meaning can be lost in communication.

The principle to remember about fidelity is to be especially alert to those situations in which accuracy is a high priority. Of course, we wish to be accurate in every communication situation, but at times, as the examples indicate, accuracy is critical. In those cases, we need to take special care in formulating the message: that is, trying to think of all the things that can go wrong (in line with both Murphy's Law and Wiio's theory).

Second, when fidelity is particularly important, we need to build redundancy into the message. Redundancy adds extra information to provide a check for accuracy in the message. Most of us consider writing a check to be a situation in which accuracy is a priority. Recall that on a check the amount is written in two forms, in numbers and in words. These two forms represent a redundancy that ensures the accuracy of the message. In addition to redundancy, we should also be especially sensitive to feedback in situations demanding high fidelity. When a business sends important mail messages, they often send it registered or certified, which provides for a return certification that the mail has been received by the intended addressee.

2. *Source.* In the second set of problems, the sources of communication became important factors in determining the success of the process. The boy who cried "Wolf" once too often shows that prior reputation can affect others' interpretation of a message's meaning. A more serious problem is represented by the youthful attorney or other professionals whose age, minority status, or sex may hinder their acceptance as credible sources of information. For example, works dealing with corporate cultures note that it has been most difficult for women and minorities to become enculturated in the strong cultures of successful companies, partly because of the emphasis there on shared values.[4]

The principle to remember about credibility is to be sensitive to those situations in which one's ethos may be a significant factor in communication. You need to be aware of how a prospective listener or group perceives your credibility and be able to identify when you need to take special steps to enhance that credibility. Take the situation of women assuming leadership positions in businesses, where traditionally there has been a feeling that women are at a disadvantage because of male perceptions or prejudice. Recent studies have supported a claim that the special socialization of women in American society has given them certain advantages, as well, in assuming leadership positions and becoming credible sources of communication in the business world. Judy Rosener, in an article in the *Harvard Business Review* that stimulated a great deal of commentary, put forth the claim that women tend to use a "transformational" style of leadership, which emphasizes team-building, developing self-reliance among subordinates, and applying demo-cratic and participative decision-making. Emphasis on these skills builds the cred-ibility of women in positions of this sort, given that modern businesses incline more and more toward such participative management styles.[5] The point is to emphasize one's advantages and abilities in a given situation, rather than reminding a pro-spective audience of one's disadvantages.

These principles recommend the importance of taking an inventory of one's strengths and weaknesses and being realistic about the factors determining how others might see you. Prospective audiences may assign you credibility on the basis of your own personal characteristics or on the basis of your membership in some group. If the intended receiver has had experience with you in the past, then we can assume that your credibility is the result of these past experiences. If there have been no prior experiences, then judgments will probably be based on factors such as your credentials and appearance. You may be seen as representing some organization or group. If you are speaking to someone as a representative of the gas company, then their experiences with or attitudes toward the gas company become important. When you call on someone and tell them that you are from the Internal Revenue Service (IRS), you can count on a certain kind of response based on their perception of that organization.

Chapter 10, which deals with the making of presentations, includes a detailed discussion of the elements relating to one's perceived credibility and techniques for enhancing a communicator's ethos. The purpose here, however, is to highlight the effects that the identity and perceptions of the source can have in determining communication effectiveness.

When we transmit a message, some meaning may be lost as well. Perhaps we did not form the words clearly and distinctly or say them loudly enough for the receiver to hear them all. We may be careless in the nonverbal signs that we send because of distraction, fatigue, or some other reason.

3. *Message, Encoding.* The third set of problems included the airline disaster in which the crew seemed to encode an incorrect message. This factor concerns the selection and construction of the signs and symbols in the message.

In the case of the pilots, specific words were of special importance because of their exact denotations. Another example of this type of problem concerns com-munication related to disclosure requirements of many businesses and other orga-nizations regarding, for example, chemicals that these companies may have on their premises. In these cases, there are highly specific definitions of "toxic" substances versus "hazardous" substances, and so on. Often, the connotation associated with words can be crucial. For example, people today may object to the term *physically handicapped*, instead preferring to use the phrase *physically challenged*, which does not imply a lack of ability or competence to the extent that the term *handicapped* does. The sensitivity to such connotations explains the care that results in the terms *revenue enhancements* replacing *taxes*, or *life insurance* being used in place of the more accurate *death insurance*. Occasionally, food product marketers prefer to use the term *food energy* rather than *calories* for similar reasons.

Besides the encoding of individual words or symbols in a message, this factor also can involve the structure of an entire message. The order in which information is presented, for example, can affect how the message is received or understood. In general, those items that are mentioned first or last in a lengthy message tend to be more easily recalled by audiences; information is sometimes "buried" in the middle. Placing something first or last, then, is a way of highlighting that particular piece of information. Similarly, we should point out that material that is clearly organized and that follows an easily recognizable sequence is more readily understood and retained by listeners, as well.

The principles that flow from this concern with encoding are that one needs to be aware of the denotations and connotations of specific words selected for messages. Second, one must be alert to the possible effects of the structuring or ordering of the material in a message. Both these concerns receive more detailed treatment in Chapters 10 and 11.

4. *Channel.* The fourth set of problems concerned a channel of communication. Consider that a pipeline can carry only so much water in a given time; when a storm forces more water into the pipe, it will burst, or the water will back up, thereby causing flooding. When a communication channel is overloaded, there will be a similar breakdown. As I looked at my desk and incoming mail, for example, I felt the channels were overloaded. Serious accidents have occurred, as noted, because people or channels in control towers or emergency 911 lines were overloaded.

Presumably, each channel has a certain capacity that can be described in terms of the amount of information that channel can successfully (or accurately) convey per unit of time. Whether a channel is overloaded or not in human communications is partly a result of some subjective factors. Whether my messy desk represents a serious problem of overload or not depends on what I am expected to do with the information. If the mail all appears to be routine or even junk mail, there is no real problem. If there is a lot of new, unexpected, and urgent information, though, there is a problem. The capacity of a channel, therefore, depends on factors such as newness of the incoming information, how unexpected or unpredictable it appears to be, how complex or difficult to understand it seems, and what action needs to be taken. Such concerns are often significant in analyzing the flow of communication in organizations, as is indicated in Chapter 2.

Beyond the question of flow or overload, the channel that is selected to carry a particular message can also become an issue. People seem to prefer to receive some messages face-to-face rather than through memorandums, for example. In many corporations, there appears to be a tendency among upper management to rely on written media of communication when employees often prefer more direct communication. Many contemporary organizations increasingly include electronic and computer-based media of communication, or Computer Mediated Communication Systems (CMCS). These systems allow for E-mail, voice mail, computer conferencing, bulletin boards, and so forth. In addition, there are conference telephone calls, videoconferencing, and internal, corporate television. Occasionally, such media are selected mainly because of the prestige or the high-tech gloss: in other words, for the message conveyed by the use of a particular channel. Chapter 12 considers these issues in some detail.

Third is the strong possibility of noise in the channel, that is, some interference that makes it difficult for others to hear or understand what we have said. For example, conversing in a noisy restaurant can affect the outcome of a business lunch because of misunderstandings arising from such interference. Noise in the channel was one of the main concerns of Shannon and Weaver in developing their model of communication: They were concerned with ways to encode messages so that distortions caused by noise could be overcome. They noted that noise reduces the capacity of a given channel to carry information and that repeating the message to increase its chances of getting through despite the noise further reduced such capacity. In a crowded, noisy room we find that in fact it takes longer to exchange information back and forth because of the need to speak more slowly, carefully, and to repeat often.

An important principle is to understand the dangers of overloading channels, to be aware of the capacity of channels for carrying your message. Second, be aware of the perceptions that people may have of certain media themselves and that for some kinds of messages, certain channels are preferred over others. Third, be alert to the danger of noise or distractions affecting the selected channel.

5. *Receiver, Decoding.* When the message is received, some of the message will probably be lost. The listener may be distracted or may have some physical reason for not hearing all of the message clearly. One problem of addressing a roomful of people is that we cannot count on everyone to be listening all the time and with the same level of attention. That is why you need to pace the presentation of information more carefully for a group than for an individual.

When a receiver of the physical stimulus (the sound waves or light waves) translates the stimulus into a meaningful message, there is a very high probability that some of the intended meaning will be lost. It is very unlikely that other people will give exactly the same meaning to your words that you do. The point is crucial: The other person actively participates in the creation of the meaning of your message. You cannot control the decoding process of the other person. The original message will always be filtered through the receivers' experiences and meanings.

The fifth kind of problem deals with those situations in which the nature of the receiver and the factors associated with the decoding of the message became significant. Once we have sent our message through some channel, we lose control over the outcome; the receiver must decode that message. There is greater danger for lost meaning and for communication breakdowns at this point than at any other point in the communication process.

Although, in the case of the messages about tornados, the weather bureau issued correct messages, the bureau did not have control over how people may have decoded the message. When there are cultural differences between sender

Diversity in the Workplace

The Meanings of Yes and No

In high-context cultures, such as the Japanese, the setting and the circumstances are considered to be key elements in interpreting messages. A "yes" in certain contexts is to be understood as "no," or at least as "no commitment at this time." During a business meeting, a Japanese may repeat "*hai, hai,* (yes, yes)" at various points. In this context, the "yes" should be interpreted as "Yes, I understand what you are saying," not "Yes, I agree with you." There are several different ways to say "no," and none of them is a simple "no." These include, "It is very difficult," "I'll make an effort," "I'll do the best I can," and "I agree, but I will have to check with my superior."

Such problems of intercultural communication are no longer merely "academic" or interesting curiosities. Businesses and professions now operate on a global scale. The creation of new European markets, the growing economic importance of Pacific rim countries, and the interdependence of corporate concerns and professional firms require attention to these problems.

and receiver, there are even more opportunities for misinterpretations to arise. In some cultures, looking down when listening to another is sign of respect, while in other cultures, such as ours, we expect people to meet our eyes when we are talking. The student's downward glance was decoded by the teacher as disrespect in our example. Finally, the context in which the Japanese businessman was responding to the American was inaccurately decoded by the latter.

The important principle of communication here is to emphasize audience analysis: that is, giving serious consideration to all the factors that might determine how potential listeners will decode your message. Audience analysis receives further attention in Chapters 10 and 11, which deal with the preparation of business presentations. This principle highlights the importance of the approach that we call being "audience-centered." The "other" in the communication process, whether an individual or an entire audience, cooperates in the creation of the message, in that they must ultimately give meaning to the encoded and transmitted message. The whole purpose for our effort at communicating is to induce others to create a certain message and, probably, to give a certain response as a result of that message. Otherwise, we are just "talking to ourselves."

One must bear in mind that each of us processes incoming messages through a set of personalized filters, or conceptual filters (as shown in Figure 1-2). These filters include what we know or don't know about a subject (knowledge), how we tend to evaluate these subjects (attitudes), and general values such as truth or honesty, which may shape our response. When, for example, you tell me how much you love cats as pets, I am going to filter that information through the knowledge that I am allergic to cats. That knowledge in turn filters what I hear on this subject.

Each person with whom we deal may have had different experiences related to the subject of our message, such as me and my allergies. These experiences may shape a particular attitude that the person has toward that subject. By an attitude, we mean a judgmental or evaluative response to some entity related to a probable response someone may have to that entity. Perhaps you have developed a negative attitude toward some product, such as an automobile, because of the difficulty you once had with a so-called lemon. If you value security highly, that will filter the message that urges you to seek adventure and to cut loose from the everyday safety of your normal routine. If you value health, then related messages will receive a more favorable hearing because of your particular screening on that topic.

In other words, we should accept the conclusion that the original intended message does not get through with 100% fidelity; some meaning is always lost. When we multiply the number of receivers for the original message, we multiply the possibilities for lost meaning. This point of view explains why rumors are so distorted. The receiver of the original message becomes the sender in the next step of the process, but the receiver already has less than the total of the original message. The second receiver derives from the process only a percentage of that reduced message, and so on, through several other steps of transmission.

6. *Feedback.* Looking for feedback can help the communication process. Feedback can alert the senders of messages to those parts of the original message that have been lost. Effective communicators pay attention to feedback for just that

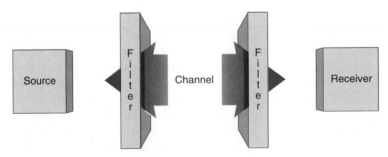

▶ **Figure 1-2**   *Filters, such as personal experience, can change or distort the message.*

reason. But, as the previous examples illustrated, feedback, which is often ambiguous, can be misunderstood. Further, the setting, especially if it involves cultural differences between sender and receiver, can complicate the process.

The opening section of this chapter included two examples of problems with feedback. In the first instance, George looked for feedback, which an effective communicator should do, but did interpret that feedback effectively. His boss's nodding was a sign that George was to continue with the presentation; it did not indicate agreement.

The first principle regarding feedback is that feedback is often nonverbal and that nonverbal cues may be ambiguous and thus subject to a wide variety of interpretations. Verbal messages, like the ones sent by George, usually have more discrete meanings (but recall that connotations, as well as denotations, differ from person to person). The nonverbal meanings of nodding, smiling, or crossing one's arms and so on are not as discrete and are much more dependent upon the context or setting. What does it mean when an audience member yawns during a presentation? There are several different meanings behind the yawning response. If you are particularly anxious about your presentation, you may interpret this as boredom or lack of interest. But in fact, the yawning person may be especially fatigued that day, responding to stuffy room conditions, or reacting to someone else's yawn.

The second principle related to feedback is that it can occur in response to different levels of meaning in the message. Note that in the second example, Smith responded to what he interpreted as emotional meanings in Jones's response. Sensing Smith's defensiveness, Jones began to respond on that emotional level as well, which led to an escalation or spiral in the heatedness of the exchange. Feedback, then, can consist of responding to the content or to other elements in the message, or both. Paul Watzlawick and his associates made this point in a very influential book, *The Pragmatics of Human Communication.*[6] They claim that each message carries both a content and a "relationship" component, meaning that any message from one person to another contains both the content (the meaning of the words or symbols) and a statement about the relationship between the two people. It would appear that Smith and Jones were having problems with feedback on the relationship level rather than on the content level.

7. *Setting.* In this kind of problem, an American executive mistook the appropriateness of a particular setting for a certain type of communication. His Japanese counterparts did not believe that a social occasion, intended to honor a guest, was the time to introduce business matters. One might have advised the executive generally against discussing business while still suffering fatigue and jet lag from the Pacific crossing. More specifically, though, communication settings are seen differently as one moves from culture to culture. This point is so important that this book devotes a feature called Diversity in the Workplace, which are examples that draw attention to the intercultural aspects of contemporary business and professional communication.

One reason for the concern about discrimination in membership in private clubs is that in the United States, business may often be conducted in informal and

▶ *Meals are often the setting for business communication.*

social settings, such as on the golf course. People excluded from these settings are therefore excluded from the communication that goes on in them.

Generally, the principle is that the message should be matched to the time, place, and occasion. First, you must be sensitive to the time: Are you or your potential partners in communication tired, in the middle of some other task, or otherwise affected by the time of the encounter? Second, you must consider the place in which the interaction takes place. Some messages are more appropriate in a locker room, some in a board room, and others in a dining room or restaurant. Such considerations as the size, privacy, or potential for interruptions in a given space may determine the nature of messages that could or should be sent. The occasion is obviously important; ceremonial occasions are usually restrictive in regard to matters that can be discussed. Informal occasions are subject to a wide range of ambiguous interpretations; one must be sensitive to how the others involved in the communication feel about the appropriateness of various kinds of messages in those settings. Formal occasions are often more clearly or definitely defined. In Chapter 10, on preparing oral presentations, we detail the analysis of communication occasions and settings.

All of these considerations are reminders that it is a mistake to take communication for granted. While some of the difficulties may be exaggerated, it is helpful to be aware of the potential breakdowns. A limitation of this view of communication, however, is that it emphasizes a linear progression in the process of communication: The message seems to follow a line from source through the channel

Problem-Solution

Matching the Setting with the Message

An important problem that communicators often face is determining whether the setting for presenting certain messages is appropriate for their content and context.

Robert L. Dilenschneider is president and chief executive officer of Hill and Knowlton, the world's largest public relations firm. In his recent book, *Power and Influence: Mastering the Art of Persuasion*, he observes that the setting shapes the message. Although firms often wish to portray a successful and upscale image, such portrayals can occasionally backfire. He describes a television story of a chemical accident and fire that destroyed much of a poor Southern town. The pictures of the devastation of the poor community were contrasted with the company's CEO answering reporters' questions in front of the company's beautiful, marble headquarters. The setting detracted from the executive's attempt to convey his empathy for the people in the stricken town. Where things are said can be as important as what is said.

Dilenschneider recommends downscaling one's image by avoiding sending messages in settings that may be seen as too opulent or imposing. Consider what the setting may suggest about your sense of your own importance and the feelings of your audience.

For other examples, see R. L. Dilenschneider (1990). *Power and influence: Mastering the art of persuasion*. New York: Prentice Hall, pp. 27–29.

to the receiver and back. The next section balances this linear view by emphasizing the mutual influence communicators have on each other during their interactions. The linear view stresses action-reaction, while the following view stresses simultaneous interaction. The linear view is more useful when considering presentations and public communications; the transactional view is more appropriate for considering interpersonal and group communication settings.

TRANSACTIONAL NATURE OF COMMUNICATION

This discussion of the problems and principles of communication highlights the fluidity of face-to-face human communication. We start out with one goal for a conversation or meeting and discover by the end that the goal has changed or that new ones have surfaced.

► ### Two-Way Communication

Communication is not usually a one-way process. The other person (or persons) involved in the interaction decodes our message, perhaps in a way we did not anticipate, the feedback leads us to consider a different interpretation, and we change our original purpose. In other words, as a result of the transaction in meanings back and forth, both parties come to a new and, at times, unexpected, understanding.

Note that the outcome is not simply that the receiver accepts or rejects our message but, rather, that the receiver suggests a reformulation of our message, just as we suggest a reformulation to the other person. We use the term *transactional* to describe the nature of this interchange, because the communication results in something new. Even in the case of a public speech or presentation, the audience feedback often leads to a modification in our original point of view or understanding. In another manner of speaking, we could say that people engaged in communication are mutually negotiating some new meaning or some new result as a consequence of that interaction. The notion of negotiation of meaning is an antidote to the constant emphasis on one-way communication, or on a view of communication as a linear process.

► ### Principles of the Transactional View of Communication

As John Stewart, who has written extensively on interpersonal communication points out, the term *transaction* is not used here in the sense of a business transaction, or the outcome of buying and selling. In the psychological sense, the term *transaction* refers to an event in which the meaning and nature of that event is determined by the active participation of people.[7] In other words, both people are engaged in submitting to the other person a definition of themselves and of the situation in which they find themselves. Stewart refers to this as a "definition-and-response-to-definition process."[8]

The relationship that develops over time results from the communication activities of the two people involved. This relationship can serve to carry the "real message." If you were to read just the words that were exchanged in the interaction, you could miss the actual meaning. For example, conversations between men and women, which appear to be rather straightforward exchanges of information, occasionally result in one or both parties becoming angry. Why? Often, it is because one person perceived the other as trying to intrude on his or her privacy or to assert control in a relationship. It is not always what is said but how it is interpreted that counts.

Therefore, we must now modify our initial view of communication as a linear process, in which a sender tries to get a message into the mind of a receiver. The steps in the preceding process should clarify that this simple idea of transference does not accurately describe what happens in human communication. When two people communicate with each other, both are simultaneously sender and receiver (as seen in Figure 1-3). The outcome of their communication is different from the initial outcomes each, separately, had hoped to achieve.

This transactional nature of communication reminds us that except in very simple, straightforward cases (say, purchasing a newspaper on the street), decoding will result in a message different from the one intended at the point of encoding. We could interpret the hypothesis of Osmo Wiio presented earlier regarding the impossibility of communicating in this way. We cannot have 100% fidelity without the luxury of mind reading. This impossibility is not necessarily all bad. In fact, the differences in meaning that result from communication is one of the main reasons for communicating in the first place: that is, to discover these differences and to create new meanings. If we did indeed all have the same codes and decoders in our heads, there would be less need for and less satisfaction in human communication.

Communication does more than convince another person that you are right; it also shows how another person sees what is right. Even in what appears to be a straightforward situation such as making a sale, the effective salesperson knows how to listen to discover the customer's needs and wants. The salesperson then tries to find a way to satisfy those needs, rather than trying to wear down the customer's resistance.

The transactional view of communication is important in understanding the dynamics of several kinds of communication events encountered in business and professional activities. For example, the key relationships between superior and subordinates and between mentors and proteges are formed through communi-

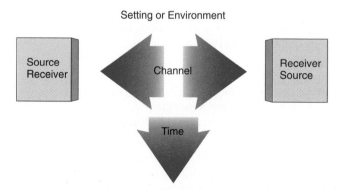

▶ **Figure 1-3**   *A transactional model of the elements and relationships in communication.*

cation transactions. Understanding what goes on in dealing with conflict, in negotiations, in various kinds of interviewing, and in group problem solving requires an awareness of the transactional nature of face-to-face communication.

SUMMARY

The elements in the model of communication developed in the previous section represent a practical approach to improving our ability to achieve certain communication goals or objectives. But by keeping the transactional model of communication in mind, we can avoid assuming too much in regard to how communication actually works, especially in the many face-to-face contexts considered throughout this text.

In order to aid in the development of practical skills, at times we emphasize the elements or linear model of communication and, at other times, the transactional model (see especially Chapter 5).

This chapter introduced a way of thinking about many communication situations. There are many different ways of looking at communication, depending upon the circumstances. We first discussed a linear model of communication, which allows us to talk about the various points in the message-sending, message-receiving process, where there can be breakdowns or problems. Also, we outlined the transactional view of communication, which attempts to overcome some of the limitations of the linear model. The transactional view points out that communication is mutual and interdependent.

Principles from Analysis of Communication Problems

There are several principles to keep in mind.

1. Be alert to situations in which fidelity is especially important.
   —Build in redundancy to enhance fidelity.
   —Be sensitive to feedback.
2. Be sensitive to situations in which credibility of the source is a special factor.
   —Emphasize special strengths, credentials.
3. Be aware of the need for care in encoding messages.
   —Take account of denotations and connotations of words.
   —Be aware of the effects of structure on the perception of the message.
4. Understand the capacity of channels of communication for carrying certain kinds of messages.
   —Be sensitive to possible responses to the media selected for given messages.
   —Be alert for noise in the channel.
5. Emphasize an audience-centered approach to communication.
   —Be aware that "others" decode the message from their own points of view.

—Be conscious of conceptual filters, such as knowledge, attitudes, and values through which people screen your message.

6. Be aware of the possible misunderstandings of feedback.
   —Nonverbal feedback may be ambiguous.
   —Feedback can be directed at different levels of meaning in the message.
7. Be aware of the need to match the message to the setting, especially the cultural setting.

Principles of the Transactional View of Communication

Keep these principles in mind.

1. Remember that communication is not a one-way, linear process.
2. Be aware that the relationship, developed over time, is important in interpreting the meaning of messages.
3. Be aware that people continually negotiate the meaning of their interactions with each other.

EXERCISES

1. Try to think of additional examples of each of the kinds of communication problems described in the first part of the chapter. For example, list situations in which fidelity is crucial; situations in which channel overload is a special problem; and so on. Discuss the principles of communication that could be used to deal with these problems.

2. Discuss the hypothetical consequences of mind reading. What would be the drawbacks of this kind of communication? What are some advantages to our indirect kind of communication?

3. Describe those situations in which the relationship between communicators is especially important. What is it about these situations that demands special sensitivity? How could it be achieved?

4. As an individual, do you find that you prefer certain channels of communication over others? In what circumstances? For what purposes? Are there messages for which the choice of channel would not make much difference? When would the chosen channel make a big difference?

5. What are your "conceptual filters" on the following topics?
   Protection of the environment.
   Classical music.
   Getting an MBA.
   High school education in the United States.
   Health care for the elderly in the United States.
   Foreign imports, such as automobiles, computers, and stereo equipment.
   Discuss how these conceptual filters influence the messages that you receive.

6. Discuss settings in which cultural differences are especially important for communication. What personal experiences have you had in which cultural differences were especially important? How did these differences affect the communication that occurred? Describe ways in which the setting for communication can influence the outcomes.

SELECTED SOURCES FOR FURTHER READING

Dahnke, G. L., & Clatterbuck, G. W. (Eds.) (1990). *Human communication: Theory and research*. Belmont, CA: Wadsworth.

Hall, E. T. (1977). *Beyond culture*. Garden City, NY: Anchor Press.

Gudykunst, W. B., & Ting-Toomey, S. (1988). *Culture and interpersonal communication*. Newbury Park, CA: Sage Publications.

Littlejohn, S. W. (1989). *Theories of human communication* (3rd ed.). Belmont, CA: Wadsworth.

Shannon, C. E., & Weaver, W. (1949). *The mathematical theory of communication*. Urbana, IL: University of Illinois Press.

Stewart, J. (Ed.) (1990). *Bridges not walls* (5th ed.). New York: McGraw-Hill.

Trenholm, S. (1991). *Human communication theory* (2nd ed.). Englewood Cliffs, NJ: Prentice-Hall.

Watzlawick, P., Beavin, J., & Jackson, D. (1967). *Pragmatics of human communication*. New York: W.W. Norton.

References

1. C. E. Shannon & W. Weaver (1949). *The mathematical theory of communication*. Urbana, IL: University of Illinois Press.
2. See especially E. T. Hall (1977). *Beyond culture*. Garden City, NY: Anchor Press.
3. Cited in Goldhaber, G. M. (1989). *Organizational communication* (5th ed.). (pp. 10–13). Dubuque: Wm. C. Brown.
4. See, for example, Deal, T. & Kennedy, A. A. (1982). *Corporate cultures*. Reading, MA: Addison-Wesley.

5. See Roesner, J. B. (1990, November–December). Ways women lead. *Harvard Business Review*, pp. 119–125.
6. P. Watzlawick, J. Beavin, & D. Jackson (1967). *Pragmatics of human communication.* New York: W. W. Norton.
7. See Stewart, J. (1990). Interpersonal communication: Contact between persons. In J. B. Stewart (Ed.), *Bridges not walls* (5th ed.). (pp. 22–24). New York: McGraw-Hill.
8. Stewart, p. 23.

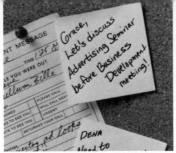

Communication in Organizations

2

CHAPTER

After studying this chapter, you should be able to:

1. Explain why communication in organizations is important.

2. Describe seven basic problems typical of communication in organizations.

3. Describe basic communication principles of four kinds of organizational theories.

4. Show the application of the organizational theories to typical problems of communication in organizations.

Overview

In the contemporary world, most professional careers are practiced in organizations or by individuals who must regularly deal with organizations. Even in private practice, a public accountant may find herself working closely with a large organization. "The corporate organization is a primary institution in modern society," write two influential theorists, "in many ways overshadowing the state in its multinational influence and in its control and direction of people's lives."[1]

Most people belong to organizations such as clubs, churches, social groups, volunteer organizations, corporations, and schools. The earliest organizations may have consisted of small hunting bands. By the time of the ancient civilizations of Egypt, Sumeria, or China, organizations had become complex and large-scale, as evidenced by the buildings, temples, and pyramids these people constructed.

Since World War II, a subdiscipline of communication study has grown up concerned especially with organizational communication. The essence of this field can be illustrated by thinking about the various levels or contexts in which communication can occur.

First, there is intrapersonal communication, which is communication within oneself (for example, when one is trying to come to a decision between two attractive options). Second, there is interpersonal communication, which is face-to-face communication usually between two people, as in ordinary conversation, counseling, or interviewing. Third, there is small-group communication, which focuses on the dynamics of communication within different kinds of groups, such as committees or work groups. Fourth, there is public communication, which is usually concerned with oral presentations. Fifth, there is organizational communication,

▶ *Communication in organizations can be both formal and informal.*

which deals with the flow of communication within an organization, often among groups or units within an organization. Sixth, there is mass communication, which is concerned with messages distributed by some form of mass media, such as advertising or broadcasting. Of course, there is much overlap among the concerns studied at these various levels. Organizational communication, for example, takes account of the other levels of communication as they occur within an organizational setting.

Whole courses and textbooks are dedicated to dealing with organizational communication. Our purpose here is not to try to condense all of that into one chapter or part of a study of business and professional communication. Rather, we are concerned with the application of various principles derived from research in organizational communication that can be applied to the various settings and problems that are the focus of this book.

◀▶ PROBLEMS OF ORGANIZATIONAL COMMUNICATION

Are there problems in organizational communication? A long tradition says that there are. One standard work on management maintains, "The foremost barrier to corporate excellence is communication, the next is planning."[2] A study reporting on opinions of employees in over 200 organizations indicated a steady decline in the evaluation of internal communication.[3] Only about 40% of the employees felt that companies did a good job of keeping them informed on company matters. Credibility of corporate communications was shown to be deteriorating; less than half of the employees favorably rated upward communication in their organization. Top management was seen as growing increasingly remote. A recent set of studies has indicated that upper management tends to overuse printed media or technology in place of face-to-face communication.

Surveys continue to show that employees feel that communication in their organizations is neither candid nor accurate, that it is often incomplete, and it is mainly top-down, with little opportunity for response.[4] In summary, people prefer more one-on-one communication in the organization but feel that their major source of communication is the informal grapevine.

Some typical problem areas in organizational communication are as follows:

1. Superior-subordinate communication
2. Vertical communication (upward and downward)
3. Horizontal communication
4. Channels of communication (formal and informal)
5. Morale or organizational climate
6. Conflict and conflict management
7. Problem solving and decision making

Communication Issues

There are several problem areas in organizational communication, as follows:

1. *Superior-subordinate communication.* The relationship between the subordinate and the superior is one of the most basic in organizations, but research reveals some typical problems in this relationship. Often, subordinates and superiors do not even agree on the nature of the task and its goals. Some superiors are seen as cold and distant and not keeping subordinates adequately informed about organizational policies and tasks. Some subordinates report that they are unsure about how they were evaluated and about how rewards are determined for the work that they do.

Some of the most-studied problems in organizational communication deal with the openness and trust exhibited in this relationship between superior and subordinate, the power or status differential perceived by the parties involved, the effectiveness of the superior to influence others, and the differences between superior and subordinate in their vocabularies, or decoding. Recent studies have focused on the variables of sex and ethnic differences between superiors and subordinates (recall the Rosener study of women leaders referred to in Chapter 1). Increasingly, intercultural variables will have to be considered as well. Some studies suggest, for example, that people brought up in a culture in which Confucianism underlies central values prefer a more formal, hierarchical relationship with their superiors than those who have grown up in a culture such as that in the United States, in which people typically prefer more informal relationships with their bosses.

The relationship between superior and subordinate touches upon important issues for communication within an organization. For example, motivation is felt to be very important in getting the best productivity out of a work group. The superior must know the best ways to motivate the particular group of people comprising his or her subordinates. Closely related to motivation is the need to regulate the work and behavior of people, or to get compliance.

2. *Vertical communication (upward and downward messages).* Vertical communication has already been cited as a special problem in most modern organizations. As stated earlier, employee surveys point to dissatisfaction with the upward and downward flow of messages.

First, downward communication is seen to be strictly one-way, with little opportunity allowed for feedback. There is the often-cited "My door is always open" myth related to this problem. But this myth overlooks the fact that a higher status person normally has to seek out communication with someone of lower status. By placing the responsibility for initiating communication on a person of lower status, the higher-status person may effectively avoid communicating.

Second, downward communication is seen as relying upon inappropriate media or channels. Recall from the first chapter that in selecting a channel, one is making a decision that can determine how well the communication succeeds. Employees report that upper-level managers tend to use written forms, such as reports and memoranda, for their downward communication, while more personal, face-to-face channels are preferred by employees. Of course, the executives prefer the written form because it appears to be more efficient and cost-effective. Some corporations have compromised with the use of company internal television, through videocassette or direct broadcast. In general, upper management tends to be overly optimistic about the effectiveness of their downward communication.

Upward communication is seen to be a problem for at least two reasons. First, the channels often do not seem to be there. Second, the climate or culture of the organization does not seem conducive to accepting open and candid upward communication. Many organizations have the ever-popular suggestion box, which allows occasionally for anonymous feedback from the lower levels. Other organizations encourage with bonuses suggestions that result in increased productivity or quality.

One major source for feedback has been exit interviews (formal interviews with people who are leaving the organization) at which point supervisors try to discover what may be sources of dissatisfaction. Of course, these interviews tend to come rather late in the game, since the person being interviewed has already been lost to the organization.

3. *Horizontal communication.* At first glance, communication among people at about the same level in the organization should seem less difficult than vertical communication. Still, there are problems in this area as well. For example, in some organizations, the people in the office next door to yours may have the piece of information that you need to complete a task, but if the inhabitants of these two offices never communicate, the information will not be shared. To communicate

Problem-Solution

The Whistle-Blower and Obstacles in Upward Communication

When upward communication appears to be closed, but employees feel that a serious or dangerous matter is being overlooked, they might engage in the process of whistle-blowing. Whistle-blowing is an employee's disclosing to outside people or agencies some organizational activity that the whistle-blower believes to be illegal, illegitimate, unethical, or possible damaging to public health or safety. Normally, such whistle-blowing occurs after internal efforts at upward communication to correct the problem have been exhausted. Obviously, the whistle-blower can be subject to retaliation, such as dismissal, poor evaluations, and the like, although there are now some legal protections for whistle-blowers. Some states have mandatory reporting requirements, for example, for health care providers, meaning that there can be a legal duty to blow the whistle in some cases. Article VI of the Institute of Internal Auditors' Code of Ethics requires the reporting of fraud or unlawful practices.

Scientists and engineers represent another group that has produced a large number of whistle-blowers in recent years. Some corporations have developed a system that encourages dissent about product safety. Many states have enacted "public policy exceptions" to protect employees from being fired for disclosures that are intended to protect public safety.

Good summaries of cases of whistle-blowing in various settings and industries can be found in R. Nader, J. Petkas, & K. Blackwell (1972). *Whistleblowing*. New York: Grossman Publishers, which presents results of a June 1971 conference on the problems faced by whistleblowers, and Alan F. Westin, Ed. (1981). *Whistle Blowing! Loyalty and Dissent in the Corporation*. New York: McGraw-Hill Book Co.

with someone in accounting, people from marketing may have to send the message up through their manager to the top level; from there, it is sent back down to accounting, which is a long and time-consuming route. This situation may be especially common in organizations that emphasize hierarchy and going through channels.

Another problem with horizontal communication is often the lack of shared interests and technical expertise between different parts of the organization. Engineers are interested in talking to other engineers but not to public relations staff. Or, interdepartmental communication is simply not part of the culture, especially within larger organizations.

▶ *Physical layout can affect horizontal communication.*

In addition, there may be problems related to turf protection. You may hear someone say that we don't want those people in the other group hearing about our problems, nor do the members of one department want others to have a good idea about their plans. In organizations in which there is great deal of competition for budget or other similar resources, there may be further inhibition on cross-departmental communication of this sort. Quality circles are attempts to overcome some of these problems. Quality circles are informal groups including supervisors and workers intended to discuss ways to improve quality in production by regularly bringing together people involved in different stages of an operation. While such groups were begun in the United States, they are now closely identified with Japanese management techniques.

4. *Channels of communication (formal and informal).* Organizations depend upon the flow of communication through their channels. First, information coming in from the outside must be absorbed. The organization needs to know whether people are buying their products or using their services, if there are potential changes coming in the demand for products and services, and the like. A lot of incoming information may also be inconsequential. Decisions need to be made about which messages to keep, where to send them, and what to do about them. Inside the organization, messages have to flow from one part to another. For example, production needs to know how many widgets have been promised by sales; personnel needs to know how many people marketing plans to hire; and so on. The flow of these messages throughout the organization depends upon the channels of communication.

The basic concerns about channels of communication, as we saw in Chapter 1, were *load* (especially overload) and *noise*, or potential distortion in the channel. A typical problem with organizational communication is the overloading of a particular channel, which leads to a bottleneck in the processing of information, and, even worse, a loss of information. One office, for example, with a very small staff may have responsibility for processing all incoming requests or calls, regardless of the nature or purpose of those calls. One secretary may become responsible for screening all information passed through a particular part of an organization.

An unforeseen consequence of computers was the huge amount of data such systems could generate. A feeling developed that if the data could be generated, it must be useful, so human beings found themselves inundated by piles of printouts. Instead of increasing the efficiency of handling data, computers had added to the problem of overload.

A problem similar to overload is noise, which means any random interference or distortion in messages passing through a communication channel. Noise can be introduced into a channel when several people are linked into it, as each might add to or subtract from the original message as they pass it on to someone else. This results when people feel they know how to "correct" or "interpret" the message that has been received from a supervisor or higher-up.

Notice how this problem is interrelated with some of the problems of upward-downward communication discussed already. When a department head explains a new policy passed down from the vice president about new forms for budget reporting, the department head may add details in the hope of clarifying the message. Occasionally, the department head may try to soften directives from above in order to maintain a pleasant relationship with co-workers: for example, "Now this requirement isn't directed really at us, but it's those other people in department X who need to pull their own weight."

Channels of communication in an organization include formal and informal networks. A network is a pattern of relationships that provide contact among various groups or departments. The links of a network are the people who carry information from one group to another. A network analysis can indicate whether an organization's networks are too long, or bottlenecked, or characterized by sufficient back-up or redundancy. Are the people serving as links overloaded? Are there unconnected groups outside the loop? Is there more than one network for passing important information through the organization? Are there too many links so that everyone has to filter too many messages?

In addition to the formal networks (as shown in Figure 2-1) that a corporation may build into the organization to provide for the flow of communication, there are of course many informal or unintended networks that develop too. These informal networks can serve as a *grapevine* for carrying rumors and gossip. The term *grapevine* developed during the Civil War in the mid-nineteenth century when telegraph wires were strung haphazardly over bushes from the front lines to the rear, resembling the stringing of a grapevine. Today the term refers to haphazard, unplanned communication systems that crisscross the planned networks of the company organizational chart.

The studies of employee's feeling about communication inside corporations, cited early in this chapter, indicate that most employees report that much of their information in the organization comes from the grapevine while they would prefer

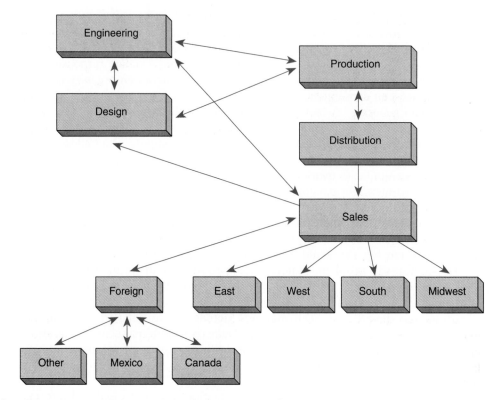

▶ **Figure 2-1**   *Formal networks within a hypothetical organization. Arrows show the direction of communication.*

more direct channels. The problem with rumors is that they are usually based on partial or ambiguous information; there is no systematic way to check on their accuracy or completeness. Rumors tend to be rife in times of crises, change, or uncertainty, when people feel a great need for information but find that it is restricted or heavily censored.

5. *Morale or organizational climate.* A major determinant of satisfaction and morale within an organization is the quality of communication within it. The term *climate* refers to a general attitude that an organization's members have toward the work and communication environment.

While it has been one of the richest and most widely studied constructs in the field of organizational communication, there is some vagueness concerning the exact meaning of the term *organizational climate*, or *communication climate*.[5] Climate concerns the perceptions of individuals within the organization about important or enduring qualities associated with working in that organization; in other words, it relies upon subjective judgments or evaluations reported by those individuals. Communication climate concerns people's judgments or feelings about the nature of communication within the organization.

Obviously, these judgments could vary within the same organization, depending upon someone's position in an organization. Those in higher levels may report more positive feelings about the climate of that organization than people in lower levels, for example, because they receive more rewards, feel that they have more control over the organization, and so on. Furthermore, the attitude toward climate could vary for an individual depending upon whether attention is focused on the level of interpersonal communication (with co-workers or supervisors), of group communication (within a team or department), or organizational level (communication from other parts of the organization).

Problems of climate or morale could result from several communication factors. An ideal communication climate would be characterized by such factors as supportiveness in the communications within the organization, expressions of trust and confidence in organization members, openness and candor in interpersonal communication, and messages that indicate participative decision-making and high-performance goals.[6] Presumably, the absence of these characteristics in an organization could result in dissatisfaction. For example, a climate of defensiveness could mean that people are afraid to express opinions, thus stifling open discussion of problem-solving ideas. Climate could therefore limit productiveness and efficiency.

Again, we should note that communication climate interrelates with other features of organizational communication: superior-subordinate communication influences climate, as well as upward-downward and horizontal communication. A lack of agreement about the purposes and goals of the organization could undercut the feelings about the climate.

6. *Conflict and conflict management.* In any group, there will be misunderstandings, disagreements, and conflict. In large organizations, the possibilities for conflict are greater.

Some organizations include built-in conflict as an expected part of the system. Budgeting processes may work to bring about competition among various units within the organization for scarce resources, such as personnel, money, or equipment. The U.S. legal system is an example of an institution based upon built-in conflict. The prosecution and defense are a necessary part of the system. These examples are reminders that conflict is not necessarily a bad thing to be avoided. Conflict can energize people, bring problems out into the open, and force people to do a reality check. Avoiding such conflict could have negative consequences. (This point is further developed in Chapter 13.)

Conflict can also be a problem. For example, it can lower morale and create a defensive climate, in which people communicate less to avoid personal feuds. Conflict can lead to the creation of a standoff. Other debilitating effects of organizational conflict include reducing information exchange, as people withhold information from the "other side" to gain an advantage, creating isolation, as people stop talking to each other, and resulting reductions in job satisfaction and productivity.[7]

Through formal or informal negotiation and bargaining, interorganizational conflicts and the associated creative tension can be managed. Negotiation and

▶ *Negotiating is a typical method for dealing with conflict.*

bargaining methods place special emphasis on the communication skills related to conflict management. We will deal specifically with these techniques in the chapter dealing with negotiation and mediation (see Chapter 14).

7. *Problem solving and decision making.* In his book, *The Work of Nations*, Robert B. Reich forces us to consider the globalization of work and business in the coming decades. He foresees three main categories of jobs in this future: "routine productive services, in-person services, and symbolic-analytic services."[8] People in the first two categories will find that they must increasingly compete on an international labor market, as corporations become global, rather than national, entities. Those in the third group must also compete in this way, but Reich feels that Americans are ahead of the curve in developing leadership in this area.

The third type of worker, the symbolic analyst, receives the most attention in the latter third of Reich's book. These people exhibit skills associated with "all the problem-solving, problem-identifying, and strategic brokering activities . . . ," including planners, communication specialists, consultants, and the like. The actual nature of their work is somewhat hard to specify, but the importance of this group highlights the significance of special abilities in manipulating symbols for creative problem solving and decision making.

The skills Reich highlights are the very communication skills needed for problem solving and decision making in complex organizations. We draw a definite connection between problem solving and decision making, because we believe that making a decision is, at base, the result of solving a problem. In too many organizations, problem solving and decision making are not the result of a rational, systematic method. Many groups tend to use what are called "inertia-activation" strategies, which involve waiting until the problem is so big that people must act. Reactive, rather than proactive, problem solving is often the norm.

Herbert Simon and his colleagues at Carnegie-Mellon University in a series of studies on organizations referred to "bounded rationality" as a way of describing real-world decision making. Bounded rationality assumes that people within organizations, faced with a problem or a decision to be made, search only long enough to find the first possible solution that might work, instead of looking for the best option among many solutions. This tendency to take the first satisfactory answer that comes along is termed "satisficing" by Simon and others.[9]

The process of problem solving and decision making in organizations may be flawed for various reasons. Incentives may focus on certain activities rather than others, so that decisions will favor those activities. For example, in many colleges and universities, research and publication activities of faculty members are rewarded more than teaching, which is more difficult to evaluate. Faculty therefore decide to spend their time and resources on publications. In some large industries, bonuses for executives are based upon quarterly profits, which tends to emphasize a short-run mentality in decision making, at the expense of long-term building.

Communication Problem Highlights

The typical problems that recur in studies of organizational communication fall into the areas described earlier.

In the next section, we provide an overview of some of the major theories concerning organizations and organizational communication and show how each looks at these typical problems. Many of the problems mentioned here, however, will be continuing themes throughout the text. Superior-subordinate communication, for example, receives a great deal of attention in Chapter 5, concerning interpersonal communication on the job.

THEORIES OF ORGANIZATIONAL COMMUNICATION

Because of the importance of modern organizations, especially in the life of industrialized nations, they have been the subject of a great deal of study. Some theories have been influential and still form the basis for the practices of those who operate within many organizations. The theories provide people with some guidance for managing organizations and trying to deal with the various sorts of organizational communication problems already discussed.

The theory operative in any given organization will significantly affect the nature of the business and professional communication in that organization. For ease in summarizing these various theories, we use four basic categories that are generally recognized in the fields of organizational theory and organizational communication:

1. Classical and scientific management
2. Human relations and human resource development
3. Systems theories
4. Corporate cultures

▶ ### Classical and Scientific Management

Classical management theory is dominated by three major figures: a German, Max Weber; an American, Frederick Winslow Taylor; and a Frenchman, Henri Fayol. Most of their work was done in the late nineteenth or early twentieth centuries, but their theories continue to be influential.

Weber's examination of modern bureaucracy appears in the context of describing three types of authority in social organizations: the legitimate or bureaucratic type, traditional authority, and charismatic authority. Traditional authorities are chiefs or feudal lords whose authority is based on their descent or family or some other traditionally sanctioned method. Charismatic leaders are those who are set apart from most people because of some special aura, usually a spiritual quality, such as prophets or heroes.

The bureaucratic type is of most interest to us here. Such leaders hold their authority on the basis of their position in a legally constituted hierarchy; they derive their authority from the position rather than from their personal identity. They occupy that position because of certain documented qualifications, such as degrees or special certifications showing an education or training for that position. Should they leave that position, they do not take their authority with them; rather, it is assumed by the next occupant of the position. In these ways, power or authority

Early Organizational Theorist: Max Weber

Max Weber, 1864–1920, was a professor of Economics in Germany and Austria and a major contributor to the development of the then-young field of sociology. One of his major concerns was the growth of modern bureaucratic organizations, and it is his description of bureaucratic structure and authority that forms the basis for classical management theory. Two of his works are well known in English: *The Protestant Ethic and the Spirit of Capitalism* and *The Theory of Social and Economic Organization*.[10] The second book contains the important discussion of bureaucracy.

is based on the organization rather than on the individual characteristics of the traditional or charismatic leaders.

Weber set forth a list of principles generally governing bureaucratic organizations; these principles are largely applicable to many present-day bureaucracies.[11] Most of these characteristics (such as written rules as the basis of authority, hierarchical structure, objective criteria for selection of people in the bureaucracy based on education or training, files of written records) are familiar to people who work in modern organizations. We take for granted that when we apply for a position in such an organization there will be a written job description, a written contract spelling out expectations, and that the selection will be based on bona fide objective qualifications. In fact, the absence of these items may be illegal under some circumstances. So, although the term *bureaucrat* may have negative connotations, we still expect our organizations to follow many of the principles of the bureaucrat.

While Weber was developing theories dealing with the structure and functions of modern organizations, Frederick Winslow Taylor, 1856–1915, became famous for his scientific analysis of work and management. After giving up plans to study law, Taylor went into machine shop work and rose to be chief engineer of a steel firm in Philadelphia. He then became a consulting engineer for most of the rest of his career, working on the ideas of scientific management with which he became closely associated.

Taylor insisted that management or administration should be considered a distinct profession that was basically the same regardless of the nature of business involved. He maintained that the "best management is a true science, resting upon clearly defined laws, rules, and principles, as a foundation."[12] Taylor's principles were seen as a reform not only for the efficiency of business, but for the welfare of laborers as well. Training and the standardization of work days, hours, and pay were all advances over the working conditions of industrial workers in the 1880s and 1890s. Clearly, Taylorism, or scientific management, emphasized vertical, formal communication. Taylor specified, "The work of every workman is fully planned out by the management at least one day in advance, and each man receives in most cases complete written instructions, describing in detail the task which he is to accomplish, as well as the means to be used in doing the work."[13]

Taylor's ideas spread to other countries: in France, an organization known as the *Conference de l'organisation Francaise* was formed to introduce his ideas to French industrial concerns. Here, Taylor's theories met those of the third founder of the classical management school, Henri Fayol. A contemporary of Weber and Taylor, he was chief executive officer of a large French mining and metals firm for 30 years, making a major contribution to the French war effort in World War I. His company became famous for the quality of its administrative staff, and so Fayol became a consultant trying to propagate his principles for administration.

Fayol's principles complement both those of Weber and of Taylor. These principles were derived first from the notion that administration was a distinct occupation based on systematic methods that could be taught; people could be trained to be effective administrators. Fayol wrote that administration "embraces not only the public service but enterprises of every size and description, of every

Taylorism and Standardization

Taylor believed that by standardizing tools and procedures, work could be made much more productive. He noticed, for example, that day laborers who worked shoveling coal for a steel plant usually brought their own shovels from home, which, of course, were of all different kinds, shapes, and sizes. By issuing standard shovels, the shape of which he had carefully calculated, Taylor found that the shovelers could handle significantly more coal in a day than before. By studying workers' physical movements, he found a standardized method for lifting and throwing the coal that was more efficient and taught it to the shovelers. Having done this, he found it was also more efficient to keep the trained workers longer, so workers were hired for periods longer than the former single days. These principles, standardization of tools, procedures, training, and job tenure, became some of the principles of the new scientific management, which was also known as Taylorism. The standardization of procedures of a job led to the association of Taylor with what we now call "efficiency experts," and time-and-motion studies.

form and every purpose." Further, he continued, "All undertakings require planning, organization, command, co-ordination and control, and in order to function properly, all must observe the same general principles."[14]

Fayol's administrative principles included the following concepts:

1. Division of work (as into departments, such as accounting, production, sales, and so forth, or at a university, sociology, history, economics, literature, and so on).

2. Unity of command, meaning that each subordinate should report to one and only one superior; in addition, authority should be delegated to each office sufficient to carry out its responsibilities.

3. Line of authority, meaning that there is a "scalar" chain of command running from the top to the bottom of the organization (compare the typical organizational chart found in most corporations today [see Figure 2-2]).

4. Stability of personnel tenure, meaning that the organization could count on the same people being in the same jobs for a predictable period of time.

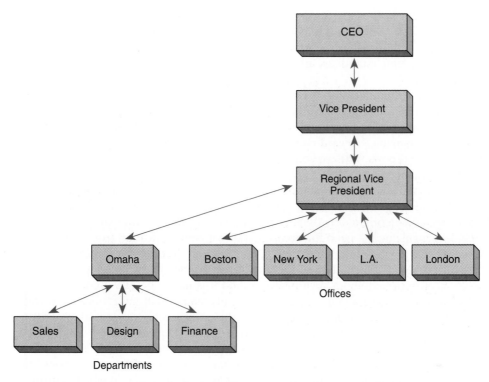

▶ **Figure 2-2** *Diagram of classical managed organization. Stress is placed on organization to produce a product or accomplish a task most efficiently. Orders pass from superiors to subordinates and reports from subordinates to superiors.*

5. Esprit de corps, referring to morale, something like organizational climate shared by the members of the "administrative team."

While Taylor had looked to scientific analysis and organization of the work of production, beginning at the level of the workers, Fayol began at the top with an analysis of the functions of executives.

Although developed at the end of the last century and the beginning of this one, these principles of bureaucratic organization and scientific management and administration continue as the basis for government agencies, corporations, businesses, and educational institutions.

Application to Communication Problems. Followers of the classical management school see each of the organizational communication problems from their view of the functioning of the organization.

First, in regard to superior-subordinate communication, these theorists emphasize formal rules and procedures for such interchanges. At the lower levels of the organization, much of the communication involves training workers in tasks and directing them in their performance. The communication, in other words, would be mostly work related and impersonal. At higher levels of the organization, the emphasis is on formal work matters; written records are important and many meetings and understandings are followed by a written memorandum formalizing results.

Vertical communication is emphasized, especially in terms of communicating plans and directions for completing the tasks of subordinates. Again, written messages are important for maintaining records, although communication is not limited to written channels. Upward communication is usually in the form of progress or performance reports. Otherwise, upward communication is at a minimum in these kinds of organizations.

Horizontal communication is limited by departmentalization and chain of command. A message from someone in one department must be passed up the line above the person originating the message, then down the other line to the recipient. Fayol, recognizing the need for occasional direct communication from someone in one unit to a person of the same rank in another unit, allowed for something called "Fayol's bridge," which allowed for such direct connections. Still, superiors need to be kept informed about such bridging, and it is not to be overused.

The channels of communication in classically managed organizations are formal and subject to easy record keeping; hence, the emphasis already noted on written memoranda and the like. Typically, phone logs are kept in order to maintain a record of these kinds of contacts. As the Watergate incident in the 1970s revealed, such formal record keeping could extend to tape recordings of conversations and meetings. Oral communications are usually structured meetings in which a formal, prepared, and scripted presentation is made to an assembly of workers or other subordinates. Face-to-face communications, in other words, are often public address situations rather than open discussions, thereby allowing for maximization of upper-management control. Other channels of communication include formal bargaining processes between management and unions.

Morale and organizational climate are probably seen in different ways depending upon one's location in the hierarchy. At the lower levels, when morale is a concern, managers believe it can be maintained through equitable treatment in wages or salary and work load. At upper levels, salary is seen as a major determinant of job satisfaction. Emphasis, therefore, is on tangible rewards, such as bonuses, vacations, and salary to maintain a positive work climate.

Conflict is formalized and regularized through a union-style bargaining process for those in the lower levels (the so-called bargaining unit employees). There may be formal budget hearings or similar meetings to allow managers to present their cases to higher-ups, but there is probably no direct give-and-take concerning the division of resources. It is assumed that most conflicts will be resolved by someone in higher authority.

Problem solving and decision making are handled through formal procedures. There may be a programmed decision-making process, in which one follows a standard format: If A happens, try B; if that doesn't work, try C; and so on. Offices are designated for dealing with specific kinds of problems and decisions, with little flexibility. If news reporters call, they are to be referred to the public relations department, for example. The emphasis is placed on having structured responses to problems, written procedures for making decisions, and so on.

Human Relations and Human Resource Development

This school of management was partly a reaction to the impersonal nature of the classical management theories. Where the classical theories had emphasized the task, the human relations approach focussed on human needs as a factor in getting the work done.

Evidence for the importance of informal factors, such as workers' interpersonal communication, morale, and feelings, appeared in a famous set of studies conducted by a team from the Harvard school of business under the leadership of Elton Mayo.

The human relations movement led to some conclusions that differed from those of the classical management approach. First, it appeared that material incentives, such as pay and bonuses, were not the only significant motivators. People were also driven by personal rewards, such as attention, praise, high morale, compatible work partners, and so on.

Second, they felt that the group in which a person worked exercised some control over that person's output and feelings about the job. It seemed that people did talk to one another during work and that such talk had its effects. The human relations approach consequently began to deal increasingly with group dynamics.

Third, given the importance of the informal work group, it was important to communicate with informal group leaders and to discover how group norms were established. In other words, the idea developed that caring for the feelings of the

---

The Hawthorne Studies

The Hawthorne studies began in 1927 at the Hawthorne plant of the Western Electric Company near Chicago. Researchers had hoped to look at the effects of environmental conditions, such as lighting, on the productivity of assembly workers. Unexpectedly, the researchers discovered that production increased both when lighting was increased and when it was decreased. Further investigation led to the conclusion that the production increases were the result of the workers' perception that they were important enough to be the subjects of attention; physical conditions weren't the issue at all. Mayo and his colleagues then began to focus on the importance of these human issues related to work performance.

workers should result in higher rates of production, or that caring was good business. Mayo thus became the father of the human relations approach and the field of industrial psychology.

The human relations theory placed attention on the human element in production. People, unlike machines or raw material, required special treatment and could make up the corporation's most important resources. Unlike machines and materials, people could be motivated and their skills could be upgraded by training. Later theorists in this tradition refined these concepts and moved toward more emphasis on training and developing the skills of workers. This accounted for the later shift in emphasis from human relations to human resource development.

Some theorists who can be considered refiners of the original human relations insights include Douglas McGregor, Rensis Likert, Robert Blake and Jane Mouton, and Frederick Herzberg.

McGregor was influenced by the work of Abraham Maslow, who postulated that the needs that motivate individuals are organized in hierarchical structure. Maslow has become a commonplace resource in management training today, as has his famous hierarchy. In short, Maslow believed that people had to satisfy lower-order needs, such as the physiological needs for food, clothing, and shelter, before they could turn their attention to higher-order needs, such as the need for affection or affiliation, esteem of others, or, the well-known pinnacle of his needs hierarchy: self-actualization. If a person is starving or needs shelter or protection, he or she will not be concerned about personal esteem. In order to motivate people, therefore, Maslow maintained, one has to know where they are in terms of their needs.

McGregor took the idea of Maslow's hierarchy of needs and used it to contrast the theories of the classical management school and the human relations school. The classical theorists, he believed, tried to motivate people by appealing to the lower-order needs, for security or pay to provide for food, clothing, and shelter. The human relations managers, on the other hand, appealed to motivators that came from the higher levels in Maslow's hierarchy (esteem, belongingness, or self-actualization), interpreted to mean participation in making decisions, or in contributing directly to the direction of the organization.

McGregor differentiated between the two views of motivation by designating them Theory X and Theory Y. Theory X was applied to the classical theorists who believed that people were motivated by incentives such as pay, or disincentives, such as threats to discipline them by docking their pay, or even worse, by firing them. Theory Y referred to McGregor's preferred style of treating people: that is, assuming they enjoyed having meaningful work to do, appreciated involvement in decision making, and were motivated by a sense that they were treated as important or worthwhile. The two theories, X and Y, therefore represented one's view of human nature; in fact, McGregor referred to these views as "cosmologies," or views of the universe. Theories X and Y are not, he insists, managerial strategies but sets of underlying beliefs.[15]

Rensis Likert increased McGregor's two theories of human management to four systems. System 1 was close to Theory X in its view of human nature and work, while system 4 was close to Theory Y. In system 1, management simply does not trust their subordinates; order is maintained through giving orders and directions, backed up by threats or rewards. Communication is mostly downward, as one might expect.

Likert's systems 2 and 3 are intermediate between the extreme directiveness of system 1 and the open, participative style of system 4. Research carried out by Likert and his associates suggested that the most productive operations were those run along the lines of the system 4 style of management. The key factor that Likert emphasized in indicating successful system 4 organizations was Participative Decision Making (PDM). In an organization with PDM, employees felt that their suggestions were taken seriously and that they actually did have some significant voice in management decisions.

A further refinement in the human relations approach resulted from the work of Robert Blake and Jane Mouton at Ohio State University. According to theories of group dynamics, communication within a group can focus on one of two ends: improving the interpersonal climate within the group (which group dynamicists referred to as "group maintenance" function) or completing the job at hand ("task" function).

Similarly, Blake and Mouton in their research looked at two factors that could be emphasized by leaders or managers: a concern for people (human relationships) or a concern for production or the task. They laid out a grid on which one could plot from 1 (low) to 9 (high) a manager's concern for people along one axis and a manager's concern for production on the same 9-point scale on the other. In this way, one could envision 81 different leadership orientations resulting from the 9 × 9 matrix.

These researchers identified five general, or "pure," leadership styles at the corners and the center point on their grid. They believed that "Each of these five theories defines a definite but different set of assumptions regarding how individuals, in fact, do orient themselves for managing situations of production that involve people."[16]

Someone who is high on concern for production but low on concern for people would be very similar to the Theory X person in McGregor's theory or system 4 management in Likert's. This person is concerned only with production with almost no interest in human relationships. On the other hand, someone interested only in the human relationships and with no concern for production at all is referred as a "country club" leader. Someone in the middle of the grid, who is moderate on concern for both production and for people, is a "middle of the road" leader, pushing just enough to get things to done, but paying some attention to morale, as well.

The best kind of leader, according to Blake and Mouton, is high on both concerns: production and people. This sort of person was a team leader, following many of the principles of Theory Y or system 4. The grid system of Blake and Mouton allowed for a more flexible manner of distinguishing types of managerial style, recognizing that people tended in one direction or another, but were seldom all Theory X or all Theory Y. These theories also suggest that there may be no one best style of management, which foreshadows some of the contingency theories that will be discussed later.

A related theory, developed by Frederick Herzberg, is called the "motivator-hygiene" theory from an analogy with public health. In public health, hygiene factors are those things that provide the general environment that permits good health. Sanitation systems, school inoculation programs, and the like provide the conditions that prevent the outbreak of epidemics, but they do not ensure that a given individual will be especially healthy, just not seriously sick. Similarly, according to Herzberg, factors in the workplace that address the lower-level needs of employees, such as pay, working conditions, benefits, and the like are merely hygiene factors. Their absence would cause serious dissatisfaction, but their presence does not guarantee a high degree of motivation. If such tangible or physical incentives cannot provide much motivation, then "motivators" have to be something else. The "something else" is derived, as in McGregor's theory, from the higher levels in Maslow's hierarchy of needs. People are motivated by the challenging or interesting nature of the work, by responsibility they have in their work, by satisfaction they derive from the work, and so on.

Herzberg's conclusions are considered surprising by some people because of the way that he downplays money as a motivator. Many feel that really large salaries can be significant motivators. Herzberg may answer that in most organizations, the line workers are not ever going to receive raises so much more than others of their rank so as to be all that significant. Even if that should happen, fellow workers would be so discouraged or dissatisfied by the discrepancy that their lack of motivation would more than offset the motivation felt by the one lucky worker.

Application to Communication Problems.   The ways in which the human relations and human resource theories would deal with the various communication problems discussed in the first part of this chapter are clear. After all, these theories emphasize communication as a remedy to many of the weaknesses they perceived in the classically managed firm.

First, superior-subordinate communication is given special attention, with the hope of improving its quality. Superiors should exhibit human warmth and trust when communicating with subordinates. Subordinates, it is hoped, will feel that they are trusted, that there is a genuine openness in communication, and that their superior is not defensive or threatening. Superiors should make it clear that suggestions, and even criticisms, from subordinates will be tolerated and accepted.

These principles should also apply in vertical communication, which should be encouraged. Both upward and downward communication should allow for discussion of personal matters or for matters that show a concern for human needs and not just business.

Similarly, horizontal communication should be welcomed and open. People should feel free to express their feelings to one another and to confront one another about personal relationships as well as about formal work matters.

The channels of communication favored in human relations and human resource approaches are more personal and face-to-face than those in classical management. Instead of the impersonal memos and public addresses that characterize the classical approach, there are meetings, conferences, groups, and discussions. So much upward-downward, horizontal, personal and impersonal communication could lead to overloaded channels throughout the organization. Informal networks may arise alongside the more structured channels with ease, however, and will probably not be discouraged.

Presumably, under the human relations type approach, there is much more concern with climate and morale than under the more bureaucratic systems of classical management. The ideal organizational climate has all the features of the Theory Y or system 4 organization. In the same vein, conflict would be dealt with openly, probably through group discussion, rather than with a higher-up making a decision. There may be more open negotiation and bargaining going on throughout the human relations type organization.

Decision making, as indicated already, occurs through the participation of everyone involved in the consequences of the decision. Efforts are made to provide people with the information they need to understand the ramifications of the problem so they can participate in a meaningful way. Obviously, all of this takes more time and effort than the Theory X method of simply making a decision without wide consultation.

Systems Theories

Another trend in the development of organizational theories is based on a set of ideas labelled systems theory or general systems theory. This approach conceptualizes the necessary features of any organized system, whether it be a living organism, a basketball team, or General Motors.

Biological Basis for Systems Theory

A biologist, Ludwig von Bertalanffy, is most closely associated with the development of the systems theory line of thinking, and he is the person who coined the term *general systems theory*. Von Bertalanffy was struck by the fact that living systems are made up themselves of other systems, which in turn are made up of smaller systems, and so on. The human body is composed of the circulatory system, the digestive system, et cetera, with each system operating to fulfill some specific set of functions for the organism. Von Bertalanffy reasoned that what applied to the patterns of systems in living creatures could also apply to other kinds of systems.

A system is more than the sum of its parts. It consists of a pattern of relationships, a structure exhibiting the following characteristics. First, the system exists within an environment. The environment contains that material, such as food, energy, and information necessary for the maintenance of the system. Second, the system itself is separated from the environment by a boundary, which can vary in its permeability, or to how much it allows things to flow back and forth from inside the system to outside in the environment. If the boundary is too permeable, the system will not be sufficiently distinct from the environment to continue its separate existence. If the boundary is too tight, the system becomes what is termed a *closed system*, with consequences we will discuss shortly. Third, the system itself is made up of smaller subsystems, separated each from the larger environment of the system by its own boundaries. Each subsystem is made up of its own subsystems, and so on down to the level of individual elements or people. In this way, the subsystems are arranged hierarchically. The elements and subsystems are interrelated with each other throughout the system.

Systems theory was seen as a useful approach for studying human organizations because they are clearly systems as the theory defines them. The most influential application of systems thinking to organizational theory is *The Social Psychology of Organizations*, by Katz and Kahn, first published in 1966, and followed by a second edition in 1978. These writers describe the structure and functions of organizations in terms of "open systems." Recall that a closed system is one whose boundary does not permit any interchange with its environment. Such a system will gradually run down, losing its energy and vitality, because it cannot take in energy from the environment or expel waste products into the environment. Such a system inevitably tends toward entropy, a situation that lacks order or pattern.

An open system, on the other hand, allows the exchange of material, energy, and information with the environment, such as when you breathe in oxygen and expel nitrogen. Without this ongoing interchange with your environment, you would tend toward an entropic state, or death. It is through interchange with the environment that the open system is able to maintain its existence.

We can apply this thinking to organizations. If an organization never takes in new members, shuns outside information, and cuts itself off from interaction with other people or organizations, it is probably moribund. A vital organization is one that searches out new blood, looks for new ideas, and stays current.

Open systems are therefore maintained by communication with the environment and by communication among its various elements and subsystems. Katz and Kahn described an organization as using *input*, or taking in materials, energy, information from the outside; *throughput*, which refers to the operations on that material, energy, and information within the organization; and *output*, the product that it sends back out into the environment. As a result of this interchange, open systems exhibit the following characteristics:

1. *Cycle of events*. The organization moves through the *input-throughput-output* phases in repeatable or ongoing cycles. The throughput phase involves the transformation of the material, energy, and/or information into some new configuration or product. This product in turn becomes input for some other part of the system or is sent back across the boundary as output.

2. *Equifinality.* This term refers to the fact that after some time, systems engaged in a similar activity in a similar environment will resemble each other in significant ways. Because they are interchanging input and output with the environment, the systems are not restricted to their original state. Each generation doesn't have to reinvent the wheel or the computer. Each new business in an industry can use the experience of others and build on that experience.

3. *Homeostasis.* This term suggests the idea of the "same state." The concept refers to the ability of open systems to remain in balance with their environments as a thermostat maintains a room's steady temperature, as shown in Figure 2-3. For example, human bodies all tend to maintain an internal body temperature of

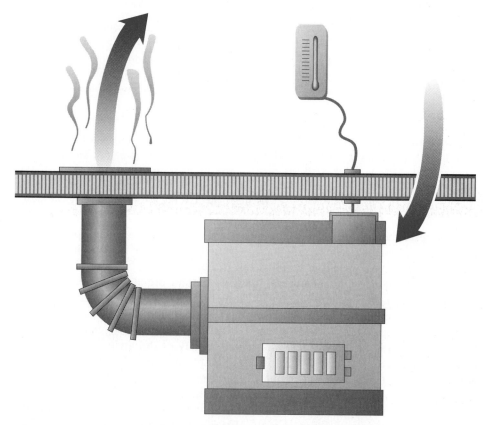

▶ **Figure 2-3**   *A simple system consisting of a furnace and a thermostat. As the room heats up, the thermostat turns off the furnace. As the room cools down, the thermostat starts the furnace.*

98.6°F, regardless of the environmental temperature. The body uses feedback from the inside and outside temperatures to help it to use energy to heat or to cool off in order to keep that temperature steady. An organization, on the other hand, tries to maintain some balanced state that permits it to remain in existence or to grow. The steady state desired could be one of 10% growth in sales per year, for example.

One of the noticeable differences between this view of organizations and those represented by classical theory or the human relations approach lies in the emphasis placed on the interrelationship between the organization and its environment. Both the classical and human relations schools tend to look upon organizations as virtually closed systems, taking account mainly of internal activities. The systems approach, on the other hand, requires us to look at the ongoing process of interaction of the organization with other systems. There is more focus on feedback, both internal and external, and on the role of boundary-spanning individuals who bring information into the system.

A second difference between systems theories and the two previously discussed is in the view of the organization as a dynamic, living entity. The organization is not static, but something that experiences growth, maturation, and possibly even death. A set of related theories has been developed, in fact, that look more closely at these aspects of open systems and their dependence on the environment and their life cycles.[17]

Contingency Theories.   In addition, some concepts from systems theory have been usefully applied in what are referred to as *contingency theories*. Contingency theorists take the view that the nature of the environment and structure of the system influence the appropriate strategies managers should adopt. The concept of equifinality holds that organizations with similar purposes in similar environments will come to resemble each other, regardless of how they started out. This idea suggests there will therefore be different strategies depending upon factors such as the resources available, the nature of the task, and the relationships among the people in the organization carrying out the task.

One contingency is that between mechanistic and organic organizations. For well-defined tasks in stable, relatively unchanging environments, mechanistic organizations are preferable. These organizations follow regular hierarchical, chain-of-command principles, such as those evoked in the classical management theories. Communication is mainly vertical, consisting largely of the giving of instructions and the announcing of decisions. In unstable, rapidly shifting environments, in which the task is not clearly spelled out, organic organizations are more appropriate. Organic organizations operate with more open communication, with "lateral rather than a vertical direction of communication through the organization, communication between people of different rank, also, resembling consultation rather than command. . . ."[18]

Joan Woodward's contingency theory, which employed the mechanistic-organic distinction,[19] developed from a study that focussed attention on the relationship between the technological complexity of operations and the nature and structure of organizational communication. She identified three kinds of operations: small-scale operations, like print shops or tailors; large-scale manufacturing, assembly-line operations; and what she termed "continuous process production," such as chemical plants or oil refineries. The assembly-line operations tended to display reliance on little communication, with emphasis on vertical, written communication when it occurred. The other two kinds of organizations exhibited more open communication, with verbal preferred over written.

Fiedler's contingency theory takes account of the following variables, or contingencies: the orientation of the leader and the "favorableness" of the situation. As with the Blake and Mouton grid, the leader's orientation could be toward the task (getting the job done) or toward interpersonal relationships within the group. The term *favorableness* refers to the degree to which the leader is able to exert influence over the group. The task could be clear and well structured or not, and the leader-follower relationship could be good or bad. A highly favorable situation is one in which the task is clear, the relationships are good, and the leader has a strong power position; a highly unfavorable situation is one in which these conditions do not exist. Many cases fall in between these extremes. The appropriate leadership style depends upon the favorableness of the situation. In both highly favorable and highly unfavorable situations, a directive, task-oriented leader is more effective; in the moderate situations, a leader more oriented to human relationships is preferred.[20]

The various contingency theories are derived from the point that systems must be seen in interaction with their environments. There is no single correct or more effective style of managerial communication; it depends upon contingencies in the environment, such as clarity or certainty of information about the task, or the kind of technology involved. In some cases, a classical management style, directive, formal, and task-oriented, is needed; in others, the more open, participative style of the human relations approach is best.

Applications to Communication Problems. The systems approach places importance on communication, since a system is maintained by its patterns of communication, and the open system idea emphasizes communication between the system and its environment. Concerning the specific nature of communications within the system, though, the contingencies of the system call for varying responses. The contingency theories imply that there is no right or wrong way to deal with organizational communication problems. Communication is often treated as a variable rather than as something that can be improved or made more effective.

The nature of superior-subordinate communication, for example, depends upon the nature of the task, the environment, and the technology employed by the organization. Vertical communication and horizontal communication are recommended for certain situations, but not for others. Vertical communication is associated with so-called mechanistic organizations; horizontal communication, with organic organizations.

The channels of communication and their capacity are of special concern in systems theories. The system depends upon the flow of communication through the network of subsystems and through boundary-spanners with the environment. Monitoring feedback is considered an important activity in the systems perspective.

Problems of morale and climate, as well as those resulting from conflict, within the organizational system are variables affecting the system's operation. In other words, climate and conflict tend not to be seen as something that one tries to deal with or to change. Rather, these factors are contingencies that can be used to determine what particular pattern of communication is appropriate. On the other hand, the systemic emphasis gives attention to the notion that conflict or poor morale in one part of the system can have negative effects throughout the whole system.

Problem solving and decision making are seen from the point of view of decision theories, which look to the relationships among environmental needs and the internal information processing of the organization. Decision making becomes a process limited by the realities and the contingencies, including incomplete and often uncertain information. The point is that, within the systems perspective, efforts will be made to build a decision-making process into the system. According to these theories, it is understood that information is not processed in a vacuum but in relationship to other subsystems and to the environment of the whole system.

▶ ### Corporate Cultures

The system theories of organization were especially influential during the 1970s and 1980s, but some theorists came to feel that this approach was overly abstract and tended to overlook actual human behavior in organizations. One answer to the abstractness of these theories was the development of the cultural approach for analyzing organizational behavior.

The concept of culture is borrowed from the field of anthropology and used here analogously. In anthropology, a culture refers to a fundamental characteristics of identifiable human groups. To speak of a group's culture means to speak of that group's language, religious and value systems, typical life and economic styles (fishing, hunting, farming, herding), products, and artifacts. Such cultures are often ethnically based.

Corporate cultures consist of unique patterns of behavior and values characteristic of individual organizations. A culture in this sense is less exact in conception than a system and is based more on stories intended to illustrate the organization's uniqueness. The cultural approach looks at the lived experience of the people constituting the organization.

Terence Deal and Arthur A. Kennedy try to make explicit the features of "culture." Their terminology is more informal and less scientific than the writers in the other traditions.[21] This use of language is partly the result of writing for a general or lay audience and partly an effort to show culture as informal, and vaguely or imprecisely felt by organization members.

The elements Deal and Kennedy identify as making up culture include the business environment, values, heroes, rites and rituals, and the cultural network. Information about values and heroes are passed on through myths and legends as

▶ *Corporate cultures such as Ben & Jerry's Ice Cream can be very distinctive.*

recounted by storytellers and priests. They highlight the symbolic purposes of corporate activity as opposed to the supposed functional purposes. The symbolism is important in inculcating and maintaining adherence to certain important bedrock values in the strong culture. The positive evaluation of symbolism is one of the important departures of the cultural approach, which distinguishes it from the functional approaches of other organizational theories.

Deal and Kennedy describe four types of tribes that exist in various environments. The use of the term *tribe* indicates how the authors have popularized the anthropological analogy; most cultural anthropologists avoid the term *tribe* because of its negative associations. The so-called tribes are reminiscent of some of the contingency theories discussed above, since they are determined by environmental conditions. (We will usually refer to them as types of cultures.)

The "tough guy-macho" culture usually exists, Deal and Kennedy claim, in highly competitive, risky fields, where the star is the tough, decisive loner. In the "Work hard-play hard" culture, the hero is the team player, who emphasizes group-sharing and fun. The "Bet your company" culture favors the technical expert who can plan. The "Process" culture focuses on processes, how things are done. The "hero" is the person who knows the precedents and regulations.

There has been some slippage or even confusion concerning the concept of organizational culture. Culture is used in some instances to refer to the backdrop against which organizational communication takes place; at other times, culture is

Corporate Culture at Ben and Jerry's

Some corporations go out of their way to create the message that they are different and to make that difference part of their corporate culture. Ben and Jerry's Ice Cream, founded by Ben Cohen and Jerry Greenfield in the late sixties, is one such organization. Ben and Jerry's corporate culture combines responsibility and playfulness. At their ice cream plants, located in a number of small towns such as Waterbury and Springfield, Vermont, the company involves itself in community affairs. Truckload sales provide free ice cream to charitable organizations for fund-raisers. On weekends, recent-run movies are shown on sides of the plants for anyone who cares to come and see them.

Moreover, part of the proceeds from the Peace Pop, one of the company's products, are donated to further the cause of world peace. In 1992, the focus of the company's mission statement was to "Leave no child behind," and a number of programs have been developed to aid the Children's Defense Fund.

The employee culture is nontraditional. For example, the highest paid member of the organization receives no more than five times the salary of the lowest paid worker. Just working in an ice cream plant has its own benefits. Each employee receives a certain number of free pints of ice cream each week. The Joy Gang provides organized fun on the job, following Jerry's motto, "If it's not fun, why do it?" Every Friday, employees are given free cookies.

treated as something that can be changed or manipulated by managers to bring about desired results. "Symbolic managers," those who are especially sensitive to the cultural characteristics of the organization, can change the values or heroes or other aspects of the culture in order to effect desired change.

The concept of corporate culture can be used to analyze the nature and effectiveness of communication within an organization. We can apply the concepts to gain an impression of how well an organization deals with communication problems. For example, we could begin with an effort to determine whether there is strong consensus concerning the values communicated throughout the organization. In strong cultures, there should be clear consensus about positive values; weak cultures lack such clear agreement. One could consider the heroes that are held up for emulation in the firm. Do they embody the values that are positive and that sustain the organization?

We can continue with a description of the storytellers and their stories, the priests who maintain the traditions of the organizational culture, the rituals and ceremonies that enact the values and traditions, and so on. Peters and Austin pay special attention to language, including terms used to designate clients (customers or problems or pains).[22] In academia, we tend to refer to research opportunities and teaching loads. (What do these terms suggest about the cultural values of a

Diversity in the Workplace

Corporate Culture and French Culture

The problems of developing a strong corporate culture are multiplied when corporate cultures and national cultures clash. Following a takeover of a French firm, General Electric (GE) attempted to inculcate its corporate culture through a training seminar. GE required the French participants to wear company t-shirts emblazoned with a GE slogan. The French were horrified by what they saw as a totalitarian effort at forcing everyone to wear uniforms.[23] This effort to instill a particular corporate culture, therefore, ran into national cultural fears.

In contrast, in its efforts to establish the new Euro-Disney theme park near Paris, Disney Corporation made special efforts to involve French-speaking negotiators and to show sensitivity to French cultural concerns. The Euro Disney Resort includes Euro-Disneyland, which comprises a Main Street USA, Fantasyland, Frontierland, Adventureland, and Discoverland. The resort represents a $4.4 billion venture. There will be a special exhibit featuring Verne, the French science-fiction author of *Journey to the Center of the Earth* and *20,000 Leagues under the Sea*. Besides ensuring that French-speakers handled the negotiations, Disney made a point to use local consultants to guide them through the maze of French licensing requirements. In addition, the exterior of the restaurants will reflect French architectural styles, even though the interiors may feature Key West-type seafood or American western steaks and barbecue.

See D. Scimoe (1991, May). Mickey Mouse is coming to town: Euro Disney resort to open in 1992. *Europe*, 306, 17–18.

university?) The culture's vocabulary provide a set of features to look for, a way of forming an overall impression of the health of an organization's communication.

In addition to this use of the organizational culture idea, there has been an effort to take into account real, anthropological cultural differences in organizational communication. The idea of organizational or corporate culture leads naturally to a consideration of the effects national culture has on tendencies for certain kinds of organizational cultures to develop. Given the relative success of Japanese exporters in world markets, and especially in U.S. markets for cars and electronics, Americans have become fascinated with Japanese culture. Hence, there has been attention to Japanese management theories, Theory Z, lifetime employment, and the like. Corporate culture, then, can be used in the original sense of culture, rather than metaphorically when referring to these kinds of phenomena.

Application to Communication Problems.   Someone looking at organizational communication problems from a cultural point of view would try to see them in relationship to the organization's traditions and values. Preference is given to the symbolic manager in superior-subordinate communication, one who is sensitive to the importance of symbolism and upholding the culture's values when dealing with subordinates. That relationship and the nature of vertical communication may depend upon the kind of culture that organization represents. The "work hard-play hard" culture, for example, calls for a leader who is warm, open, and caring. Horizontal communication is obviously to be favored in the team-building atmosphere of this culture, as well.

The channels of communication preferred also vary depending upon the culture. Meetings and long conferences are the preferred medium of communication in the "bet your company" culture. The goal in this setting is to ensure that all bases have been covered, every contingency thought out in advance; hence, the emphasis on long discussions. "Process" cultures also favor meetings and the ability to follow proper procedures in handling such meetings. One also looks for rituals and ceremonies as means of expressing the culture's values. A ritual is a recurrent activity carried out in part for its symbolic value; a ceremony is grander and celebrates the heroes and, thereby, the core values of the corporate culture. One who follows a corporate culture approach, therefore, would emphasize rituals, ceremonies, and heroes as media for symbolic expression.

Conflict and decision making are similarly handled differently according to the nature of the corporate culture involved. The team-building cultures are concerned with settling conflicts in ways that maintain the group's solidarity. They hope to maintain a positive, accepting organizational climate. Presumably, there is less concern for such a climate in the tougher cultures.

Decision making and problem solving are carried out in ways congruent with the culture and values of the organization. For example, Deal and Kennedy stress the importance of recruiting heroes to help to give legitimacy to the process of decision making. Once a decision has been made, it is important to carry out in ways that do not seem threatening to the traditions or culture. Rituals should be developed to help gain acceptance for the decision and to symbolize the cultural sanction for the decision that has been made.

SUMMARY

Organizational communication has become a subdiscipline in the field of communication. Several theories have been developed concerning organizational principles and structure and their relationship to communication within organizations. These various theories suggest approaches to the many kinds of communication problems that can occur in organizations. In this chapter, we looked at seven varieties of organizational communication problems and considered some of the ways that these problems would be dealt with, given the assumptions of different kinds of organizational theories.

The theory operative within an organization, whether knowingly selected or not, determines to some extent the nature of communication within that organization. Further, the theoretical approach taken by an observer or analyst trying to understand communication within an organization will focus certain things and perhaps neglect others.

The seven types of organizational communication problems discussed in the chapter follow:

1. Superior-subordinate communication
2. Vertical communication
3. Horizontal communication
4. Channels or media for communication
5. Morale or communication climate in organizations
6. Conflict and conflict management
7. Problem solving and decision making

•

EXERCISES

1. List all the organizations to which you now belong or have belonged. Discuss your list with others; what does your list indicate about the definitions people have for organizations? What are the features of these groups that lead us to call them organizations?

2. Discuss the nature of communication problems in organizations. What seem to be some basic causes for these problems? Select one of the four types of organizational theories and use its principles to troubleshoot the problems of communication that you have experienced in organizations.

3. Differentiate internal communication in firms following a scientific or classical management theory and those following a human relations approach to management. Summarize how a management philosophy can affect internal organizational communication.

4. Why is communication particularly important in theories that take a general systems approach to organizations? What is the distinction between a mechanistic and an organic system? Show how these differences are significant for the communication climate in a given organization. Describe organizations to which you belong that could be considered to have the communication characteristics of organic or mechanistic organizations.

5. What is meant by the term *culture* as applied to corporations or other organizations? What are some of the noticeable features of corporate culture? If one were taking a cultural view of organizations, what kind of communications would one want to observe? Describe the organizational culture of one of the organizations to which you belong. Explain why it is a strong or weak culture.

6. Research a corporation or other organization, though the library or, if possible, by a site visit. What are your initial impressions concerning the nature of communication within that organization? What evidence have you used to come to these conclusions?

Communication Case Problem: "We're for Sale."

In December 1990, Chrysler Corporation announced that it would be putting up for sale its subsidiary company, Gulfstream Aerospace of Savanna, Georgia. The founder and CEO of Gulfstream intented to buy the company himself.

When Mr. Paulson first sold the company (eventually to Chrysler) in 1985, rumors shot through the company, leading to abysmal morale and many unnecessary resignations. There were widespread fears that massive layoffs would result, new managers, perhaps even foreign managers, would be brought in, upsetting the well-established and highly positive Gulfstream corporate culture.

How should Mr. Paulson handle this latest situation? How can rumors and fears similar to those in 1985 best be dealt with? For further details, see the story by Claudia H. Deutsch, *New York Times*, March 4, 1990, regarding Paulson's solution.

SELECTED SOURCES
FOR FURTHER READING

Blake, R., & Mouton, J. (1964). *The managerial grid*. Houston: Gulf.

Burns, T., & Stalker, G. M. (1961). *The management of innovation* (2nd ed.). London: Tavistock Publications.

Cherrington, D. J. (1989). *Organizational behavior: The management of individual and organizational performance*. Boston: Allyn and Bacon.

Cummings, H. W., Long, L. W., & Lewis, M. L. (1987). *Managing communication in organizations: An introduction* (2nd ed.). Scarsdale, NY: Gorsuch Scarisbrick.

Cyert, R. M., & March, J. G. (1963). *A behavioral theory of the firm*. Englewood Cliffs, NJ: Prentice-Hall.

Deal, T., & Kennedy, A. A. (1982). *Corporate culture: The rites and rituals of corporate life*. Reading, MA: Addison-Wesley.

Drucker, P. F. (1974). *Management: Tasks, responsibilities, practices*. New York: Harper & Row.

Farace, R. V., Monge, P. R., & Russell, H. M. (1977). *Communicating and organizing*. Reading, MA: Addison-Wesley.

Fiedler, F. (1967). *A theory of leadership effectiveness*. New York: McGraw-Hill.

Herzberg, F. (1966). *Work and the nature of man*. Cleveland: World Publishing.

Jablin, F. M., Putnam, L., Roberts, K. H., & Porter, L. W. (Eds.) (1987). *Handbook of organizational communication: An interdisciplinary perspective*. Newbury Park, CA: Sage Publications.

Katz, D. & Kahn, R. L. (1966). *The social psychology of organizations*. New York: John Wiley.

Katz, D. & Kahn, R. L. (1978). *The social psychology of organizations* (2nd ed.). New York: John Wiley.

Koestler, A. (1967). *The ghost in the machine*. Chicago: Henry Regnery Company.

Likert, R. (1967). *The human organization*. New York: McGraw-Hill.

March, J. G. & Simon, H. A. (1958). *Organizations*. New York: John Wiley.

McGregor, D. (1960). *Human side of enterprise*. New York: McGraw-Hill.

McGregor, D. (1967). *The professional manager*. Eds. McGregor, C., & Bennis, W. New York: McGraw-Hill.

Peters, T. J. & Austin, N. (1985). *A passion for excellence: The leadership difference*. New York: Random House.

Peters, T. J. & Waterman, R. H., Jr. (1982). *In search of excellence: Lessons from America's best-run companies*. New York: Harper & Row.

Scott, W. G. & Hart, D. K. (1979). *Organizational America*. Boston: Houghton Mifflin.

Taylor, F. W. (1934). *The principles of scientific management*. New York: Harper & Brothers.

Weber, M. (1947). *The theory of social and economic organization* (A. M. Henderson and T. Parsons, Trans.). New York: The Free Press.

Weick, K. E. (1979). *The social psychology of organizing* (2nd ed.). Reading, MA: Addison-Wesley.

Woodward, J. (1965). *Industrial Organization: Theory and Practice*. London: Oxford University Press.

▶

References

1. Deetz, S. & Mumby, D. K. (1990). Power, discourse, and the workplace: Reclaiming the critical tradition. In J. A. Anderson (Ed.), *Communication Yearbook 13* (p. 19). Newbury Park, CA: Sage Publications. For a critical view of the role of organizations in our lives, see Scott, W. G. & Hart, D. K. (1979). *Organizational America*. Boston: Houghton Mifflin.

2. Blake, R. R. & Mouton, J. S. (1964). *The managerial grid: Key orientations for achieving production through people* (p. 3). Houston: Gulf.

3. Morgan, B. S., & Schiemann, W. A. (1983, March). Why internal communication is failing. *Public Relations Journal*, pp. 15–17.

4. McCathrin, E. Z. (1989, July). Beyond employee publications. *Public Relations Journal*. p. 15.

5. Falcione, R. L., Sussman, L., & Herden, R. P. (1987). Communication climate in organizations. In F. M. Jablin, L. L. Putnam, K. H. Roberts, & L. W. Porter (Eds.), *Handbook of organizational communication: An interdisciplinary perspective* (pp. 195–196). Newbury Park, CA: Sage Publications.

6. Falcione, Sussman, and Herden, p. 201.

7. Cummings, H. W., Long, L. W., & Lewis, M. L. (1987). *Managing communication in organizations: An introduction* (2nd ed.). (pp. 164–165). Scarsdale, AZ: Gorsuch Scarisbrick.

8. Reich, R. B. (1991). *The work of nations: Preparing ourselves for 21st century capitalism* (p. 177). New York: Alfred A. Knopf.

9. March, J. G., & Simon, H. A. (1958). *Organizations*. New York: John Wiley.

10. The English title for what was part of a larger German work, titled *Wirtschaft und Gessellschaft*.

11. Adapted from Weber, M. (1947). *The theory of social and economic organization* (pp. 333–334). (Henderson, A. M., & Parson, T., Trans.) New York: The Free Press.

12. Taylor, F. W. (1934). *The principles of scientific management* (p. 7). New York: Harper & Brothers.

13. Taylor, p. 39.

14. Fayol, H. (1937). The administrative theory in the state (Greer, S. Trans.). In L. Gulick & L. Urwick (Eds.). *Papers on the science of administration* (p. 101). New York: Institute of Public Administration.

15. McGregor, D. (1967). *The professional manager* (pp. 13–14). Eds. C. McGregor and W. Bennis. New York: McGraw-Hill, pp. 39–41.

16. Blake and Mouton.

17. Such newer theoretical approaches are summarized well in Euske, N. A., & Roberts, K. H. (1987). Evolving perspectives in organizational theory: A communications perspective. *Handbook of Organizational Communication* (pp. 52–61). These theories include resource dependency theory, which looks to how organizations strive to gain control over resources in their environments; population ecology and life cycle theories

that emphasize a biological, evolutionary metaphor; and institutionalization theory, which deals with organizations conformity with norms and expectations of environments.

18. Burns, T., & Stalker, G. M. (1961). *The management of innovation* (2nd ed.). (p. 121). London: Tavistock Publications.

19. Woodward, J. (1965). *Industrial organization: Theory and practice* (pp. 23–24). London: Oxford University Press.

20. Fiedler, F. (1967). *A theory of leadership effectiveness* (p. 13). New York: McGraw-Hill.

21. Deal, T. & Kennedy, A. A. (1982). *Corporate culture: The rites and rituals of corporate life.* Reading, MA: Addison-Wesley. Deal and Kennedy's treatment, as shown by their use of terms, is somewhat popularized; more academic discussions of corporate or organizational culture can be found in P. J. Frost, L. F. Moore, M. R. Louis, & J. Matin, Eds. (1985) *Organizational culture.* Beverly Hills, CA: Sage Publications, or, J. A. Anderson, Ed. (1990). "Section one," *Communication yearbook 13.* Newbury Park, CA: Sage Publications.

22. Peters, T. & Austin, N. (1985). *A passion for excellence: The leadership difference* (pp. 281–282). New York: Random House.

23. See related story (1990, July 31), GE's culture turns sour at French unit, *Wall Street Journal*, p. A10.

Effective Listening Processes

3

CHAPTER

After studying this chapter, you should be able to:

1. Explain why listening is important to successful communication.

2. Distinguish listening from simple hearing.

3. Identify different kinds of listening situations.

4. Explain the steps in the listening process.

5. Understand typical problems that prevent effective listening.

6. Apply principles for improving comprehensive listening.

7. Apply principles for improving critical listening.

8. Apply principles for improving empathic listening.

Overview

Everyone likes a good listener, and no one seems to like a poor listener. Recall from the Preface that listening headed the list of skills most often mentioned by business leaders as necessary for success in their businesses. In a survey conducted by the authors of training directors for corporations, we found that nearly one-half (49.1%) reported that they either planned or were already doing listening training in their firms.

This chapter continues to emphasize the transactional nature of human communication. Before turning our attention to the production and presentation of messages in later chapters, we look first to the process of receiving, decoding, and interpreting messages: that is, the process of listening. We consider this topic before others for two good reasons: first, in order to develop the skills of comprehension, interpretation, and retention that characterize good listening; and second, in order to improve message-producing skills by becoming sensitive to how listeners deal with our messages.

In other words, we should strive to learn effective listening skills for their own sake, because such skills will enhance our personal effectiveness: Good listening is good business. A second benefit is that attention to the listening side of the

▶ *Listening is an essential skill.*

equation ought to make us more effective in formulating and delivering messages. Listening is a skill general to all interpersonal communication situations and contexts. For these reasons, we place this examination of the processes of listening upfront.

Today, it is commonplace to say that listening is important and that many problems result from poor listening. Recent surveys continue to highlight the need for effective listening skills. Corporations such as Sperry, IBM, and others organized structured training programs for their employees. Organizations often call in consultants to help train people in becoming more effective listeners; in fact, one of the authors serves occasionally in this capacity, giving listening workshops for both corporate and nonprofit agencies.

▶ **Listening Can Be Taught**

Surveys and activities such as those described focus on the aspect of human communication often taken for granted: listening. They also indicate a belief that listening can be improved by education or training and that effective listening can be learned. This point reminds us that listening is not just a passive activity, or something that happens or doesn't. The passive view of listening suggests that some people are born good listeners while others are not. Of course, certain aspects of listening behavior result from one's physiological or psychological makeup. For example, basic intelligence or abilities in verbal recognition and memory retentiveness may be little affected by a workshop or a single course in listening. Vocabulary and familiarity with the speaker's words will also affect the listener's comprehension and retention of verbal material. Physical hearing acuity is another obvious factor in listening that may not be subject directly to training. Still, there are techniques for overcoming bad habits that we have fallen into as listeners.

Diversity in the Workplace

European Advisory Councils

Several large American corporations have set up advisory councils in Europe in order to listen and to find out what is seen as important in international markets. These councils, made up of business, government, academic, and professional experts, have reportedly been used by as many as 300 companies. General Motors has found its advisory group so helpful in Europe that the company plans to institute others in places such as Australia. IBM has similar councils in Asia and Latin America as well as in Europe.

Discussions at council meetings are generally free-wheeling, covering cultural and related topics, rather than dealing with specific policy or business. The American executives in attendance are there mainly to listen.

For more information, see C. H. Deutsch (1990, June 24), Soliciting the foreign perspective (p. F25). *New York Times*.

Hearing versus Listening

In stating that hearing acuity is important for good listening, we need to be clear about the distinction between "hearing" and "listening." By hearing, we mean the physical receiving of the sound waves by the receptor organs (the ears) and the operation of the human hearing system. By listening, we mean the mental and interactive processes of attention-giving, recognition of the symbolic meaning of the physical stimuli, understanding, retaining, and acting upon that understanding. Obviously, there is a direct link between hearing and listening: If you can't hear, you can't listen. Hearing is the first step in the listening process.

TYPES OF LISTENING

Up to this point, we have spoken of listening in an undifferentiated way, as if there were one type of listening. In fact, there are many different contexts and purposes for listening. What is often overlooked in the popular literature concerning listening is that different listening situations call for different kinds of listening skills.

Let's go back to the opening line of this chapter ("Everyone likes a good listener"): What is meant by the term *good listener*? Consider a person you know whom you would describe as a good listener. Why do you select this person? What does he or she do that you associate with good listening? When we ask this question of students or others, people invariably describe someone who is sympathetic. On the other hand, when executives say that employees are not good listeners, do you think that they have the same characteristics in mind? When teachers complain about the listening habits of students, are they thinking of the same attributes? These examples suggest that there are different kinds of listening, which are appropriate to different needs and circumstances. The teacher is thinking of listening and being attentive (probably quiet) and retaining what is said in class. The person describing a personal problem to someone is probably not concerned with the listener's retaining the specifics of what is said in order to pass a test. The executive may not be too concerned about the sympathetic feelings of the employees as they listen.

We cannot approach the subject of listening systematically until we distinguish these various listening situations. Principles and skills emphasized in one type may not be in another. Distinctions of this type have been reported in research dealing with the psychology of language processing: "The orienting task of the understander has been found to affect the representation that is extracted from the discourse."[1] In other words, what we listen for and how we listen is affected by our expectations concerning the nature of situation, whether it is conversation, entertainment, or education.

Appreciative Listening

Some listening is done for pleasure. Such listening could involve listening to a play, watching a film, or conversing with friends. By definition, these situations are supposed to be less like work and less demanding than other types of listening. We can, however, improve our skills in these situations and thereby enhance the associated pleasure. For example, a course in theater appreciation or criticism may heighten one's awareness of the features that make for good theater: the effects of staging, direction, setting, acting skill, and so on. A course in film history or criticism could make one more aware of the techniques of good film-making; many people report that they derive much more pleasure from films and plays as a result of such training. Similarly, some education in music history and appreciation makes for more enjoyable concert going. Even at this level, therefore, listening skills can be improved.

Comprehensive Listening

Comprehensive listening means listening to learn. The emphasis is on comprehending and retaining material. This is the situation that most people have experienced in schools, especially when listening to lectures. Much of the training and information given in business and industry uses similar lecture methods, although the lecturer may be on videotape or film, rather than present in person. When interest first developed in overcoming bad habits of listening, this was the kind of listening people had in mind. This type of listening is said to be effective when the listeners are able to perform some task described in the presentation or pass an examination showing that they understand and remember the important parts of the presentation. Listening-comprehension tests are usually aimed at this level of listening.

Critical Listening

Critical listening refers to listening that we do when we need to make some kind of decision or judgment based upon what we have heard. For example, if you were going to attend a debate between two candidates running for office, this would be a critical listening situation. In this case, you are not listening just to be able to retain what each candidate says. Rather, you are listening in order to determine which candidate deserves your vote. Similarly, if you are shopping for a new car, you will listen to the sales pitches of competing salespeople in the different show-rooms. The point here is to be able to pick out the best reasons and arguments that each salesperson or each candidate makes. When we call this critical listening, we do not mean listening to criticize, then, but to make critical judgments.

Empathic Listening

The fourth kind of listening refers to those situations in which someone needs a sympathetic ear. The term *empathy* contains the Greek root, pathos, which denotes feelings, emotions. We see this root in many English words: For example, apathy means absence of feelings; sympathy means to feel the same as; and empathy means to feel within, as if you were in the same position as the other person. In this situation, you listen in such a way that the other person can feel that you understand and can identify with the feelings that other person is expressing. This kind of listening requires a person who can be noncritical and nonjudgmental: that is, one who does not appear to be listening in order to evaluate the speaker. The emphasis is on acceptance and helpful understanding.

We will not concern ourselves here with the listening for appreciation situations but will concentrate on the other types. Hence, we will discuss three types of listening: comprehensive, critical, and empathic.

The distinction among these types is important to understand because each calls for a different kind of skill. It is possible, even probable, that a person good in one type of listening will not necessarily be good in another. For instance, a good critical listener, who is very good at picking apart arguments and evidence, may not be the best person to go to when you want to talk out a personal problem. In fact, you hope that a good empathic listener will refrain from being too evaluative or too critical. Some people may be very good at retaining what they hear but not particularly critical when it comes to analyzing what they have remembered. A truly effective communicator is able to recognize which type of listening is called for by a particular situation and to enact the appropriate listening behaviors.

On the other hand, all three types of listening situations are not completely distinct. Of course, there are basic similarities in all listening and in all contexts of processing incoming messages and sending feedback in response to those messages. The point is that different aspects of listening are emphasized over others, depending upon the purpose and the setting. Still, empathic listening requires good comprehending skills; being an effective critical listener also requires the abilities to comprehend and retain the message. Learning content requires skill at differentiating important points from less important points or for recognizing and remembering the evidence and support used for various points, skills associated with effective critical listening.

PROBLEMS OF LISTENING

Corporations such as Sperry, Xerox, and others became concerned about listening in recent years because they considered that much listening was ineffective. Listening training is now a regular part of many firm's employee development programs. Problems may hinder any or all of the three kinds of listening situations that concern us. A lack of good empathic listening, for instance, could be at the heart of a perceived problem in superior-subordinate communication, one of the organizational communication problems referred to in the previous chapter. If a co-worker or a superior is not seen as a good empathic listener, there may be deleterious effects on the organization's climate or morale. What may be seen as a problem in downward vertical communication could be a result of ineffective listening habits of members of the organization. Proper instructions or explanations are being given, but people have not been well trained in comprehensive listening. Decision making or problem solving may be hampered by a need for better critical listening on the part of decision makers. Many problems, therefore, can be traced to inadequacies in listening processes and behaviors.

In order to understand the kinds of problems that occur in listening, we begin with a discussion of the nature of the listening process; then we consider typical barriers to effective listening; and finally, we turn to problems more specific to each type of listening situation.

The Nature of the Listening Process

Listening focuses on a special part of the process of human communication. If you think of the linear model of communication, like that introduced in Chapter 1, listening refers to the behaviors on the right side of that model—the internal processing of the incoming message by the receiver, the listener.

When we engage in communication, as stated earlier, each of us becomes simultaneously a sender and a receiver of messages. Listening is thus an interactive process. How we listen is influenced by the ongoing flow and interchange of verbal and nonverbal cues occurring as a part of the interaction. The listener does not process the incoming material in isolation, but in response to the interaction with the speaker, as well as others who may be present as other listeners. The human receiver is very different from a radio or television receiver. The television receiver cannot change channels at will nor *intentionally* distort or filter out incoming messages. The human receiver is not as simple, because a person actively participates in forming the message that is received. We can tune out a speaker, and we can select to listen only to certain parts of what is said.

In the linear model of communication developed in the first chapter, we noted that the signal coming through the channel was received and decoded before reaching the destination, or the mind of the other person. In response to that decoded message, feedback was sent. Now we look at these steps in a little more detail.

1. *Message is received.* The first step in the listening process involves simple hearing. The receptor organ, the ear, picks up the vibrations in the air waves recognized as speech sounds. Although it may appear to be a passive activity, the act of hearing speech is not quite so simple.

First, we should clarify the differences between listening and reading and between speech and writing as media of communication. When you look at a written page, such as this one, many visual cues may aid you in grasping the page's meaning. There are punctuation marks, paragraphs, numbers, and section headings, which tell you how the various words relate to one another. You can go over the page at your own speed, reading quickly or slowly; you can go back and reread parts in order to get the whole sense. If you were listening to this page, you would get the words one at a time; you would not see them all laid out with relationships visually indicated. When you got to the end of a sentence, you would have to remember the beginning; you couldn't reread. You would have to listen at the pace of the speaker, whether fast or slow.

We are usually unaware of our active role as listeners, because so much of what constitutes hearing occurs automatically, at a level out of our conscious awareness. To begin with, the units of sound of speech, called phonemes, are not really as discrete and separable as are the written letters on a page. As one text on the psychology of language puts it, "Rather than being spaced out like beads on a string, the acoustic cues for different speech sounds overlap and intermesh, so that a vowel sound might provide clues to the identity of both the preceding and the following consonants."[2]

When we have learned a language, we have learned to hear specific sounds called phonemes, which are roughly approximated by letters in an alphabet. Much of what we hear is influenced by the linguistic context and by our own expectations. Experiments have shown that people will fill in phonemes, or letter sounds, that are left out in speech, and actually "hear" the missing sounds. We can therefore understand speech even when the sound is faint or when there is noise because of this tendency to fill in the anticipated parts.[3] Before becoming consciously aware of the speech, we have already begun to "correct" it to fit with our auditory filters. We hear what we expect to hear. This partly explains our difficulty in listening to a foreign language, even after we have studied it in school; we need to get used to the patterns of speech sounds, the rhythm, and the typical combinations, in order to start hearing. It is easier to understand the speech of a close friend or relative than that of a stranger, because you have become accustomed to the intimate's characteristic patterns and phrasings.

2. *Message gets attention.* We cannot say that a message is actually received in a communicative sense if it is not attended to. At this stage, attention is directed to the message: It is perceived as being a message. A great deal of information is available for our attention in our surroundings at any one time. In order to function, we need to develop habits of excluding much of this information and dealing with only a small, selected part of the available information. We have to learn to exclude a lot of information in order to make sense of what's going on around us.

When several spoken messages are sent simultaneously to a person, the listener can pick out one and exclude the others if the messages are coming from different locations, or are at differing volumes, or spoken by different voices (say, male versus female). In other words, some physical distinction allows us to exclude some messages and give attention to others.[4] The excluded messages are not entirely unheard, however, as experiments indicate that people will notice items such as their own names when spoken in the message that is not being attended to. Certain items can call attention to themselves because of our special interests or needs, even while attending to something else. A friend recalls being involved in conversation with one person at a gathering and suddenly hearing a reference to the small college in the Midwest that he attended years before. The college's name, in this instance, gained his attention while he was engaged in giving attention to another message. While it is easy to think of listening as a passive process, the listener must be active in selectively choosing the stimuli, or the messages that will be processed. Selective attention can be a significant barrier to listening.

3. *Message is given meaning.* Once the incoming stimuli have been identified as speech that should receive our attention, the next step is to determine the meanings of the words and the overall message. This decoding process appears to be influenced by expectations and the effects of context, as are hearing and attending. We learn to listen to phrases or utterances rather than to individual words or phonemes. When someone says, "It's going to be a nice day," we anticipate the ending of the sentence and have little difficulty decoding "day." Not only do we anticipate and hear certain phonemes, but we also fill in parts of the message based on our expectations. If the person were to substitute "giraffe" for "day" at the end of the sentence, it may take us a moment to get the meaning. Decoding may be more difficult for unexpected material or parts of messages, not just unfamiliar parts.

The trickiest aspect of decoding is the matching of the vocabularies and the dictionaries of the speaker and listener. To recall an earlier analogy, the "decoder rings" probably do not match, at least not perfectly. The listeners must assign meaning to the words and message based entirely upon their own stock of meanings and definitions. Meanings are affected by the connotations that the listener places on the terms used by the speaker. The listener, in decoding, *actively creates* the message as far as the listener is concerned. The person sending the message may be unaware of the connotations or private associations that the listener may have for selected words.

4. *Message is interpreted and evaluated.* Sounds and words are combined into a meaningful unit related to the listener's past experiences or present needs. At this stage, we say that the listener gets (or does not get) the point. Philosophers such as John Searle have advocated a theory of language use that is called speech act theory. This theory holds that the meaning of language is not found in the meaning of individual words: The meaning of words varies with the context. The smallest unit of meaning in a language, according to this theory, is the act performed by the use of language. When the listener is able to determine what the speaker is trying to accomplish by using speech (the speech that the listener hears), then the listener is getting the message. In interpreting the message, the listeners try to determine what the intended purpose of the message is and how that purpose fits with their own needs, values, and experiences.

The listener evaluates the message to determine whether it is useful, worth remembering, interesting, amusing, or seems true or accurate. The listener must determine whether the speaker is serious or not, or whether the speaker is trying to use irony, exaggeration, or sarcasm. The listener must consider the literal and hidden meanings contained in the message.

The stage of interpretation and evaluation is probably when the internal cognitive structure of the listener becomes most relevant. This cognitive structure consists of the listener's knowledge or beliefs, attitudes, and values.

Knowledge. Our interpretation of a message can only be in terms of what we know or think to be true. If we don't know the subject well, we will have trouble following a lecture about it. The listener must be able to relate the message to a frame of reference. A visiting lecturer reports puzzled looks from the audience when he discussed the political views of Adlai Stevenson; he finally realizes the students have not heard of Adlai Stevenson before.

Attitudes. Attitudes act as an important cognitive filter through which incoming messages are processed. An attitude refers to an evaluative response to a specific item. For example, if someone believes that Columbus's voyages to the New World led to exploitation of or the destruction of a way of life or peoples, he or she will listen in a certain way to your speech about Columbus and tend to interpret and evaluate your message in perhaps a more negative way than you had intended.

Values. Values refer to general, long-term guides about what is good or bad, about what should be sought out and what should be avoided. Someone may value health over wealth, for example. If someone places a greater premium on a less stressful life-style, that person may be unimpressed with your call for a workaholic life-style in pursuit of fame and fortune.

How the listener understands the message, then, is affected by the elements of cognitive structure, especially knowledge, attitudes, and values.

5. *Message is retained or assigned to memory*. When we say that the message is remembered (or not), we need to be clear about the different kinds of memory we seem to have. In order to get through steps 1 and 2 (recognizing language and assigning simple meanings to words and sentences), we have to place incoming stimuli in short-term memory. This short-term memory is like working memory, or the amount of remembering that we have to do in order to get us through a phrase or sentence. To get the meaning of the last part of a sentence, I must remember what was said in the first part. This kind of short-term or working memory seems to be able to hold about two sentences worth of material, just enough to get through the simple processing of the incoming words.

Some of the incoming messages are assigned to long-term memory as well. We usually say that learning has occurred when a message has been placed in long-term memory, from which it can be quickly recalled as required, say, for an examination. People who do well at television quiz shows such as "Jeopardy" are said to have not only many things stored in long-term memory but quick recall as well.

Again, context and experience affects how well material is remembered. For example, after an interval, perhaps a week, it has been shown that people "remember" events or things that were supposedly said at a gathering or a restaurant based not on what actually happened but on what was only implied or would have been plausible for that situation.[5] Plausibility and expectation therefore influence what is placed in long-term memory. Familiar patterns of words or experiences are more easily recalled after time than unfamiliar patterns. The listener's needs affect what parts of the message are retained. In one study, people listened to a story that involved some details about a house: that it had a leaky roof, contained a coin collection, and so on. Listeners were told that as they listened, they were to think of themselves as burglars or as home buyers. The details that were remembered tended to be correlated with those identities. The "burglars," for instance, recalled the coin collection but not the leaky roof, while the home buyers were more likely to remember the leaky roof.[6]

6. *Message is responded to; feedback is sent.* We do not really know whether or not listening has occurred until the listeners do something to indicate that they got the message. Feedback becomes the check on whether or not the comprehensive listener learned the material or not. The feedback sent by the critical listener indicates whether or not the listener did apply logical tests to the message. In empathic listening, feedback is especially important since it represents the empathy that the listener is feeling for the speaker. So, although it may seem strange to include the sending of feedback as part of the listening process, it is an essential component if we are to assess the quality and effectiveness of listening.

A listener's feedback can be nonverbal or verbal. While listening to a lecturer, we may provide continuous eye contact, head nodding, or even note-taking to indicate that we are absorbing the content of the lecture. On a less serious note, in the first movie involving the character Indiana Jones, who portrayed a professor of archaeology, one female student provided a kind of feedback by having the words "I love you" written on her eyelids so that when she closed her eyes during his lecture, he would get that feedback. Recall that in the examples of communication problems in the first chapter the teacher misunderstood the nonverbal feedback from one student, because in the teacher's culture, proper feedback while listening required continuous eye gaze at the face of the speaker.

In empathic listening, we expect more verbalized feedback, as we will see in the discussion concerning techniques for that kind of listening later in this chapter.

The empathic listener not only exhibits a respectful, sympathetic demeanor non-verbally but also asks questions and indicates acceptance and understanding throughout the interaction.

Highlights of the Nature of Listening.   These six steps in the listening process (as shown in Figure 3-1) indicate the nature of that process and remind us that listening is far from a passive or uninvolved activity. People tend to overlook the role that the listener plays throughout interaction in shaping and determining the messages ultimately received and understood by the listener. We can listen only from our own point of view.

It is important to take special note of the influence of context and the listener's experience and expectations in shaping that message. Even at the point of entry, at the point of hearing and recognizing air waves as language, expectations and context have an effect.

Finally, note that much of listening is an interactive process. The listener is not immobile or mute during the period of listening. Varying amounts of feedback are being sent on a fairly continuous basis that could influence the speaker and could shape the message that will be received.

Selectivity in Listening

We can imagine breakdowns interfering in listening at various steps in this process. Noise or physical distractions in the listener's environment can disrupt the incoming message, thus interfering with the physical receipt of the message. Attention may be misdirected or insufficient for the listener to get the whole message. A person worrying about the funny noise that his or her car was making on the way to the meeting is not going to give full attention to the presentation. Perhaps most problems occur at the points at which meaning is assigned to the message (decoding) and at which the message is interpreted and evaluated. The meaning that I give to the term *free market* may not be the same given by an economist, a student, or the developer of shopping malls.

These potential problems of listening have captured the attention of advertisers and political campaigners, who recognize three barriers to deal with in winning

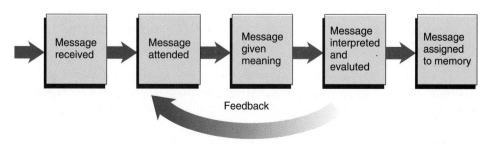

Figure 3-1   *Six elements in the listening process.*

▶ *Noise can lead to special efforts at selecting incoming messages.*

over their publics. These barriers are: selective exposure, selective perception, and selective retention.

1. *Selective exposure.* By selective exposure, we mean people will expose themselves only to messages that will confirm their existing beliefs or attitudes. A political partisan will probably not attend political rallies for the other side, except in the capacity of a heckler. There is a tendency to seek out information that reinforces decisions already made.

2. *Selective perception.* Selective perception refers to the tendency to understand or comprehend messages in a way that fits with preexisting attitudes and beliefs. If you say that you agree with part of what I say, I may perceive only that you agree with me and report that to other people. A constant complaint of politicians or others in the news is that the news media quote only part of what they say, and take it "out of context," which tends to provide a selective view of their position.

3. *Selective retention.* The third problem, selective retention, means that we are more likely to recall those parts of a message that fit with our needs, beliefs, and values. We have noted that people listen with particular points of view and will recall more easily those things that are anticipated, are congruent with beliefs, or fulfill the listener's needs.

These problems of selecting parts of messages in various stages of the listening process operate at the face-to-face, interpersonal level of communication as well as at the level of mass communications.

Barriers to Effective Listening

◀

Over the years in various listening workshops, the authors have asked people to brainstorm about what they believe are some of the main barriers to good listening. Here, we refer to those barriers not due to physical hearing but those barriers that are potentially under our control as we communicate with each other. The lists tend to be similar and point to some typical, recurring problems:

Typical Brainstorming List of Listening Barriers:

> Speaker's rate or tone of voice
> Speaker's accent
> Speaker's distracting mannerisms
> Room too hot, too cold
> Use of jargon, technical terms, "technospeak"
> Unfamiliar subject
> Boring speaker, subject
> Subject is "old hat," heard it all before
> Listener's fatigue
> Competing noise
> Other people in room
> Emotional subject (cancer, for example)
> Mind wandering, lack of concentration
> Listener feels insecure, intimidated
> Lack of respect for speaker
> Listener's anxieties, worries
> Disagreement with speaker, debating the speaker
> Concern with speaker's errors (pronunciation, grammar, facts, et cetera)

Do these things sound familiar? Such a list points to some important issues that can be generalized for most listening situations. We will first look at some of these general problems and then turn to problems more specific to each other in three situations: comprehensive, critical, and empathic.

1. *Speaker's mannerisms.* Habits of the speakers themselves often come up as a perceived barrier to good listening. In this situation, listeners allow themselves to be distracted by some aspect of behavior of the other person. In the list above, we see such things as the speaker's accent (regional or national), and the rate at which the speaker talks (too fast or too slow). Other mannerisms include being too loud or too soft or repeating certain fillers or phrases, such as "naturally,"

"hence," "we can obviously see," "ahem," and the like. The speaker is seen by the listener as carrying all the responsibility for the communication in this situation, while the listener is not seen as being responsible for the outcome of the communication. Listeners need to become aware of these distractions and try to overcome them in order to get more out of such listening situations.

2. *Power or status differences*. Sometimes the other person's status speaks so loudly that listeners cannot hear the words. This barrier works on both sides of the status or power divide. If a lower-status person feels threatened or intimidated in the presence of the higher-status individual, listening will be impaired. Of course, the higher-status person may not be in the habit of truly listening to the subordinates either. We have already noted the myth of the "open door." How could there be a problem of communication, the higher-status person says, "My door is always open." But, a door appears more open from the inside than from the outside. One manager of a branch bank reported that when he brought in tellers for their annual performance evaluation, he felt that they listened only when he got to the "bottom line," that is, the raise they were to expect for the coming year. He admitted that when he goes downtown for his own appraisal interview, he finds himself suffering from the same hearing problem.

3. *Differences in communication style*. Problems of style are seen in complaints about the speaker's language, mannerisms, perceived errors, and so on. One person may treat a conversation or interview with great casualness, while the other person expects more formality. Breakdowns in communication between people from different nations or cultures often manifest themselves as differences in communication style. Businessmen from Japan or parts of Europe or Latin America may be put off by an American businessman's habit of "coming straight to the point." If the speaker seems too pushy or aggressive, some listeners may tune out that speaker. Other listeners may tune out a folksy style, or one that seems vulgar or disrespectful.

4. *Language differences*. Of course, if the vocabularies of the people engaged in the interaction differ in significant ways, there is a strong possibility of communication breakdown. Problems of status differences can interact with this factor to heighten the problem. A subordinate may not wish to admit to a higher-status person that he or she does not understand all that is being said. It might seem easier and safer to nod and appear to agree and hope to find someone who could explain it all later. Students may be reticent about clarifying the meaning of words used in a classroom discussion because they don't want others to know that they aren't sure of the meanings of certain words.

Specialized languages, jargons, slang, or technical terminology can interfere with listening. People in specialized occupations may not realize that they habitually use "expert" words that may be unfamiliar to others. A friend, in seeking the reason for a flight delay, was told by airline personnel that the delay was due to a lack of "equipment." It was some time before he realized that the equipment in question was an airplane. Physicians may use medical or technical terms for conditions that can mystify patients who, again, may be reluctant to question the doctor. Unless we are in the business, we may be unaware that insurance policies are considered products. At Walt Disney World, all employees are referred to as "cast members." Each profession and organization tends to develop an in-language that becomes habitual for those people. One of the signs of a corporate culture, you may recall, was the development of special symbols and titles of this sort.

5. *Stereotyping and labelling.* This barrier is often reported by people in service occupations. Service people tend to categorize clients or customers by types of problems or personality. When a call comes in, the service person may, without really thinking, place the call in one of several typical categories: "Oh, oh, the lady with the cat problem" again. After applying the label, however, it becomes very difficult to keep listening for the details of this particular case. This is the trap of "I've heard it all before." People who deal with customer problems or service needs have told us that such categorization can become a real problem, even though they know that they are doing it in order to speed up service and to deal with several problems at once. They also know that they tend to miss important details that set each call apart from all the others. Professionals who deal with recurring

▶ **Figure 3.2** *Stereotypes can be a barrier to effective listening.*

kinds of problems, like lawyers, accountants, dentists, and so on, report that they must struggle against this same tendency.

Expectations play an important role in determining what we hear. Stereotypes are a good example of expectations affecting communication. When we listen to a member of a particular ethnic group, national background, or member of a coculture, such as someone in a wheelchair, for example, we may expect to hear certain things. We may listen based upon our expectations concerning members of those groups and therefore not really listen to what is actually said.

6. *Nonverbal distractions*. Such distractions are a special problem in prolonged listening situations, such as listening to a long speech or lecture. The presence of other people can also be a distraction. People report that in a crowded room, with people close to them, they have more difficulty concentrating on the speaker. If these other people are talking, making noise, or engaging in some other distracting behavior, it is even more difficult to listen. There may be one particular person who gets our attention: someone we are surprised to see, or have not seen for a long time, or are especially attracted to. As mentioned already, speaker mannerisms can themselves be nonverbal distractors. One friend recalled a chemistry class in college in which the students quickly became aware of the lecturer's habit of constantly pacing back and forth in front of the hall. Some of them began to wager on the exact number of turns that would be completed each class; soon they were not listening to too much chemistry.

7. *Lack of interest*. The discussion of attention in the listening process shows that people tend to focus attention on the basis of felt needs. If you feel you need the information, you will listen more carefully than if the need is not clear. The listener decides whether this topic or this speaker is interesting or not; the interest of a subject is not inherent in that subject. Some may feel that because of the professional entertainment that they constantly receive through the media, especially television, speakers and lecturers should be as interesting, that is, as entertaining. There should be some distinction between interesting and entertaining presentations, although they are certainly not incompatible. One danger is that after tuning out mentally, the listener may miss it when the speaker has moved on to something that is important or interesting to the listener. Recall that anticipation is an important factor in hearing and listening. The expectation of boredom can be a self-fulfilling prophecy.

8. *Lack of knowledge*. Listening will be less than ideal when the listeners feel lost or that the subject is beyond them. Sometimes what is perceived to be lack of interest or concentration on the part of listeners may actually result from unfamiliarity with the topic. An interview or a conference is always more interesting and productive when the participants have come well prepared, are up on the information necessary to follow, and contribute to the encounter. Communication, as we have stated, is a reciprocal process, and all parties need to know what is being discussed. Again, this barrier often reinforces some of the others in this list. Use of unfamiliar terms (language barriers) by a speaker may lead listeners to conclude that they lack the knowledge to follow the presentation. Status differences can inhibit listeners in acknowledging gaps in knowledge that a speaker could fill in. Or, lacking the feeling that the subject is really interesting or relevant, the listeners may not try to overcome the knowledge gap.

9. *Routinization.* This barrier is one that often interferes in everyday life as well as business. As we accumulate experiences, we begin to see patterns or routines. Of course, this is necessary in order to deal with the complexity of our lives and careers. Because the routine seems familiar and predictable, though, we don't feel the need to concentrate too much on them. We have all experienced driving through a familiar part of town without really remembering whether we stopped at that last stop light or not. As we tend to categorize or stereotype people, we come to routinize our activities, so that we can sit through an entire meeting or class without really listening to what is going on. Just as unfamiliar subjects or situations can lead to listening difficulties, so can those subjects or situations that seem too familiar. We suddenly find ourselves thinking, "Here we go again."

These sorts of problems can interfere with listening in conversations, interviews, meetings, classes, training sessions, and so forth. Many difficulties seem to result from the mistaken assumption that the listener is not an active partner in the communication process and that the obligation for effective listening lies only with the speaker.

Now let us turn to problems specific to the three special kinds of listening situations: comprehensive, critical, and empathic listening.

COMPREHENSIVE LISTENING SITUATIONS

The pioneer in the study of comprehensive listening was Ralph G. Nichols at the University of Minnesota. Over a period of years, he completed a series of studies aimed at isolating the habits of good and poor student listeners. These studies provided much of the material that continues to provide the basis for effective listening training today. Nichols developed a series of listening comprehension tests that allowed him to identify the most successful and the least successful listeners in several entering freshman classes at the university. During their orientation sessions in the first year, these students would listen to short lectures and then be tested on their contents. This type of procedure provides a good example of what we mean by comprehensive listening, or listening to learn. As a result of these tests, Nichols was able to pick out the most effective and least effective listeners in each freshman class. He then interviewed both groups, hoping to discover some significant differences in how these two groups listened to the lectures as a way of isolating the good and bad habits of comprehensive listening.

▶ ### Habits of Effective Comprehensive Listening

After several years of testing, Nichols felt that he could identify areas of differences between the so-called good listeners and bad listeners. These habits or techniques of good listening represent solutions to the barriers to good listening for comprehensive listening.

1. *Find areas of interest.* Nichols observed that the poor listeners were more easily bored than were the good listeners. The students in the poor category often gave the "boring" response as their main difficulty in listening to the lectures. The good listeners apparently figured that they should try to find something that could be interesting in the lectures, if for no other reason than to avoid wasting their time.

2. *Judge content, not delivery.* Nichols found that speaker mannerisms, one of the general problems referred to in the previous section, was a major stumbling block for the poor listeners. They seemed to be easily distracted by what they found to be offputting speaker habits. The good listeners seemed better able to make the effort to overcome the distractions of poor delivery, diverting gestures or other nonverbal cues (for example, tapping a pen on the lectern, pacing back and forth, and fiddling with note cards or sheets of paper).

3. *Hold your fire.* It seemed that the poor listeners tended to overrespond to points that they disagreed with in the lectures. They might tune out a speaker who touched an "emotional trigger" or in some way treaded upon a listener's opinion. Many people have developed the habit of debating the speaker; this habit is often mentioned in listening seminars.

Nichols separated this point into two recommendations: Avoid debating the speaker until he or she is finished, and avoid emotional responses.

4. *Listen for ideas, rather than for isolated facts or details.* According to Nichols, the poor listeners seemed to listen especially for the facts: They were fearful they would miss some name, date, or battle. Meanwhile, the good listeners concentrated on the overall point, the broad generalizations, and concepts.

Poor listeners seemed to have related difficulties with note-taking. The poor listeners tried to write down everything (or gave up, and wrote down nothing) because they weren't sure they could distinguish the important points from filler. If they didn't write down everything, they tried to outline the lecture, which can be frustrating in the listening situation. The good listeners would think of "generalization and supporting facts." They might even take their notes in that fashion, drawing a line down the middle of the page, with one side labelled concepts or generalizations, and the other side facts, lined up against the appropriate generalization. This technique also gets away from trying to reconstruct the lecturer's outline while hearing it for the first time.

Again, you should be aware that we have combined two of Nichols's points

Taking notes with a purpose

Note-taking should reflect the type of material that the receiver is listening to and the intended use for that material. For example, the critical listener should separate generalization or assertion from support. An easy way to do this is to divide the paper in half with one side of the page labeled concepts and the other side labeled "facts" or "support." In a complex argument, two columns might be used to show support, as shown below.

Generalizations	Support
XYZ Corporation should close the Springfield Plant.	The Springfield plant is losing money.
	Production is lagging.
	Plant efficiency cannot be increased.
	There was a $22 million loss in the fourth quarter.
	The new Dayton plant produces at 22¢ per unit vs. 28¢.
	The plant is outdated and needs renovation totalling $500 million.

into one here by putting the idea of flexible note-taking with the notion of listening for ideas rather than facts.

   5. *Work at listening.* The poor listeners that Nichols spoke with were misled by the physical setting of speaking and listening into thinking of listening as an easy, passive activity. They would let the words wash over them and assume that they would be comprehended and assimilated without any real effort on their parts. Effective listeners realize that they will have to expend some effort. One needs to take a physical position that enhances the possibility that concentrated listening will occur. Slumping over a couple of chairs in the back row of a room does not put one into a physical or psychological state of readiness to get the most from a lecture.

6. *Resist distractions.* This point is clearly related to the previous one: comprehensive listening requires effort. As a start, one can take a personal inventory of distraction. When you next listen to a speech, lecture, or presentation, try noting down the times when your mind starts to wander to the problems of tomorrow, the upcoming meeting, or the problems down in production, or wherever. Becoming aware of distractions and when they are likely to occur can help in resisting them.

7. *Exercise your mind.* Nichols felt that the mind, like the body, needs regular exercise to keep it in top shape. In order to improve reading speed and comprehension, one should practice with difficult material, to stretch one's capabilities. Many of the poor listeners in Nichols's interviews did not attend lectures or speeches on campus nor report watching "serious fare" on television. They were accustomed to entertaining material only. Nichols felt that the good listeners made more effort to expose themselves to demanding listening situations, and so they were in better mental shape.

8. *Analyze as you listen.* This recommendation has a different emphasis from Nichols's and others' views on "thought speed." Nichols believed that because people could think much faster than most speakers talked, there was some extra time available for the listener to think about what the speaker was saying. He therefore recommended that listeners take advantage of this thought speed to help rehearse and analyze what the speaker was saying.

It is, however, unclear how one might measure such thought speed or observe it, for that matter. The psychological study of attention suggests that each of us has a certain capacity for attending to stimuli. We can probably switch attention rapidly among tasks, and the redundancy most speakers use allows us to switch attention to tasks such as summarizing a point previously made by the speaker. But this use of our time differs from thinking in the spaces between the speaker's words, and thereby not missing any of the words. For these reasons, we prefer to think in terms of shifting attention now and then to an analysis of what we are listening to.

Such analysis has the advantage of reinforcing the points that the speaker is making, because the listener processes them more thoroughly, repeating or "rehearsing" them. For example, one technique is to briefly summarize what has been said up to a particular point in the presentation. A good speaker, of course, does this for listeners as well.

▶ ## Principles of Comprehensive Listening

Another technique Nichols suggests is to try to predict where the speaker is going next. He felt that if listeners predicted correctly, then the point was further reinforced and more likely to be retained. Of course, if the listener's prediction is incorrect, a loss of concentration might result.

Other useful techniques of comprehensive listening include making a mental note of the evidence or support that a speaker uses to back up a point made and trying to think of additional examples or pieces of evidence that would make the same point. If you do succeed in thinking of additional examples or applications of the speaker's point, this approach should reinforce that point and ensure better retention.

You also may listen as if you were going to have to report the contents of the presentation to someone else within 8 hours. This technique is effective for focusing on the content of the presentation.[7]

In a useful book on listening, *Listening: A Practical Approach*, James J. Floyd includes similar ideas to improve comprehensive listening.[8] He refers to the apprehension that a listener may have when approaching some listening situations. This fear of failure results from a feeling that the material will be too difficult. Listeners can respond to such situations in several ways. They can admit failure; they can dismiss those speeches or situations as trivial or boring; or, they can avoid these situations altogether. Floyd's preferred approach, however, is to keep exposing oneself to those situations in order to learn from them. He also suggests that listeners do some outside or background preparation prior to entering such situations. Floyd indicates the importance of vocabulary in listening effectively. The most rewarding way to expand one's vocabulary is to read widely, so that new words are presented in context rather than in isolation.

Some generalizations regarding practical steps to improve comprehensive listening follow:

1. Be aware of the barriers that are especially troublesome for you. Listening difficulties are individualistic. Try to inventory your own listening problems. Developing awareness is an important step in overcoming such barriers.

2. Listen as though you will have to paraphrase what is being said. When listening to longer presentations, be ready to paraphrase at least the main ideas and overall pattern of the presentation, rather than specific details such as names, dates, and so on. Remember to listen for ideas rather than for facts.

3. Approach the listening situation with a positive frame of mind. Self-fulfilling prophecies seem to apply to listening: If you expect to be bored, you will be.

4. Expect to work at listening. Of course, if you listen with the notion that you will have to paraphrase what is being said, this should raise your effort level automatically. Work at overcoming distractions, such as the speaker's delivery or nonverbal mannerisms.

5. Read more challenging material than you would normally select in order to build up your vocabulary and knowledge. It is especially important to do some background reading prior to listening to a difficult subject.

6. Practice different methods of note-taking, such as paraphrasing main points, listing ideas and supporting facts separately, and so on.

7. Concentrate on summarizing the presentation as you listen. If possible, think of additional supporting material that would fit with the point that the speaker is making. Avoid trying to refute the speaker. Try not to be to turned off by remarks you disagree with.

8. Expose yourself on a regular basis to what you feel are difficult listening situations

When these techniques were practiced as part of listening workshops, participants who concentrated on ideas rather than facts reported the most immediate gain in listening comprehension. After listening to a series of difficult, expository passages, several people were surprised to find that they could remember the details much better when they had not concentrated on them but instead had tried to remember the main points and what supported those main points.

Improving listening comprehension requires practice and work, and there is no quick fix. Reading about these techniques is not enough: Such principles are only guides for more effective comprehensive listening.

CRITICAL LISTENING SITUATIONS

The point of critical listening is to listen in order to analyze the arguments being presented in order to make a decision. There is less concern with listening to remember all the important content. It may not be necessary to remember much of the presentation at all once you have decided how you will vote, what you will buy, or which alternative you will choose. The basic purpose in critical listening, then, is to pick out the *conclusions* that you are being asked to draw and the *reasons* that are presented to support those conclusions.

In the next sections, we cover the following techniques to aid in enhancing critical listening:

Recognizing assertions
Recognizing types of support
Distinguishing facts, inferences, and judgments
Recognizing excluded choices
Recognizing statements of allness
Recognizing use of suggestion

Arguments versus Assertions

Think of an argument as a conclusion combined with reasons for that conclusion. A conclusion without reasons to support or justify it is called an assertion, or an unsupported assertion. The first step in critical listening is to identify and separate the arguments from the assertions.

Since assertions are not supported, there is no reason for you, the listener, to accept them, unless you choose to do so. Some assertions may fit well with your existing beliefs about the world or as fundamental theories about reality. If you are going to accept these points without support, you should at least be aware that you are doing so and not allowing questionable assertions to be slipped by you as basic axioms.

A speaker may assume that people in the audience will accept some generally understood axioms or values because of the culture in which they live, how they make a living, or the level or nature of their education. We would not expect a speaker to justify the assertion that small children should not be mistreated. We may not agree, later in the presentation, with the definition of "mistreating," but we will accept the fundamental assertion without argument. On the other hand, should a speaker assert with no support that it is necessary to protect some industries from foreign competition, we may or may not accept that assertion. Assertions, therefore, are not necessarily wrong or bad; they just should be recognized for what they are, to the extent possible.

Arguments and Support

Once we have recognized that a point is or ought to be an argument rather than an assertion, we then listen for the support. First we must be ready to separate out the conclusion from the support—which is not always as simple as it may sound. The word *conclusion* implies something that should come at the end, but in real life people do not always place the conclusion there. They may place it first or even leave it out on the understanding that the listener will infer the correct conclusion from the evidence. In the following example, the conclusion is implied in the middle of the argument:

> If the current method of electing a president, by the Electoral College, were completely democratic, then each person's vote would count equally; but because of the distribution of votes based on congressional seats for each state, a person's vote in a small state counts more than a person's vote in a large state.

Here the speaker is hoping we will draw the conclusion that the Electoral College is not a completely democratic way to elect a president. The reason supporting the conclusion runs as follows: In a complete democracy every vote counts exactly the same as every other vote. But the votes in the Electoral College are distributed according to each state's representation in Congress, where every state gets at least two senators in addition to members of the House of Representatives, regardless of the state's size. Senators from minimally populated states, like Wyoming, represent many fewer actual citizens than senators from heavily populated states, like California. Notice how much of the reasoning as well as the conclusion is implied in this argument, which requires the listener to be familiar with the voting arrangements in the Electoral College and the Congress. The speaker's argument is based on a definition and facts that relate to that definition.

In our experience, many speakers and lecturers tend to place the conclusion to the argument first, and then give the reasoning and evidence to support it. Take the following argument:

> Boys' clubs are important because they help to reduce juvenile delinquency. While the boys are participating in sports, recreation, or crafts, they are less likely to be at loose ends, hanging out in the streets, and getting into trouble.

The conclusion claims that boys' clubs are important. The reason is that they reduce juvenile delinquency. The rest of the argument presents an explanation of the mechanism, the way the clubs work, which is given as the cause for the reduction in delinquency. This argument would be strengthened by statistics that show a decline in juvenile delinquency in areas in which boys' clubs have been located.

In the first two instances of argument just given, the reason for the conclusion was based on, first, a *definition*, and, second, on an *explanation* of how something works. Then evidence had to be produced to show that in the specific cases discussed, the facts did meet the definition or did accord with the explanation of cause and effect. As we saw, the second argument needed more data. A critical listener ought to be able to identify these types of arguments and to ask whether the specific evidence is sufficient to justify the definition or the explanation.

Occasionally, an argument is not based on any explanation, but simply on the audience's willingness to accept that one thing indicates another, as follows:

> NATO, set up after World War II, has been successful in keeping the peace. After all, there have been over 200 armed conflicts in the world since 1945, but not a single one in Europe.

The force of this argument derives from the listener's accepting the lack of war or "armed conflict" as a *sign* that indicates NATO has worked. The critical listener must evaluate whether this sign is an adequate sign or not of what the speaker hopes to prove.

In the next example, the reasoning to justify the conclusion is a little different from the first cases:

> A voice-mail system would be effective and productive for our firm. It has been set up by our competitor, XYZ Corporation, and it has proven very useful. The company reports improved ratings of satisfaction and efficiency from customers and vendors.

The speaker here maintains that what works in one place should work in another; this is argument by comparison or by analogy. The critical listener first recognizes that the reasons are based on comparing two or more like situations and then checks to see whether the things being compared are comparable. It could well be that the competing firm is not at all similar to the speaker's. If so, then the argument would not be very strong. The critical listener demands that when things such as this are compared, they must be shown to be alike in all relevant respects. The important point here is relevance.

In the following argument, the speaker hopes to convince the listeners by giving examples that support the point:

> Computers have many educational uses. They can teach logical thinking through elementary programming; they teach problem-solving skills, as in debugging simple programs; and they can enhance writing skills through word-processing programs.

Someone listening critically to this argument might ask whether enough examples have been presented to justify the conclusion. Are these examples relevant to proving the point? Are there better ways to teach the same skills than by using expensive computers? After picking out the conclusion—that which the speaker wishes to prove—the listener then must evaluate the quality of the examples to see whether they justify the speaker's conclusion.

This next argument proceeds in an opposite direction from the last example and relies upon assumptions that the listeners may accept as fact:

> Of course she's a good student; she's a chemistry major.

The speaker here hopes that the listener will grant the premise that all chemistry majors are good students. This is a broad generalization that may or may not be true. Statements of this kind, as we will mention in the discussion on "allness," are rarely true. If no other support is offered for this conclusion, a critical listener would probably reject the support as inadequate.

The critical listener, then, should be able to pick out the conclusion that is being claimed in an argument, decide upon what basis a conclusion is being made, and analyze the evidence used to support this claim in each specific case.

In the examples above, the bases for conclusions were as follows:

Definition (of democracy)
Casual explanation (of how boys' clubs work)
Sign (of successful peacekeeping)
Analogy or comparison (with other voice-mail systems)
Generalization from a series of examples (of computer uses)
Deduction (from what is true of the whole group is true of any member of that group)

Once the conclusion has been identified and the basis for the argument figured out, the listener then should listen for the evidence that the speaker marshalls. Evidence refers to the specific details that are used for each conclusion argued by the speaker. There is a more detailed discussion of the kinds of evidence that can be used for support in the chapter on putting together presentations, particularly the discussion on statistics, uses of authority evidence, and facts in Chapter 10 (see pp. 317–322).[9]

Facts, Inferences, and Judgments

In addition to distinguishing arguments from assertions and to identifying conclusions and types of arguments, critical listening requires recognizing the difference between statements of fact, inferences, and judgments.

Statements of fact are intended to be reports of actual observed or observable states or events. Facts, therefore, are based on direct observations.

Inferences are, in a sense, educated guesses in which we infer a certain unobserved state of affairs on the basis of outward or observable evidence. For example, if I see a person, whom I don't know, around 19 years old buying books in the university bookstore, I may tell someone else, "I saw a student buying books today." In fact, I have no direct proof that the purchaser was a student; my statement was therefore not a statement of fact, but a statement of inference. Many of the statements that speakers and even listeners typically treat as statements of fact are really inferences. People draw conclusions based upon past experiences and associations and then report these conclusions as if they were the actual events that were observed. A careful critical listener would be alert to those instances when speakers treat inferences as facts. Finally, a judgment is an evaluation that listeners place upon either facts or inferences.

When we say that a fact is the report of an observation, we probably need to add some qualifications to that statement. Some facts are accepted as facts that can no longer be directly observed. For example, we accept that Columbus first sailed across the Atlantic in the year 1492. This cannot be observed any longer, but we take it as fact based upon years of reports and documentation. Similarly, we accept as fact that Julius Caesar was assassinated on March 15, in the year 44 B.C. We also accept as facts certain conclusions made by scientists that we cannot directly verify ourselves, such as the distance from the earth to the moon or the number of electrons associated with an atom of chlorine. We take as facts certain conclusions derived from the conventions of language, but which are not observable in the physical sense. Therefore, we allow as fact that something cannot be both present and not present at the same time and that something cannot at the same time be itself and its opposite. We are also likely to accept as fact reports of events in the press or the media, at least in regard to reported observations.

Facts, therefore, can include the following types: observations; historical facts; scientific facts; logical facts; and journalistic facts (the news).

Inferences go beyond the facts and draw new conclusions based upon thinking about the facts as observed or reported. On the basis of the facts, we try to draw conclusions concerning unobservable states of affairs or events. Inferences, we might say, are based upon circumstantial evidence. In order to make sense of the world, we are constantly drawing such conclusions and treating them as facts. When George says that you failed to greet him at a party because you were angry with

Problem-Solution

?...!

Critical Listening and Technical Information

In a world in which technical and scientific knowledge is growing exponentially, people have difficulty evaluating critically what they hear. Many people are reduced to parroting what the "experts" say. The physicist James Trefil confronted the problem when his 10-year-old son, after seeing a documentary about extraterrestrials' ancient visits to earth, did not take his father's skepticism about the show seriously. For the son, seeing, especially on television, was believing.

All too many people face similar problems when confronted with expert or technical information. This may especially be the case when we are considering environmental or medical risks. Will this cause cancer? How bad is cholesterol? In these cases, the best defense is probably knowledge, but that is not always practical. The second line of defense is a healthy skepticism. Finally, withhold judgment until you can do some research or get an unbiased second opinion.

See, for example, J. S. Trefil (1978, April 29). A consumer's guide to pseudoscience (pp. 16ff). *Saturday Review*.

---

him, he is drawing an inference about some internal state, your anger, without being able to observe that state directly.

A critical listener must be prepared to sift the inferences from the facts when it is appropriate. Many inferences might as well be facts as far as the force of the presentation may go. The listener needs to be alert for those inferences that make a difference. Perhaps the identity of the book purchaser in the example above as a student is important to some case that I am building: For example, students are interested in books. In that case, the factual nature of the assertion becomes relevant. I am asking you to accept that someone is a student without any proof. A listener needs to question "facts."

Judgments are statements that reflect some evaluation that the speaker applies to the facts or inferences. In addition to stating a fact or inference, the speaker says that it is either good or bad. Were we to say that the assassination of Caesar in 44 B.C. was a terrible tragedy for Rome (or a great benefit for Rome), we are going beyond the facts. Let us take the example of Columbus, whom, we agree, sailed across the Atlantic Ocean to the West Indies in the year 1492. Should we say that Columbus discovered the New World or America in 1492, we are at least making some inferences beyond the known facts. It may be that other Europeans had sailed across the Atlantic prior to Columbus's well-publicized voyage: Scandinavians under Leif Ericson, for example, or fishermen who had discovered the cod off Newfoundland but wanted to keep their find a secret. In addition, there were people already living in the Americas in 1492 who would have been mystified by the concept that they had been "discovered." One could say that as a result of this voyage, they, the native Americans, discovered Europeans. The idea that Europeans did the discovering, in other words, puts them in a privileged position: They do the discovering, the other people in the world are there to be discovered, as if they did not really exist until brought into contact with certain kinds of people. Some people would argue, therefore, that the simple statement about Columbus's discovering America expresses a value judgment in addition to an inference.

Value judgments can be attached to facts and inferences as "loaded language" that is intended to bring about an emotional response. An example would be phrasing a question as follows: Do you favor tax support for welfare freeloaders? The implication that those people who are on welfare are freeloaders is clearly a value judgment. There is a danger when we listen to loaded language or to value judgments of this sort in that we may tend to respond similarly. That is, as listeners we may begin to respond emotionally and make value judgments about the speaker that could effectively close us off to the rest of the presentation. Recall Nichols's point in regard to good comprehensive listening: "Hold your fire." When the other person uses loaded language and value-laden statements, the listener needs to recognize it and maintain objectivity.

Excluded Choices

Another tactic that a critical listener should watch for is the use of language that tends to exclude possible alternatives. Some speakers present their arguments as either-or dichotomies. Situations presented as either-or dichotomies may not be that way at all. Should a speaker say that you must decide whether to work for grades in school or to learn the material, the listener should respond that one can do both. The speaker may leave out alternatives or options, hoping to cut down the choice presented to an unattractive choice versus the preferred choice. When given a choice between two options, the critical listener tries to think of those alternatives that have been left out.

Statements of Allness

There is the old humorous proverb: "All generalizations are wrong, including this one." This leaves us with a paradox. In general, it's best to be wary of claims intended to cover entire classes of events, things, or people. Recall the earlier implied generalization about chemistry majors. With no offense to chemistry students, it seems improbable that this is always the case. The loaded language about people on welfare was intended to imply, in a similar fashion, that all people on welfare were the same. The critical listener should listen for qualifications that put parameters or set limits to generalizations of this type. As a group, it may be found that at a particular college, those students who have majored in chemistry for four years have a mean GPA slightly higher than the average for all other students who have completed the same four years. While that may be a duller statement, at first hearing, than the claim, "Of course she's smart, she's a chemistry major," it has a good chance of being more accurate.

Critical listeners should be alert to terms that imply "all," "never," "always," "none," and similar sweeping imputations of allness.

Suggestion

Suggestion is a tactic associated with propaganda. A speaker does not specifically make a particular claim but allows listeners to draw a conclusion that has never been justified or warranted. The speaker may, for example, suggest that one person is associated with other people who may exhibit characteristics that are valued negatively by the speaker and, it is assumed, by an audience. It is never directly claimed that the person in question has these characteristics; it is suggested by association with others who are thought to have them. One may hear that a congressman was in an auto accident and that he is known for his so-called life-style. There is no direct claim that the representative was drinking while driving, but there is an implication made.

Often, such a suggestion may be made by "not making it." The speaker may begin with the disclaimer that "I'm not going to impugn my opponent's motives in this case," or "I do not intend to make an issue of my opponent's having financial investments involved in this case, but . . . " Of course, the suggestion has already been made, and the speaker can claim to have taken the high road.

The critical listener is alert to assertions that are inserted as suggestions.

Highlights of Critical Listening

In general, critical listening involves paying attention to the speaker's conclusions and the methods used to justify or support those conclusions. Paying attention in this way means watching for unsupported assertions; distinguishing facts, inferences, and judgments; and being aware of statements of allness, excluded choices, and suggestion. Listing claims and the facts used to support them is a good note-taking technique to aid in keeping track of arguments and support.

EMPATHIC LISTENING SITUATIONS

While a critical listener tries to evaluate the speaker's arguments and claims, an empathic listener tries to avoid being judgmental or evaluative. The purpose of empathic listening is to "feel with," as if you were inside the other person, accepting his or her emotions, and seeing the world from his or her perspective. If you go to someone with a serious, personal problem, you don't want that person to pick apart your inferences or evidence and tell you that you are just being "illogical."

▶ *Good listeners are skilled at empathic listening.*

An empathic listener, then, listens to the feelings or human needs that are being expressed rather than trying to learn the material or to evaluate the content. Carl Rogers, a psychologist who has been very influential in the study of interpersonal communication, believes that the major barrier to mutual understanding "is our very natural tendency to judge, to evaluate, to approve or disapprove, the statement of the other person, or the other group."[10]

Empathic listening occurs in those situations in which the listener is trying to help another person better understand a problem, perform some task more effectively, or adjust to a particular environment. One might call this type of listening "interactive," since the emphasis is on the participation of the listener in helping the speaker to work through to a resolution or solution. Here, the listener directly interacts with the speaker, more than in comprehensive or critical listening, in order to seek more information or explanation or to lead the speaker to explore the problem in greater depth.

In Chapter 2, we discussed the superior-subordinate relationship. At times, this relationship calls upon one's skills as an empathic listener. A subordinate asks you for help in figuring out a way to overcome a problem that is interfering with work, or the subordinate may be having trouble adapting to a new colleague, new machinery, or new techniques. As a listener, you need to avoid making quick-fix suggestions. The other person is more likely to accept and to carry out a solution when he or she feels involved in coming up with it in the first place.

It is clear, then, how many of the general barriers to listening can adversely affect efforts at empathic listening. For example, speaker mannerisms can be a problem if the listener, rather than listening empathically, concentrates on the speaker's clothes, hand gestures, habits, eye contact, or similar distractions. Power or status differences can be barriers to this kind of listening. Not only will the lower-status person avoid seeking out the superior or feel intimidated, but the higher-status person may feel an obligation to solve the other's person's problem quickly and authoritatively, without really listening. Such differences may be complicated by other differences in language and communication style. Routinization can be a significant barrier to good empathic listening as well. The listener may try to pigeonhole the speaker or the speaker's problem too quickly in order to get on to "important" matters.

Characteristics

Two important characteristics of empathic listening are the interpersonal setting and its transactional nature. These characteristics can alert us to typical problems associated with empathic listening.

Interpersonal Setting. Empathic listening is much more likely to occur in one-on-one settings than in the group or audience settings associated with the other two types of listening discussed so far. The principles of interpersonal communication are consequently more likely to come into play in this type of listening. A relationship, after all, is central in this kind of listening: that between the speaker and the listener.

▶ *The setting can enhance the quality of empathic listening.*

One axiom of communication, as discussed in the Introduction to Part I of this text, was that one cannot avoid communicating when in the company of another person. You cannot help but send messages, even when you think that you are "passively" listening to the other person. The other person will interpret your nonverbal behavior, your so-called body language, even though you may be unaware of it. When in the role of the listener, especially that of the good listener, you must realize that you are continually sending messages that will be interpreted by the other person as meaning something. The listener's demeanor, eye contact, and body orientation toward the other person will indicate attention or interest or their opposites. Obviously, in one-to-one situations, there is considerably more obligation to maintain signs of attention to the other person than when you are part of a large audience or group. An empathic listener is more directly involved with the other person.

How people see the relationship between them is also important as part of their communication. In other words, the way that a message is encoded and transmitted includes an indication regarding the relative status, power, authority, or respect of the two people. For example, by abruptly cutting off a conversation with a subordinate with a brusque, "Here's what you do in this case . . . ," a superior clearly communicates something about the relationship. That "something" will be interpreted by the subordinate as indicating that the superior does not really respect him or her and is not willing to take the time to find out what the real problem is. Empathic listeners must be aware of the sometimes unintentional meaning that could be ascribed to the behavior accompanying their spoken words.

In the situation of empathic listening, then, the interpersonal relationship and the nature of interpersonal communications are more likely to be complicating factors than was the case with comprehensive or critical listening.

Transactional Nature.   Our approach of empathic listening also harkens back to the discussion in Chapter 1 regarding the transactional nature of communication. This transactional view is especially important in empathic listening. Rather than concentrating on just one point of view prevailing, that of the designated speaker or sender, the transactional view reminds us that the result of interaction is something new and beyond the messages intended by either party at the start of the interaction. The new outcome of communication is possible as a result of empathic listening, or what John Stewart and Milt Thomas have called "dialogic listening."[11] The outcome of such listening is a new product, the result of what Stewart and Thomas call "active involvement" on the part of the listener. In dialogic listening, the listener and the other person concentrate on what is "in front of" the two and what is "present" in the current interaction. In "monologic" listening, each person is, in effect, presenting a monologue, concentrating on a single point of view. In dialogic listening, there must be trust that there are no hidden agendas present. This kind of listening places a premium on trust, honesty, and openness.

This transactional view of empathic listening can be further clarified by relating it to creating an atmosphere that allows for confirming rather than disconfirming communication. When we go to someone and expect that person to be a good listener, we want to be taken seriously as respected human beings. Martin Buber, the great Jewish theologian, has been influential in this approach to interpersonal communication and listening. He believes that we can treat other people either as objects (things) or as subjects, unique individuals who cannot be categorized. Treating people as subjects underlies effective empathic listening.

When we confirm another person, we affirm that he or she is unique, unlike others, and respected as an individual personality. We say, "Don't treat me as you do someone else; I'm different." At the same time, we say, "My problem is different, my problem is unique." Each of us wishes to be treated in this way, and so does each person who comes to us and asks us to listen. Carl Rogers often spoke of allowing for situations in which he was completely open to others, not letting preconceptions determine how he would respond. Rogers noted that being self-conscious was particularly detrimental to listening in a truly open and effective way.

Empathic listening, therefore, can be derailed by indifference, imperviousness, or disqualification, according to Kenneth Cissna and Evelyn Sieburg.[12]

Indifference means that the listener simply avoids interaction by seeming to be indifferent to the presence or the problem of the other person. Such indifference can be communicated by using impersonal language in the conversation, such as, "It is the company's policy in these situations to do such-and-such." Personal pronouns or statements are avoided. There may be physical cues, such as the avoidance of eye contact or remaining seated behind a desk, seemingly distracted by other work.

Imperviousness means that the listener does not let the point of the view of the speaker get through. The listener may respond, "Oh, you don't really mean that," or, "What you really mean is something else." The listener may deny the other the right to feel a certain way or have a certain opinion, by responding, "After all this company has done for you, you really shouldn't feel that way."

Disqualification refers to listener behaviors that seem to deny the qualifications of the speaker or even to disqualify the listener's responses. A listener could respond by making some irrelevant comment or going off on a tangent to avoid engaging the speaker in dialogue: "You know, it's interesting your bringing up this problem about the work schedule . . . why, just the other day, I was thinking of a time management seminar I attended in Atlanta . . . or was it Nashville . . . somewhere like that . . . but wait, I think it's time for my other meeting."

Empathic listeners are not concerned with imposing their own solutions on others but, rather, they allow solutions to grow out of the give and take nature of the interpersonal transaction. Dialogic listening and listening to confirm the other person characterize this approach to listening.

Techniques for Empathic Listening

It may seem ironic to suggest techniques to improve empathic listening, given that the very idea behind empathic listening is to adopt an attitude of openness to the other person and to the unfolding situation. The concept of techniques suggests that there is something premeditated to one's listening. On the other hand, most people can be helped to understand the nature of this approach by thinking of and practicing some methods that help us see how one can avoid appearing judgmental and evaluative.

In general, the techniques of empathic listening call for avoiding expressing judgments and conclusions and for allowing the other person to explore and express personal feelings about a situation as completely as possible. These behaviors can be thought of under three clusters of activities, labelled the "recognition cluster," the "acknowledgement cluster," and the "endorsement cluster."[13]

Recognition is signalled through the nonverbal behaviors of looking at the other person, establishing nonthreatening eye contact, and allowing the other person plenty of time to engage in the conversation. Acknowledging the other person does not necessarily mean agreeing with him or her but, rather, letting the other person understand that you have understood and appreciated his or her viewpoint. Rogers suggested an exercise in which each person had to explain what the other person had just said, to the other person's satisfaction, before presenting another statement. Such an exercise can be difficult, but it does force the listener to come to grips with the other person's point of view.[14]

Endorsing does not necessarily imply agreement but rather allowing others the right to express their feelings or opinions. Denying others the right to feel a certain way or to express a certain opinion is the opposite. The idea is to accept the others as they are.

The theories of Watzlawick, Rogers, Buber, and others that the feedback one sends is especially important to the creation of the nonjudgmental, nondirective atmospheres desired have already been mentioned. Some specific kinds of verbal feedback to enhance empathic listening include the following:

1. *Paraphrasing.* It may be helpful for the other person to hear back what has been said phrased in the way that the listener heard or understood it. The paraphrase is also used to acknowledge that the listener has understood what the other person is saying. As with the giving of most such feedback, one needs to avoid overdoing this. The speaker may become annoyed should you do nothing but constantly refrain, "I hear you saying this . . . " In other words, this or any similar technique can become a routinizing habit.

2. *Clarifying.* This feedback asks the other person to define terms more completely or to give some more explanation. For example, if Ralph says that he cannot work with George, does this mean that he cannot do a specific task with George, or that he cannot do anything at all when George is in the room? Again, asking for more information also indicates that you are not closing off communication. The other person may need to clarify the problem in his or her own thinking, and your feedback may allow that to happen.

3. *Leading and asking open-ended questions.* This kind of feedback normally consists of asking open-ended questions in order to expand the subject under discussion. You may wish to broaden the scope of the conversation to find out how widespread this problem appears to the other person. In counselling a student who is having trouble with cost accounting, for example, an adviser might ask whether the student has had similar problems with other subjects or examinations. It may be possible to find that the student has generalized "test anxiety" that is exaggerated in the case of accounting. Possibly, the student suffers this kind of problem with any subject concerning calculations, such as statistics or mathematics. The idea is to take the discussion away from an immediate situation, which may be loaded with feelings of inadequacy or fear, and to try approaching the problem from a new angle. This new angle may be less threatening to the speaker.

4. *Specifying*. Specifying involves going in the opposite direction from the previous one. Should the discussion seem to be too vague or general, one may begin to ask for specific instances or cases. The listener, in other words, needs to remain flexible and to be aware of when one approach may be more fruitful than another.

5. *Summarizing*. Providing a summary may be useful feedback for the listener as well as for the speaker. A summary may allow both participants to see inter-relationships among points or problems that might otherwise have been overlooked. One can simply begin with a simple statement of, "Here's where we seem to be . . . " and go on from there. This approach can allow for a breather, for both people mentally to catch their breath and take stock of what has been covered up to that point. A summary can also lead to a refinement or a redefinition of the problem.

Highlights of Empathic Listening

The feedback techniques just discussed should be practiced with an attitude of conveying a sincere concern with the other person's worth and particular problem. Of course, the techniques can become habitual responses themselves. That is why we stress that a desire for open communication must precede empathic listening. Clearly, the disadvantage to such empathic listening is that it takes considerable time and effort on the listener's part, which may not be possible nor appropriate. Recall the discussion in Chapter 2 about the contingency theories of organizational communication. Empathic listening, then, may be an ideal that is not always attainable.

SUMMARY

During the course of your career, you will probably spend more time listening than talking. The subject of listening can be studied systematically, and it is possible to improve listening. Of the four types that we distinguished at the start of the chapter, three—comprehensive, critical, and empathic listening—are probably most relevant in business and professional settings.

The principles of comprehensive listening are summarized here:

1. Be aware of troublesome listening barriers.
2. Listen as though you will have to paraphrase what is said.
3. Approach the listening situation with positive expectations.
4. Expect to work at listening.
5. Read more challenging material.
6. Practice different methods of note-taking.
7. Summarize the presentation as you listen.
8. Expose yourself to difficult listening situations.

The principles of critical listening follow:

1. Distinguish arguments from assertions.
2. Look for how arguments are supported: by basis for the reasoning; definition; causal explanation; sign; analogy or comparison; generalization from specific examples; deduction; and by the evidence and facts behind the reasoning.
3. Distinguish facts, inferences, and judgments as you listen.
4. Watch for excluded choices.
5. Listen for statements of allness.
6. Be aware of suggestion.

The principles of empathic listening are as follows:

1. Be aware of the importance of interpersonal relationships.
2. Be aware of the transactional nature of empathic listening.
3. Practice techniques for feedback in empathic listening: paraphrasing; clarifying; leading and asking open-ended questions; specifying; and summarizing.

EXERCISES

1. Make a list of the barriers to good listening that most affect you as a listener. What barriers characterize people with whom you live or work? What strategies can you use to overcome these barriers?

2. Take a controversial issue, such as the pro-choice, pro-life debate in regard to abortion rights in the United States. Write an inventory of obstacles to your own critical listening on this issue. Arrange to listen to presentations on both sides of the issue and try to prepare an objective, critical analysis of both presentations. What was difficult for you?

3. Attend a lecture or speech and try the following note-taking techniques. Divide a piece of paper in two: List generalizations on one side and facts supporting them on the other. Evaluate how effectively this seemed to work for you. Try other note-taking techniques discussed in this chapter. Do they work as well or not as well?

4. Attend a lecture or speech and make a note of each time that you found your mind wandering. What were some of the main causes for distraction?

5. For a group exercise, discuss a controversial issue (local or national) and use Rogers's paraphrase rule: Before one person can make a point, he or she has to report, to that speaker's satisfaction, what the previous speaker said.

6. For another group exercise, get in groups of three or four. One person presents a problem he or she is having (real or imaginary); one person serves as the listener and may use only the five techniques for feedback; and the others listen to report to the listener and speaker what they observed. As time permits, rotate the roles through the group.

Communication Case Problem: Client Corrections

You are managing a group of tax accountants who are preparing taxes for a number of corporate clients. You notice a large number of second and third client interviews and conferences because of errors or misunderstandings in putting together verbally supplied information with computerized information.

You feel that a retreat or workshop should take place to improve the listening of your accountants in their interviews with clients. Describe specific objectives for the one-day workshop and organize its activities and training.

SELECTED SOURCES FOR FURTHER READING

Barker, L. L. (1971). *Listening behavior*. Englewood Cliffs, NJ: Prentice-Hall.

Buber, M. (1970). *Martin, I and Thou*. W. Kaufman, Trans. New York: Scribner.

Cissna, K. M. L., & Sieburg, E. (1990). Patterns of interaction confirmation and disconfirmation. In J. Stewart (Ed.), *Bridges not walls*, (pp. 237–245). New York: McGraw-Hill.

Ellis, A., and Beattie, G. (1986). *The psychology of language and communication*. New York: The Guilford Press.

Floyd, J. J. (1985). *Listening: A practical approach*. Glenview, IL: Scott, Foresman.

Herrick, J. A. (1991). *Critical thinking: The analysis of arguments*. Scottsdale, AZ: Gorsuch Scarisbrick.

Nichols, R. G. (1957). *Are you listening?* New York: McGraw-Hill.

Rogers, C. R. (1961). *On becoming a person*. Boston: Houghton Mifflin.

Singer, M. (1990). *Psychology of language*. Hillsdale, NJ: Lawrence Erlbaum Associates.

Stewart, J., & Thomas, M. (1990). Dialogic listening: Sculpting mutual meaning. In J. Stewart (Ed.), *Bridges not walls* (pp. 192–209). New York; McGraw-Hill.

Taylor, A., Meger, A., Rosegrant, T., & Sample, B. T. (1989). *Communicating* (5th ed.). Englewood Cliffs, NJ: Prentice-Hall.

Underwood, G. (1976). *Attention and memory*. Oxford, UK: Pergamon Press.

Watzlawick, P., Beavin, J., & Jackson, D. (1967). *Pragmatics of human communication*. New York: W. W. Norton.

References

1. Singer, M. (1990). *Psychology of language: An introduction to sentence and discourse processes* (p. 18). Hillsdale, NJ: Lawrence Erbaum Associates.
2. Ellis, A., & Beattie, G. (1986). *The psychology of language and communication* (p. 214). New York: The Guilford Press.
3. Ellis and Beattie, pp. 218–219.
4. Underwood, G. (1976). *Attention and memory* (pp. 211–212). Oxford: Pergamon Press.
5. See Ellis and Beattie, pp. 245–246.
6. Ellis and Beattie, p. 243.
7. Steihl, L. K. (1980, May 26). *U.S. News and World Report*, p. 66.
8. Floyd, pp. 79–81.
9. A helpful source for critical listening in this regard. (1991). In Herrick J. A. *Critical thinking: The analysis of arguments* (esp. Chap. 1). Scottsdale, AZ: Gorsuch-Scarisbrick.
10. Rogers, C. R. (1961). *On becoming a person* (p. 330). Boston: Houghton Mifflin.
11. Stewart, J., & Thomas, M. (1990). Dialogic listening: Sculpting mutual meanings. In J. Stewart, (Ed.), *Bridges not walls* (5th ed.), (pp. 192–210). New York: McGraw-Hill: see also Floyd's discussion of dialogic listening, pp. 121–122.

12. See Cissna, K. N. L., & Sieburg, E. (1990). Patterns of interactional confirmation and disconfirmation. In J. Stewart (Ed.), *Bridges not walls* (pp. 240–244). New York: McGraw-Hill.
13. C. Sieburg, p. 244.
14. Rogers, pp. 332–333.

Intercultural Communication in Business and the Professions

●

4

CHAPTER

After studying this chapter, you should be able to:

1. Explain the impact of a multicultural environment on professional lives.

2. Define and explain the meanings of "culture" and "intercultural communication."

3. Be sensitive to differences of subcultures and cocultures.

4. Avoid cultural stereotyping.

5. Give reasons for the difficulty of intercultural communication.

6. Explain the effects of cultural differences on language and thought.

7. Show the importance of the context in interpreting the meaning of communication.

8. Describe the effects of various cultural dimensions on intercultural communication.

Overview

We live and work in an increasingly muticultural environment. One reason for this is the sophistication of current communication technologies. When we awaken, for example, the early morning news tells us what happened to the Nikkei Index (the Tokyo stock exchange's equivalent to the Dow Jones Index). Thus, we are reminded how we are enmeshed in an international web of complex interrelationships. Events in other parts of the globe can have instantaneous effects on our own careers and lives as messages now flash across continents and oceans.

▶ *Business has become global.*

IMPORTANCE OF INTERCULTURAL AWARENESS

The increasingly multicultural nature of our professional lives results from the move toward multinational businesses and organizations. The emergence of the "cross-cultural corporation" has created a new awareness of the importance of understanding other cultures.[1] Communities in the U.S. Midwest and South now compete with one another in the effort to attract foreign-owned and -managed plants. In Tennessee, Indiana, Ohio, and other states, American auto workers now work side by side with Japanese co-workers and managers. Corporations routinely set up international operations, with shops and facilities in Latin America, the Caribbean, and Europe or Africa. The proliferation of international NGOs (nongovernmental organizations) concerned with science, economic development, social problems, and the like mean that more and more Americans are in contact with people from other countries and cultures.

A second reason for the increasing multicultural nature of work is that there is more heterogeneity in the workplace than ever before as a result of increased opportunities for minorities and women. Demographic projections indicate that by the year 2000, 85% of the net increase in the American work force will be made up of women and minorities.[2] By that same year, women will probably make up 63% of all people working in the United States.[3] The expansion of opportunity for all people—regardless of race, ethnic or national background, sex, religious affiliation, age, or handicap—will have a significant impact on interpersonal communication in the contemporary organization.

Third, political and economic changes have been happening throughout the world over the last several years, and these trends can be expected to continue. During the 1980s, for example, the world saw the economic rise to prominence of the Pacific Rim. In addition to Japan, other Asian economies, including Korea, Singapore, Malaysia, Thailand, Hong Kong, and Taiwan, began to take their place as major players in the world economy. Western Europe continues toward political as well as economic integration, thereby creating a vastly enhanced market and economic power. Changes in Eastern Europe, with the end of communist rule there, and the revolutionary changes in the former Soviet Union represent challenges to our ability to communicate and deal with these cultures and their governmental and other organizations. The Middle East will continue to be significant for energy resources into the future. In the Third World, there are movements toward more open systems, both economically and politically. The Republic of Nigeria, for example, the most populous nation on the African continent, is one of the major oil-producing nations in the world (as is potentially the African nation of Angola). Latin America and the Caribbean region will continue to be important markets and producers in this hemisphere. Finally, our involvement with these other areas of the world will grow, not just because of business and economic connections, but also because of growing awareness and involvement in cultural affairs.

Multicultural settings are, therefore, growing in importance for at least these four reasons:

1. Changing technologies of communication.
2. Growth of multinational (cross-cultural) businesses and organizations.
3. Increasing heterogeneity in the workplace.
4. International political and economic changes.

▶ *Multinational businesses affect many people in the heart of the United States.*

One article concerning management in these times summarized these points, "The growing population of international students and employees in the United States, disproportionate trade deficits, the popularity of international acquisitions and joint ventures, and increasing international interactions among companies today force leaders in U.S. organizations to learn to interact and to communicate more efficiently with a greater variety of cultures."[4]

Cultural awareness plays a role in many of the communication interactions and settings discussed throughout this book, including interviewing, group communication, conflict management, negotiation, and so on. Next, we discuss a few basic principles underlying intercultural communication.

◀▶ CULTURE AND INTERCULTURAL COMMUNICATION

An explanation of culture must precede an understanding of cultural factors of communication. The concept of culture comes from the field of anthropology. A variety of definitions have arisen to explain the term *culture*.

Generally, culture refers to a set of patterns of human behavior. These patterns are characteristic of identifiable groups. Perhaps the most obvious of these patterns is the language spoken by a particular group of people, such as French, Lithuanian, Algonquin, or Thai.

In addition to language, there are many other systems that distinguish the different cultural groups in the world, such as typical occupations. The Fulani people of West Africa, for example, are mostly herders of cattle and goats. Cultures may have characteristic ways of organizing their homes or cities. Religious beliefs and systems are other patterns that can be associated with cultures. For example, Islam is associated with many Arabic cultures as well as with Turkish, Iranian, Malaysian, Indonesian, and many African cultures. In addition, belief systems and values are organized into patterns and systems in each culture. For example, the U.S. culture has usually valued progress and the belief that things will improve in time. Other cultures place more value on the concepts of tradition and stability. Particular forms of clothing, music, family and marriage arrangements, furniture, and humor may characterize human culture as well.

Cultural systems developed to provide people a sense of security and predictability. Imagine how difficult life would be if each day you could not be sure what language people would speak or what rules would govern people's interactions. As children grow up in a particular culture, they learn these various systems and thereby learn what to expect from others and what is expected of them. These expectations become second nature.

Communication is inextricably bound up with culture. Communication works when we can predict the actions and responses of others. Again, at the most obvious level, the authors are writing in the English language on the assumption that you, the reader, will be able to understand English and, therefore, our message. When people formulate messages to send to others, they predict, "If I were that other person, I would understand what was meant by saying this—so that is what I will say." In other words, communication between people depends upon the ability to make predictions about each other. Cultural systems normally provide this kind of predictability. Take the preceding example about the value of progress in the U.S. culture. If we predict that you value progress, then we will will try to get you to agree to something that we want by pointing out that it will contribute to progress. If you did not value progress, then our prediction would fail in this case, and our communication would be less successful. The patterns of behavior and value systems that we learn as children provide us with the ability to make such predictions. Now we turn to a definition of the term *intercultural communication*.

Intercultural communication occurs when two or more people from different cultures exchange messages. These messages are filtered through a set of cultural expectations by the people involved. The predictions that they make are shaped differently by the people's different cultural environments. The more different the two cultures involved are, the more the cultural filters will change and distort the messages being exchanged: Figure 4-1 shows cultural filters affecting messages.

There are degrees of difference among various cultures. Clearly, the general U.S. culture is similar to the culture of English-speaking Canadians. On the other hand, the general culture of the United States is much more dissimilar to the culture of the Chinese or the Zulu of South Africa. As a consequence, one would expect that there would be more barriers to effective intercultural communication between an American and persons from the latter two cultures. The Canadian and U.S. citizens share similar life experiences, environments, work and occupation styles, language, living arrangements, entertainment preferences, and so on. A Canadian, on the other hand, would probably share none of these similarities with a Chinese or Zulu.

Subcultures and Cocultures

While we have a good idea of what is meant by the English language and when people are speaking English versus French or some other language, we also understand that there are different kinds of English. There are regional variations, for

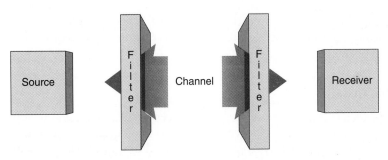

▶ **Figure 4-1** *Cultural filters change or distort the message.*

example. Pronunciation is different in Ontario, Canada compared to Massachusetts to South Carolina to Texas. There are differences in vocabulary or word meanings (dialect) as well. For example, is something a bucket or a pail? Do you carry groceries in a sack, a bag, or a tote? Do you hold papers together with a rubber band or gum band? The British "ascend" buildings in lifts whereas Americans "go up" in elevators.

Just as there are varieties of English still recognized as English, there are variations within large cultures that are recognized as subcultures within the larger culture. These subcultures can be associated with occupations. Engineers and accountants, for example, develop specific ways of talking, typical value systems, and patterns of behavior. There can be regional or life-style subcultures as well. Farmers from different parts of the country, for example, find that they share a subculture and when they meet each other have some immediate shared experiences to draw upon.

There are also generational subcultures. People over the age of 65, for example, constitute an identifiable group with shared experiences and needs. These experiences lead group members to develop characteristics of a subculture: a shared way of talking, shared value systems, living arrangements, and even clothing styles. Similarly, young people (say, junior high students through college age or early twenties) can be thought of as sharing a subculture. In Chapter 2, we talked about corporate cultures, which can be thought of as small subcultures, such as IBM or Apple. The point is that people from the same subculture can usually communicate more easily with each other than they can with people from different subcultures.

In addition to subcultures, there are cocultures, which are cultural groups that exist alongside the larger culture. For example, in addition to being members of the U.S. culture, African-Americans belong to their own coculture as well. Some, like the popular writer Deborah Tannen, would argue that women constitute a coculture alongside the general U.S. culture. Others point to the handicapped or physically challenged, the deaf, Native Americans, various Asian American groups, Hispanics, Chicanos, and Latinos as examples of cocultures within the U.S. culture. Members of each of these groups share significant patterns of behavior and experiences with other members. In effect, they participate in two (or more) cultures simultaneously.

As noted, expanding opportunities and the increasing pluralism of U.S. business and workplaces mean that members of these cocultures and the general culture are being brought together more often than in the past. The need for sensitivity to the communication patterns and differences of these various groups therefore becomes more important.

▶ **Variability within Cultures**

In introducing the idea that there are cultural differences that affect communication among people, we run the risk of stereotyping. There is the danger of generalizing in ways that lead to negative portrayals rather than to cultural sensitivity. You are aware that within your own social and cultural group there is diversity among the people you know. All within your group tend to speak the same language,

Problem-Solution

American with Disabilities Act of 1990 (ADA)

The handicapped or physically challenged can be considered a coculture. The Americans with Disabilities Act (ADA) of 1990 establishes a commitment to meet the special needs of members of this coculture, which include accommodations to facilitate their communication in business and professional organizations. Complying with the ADA's requirements should help to solve the problems that these people often face in their interactions with others.

In January of 1992 the requirements set down in the ADA became effective. The ADA requires that buildings be made accessible to those with physical limitations or restrictions. In addition, the law intends to help the approximately 43 million Americans who have physical disabilities gain entry to employment on an equal footing with other Americans. Some of the noticeable changes include requirements that ATMs (automated teller machines) be set low enough to accommodate people in wheelchairs. Service counters similarly should be low enough to be convenient to anyone who has a physical disability. Directions or even menus should be in braille to serve the blind, or at least someone needs to be present to read the material to visually impaired persons.

At this time, businesses are not required to go beyond reasonable physical modifications that do not impose "undue hardship" on the business.

While over 100 articles have recently appeared in the business literature concerning the ADA, useful summaries include B. L. Kornblau and M. Ellexson, Hiring employees under the disabilities act. *Risk Management*, 38:11 (November 1991), 38–50; and W. E. Barlow, Act to accommodate the disabled. *Personnel Journal*, 70: 11 (November 1991), 119–124.

place similar values on education and life goals (such as success probably defined as material success), dress in similar ways, use gestures and facial expressions in predictable ways when communicating with each other, and so on.

The term *stereotyping* refers to a tendency to judge people as a category based upon a single characteristic, such as nationality, ethnicity, skin color, sex, and so forth. Such judgments typically are based upon ill-informed expectations about all people who share a certain characteristic. These judgments almost always are value judgments: These people are good or bad, smart or dumb, dependable or not dependable, and the like.

There are real dangers in generalizing. In the 1990s U.S. professionals are highly aware of the business challenges represented by the growing economies of the Pacific Rim. In relation to this, Americans may display a related tendency of assuming that all the cultures of the Pacific Rim countries are the same. Philip West, a guest editor for *Business Horizons* magazine and professor of Modern Asian studies, warns against such a simplification. He asserts that the different nations and cultures of Eastern Asia are diverse. Therefore, what works for doing business with the Japanese may not be applicable for the Singaporeans, or the people of Taiwan, Hong Kong, Thailand, Indonesia, or the Philippines. (Australia and New Zealand, by the way, are geographically part of the Pacific Rim, as well.)[5]

When we discuss the principles of intercultural communication, therefore, it is important to bear in mind that there is variability within cultures. People are still individuals despite their membership in a culture, a coculture, and a corporate culture. Individuals' actions and communications, of course, are never entirely predictable. There is a difference between recognizing that members of cultures may use language and gestures differently from members of other cultures and making broad generalizations, or stereotypes. In fact, the goal of developing cultural sensitivity is to withhold judgment, whereas the tendency of stereotyping is to rush to judgments.

▶ ### Highlights of Culture and Intercultural Communication

Culture refers to the sets of patterns of human behavior that groups of people have developed over hundreds or thousands of years in order to organize and make their lives more predictable. Language may be the most obvious of such patterns.

Intercultural communication refers to the situation in which people from different cultures try to communicate with each other. Their varied expectations or predictions, learned in their own cultures, can create barriers to their understanding one another.

Within or alongside large cultures, there may be subcultures and cocultures. Also, there will always be diversity and variability within cultures because individuals are unique. Being sensitive to cultural factors in communication should lead to withholding of judgment rather than to stereotyping.

◀▶ ## PROBLEMS OF INTERCULTURAL COMMUNICATION

Because culture serves to make our lives more predictable, communication across cultures reduces our ability to predict. Misunderstandings are likely because people are not aware that their partners in communication are playing by a different set of sometimes-unstated rules. There are three major problems that create barriers in intercultural communication:

1. It is difficult to imagine other perspectives.
2. Most cultural assumptions are out-of-awareness.
3. People assume that "All people are the same."

One of the first problems in dealing with communication across cultures is that people have learned their own cultural patterns so well that it becomes difficult for them to imagine a different perspective. Recall the earlier statement that one learns a culture's systems from childhood. People assume that the way they have learned to behave is the natural and normal way to act. Other behaviors are seen as somehow abnormal. In other words, we come to conceive of our own culture as human nature. If other people behave differently, their system must somehow go against this so-called human nature.

A second, closely related problem of intercultural communication is that so much of these learned patterns of culture are out of our conscious awareness. After you have learned to ride a bicycle, for example, you no longer think about it when doing it: You are no longer conscious of the continual adjustments of your weight or the handlebars in order to maintain your balance. Similarly, after you have learned your culture's language, style of walking, nonverbal communication systems, value system, and so forth, these things are no longer brought to your conscious attention.

One of the best examples of this situation is the difference in conversational distances between North American and Latin American people. North Americans are comfortable with about a 3- to 6-foot separation for a casual conversation; people from certain Latin American cultures are comfortable when the distance of separation is much less. The North American keeps backing away from the Latin American, who keeps edging closer simultaneously. Neither person is aware of ever having learned to feel comfortable at certain distances in such sit-

▶ *Diversity in organizations requires sensitivity to conversational rules.*

uations; rather, they are probably aware of their own discomfort and blame it on the pushiness of the one or the standoffishness of the other.

Recall the example of the teacher talking to the African-American student in Chapter 1. This is another example of a case in which neither participant in the interaction is aware that there are different expectations and different rules involved. In fact, neither person is probably even aware that there *could* be different rules for eye contact during conversations. These rules are learned in the way that we first learn language as children, by imitation without the awareness that there are regular rules being learned with the imitation.

A third problem in intercultural communication is the assumption that all people are essentially the same and that any differences should be downplayed or ignored. While this assumption may be based on good intentions, it prevents awareness of differences in cultural codes of communication. One anthropologist believes, "The 'they are just like the folks back home' syndrome is one of the most persistent and widely held misconceptions of the Western world, if not the whole world."[6]

Familiarity is not always the answer: One can visit another country or culture without developing an understanding or sympathy for the other cultural perspective.[7] If one continues to see the other culture as less valid than one's own, then all the observations will be interpreted from that point of view. Contemporary African writers, for example, often have commented on the "colonial misunderstanding" that continued to exist between the French or British colonial officers and the Africans or Indians among whom they lived for years.

The Nobel Prize-winning Nigerian playwright, Wole Soyinka, in his play, *Death and the King's Horseman*, provides an excellent example of such misunderstandings. In the play, the British honored a naval captain who chose to go down with his ship (commit suicide, in other words) but considered an African leader to be immoral for trying to commit ritual suicide to fulfill the traditions of his people. Choosing death voluntarily was considered honorable in one case and dishonorable in another from the perspective of one culture (the British), which the British colonial officers assumed to be universal. The communication between the Africans and the British in the play are never quite on the same wavelength because of the inability of either side to comprehend that the other could see things only through its own set of cultural assumptions. In this case, cultural filters become cultural blinders.

◀▶ IMPROVING INTERCULTURAL COMMUNICATION

The remainder of this chapter brings out factors that are particularly significant in intercultural communication. The goal is to raise awareness of the major issues and pitfalls that can affect communication across cultures. Specifically, this section deals with the following two communication factors: language and thought; and the importance of context in determining meaning (that is, differences in high-context versus low-context cultures).

Next, the discussion takes up other major dimensions used to distinguish communication activities in one culture from those in another. When preparing to engage in intercultural communication people should be aware that communication can be significantly different from that in their own cultures on the following dimensions:

1. Individualism versus collectivism
2. Immediacy: high contact versus low contact
3. Uncertainty avoidance
4. Gender: masculinity versus feminity
5. Independence versus intimacy

As noted earlier, nonverbal messages are often culture-bound and therefore important aspects of intercultural communication. For example, the use of time and space for communication are often quite different across cultures. (Chapter 6 is devoted to nonverbal communication. Most of the discussion of nonverbal elements, such as time and space differences, in intercultural communication is treated there rather than in this section.)

Bear in mind that the text discussion returns to intercultural issues repeatedly in the contexts of business and professional communication as well. The purpose here is to set forth some of the most widely accepted principles relating to cultural effects on interpersonal communication

Language and Thought

Earlier, we noted that language is one of the most obvious markers of culture. We often think of cultures as being coextensive with some languages: The Finnish culture comprises those people who speak Finnish, for example. Unlike many of the out-of-awareness aspects of culture, we are immediately aware of someone speaking a language other than our own.

Linguistic Determinism.   Language provides the means for us to think and to talk about the world and our lives in it. An important question for intercultural communication concerns whether or not what is expressed in one language can successfully be translated into and expressed in another. If we read a book translated from Japanese, are we really experiencing the book in the same way as those people who read it in the original language?

Scholars have long debated the question of "linguistic relativism" or "linguistic determinism." The question is whether or not the language people speaks determines how they see reality in the world around them. The strongest affirmative answer to this question was made by Edward Sapir, a linguist, and Benjamin Lee Whorf, a businessman and linguist who worked with Sapir. Together, they formulated the well-known Sapir-Whorf Hypothesis, which states that the language a person speaks shapes the reality one perceives.[8] This is directly opposed to the notion that language represents the objects in reality and that the objects all look the same to people regardless of what language they speak. The Sapir-Whorf

Hypothesis suggests that reality does not look the same to people speaking different languages.

Whorf, a businessman in manufacturing, noted that there were several accidents around a storage area where gasoline drums were kept. The gasoline had been used from the drums and, therefore, they were labelled "empty." Workers would occasionally toss cigarette butts into the empty drums, causing an explosion, because the drums were empty of liquid gasoline but not of the fumes. This observation led Whorf to note that people respond to words rather than to reality per se or that language shapes people's reality. For the smokers among the workers, the drums were empty, when in fact they really were not (see Figure 4-2). When Whorf began to study the Native American language of the Hopi under the guidance of Sapir, he saw a wider application of his earlier insight. Sapir and Whorf were convinced that the grammatical concepts of the Hopis' language shaped their perceptions of the world, causing them to see the world differently from speakers of most European languages.

This hypothesis can be interpreted as saying that people notice those things for which they have a word. Usual examples include the many words that the Inuit (or Eskimo) people have for snow or that the Maasai of Kenya have for cattle. Presumably, these people are aware of many distinctions among types of snow and cattle that are not as obvious to other peoples. Or, it is often noted that the Japanese or the Hopi break down the color spectrum differently from English: Each of these languages has two separate words for different shades of black, for example, but

▶ **Figure 4-2** *Are the gasoline drums marked "empty" really empty, apparently empty, almost empty, or not really empty?*

only one word to cover the English notion of blue and green. Advertisers are aware of how people respond to words. One food company trumpeted the fact that its product had more so-called food energy than its competitors. Food energy is measured in calories, but the advertiser realized that it would not be wise to say that the product had more calories than its competitors'.

At the grammatical level, the Sapir-Whorf Hypothesis suggests that the grammatical structures of a language shape how the speakers of that language perceive time or action. The tense systems of most European languages, for example, suggest one orientation to time (past, present, and future). Other languages include tenses for near versus far-distant time (in the past or into the future), or tenses differentiating potential happenings from actual events, and so on. In the United States, the movement to avoid or to remove the gender-specific pronouns of English (as in the construction that invariably used "he" or "him" to denote people in general) indicates that people feel that grammatical terms can influence how we think. Writers now try to avoid using gender-specific pronouns.

For intercultural communication, these considerations underscore the potential difficulties when two people, who are native speakers of different languages, try to communicate with each other. If they communicate in the same language, say English, one of them is speaking a foreign language. For one participant, the ideas to be expressed must be translated from one language to another. The connotations of a word in one language are usually not equivalent to the connotations of the translated word in the other language. When the Secretary General of the United Nations announced that he would try to mediate a dispute between the United States and Iran, he was unaware that in Farsi (the Iranian language) the word *mediator* carried the connotation of a *meddler* or *trouble-maker*. Many of us recall when President Carter, on a state visit to Poland, wanted to say that he desired better relations with the Polish people. Unfortunately, translators selected from several choices a Polish synonym for the verb *desire*, which carried the connotation of desire in the sense of lust.

Americans doing business in Thailand, one of the growing tigers of the Pacific Rim, report that one should be aware that there are different languages and vocabularies in the Thai language itself. One version of the language is used for formal situations in which royalty is present. Another is used for formal settings without royalty. Further, there is an informal language for friends and coworkers; and, finally, there is a low, or vulgar, form of the language not suitable for the other situations.

Japanese represents a similar linguistic situation. First, there is the Japanese language for women, which differs from that used by men. Second, there are significant differences in pronunciation and vocabulary in Japanese, depending upon whether you are addressing a superior, an equal, or a subordinate. For example, a supervisor would address a subordinate as Smith-*kun*, but an equal level supervisor of Jones-*san*. These differences also appear as the use of a formal language (*keigo*) versus a colloquial language (*kogo*). By switching from the formal to the colloquial, a Japanese executive can carry on a more private conversation, even in front of Japanese-speaking foreigners (who have probably learned only the *keigo*, or formal language). These cases suggest the pitfalls that are possible when using a translator or when trying to learn just enough of the other language to get by.

Two solutions available for those doing business with Japanese corporations, then, are: (1) to learn the language and its nuances, or (2) to make use of translators. The second option is much more likely, given time and other limitations. Mark Zimmerman, who operated in the Japanese business world for several years, warns that it is important to check out translators carefully and to review before a meeting the vocabulary and terms that are important for your business.[9]

Matters of Style.   Besides the question of the difficulties of making accurate translations from one language to another, there are differences in cultural preferences for language styles and uses. The writer V. S. Naipaul (from Jamaica but of a Hindu Indian family living in Great Britain, an intercultural phenomenon himself) describes a conversation that he struck up on an airliner with another passenger, also Indian. Naipaul says that in the opening of their talk, he tried to determine whether it would be a Western conversation or an Asian conversation. In the second type of conversation, people discuss which personal issues, such as one's income, would be too private to bring up in a so-called Western conversation. This situation indicates that there are different cultural rules for appropriate topics of conversations.

Cultural norms will also differ regarding the correct styles for opening and closing conversations. Styles may differ in other ways, as well. For example, the Igbo people of southeastern Nigeria say, "Proverbs are the palm-oil with which words are eaten." By this, they mean that putting their statements in the form of or accompanied by well-known proverbs allows the words to be absorbed more easily, just as oil helps make dry food more palatable. Other West African peoples also greatly prize the ability to mix proverbs and familiar sayings into one's conversations. To someone unaccustomed to this cultural norm, the West African businessmen may seem to be indirect or to tell too many stories before getting to the point.

We have already mentioned the barrier often created by U.S. business people's directness in the use of language with those from cultures, such as the Japanese or Chinese, who may be more comfortable with indirection. Recall one of the problems from Chapter 1 in which the U.S. businessman wanted to begin discussing business too soon after arriving in the country. The Japanese want to know the people with whom they are dealing. For them, trust and interpersonal understanding are more important than annual reports and bottom lines. They expect a protocol or procedure to be followed in initial meetings that precede any business dealings. At a first meeting, the American guest will be ushered into a large conference room and should wait to be shown to the seat of honor (the middle of the table opposite the entrance). The first meeting will probably be a formal meeting with senior officials present, who will recount in great detail the history of their firm and its dealings with the American's company. Any hurrying of this process will undoubtedly be taken as an indication of unreliability or a lack of proper respect (and foreclose the possibility of "getting down to business"). As we will discuss later, gift-giving is inevitably associated with such a first meeting, as well.

Similarly, other cultures often have a different feeling about the directness of American debating or argumentation. The use of public speaking "for the debating of conflicting viewpoints, especially popular in election years in the West, has been generally unacceptable in the Orient."[10] This attitude is attributed partly to the belief in Confucian societies that language is ambiguous or unreliable for such purposes. Not only are Oriental cultures uncomfortable with public debate. The Finns also emphasize Finnish solidarity to the point that they report being uncomfortable with direct debate between their political leaders. Attitudes toward language and speech and what one is expected to do in language and speech, then, can differ from one culture to another.

Highlights of Language and Thought. Language is the most obvious aspect of cultural difference as well as the clearest barrier to effecting intercultural communication. Direct translation of words from one language into another is not as simple or straightforward as it may seem. Nuances and connotations are lost when one moves from the words of one language to those of another. The Sapir-Whorf Hypothesis reminds us that the language people grow up with tends to shape their perceptions of reality and, possibly, the ways that they think, and these things are hard to capture in translations. The style with which language is used also varies from one culture to another. People in one culture may prefer a style more direct or one less based on rational argument than what Americans may have experienced. It is therefore important to prepare carefully with translators ahead of time.

Effects of Context

The anthropologist Edward T. Hall has been working in the field of intercultural communication for many years. He has developed a widely accepted basis for distinguishing cultures' communication activity, which he refers to as context. He suggests categorizing cultures according to whether they are low-context or high-context.[11]

First, by the idea of context, Hall directs our attention to the way that people construct a context, a setting, for the events and behaviors that they observe. Culture functions, he claims, as a "highly selective screen" so that one's culture "designates what we pay attention to and what we ignore."[12] When we first come into the world, our environment is just one "bloomin' buzzin' confusion." Gradually, we learn to sort things out and to notice some things while ignoring others. We could not function if we constantly paid attention to all the stimuli, colors, and activity around us. We must pick out a few stimuli and focus on them to the exclusion of others. In learning a culture, we learn to pay attention to the right things from the point of view of that culture.

Of course, there are reasons not specifically cultural for paying attention to some things and ignoring others in the environment. When we are hungry, we pick out signs for restaurants or other indicators of where food may be found. When finding our way through a strange city, we pay special attention to street or interstate signs. When performing a particular task, we of course focus on the tools or material with which we are working. Managers pay attention to the overall functioning of a department or organizational unit, while particular department members pay more attention to their immediate task environment. Therefore, one's purpose, situation, or location in a hierarchy are additional factors that help determine what is seen as the context for events. Culture is another powerful determinant because often, as we have seen, it operates out of direct awareness.

Now we turn to the distinction that Hall makes between a high-context and a low-context culture. He points out that the meaning of any particular event is found in the words of the language that is used (the code) and in the surrounding setting or context. In a high-context culture, people assume that the setting, or context, carries *most* of the meaning of an event. In a low-context culture, people assume that the coded language, the words, carry *most* of the meaning regardless of the setting.[13] In low-context cultures, then, there is more tendency to "spell things out" or "to put it in writing." In the high-context cultures, more is left unsaid and people infer from the situation what is intended. Note that we are not saying that words are not important in high-context cultures or that context is not important in so-called low-context cultures; rather, there is a tendency to emphasize more context in the one and more words in the other.

Hall believes that it is possible to place most of the world's cultures on a continuum or scale running from high-context to low-context. As one might surmise, the U.S. culture is very near the low-context end. (It is not at the very end, where Hall places the German-Swiss, German, and Scandinavian cultures.) He believes that the British culture is more high-context than the American, in that things such as status and rank are indicated more subtly by contextual factors (such as accent or food preferences) than by specifics such as official positions.

Difficulties in intercultural communication arise if one person listens to the words carefully, while the other attends just as carefully to the context. The two could easily "hear" two completely different messages. The American therefore may not hear the Chinese customer say "no," because it will probably not be said "in so many words." In fact, the coded message, in words, may have been "yes," while the context was meant to indicate the opposite message. There may also be unintended emotional problems in the relationship. When someone talks down to us, he or she is essentially low-contexting us, Hall would say. Similarly, someone from a high-context culture could feel that we are talking down to them by spelling things out so completely in words when they believe that the context already provides ample information.

Zimmerman provides a good example of the importance of context versus words when dealing with the Japanese. He was visiting several Japanese companies to line up licenses for his corporation's pharmaceuticals. When he arrived at one company—one with which he had previous dealings—he received a lavish welcome, with all the senior executives present. He was then treated to a wonderful night on the town. He realized that the welcome was too lavish (the context) and that the meaning, regardless of what was said, was that the Japanese company was committed to someone else and could not do business with him.

In negotiations, the Japanese are expert practitioners of *haragei*, or communicating by feelings or intuition rather than by words. *Haragei* represents a means of communication often used by politicians and business executives in Japan: Its literal meaning is "acting (gei) on guts (hara) alone."[14] This strategy is marked by the occasional long periods of silence (*ma*, a pregnant silence) or responses that seem tangential or at best indirect. The communication that actually occurs in *haragei* is almost entirely what we would call contextual. Compared to the United States, Japan is unusually homogeneous, both culturally and ethnically. These shared cultural assumptions may account for the ability for Japanese to communicate with each other by *haragei*, by context.

American business people may be surprised to learn that details of contracts, which are low-context, are of less interest to their Japanese or Korean counterparts than the background of experiences and interactions that the two sides may have with each other. In Korea, it is expected that contracts will be regularly changed and renegotiated as the context, or conditions, change. The context, in other words, is seen as more important than the coded or written message.[15]

Highlights of Context. Context provides a further complication to the differences in language and thought noted in the previous section. Not only is the language different when we communicate across cultures, but the very function or purpose of language may vary. We need to be alert to the situations in which the context or setting speaks much louder than words. It is useful to try to find out if the other culture with which we must deal is a low-context or a high-context culture.

Dimensions of Cultural Difference

We have now seen that language and the context that surrounds the use of language are important variables of intercultural communication. Other dimensions provide useful ways to differentiate and categorize cultures and suggest ways that cultures vary in systematic ways. When engaging in intercultural interaction, one needs to be alert for variability along these lines, since it may affect or even distort the messages being exchanged.

Individualism versus Collectivism. Many researchers and theorists have noted and used the distinction between individualist and collectivist cultures.[16] The dimension has been referred to as "Among the most basic cultural dimensions."[17] In individualistic cultures, people derive their identities from their own activities and personality. People think in terms of maintaining one's own self-esteem apart from the group or family to which one belongs. It is within individualistic cultures that Maslow's highest level of motivation, self-actualization, makes the most sense. In collectivist cultures, one's identity is bound up with a significant group: The emphasis would therefore be on group-actualization. In-group relationships are more important than in individualistic cultures and people tend to draw sharp boundaries between us and them. People in the collectivist cultures also tend to place group goals and achievements ahead of individual achievements.

There appears to be some direct relationship between high-context and low-context cultures and ones described as collectivist and individualist. The cultures that Hall has designated as high-context seem to be nearly all collectivist, as well. This has led William Gudykunst and Stella Ting-Toomey to conclude, "It, therefore, appears that low- and high-context communication are the predominant forms of communication in individualistic and collectivistic cultures, respectively."[18]

Difficulties in understanding can occur when people from a highly individualistic culture, such as that in the United States, interact with people from cultures who place more value on the group. Whereas the Americans may appeal to satisfaction in achieving some personal goal, the collectivist may have some trouble understanding such an appeal. American families are often not particularly close, and often people living in U. S. cities do not even know the names of their neighbors. Therefore, Americans may not realize the importance of being accepted as a member of a group before sharing friendship or doing business with someone from a collectivist culture. Also, Americans may not realize how self-centered we may appear from another culture's point of view.

The implications of these differences are that appeals to motivate people are likely to be different in individualist and collectivist cultures. In collectivist cultures, the good of the group is placed before that of the individual, and no one wishes to stand out too much from the group.

When President Bush visited Japan in 1992 to encourage improved trading opportunities for American business, he was accompanied by several American CEOs. The Japanese media focussed on the huge salaries and bonuses that the CEOs were paid, even while their corporations were laying off workers. Japanese CEOs would never be given salaries so much greater than the average earnings of workers in their firms. In fact, they would probably be embarrassed to be singled out in that way. Neither the Japanese nor the Americans, for that matter, seemed to realize the cultural basis for motivating individuals with salaries and bonuses in the United States versus group motivation, which is more the norm in Japan.

Another implication of the difference between individualism versus collectivism is that there is a stronger group bond among work groups in collectivist-oriented cultures. American consultants working with Mexican corporations report on the difficulty of "meshing" with their Mexican counterparts; there may be a period of adjustment of a day to several weeks as the consultant gradually becomes a member of the group. It is typical for Mexican companies to provide a free main meal in the middle of the day for the workers, which comes about 1:30–3:00 P.M. Communal eating expresses collective, even familial, solidarity in contrast to the U.S. pattern of bringing one's own lunch, going out to eat, or buying something in the company cafeteria.

While it appears that the individualist cultures are predominantly Western, and the collectivist ones are non-Western, we must be alert for variability and exceptions to such generalizations. To return to the example of the Igbo of Nigeria, it is clear that individual achievement is considered laudable. The main character of Nigerian author Chinua Achebe's masterpiece, *Things Fall Apart*, is a man who is honored for his ability to overcome the life situation of his father and family. As the Igbo say, "If a child washes his hands, he may eat with kings," meaning that one can earn his or her own way through personal achievement. The "her" in the last sentence is particularly significant for the Igbo. There are well-known cases of women who struck out from the usual role of their sex and became warriors, elders, and respected members of (usually) all-male societies.

Immediacy, or High- and Low-Contact. Cultures seem to differ in terms of the level of involvement people display in conversation and other interactions with each other. This dimension is also described in terms of high-contact versus low-contact cultures. In cultures that are high on immediacy, there is more physical touching and contact during communication interactions than in the less immediate, or low-contact, cultures.

People from cultures low on immediacy appear as distant, aloof, or unfriendly to people from a culture high on immediacy. On the other hand, people from low-

Diversity in the Workplace

Diversity in the Workplace: Business in Latin America

Latin American cultures tend to be high-contact, as mentioned earlier. Professionals working in Mexico, for example, note that there is more hand-shaking—usually at every meeting—than in the United States. Mexicans exhibit more hugging and emotional displays, not only upon meeting but also in ending a relationship. A consultant has reported that she has experienced this several times after spending only a few weeks with a firm. Therefore, Americans in Mexico or other Latin American states should be aware that their normal professional demeanor can be read as aloofness or a sense of superiority that Latin American fellow professionals may resent. Note that respect is very important in such cultures, as well. Americans should not interpret these points as meaning they should become too informal or familiar, such as slapping others on the back. Rather, Americans should expect and accept closer physical distances and contact and more a sense of groupness than they are accustomed to in the United States.

contact cultures will feel threatened or crowded by "pushy" people from the high-contact cultures, or those higher on immediacy. The difficulty often is that both make emotional judgments about the other person without really being aware of what the problem is. North Americans, Northern Europeans (British, Germans, Scandinavians), and Japanese tend toward the low-contact end of the scale, whereas the high-contact cultures seem to be associated with climates nearer the equator. The Japanese examples clarify that a culture can be both high-context and low-contact. It is not known whether there is any particular explanation for this geographical distribution of these cultural characteristics.[19] Again, it is important to bear in mind that these are generalizations about tendencies within a culture; there are of course many individual differences and exceptions.

Uncertainty Avoidance.   Many researchers have noted that cultures differ according to their members' tolerance for uncertainty and ambiguity. This was one of the major dimensions of cultural variability discovered by Hofstede in a large-scale study of individuals within multicultural corporations.[20] Those cultures that avoid high uncertainty are more resistant to change. There may be more explicit and more numerous prescriptions or rules for behavior in such societies. In general, people from cultures that emphasize avoiding uncertainty prefer specialist careers in organizations rather than the generalist track, which may carry more risk. They may prefer occupations such as cost accounting or specialized engineering or technical fields in preference over sales or advertising or general administration.

People from cultures high on uncertainty avoidance are less likely to be tolerant of open conflict and competition.[21] The countries that researchers have designated as high in uncertainty avoidance are largely found in South America and southern Europe (Greece, Argentina, Spain, Chile, Portugal, for example). Countries low in concern with avoiding uncertainty tend to be grouped in South Asia (such as Singapore and Hong Kong) and in Northern Europe and and North America.[22]

Implications of the concern for uncertainty mean that some cultures will be more risk averse than others. People from these cultures may be unlikely to be motivated to become involved in entrepreneurial enterprises. People in these cultures will not be as likely to be motivated by the possibility of big returns in the face of some risk but will prefer tried and true methods. Appeals to being innovative, widely used in the United States, will probably fall flat in such risk-averse cultures, whereas appeals to tradition and experience will be more successful.

Gender: Masculinity versus Femininity.   Cultures that scored high on the masculinity index emphasized differentiated sex roles: For example, "men's work" and "women's work" were clearly designated.

The cultures high on masculinity also emphasized assertiveness, competition, ambition, and independence. People in these cultures report that work and their jobs are the central aspect of their lives and are willing to accept work's taking precedence over private or family life. A U.S. corporation recently ran a series of television commercials that emphasized that their workers thought about their work 24 hours a day, every day. They would stop in the desert on vacation to call in an idea from a remote gas station, for example. Clearly, American firms tend to reward what are sometimes called "workaholics."

The demands of the job that are accepted in one culture may be seen as interfering with family and private life in another, causing some friction within cross-cultural organizations. Cultures high on the masculinity index expect people to subordinate their private lives to the demands of the job. This expectation will probably meet with resistance in a culture that places more value on the quality of private life. Americans vacationing in France are sometimes astounded to find French businesses, even restaurants, closed on the weekends, when Americans would expect to do their best business. Many French place a higher priority on enjoying the weekend than on maximizing profits.

As noted, female roles are more clearly distinguished from male roles in highly masculine cultures. There, women are expected to be nurturant and to take the lead in care for children and family life. Japan represents a culture that appears to be highly masculine, as do Mexico and Caribbean countries as well as several central European national cultures. Many African and Islamic cultures also have sharply defined and separate roles for men and women.

Obviously, differences on this dimension could result in communication problems, particularly when women are assigned to certain roles in a culture high on masculinity. During the brief war in the Middle East between forces of the United Nations and Iraq, there were several instances when Arab allies were disturbed by roles assigned to women in the U. S. and other Western armies. In Saudi Arabia, from which the allied armies operated, women are expected to play a subordinate role in public life and are not even permitted to drive automobiles on the streets. The employment of women troops, therefore, caused strain between the Western armies and the Saudi hosts.

Within a culture as heterogeneous as that in the United States, there are often conflicting orientations on the dimension among different cocultures. First, in terms of corporate cultures, there are different professions and occupations that have traditionally been seen as masculine, particularly favoring those who are aggressive and assertive. Recall Deal and Kennedy's reference to the "tough guy-macho" cultures associated with individual sales, for example. Some occupations, such as law enforcement, construction, or mining have been seen as traditionally male occupations until recently. Efforts at integrating women into such subcultures have not always gone smoothly. Traditionally, certain cocultures have been seen as differing along this dimension, as well. Cocultures derived from Hispanic cultures or Southern European cultures have been seen as emphasizing sharp distinctions between male and female roles, for example.

Independence and Intimacy.   The linguist Deborah Tannen has analyzed the differences in the style of communication between men and women, primarily in the United States.[23] She discerns a cultural difference between the two sexes and believes that, as children, boys and girls are acculturated (that is, taught about their culture) in different ways. These differences lead to the existence of two cocultures, male and female. Her research is based on extensive observations of

▶ *Men and women may employ different communication styles.*

play groups among children, which tend to be same-sex. Such research notes that boys' games are often more competitive with emphasis on winning and losing and establishing a hierarchy. Girls' play tends toward small groups and pairs engaged in cooperative activities, such as "playing house." Through these activities, Tannen believes that males and females are initiated into different cultural worlds.[24]

These two cocultures differ, according to Tannen, on the dimension of independence versus intimacy. She explains these terms in the following way: "Intimacy is key in a world of connection where individuals negotiate complex networks of friendship, minimize differences, try to reach consensus, and avoid the appearance of superiority." On the other hand, *independence* is the key term in a world of status, "because a primary means of establishing status is to tell others what to do, and taking orders is a marker of low status."[25] Everyone, both male and female, needs intimacy and independence in their lives, of course, but women tend to emphasize intimacy, whereas men are concerned mainly with independence.[26] As a result, Tannen concludes, "If women speak and hear a language of connection and intimacy, while men speak and hear a language of status and independence, then communication between men and women can be like cross-cultural communication, prey to the clash of conversational styles. Instead of different dialects, it has been said they speak different genderlects."[27]

As with people who exhibit other cultural differences, when men and women communicate with each other (if they are speaking from different conceptions of reality), there are bound to be misunderstandings. Also, as with other cultural differences, neither person in the dialogue may be aware of what the difficulty is, so both are left frustrated and unsure of what went wrong. If women are interested in establishing rapport and negotiating relationships in a conversation, and men are more interested in establishing their status and independence, problems will result. For example, in seeking the help of someone else in completing a project at work, a woman may feel that she is exhibiting the positive quality of establishing a connection with that person, whereas a man may feel that she is indicating a lack of independence. Notice that this kind of misunderstanding could also occur between someone from a collectivist culture and coworker from a individualist culture.

Highlights of Dimensions of Cultural Difference.   This section considered some of the widely used systems that have been developed for classifying culturally significant differences as they affect communication. The point of summarizing this list of dimensions is to help make you aware of the various ways in which cultures can differ and that varying viewpoints are possible.

SUMMARY

We live in a multicultural world. The pace of technological change and the expansion of economic interconnections make intercultural experiences increasingly likely for people in business and the professions. We must be prepared to deal with an intercultural world and a multicultural workplace. More and more companies with international operations are training their people in intercultural communication. Despite efforts in this direction, however, most approaches have not gone beyond simple language instruction and teaching about local customs.[28]

A major key toward developing skills in intercultural communication is to understand that such differences are present and likely. We cannot expect everyone to speak English, and we should not expect everyone to have learned the same cultural norms about communication that we have learned. An awareness of others' cultural expectations, habits, and reasons for behavior go a long way toward improving intercultural communication.

The difficulty to finding this key lies in the fact that, by its very nature, culture operates out of our direct conscious awareness. The purpose of culture is to make our lives more predictable by allowing us to take certain things for granted. People from different cultures have learned to take different things for granted, though. Therein lies the need for heightening our own sensitivity to the possibilities of these differences. We need to be aware that not only are there significant differences between national cultural groups, but also between subcultures and cocultures associated with the larger national cultures.

This chapter has touched upon some of the important factors of intercultural communication: language and thought; the effects of context in high- and low-context cultures; and dimensions for differentiating cultural differences. These dimensions include the following: individualism versus collectivism; immediacy, or high- and low-contact cultures; uncertainty avoidance; gender, masculinity and femininity; and independence and intimacy.

The next two chapters, on interpersonal communication and nonverbal communication, will return to several of the ideas developed here.

Communication is inextricably linked with culture; in fact, culture is often embodied in the way that people communicate. Not only do cultures have different languages, they also communicate in terms of different value systems and expectations about relationships, as well as about how conversations and communication episodes should proceed and about the use of nonverbal communication.

EXERCISES

1. Explain factors that are leading to an increasingly interdependent and multicultural work environment. Discuss the intercultural contacts that are significant for your school, company, and organization. What sort of international and intercultural contacts are important in your state, city, or region?

2. Write a definition of culture. Compare this definition with those of others in the class. What elements are especially important for communication? List the communication problems that you or people you know have experienced as a result of intercultural differences.

3. List the subcultures and cocultures to which you belong and to which your group of friends belong. How do these identifications result in problems in communication with those from other subcultures and cocultures? To what extent do people with physical disabilities constitute a coculture that experiences some special problems in communicating with members of the larger culture? Discuss whether the terms *the young* or *the aged* seem to represent cocultures with similar problems.

4. Explain the difference between "stereotyping" others and being alert for intercultural differences. Look for examples of stereotyping of people from different cultures or cocultures. Describe situations in which these differences cause difficulties in communicating.

5. Discuss situations that you have observed or read about that illustrate communication expectations resulting from the various dimensions of intercultural communication described in this chapter. To what extent do you find that women and men represent different cultures in terms of some of these dimensions?

Communication Problem: Accessible to Communication?

Conduct a floor-by-floor inventory of an important building on
your campus, such as the main library. Make a note of obvious
obstacles for someone in a wheelchair. Then make a special study of
check-out counters, study carrels and desks, copy machines, and on-
line terminals in the reference room and elsewhere. Are these
facilities set up so that a person in a wheelchair would not feel
inconvenienced or, worse, put down, when using them? How
would such a person feel in the stacks, where books on upper
shelves could be well out of sight, let alone out of reach?

Develop a plan for improving how a physically challenged
person would feel using the facilities you have inventoried. How
could you improve the messages being sent to members of this
coculture by the facilities and setup of this building?

SELECTED SOURCES
FOR FURTHER READING

Asante, M. K., & Gudykunst, W. B. (Eds.). (1989). *Handbook of international and intercultural communication*. Newbury Park, CA: Sage Publications.

Berger, M. (1987, July–August), Building bridges over the cultural rivers. *International Management, 42*:7–8, 61–62.

Borden, G. A. (1991). *Cultural orientation: An approach to understanding intercultural communication*. Englewood Cliffs, NJ: Prentice-Hall.

Braithwaite, D. O. (1991). "Just how much did that wheelchair cost?": Management of privacy boundaries by people with disabilities. *Western Journal of Speech Communication, 55*, 254–274.

Condon, J. C., & Yousef, F. (1975). *An introduction to intercultural communication*. Indianapolis: Bobbs-Merrill.

Dodd, C. H. (1991). *Dynamics of intercultural communication* (3rd ed.). Dubuque: Wm. C. Brown.

Gudykunst, W. B., & Ting-Toomey, S. (1988). *Culture and interpersonal communication*. Newbury Park, CA: Sage Publications.

Hall, E. T. (1977). *Beyond culture*. Garden City, NY: Anchor Press.

Hendle, C. G.; Fennell, B. A., & Miller, C. R. (1991). Understanding failures in organizational discourse: The accident at Three Mile Island and the shuttle Challenger disaster. In C. Bazerman & J. Paradis (Eds.), *Textual dynamics of the professions*. Madison, WI: University of Wisconsin Press.

Kim, Y. Y., & Gudykunst, W. B. (Eds.). (1988). *Theories in intercultural communication*. Newbury Park, CA: Sage Publications.

Kluckhohn, C. (1962). *Culture and behavior*. New York: The Free Press.

Kluckhohn, F. R., & Strodtbeck, F. L. (1961). *Variations in value orientations*. Evanston, IL: Row, Peterson and Co.

Knotts, R. (1989, January). Cross-cultural management: Transformations and adaptations. *Business horizons*, *32*:1, 29–33.

Kroeber, A. L., & Kluckhohn, C. (1963). *Culture: A critical review of concepts and definitions*. New York: Vintage Books.

McCreary, D. R. (1986). *Japanese–U.S. business negotiations: A cross-cultural study*. New York: Praeger.

Naipaul, V. S. (1981). *Among the believers: An Islamic journey*. New York: Vintage Books.

Richardson, B. M., & Taidzo U. (1981). *Business and society in Japan*. New York: Praeger.

Samovar, L. A., & Porter, R. E. (Eds.). (1989). *Intercultural communication: A reader* (6th ed.). Belmont, CA: Wadsworth.

Soyinka, W. (1975). *Death and the king's horseman*. New York: Hill and Wang.

Tannen, D. (1990). *You just don't understand: Women and men in conversation*. New York: William Morrow.

Ting-Toomey, S., & Korzenny, F. (Eds.). (1989). *Language, communication, and culture: Current directions*. Newbury Park, CA: Sage Publications.

Yum, J. O. (1988). The impact of Confucianism on interpersonal relationships and communication patterns in East Asia. *Communication Monographs*, *55*, 374–388.

Zimmerman, M. (1985). *How to do business with the Japanese*. New York: Random House.

▶

References

1. Zey, M. G. (1988). A mentor for all reasons. *Personnel Journal*, *67*:1, 46–51.
2. Haight, G. (1990). Managing diversity. *Across the Board*, *27*:3, 22–29.
3. Dreher, G. F., & Ash, R. A. (1990). A comparative study of mentoring among men and women in managerial, professional, and technical positions. *Journal of Applied Psychology*, *75*, 544.
4. Knotts, R. (1989, January). Cross-cultural management: Transformations and adaptations. *Business Horizons*, *32*:1, 29–33.
5. West. P. (1989, March–April). Cross-cultural literacy and the Pacific Rim. *Business Horizons*, *32*, 3–5.
6. Hall, E. T. (1977). *Beyond culture* (p. 63). Garden City, NJ: Doubleday/Anchor Books.
7. "Research does not confirm this simplistic notion [that contact itself is the answer]; contact between nations has, more often than not, actually exacerbated existing antagonisms." Barnlund, D. C. (1989, March–April). Public and private self in communicating with Japan. *Business Horizons*, *32*, 32.
8. Sapir, E. (1921). *Language: An introduction to the study of speech*, New York: Harcourt, Brace & World; and Whorf, B. L. (1956). *Language thought and reality*, New York: Wiley.

9. Zimmerman, M. (1985). *How to do business with the Japanese*. New York: Random House.

10. Becker, C. B. (1991). Reasons for the lack of argumentation and debate in the Far East. In L. A. Samovar & R. Porter (Eds.), *Intercultural communication: A reader* (6th ed.) (p. 234). Belmont, CA: Wadsworth.

11. The concept of high and low context is most thoroughly explained in Hall's book, *Beyond culture*. Garden City, NJ: Doubleday/Anchor Books.

12. Hall, p. 85.

13. Hall, E. T. (1977). *Beyond culture*, Garden City, NY: Anchor Books. See esp. Chapter 6, "Context and Meaning," pp. 85–104.

14. McCreary, D. R. (1986). *Japanese–U.S. business negotiations: A cross-cultural study*, (p. 46). New York: Praeger.

15. "Unlike in the United States, where legalistic and contractual bonding are prevalent in business relationships, personal trust between negotiators is one major guarantee in Japan that business agreements will be honored by each firm." Richardson, B. M. & Ueda, T. (1981). *Business and society in Japan* (p. 307). New York: Praeger.

16. Gudykunst, W. B., & Ting-Toomey, S. (1988). *Culture and interpersonal communication* (p. 210). Newbury Park, CA: Sage Publications.

17. Hecht, M. L., Andersen, P. A., & Ribeau, S. A. (1989). The cultural dimensions of nonverbal communication. In M. K. Asante & W. B. Gudykunst (Eds.), *Handbook of international and intercultural communication* (p. 169). Newbury Park, CA: Sage Publications.

18. Gudykunst and Ting-Toomey, p. 44.

19. Andersen, P. (1991). Explaining intercultural differences in nonverbal communication. In Samovar, L. A. & Porter, R. E. (Eds.), *Intercultural communication: A reader* (6th ed.) (p. 289). Belmont, CA: Wadsworth.

20. Hofstede, G. (1984). *Culture's consequences*. Newbury Park, CA: Sage Publications.

21. Gudykunst and Ting-Toomey, p. 47.

22. Hecht, Andersen, and Ribeau, p. 175.

23. Tannen, D. (1990). *You just don't understand: Women and men in conversation*, (p. 26). New York: William Morrow.

24. Tannen, pp. 43–47.

25. Tannen, p. 26.

26. Tannen, p. 26.

27. Tannen, p. 42.

28. Berger, M. (1987, July–August). Building bridges over the cultural rivers. *International Management*, 42:7–8, 61–62.

Communication Breakdown in Air Traffic Control System, New York City, 1991

September 17, 1991 was an especially hot day in New York City and air conditioners were drawing record amounts of electric power. Consolidated Edison (ConEd), the utility supplying the city's electricity, had an arrangement with AT&T which allowed the utility to ask AT&T to switch temporarily to its own generators for electrical power during such periods of peak demand. When the power company made the request that day, AT&T Long Distance did switch over to their own generators. The generators, however, were not working because of mechanical failure, so back-up batteries, in place for such an emergency, took over supplying power to AT&T. Unfortunately, no one at AT&T noticed that the generators were not working and that the power to keep the long distance system going was coming from batteries with a life of only a few hours.

At 4:50 that afternoon the batteries went dead. At about that time AT&T technicians realized that their crucial control center for the New York City area was on back-up battery power. The shutdown of the phone lines had an immediate and devastating effect on the area's three major airports and on air traffic in the congested northeast area. Federal Aviation Administration (FAA) air traffic controllers at the city's airports depend upon phone lines to link them with the radar control centers and radio transmitters through which they communicate with flight crews. The disruption in AT&T service meant that controllers were out of communication with arriving and departing planes at Kennedy International, LaGuardia, and Newark airports. Phone service was not restored until 1:30 A.M.

Some of the consequences and dangers of this kind of communication breakdown are explained in the video sequence. Obviously there was the very real danger of a disaster such as a midair collision or plane crash while some of the circling airplanes were out of communication with ground controllers. Over 700 flights were delayed or cancelled at the three airports during the shutdown. Had the phone outage occurred earlier in the day it is possible that business transactions, such as trading on the New York Stock Exchange, would have been interrupted with a potential loss of as much as $1 trillion in a single day.

This case brings to our attention several important points about communication introduced in this first part of the text. First, the sheer importance of communication and of the systems that support communication are emphasized. Breakdowns in communication can have severe and widespread impact.

Second, notice the centrality of the human element in a case that seems to focus on technology. If the AT&T technicians had checked the part of the building housing the electrical generators, they would have heard the alarms warning them that the generators were not working. Note that a crucial part of the system was running on batteries for six hours before anyone noticed it. The questions of human responsibility go even further. There is, for example, the question of who decided that the FAA control system would depend on one private long distance carrier instead of having its own dedicated telephone communication network. Some of these issues are taken up in later CNN video cases in this text.

Third, notice the systemic interrelatedness illustrated by this case study. An attempt to deal with a heat wave by one system, the electric utility, led to widespread unanticipated effects in several other systems. A failure in one system led to breakdowns in other systems.

For discussion after viewing the video we suggest that you consider some of the following questions: Have you ever experienced a power or telephone outage at home, business, school, or elsewhere? Have you run into "down" computers or equipment when traveling, making bank transactions, or in other activities that brought your attention to our dependence on widespread communication systems? What were the effects of this kind of disruption? Can you think of similar cases in which a seemingly unrelated event or accident had wide-ranging impact in disrupting human communication? Suggest ways to deal with the problems posed by our modern vulnerability to the technological systems that support the conduct of our business and our lives.

Interpersonal Communication in Business and the Professions

This part of the book looks at several different settings in which interpersonal and group communication is important on the job.

Chapters 5 and 6 provide overviews of the factors influencing interpersonal relations: the face-to-face, dyadic setting and nonverbal communication.

The discussion then turns to specifically practical settings in which these principles are applied: interviewing, small-group problem solving, and group leadership. The interview is a pervasive form of communication throughout business and professional work settings. Group settings are also dominant in most people's professional lives. Relevant findings on this topic are covered in this part of the text.

A second important topic related to work in or with groups concerns group leadership. Following some theoretical information, the text turns to practical matters of dealing with agendas, different kinds of work groups, as well as public discussion groups. Much of the discussion in the following chapters takes into account interpersonal effects important in communication.

Face-to-Face Communication in Business and Professional Settings

5

CHAPTER

After studying this chapter, you should be able to:

1. Explain the importance of dyadic and transactional communication.

2. Recognize typical problem areas affecting superior–subordinate communication.

3. Recognize the advantages and disadvantages of mentoring relationships.

4. Show the importance of relational communication in affecting interpersonal communication.

5. Describe the communication processes involved in how we form impressions of others.

6. Understand the function of roles and rules in our interpersonal communication.

Overview

Many communication experiences on the job involve face-to-face, one-on-one interaction. This chapter is especially concerned with face-to-face encounters that are part of an ongoing relationship. One of the most studied of these relationships in organizations is that between a superior and a subordinate. As Chapter 2 discussed, this relationship is often problematic. Undoubtedly, this relationship is central in determining the work climate and one's morale within an organization. Other relationships on the job, such as that between equals or coworkers, have been less studied. Researchers have been more likely to study communication among coworkers as group communication (beginning with the famous Hawthorne Effect study of Mayo). This relationship is discussed at more length in Chapters 8 and 9, which deal with small-group communication.

This chapter presents a review of some of the basic principles that underlie interpersonal communication. We proceed on the understanding that there are whole courses and many texts available devoted to the single topic of interpersonal communication. The purpose here is to provide an overview of the concepts that are treated more fully in these other places. The goal of this chapter is to provide

▶ *Face-to-face communication.*

enough background from the study of interpersonal communication to enhance the understanding of face-to-face communication in the workplace.

The major themes in this chapter deal with superior–subordinate communication, relational communication and theories related to relationship development, such as uncertainty reduction theory and attribution theory, and role theory and rules theories. Interpersonal communication can become a problem on the job when people are unaware of the effects of insensitive or inappropriate messages or interactions. A significant topic in which interpersonal communication can have negative effects is that of sexual harassment, which is discussed toward the end of this chapter.

Two points guiding the discussion of interpersonal communication are the concepts of dyadic communication and of the transactional nature of communication.

▶ **Dyadic Communication**

A vast amount of research and theory has been developed regarding interpersonal communication. Most of this research has focused on communication in a dyad. The term *dyad* is used to denote a pair of communicators in an ongoing relationship as opposed to a pair of people engaged in a casual conversation, as at the check-out line in the grocery store. The use of the term *dyad* also suggests that we look at the communication between the two people as constituting a system, in which there are regular and recurring patterns of interaction. The members of the dyad are therefore interdependent in their communication activities, and the dyad itself can be thought of as a unit.

The notion of a communication dyad can be applied effectively in many of the situations discussed throughout this text. Obviously, an interview is a dyadic situation, even though the relationship established between interviewer and interviewee may be relatively brief. The descriptions of empathic listening situations described in Chapter 3 essentially looked at dyads. Obviously, the interpersonal relationship is particularly important in empathic and active listening episodes. Later sections discuss the topics of conflict management and negotiation and mediation, which often take place within an ongoing dyadic relationship.

The main characteristics of a communication dyad, therefore, are as follows: an ongoing relationship, interdependent partners, and recurring patterns of interaction.

Transactional Communication

The idea of the transactional nature of human communication was introduced in Chapter 1. There, we attempted to explain that communication is not a simple one-way process of sending and receiving messages. Rather, "sender" and "receiver" are both simultaneously sending and receiving messages during the entire time of their interaction, as shown in Figure 5-1. The result of this process is the creation of a new reality, which is the product of this simultaneous sending-receiving activity. Part of the new reality that is created as two people continue to communicate with each other is the resulting relationship.

The relationship that develops and changes over time is defined as a result of the communication activities of the two people involved. This relationship can serve to carry the "real message." If one were to read just the words that had been

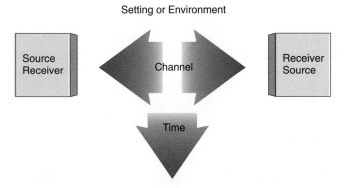

▶ **Figure 5-1** *Transactional model of the elements and relationships in communication.*

exchanged in the interaction, one could miss the actual meaning. This idea is behind the notion advanced by Deborah Tannen referred to in Chapter 4. She describes several conversations between men and women which appear to be straightforward exchanges of information but that result in one or both parties becoming angry. Why? The answer is because one person perceived the other as trying to intrude on his or her privacy or to assert control in a relationship.[1] It is not always what is said but how it can be interpreted in terms of a relationship that counts. For example, a man opening a door for a woman could be interpreted as polite caring, or it could be interpreted as indicating that the door opener has control over when the other person can use the door.

As the intricacies of transactional communication are considered throughout this chapter, examples are provided in which more serious consequences can occur when the total transaction, including the relationship message, is at odds with the surface meaning of the information exchanged.

◀▶ SUPERIOR–SUBORDINATE COMMUNICATION

The relationship and the nature of the communication between superior and subordinate are, of course, crucial in determining one's satisfaction and motivation in performing organizational duties. Superiors generally spend a good deal of the their time communicating with their subordinates: Findings consistently indicate that they spend between one third and two thirds of their time in such communication. Most of this communication is face-to-face and appears to deal with task-related matters.[2] The messages that the supervisors send usually deal with giving directions or information concerning organizational goals and procedures, providing job instructions, and evaluating the performance of subordinates. The upward communication, from subordinates to supervisors, tends to be concerned with information about the subordinates themselves, coworkers, problems, and information about things that need to be done.

To a certain extent, the nature and amount of communication between superior and subordinate depend upon where you are in an organization. At the highest levels in a large organization, executives communicate mostly with other executives and staff. In the middle ranges of an organization, middle managers deal with supervisors and department heads. The first-line managers and supervisors deal directly with the people involved in the production or service work of the organization. At the upper levels, executives usually communicate with people who are similar to themselves in terms of education, training, socioeconomic condition, and values. At lower levels, there is often more distance in status and education between superiors and subordinates.

An organization's business is a factor as well. One can draw a general distinction between those involved in production of goods versus those involved in direct service to clients or the public. Those in service organizations are usually engaged in much more interpersonal communication on the job than are production workers, and, in fact, supervisors oversee some of this communication as part of their job.

Potential Problems

There is often distortion in the superior–subordinate communication process, whether upward or downward. Problems leading to distortion discussed in the following sections include:

Amount of openness in communication
Upward distortion of communication
Language barriers
Leadership or management styles
Feedback distortions
Sexual harassment

Openness. Some distortion can result from the amount of openness (or lack thereof) as perceived by the subordinates. While subordinates report that they are more satisfied in jobs in which there is openness in this relationship (they feel free to communicate fully, good as well as unfavorable information), superiors often overestimate how open they appear to those below them. We mentioned the myth of "My door is always open; people are free to come to me at any time" earlier. Supervisors can claim to be open to communication, but in fact they may send nonverbal messages that indicate they are less willing: For example, they may schedule meetings for late in the day, allow interruptions that take them out of a conference with a subordinate, or continually postpone such meetings. Even a

▶ *Physical arrangements can serve as barriers to communication.*

supervisor's demeanor (facial looks, tone of voice, and so on) can subtly discourage a subordinate.

Some recent research indicates that how open subordinates are willing to be may partly depend upon the perception of the activities of superiors outside the immediate relationship, specifically, the extent to which the superiors are seen as involved in organizational politics. Internal politics refers to activities intended to enhance the personal or institutional power of individuals within the organization. It appears that most "subordinates feel comfortable being open in communication with superiors who are minimally or moderately involved in politics, but not with superiors who are highly involved in political activities."[3] In the latter case, subordinates may be made reluctant to express themselves in a general atmosphere of manipulation or maneuver.

Openness in communication is influenced, in other words, by perceptions of reciprocity in a relationship. Important factors include whether the climate, established by superiors, is defensive or not. In overly evaluative atmospheres, subordinates will of course be reluctant to communicate openly with superiors. Superiors must be able to communicate such openness sincerely, being aware of subtle clues they may send that would undermine their verbal declarations.

Upward Distortions.   Of course, the perception of openness (that is, the superior's receptivity to upward communication) plays an important role in determining whether the upward messages are intentionally distorted or not. It probably is not surprising to hear that most of the research supports the notion that subordinates tend to suppress or distort messages that would be considered as unfavorable, especially if the bad news reflects negatively on the subordinate. There is a natural tendency to tell the boss what you think he or she wants to hear. If the subordinate is "upwardly mobile," that is, wants to move up the organizational ladder, this tendency is often increased. Superiors, in contrast, may sometimes discount good information from subordinates and give more credence to information that may be critical of the subordinate.

Some upward communication of the subordinate to the superior is undoubtedly concerned with attempts to persuade or influence the superior: to get a favorable budget decision or promotion or raise. In some organizations, rational and logical appeals are most often used, whereas more indirect strategies are selected in others. These other strategies can include going over the supervisor's head to someone else in the organization, wearing down the other with persistent demanding, appealing to union or other rules, and so forth. It would appear that the organizational climate or organizational culture is an important determinant of the ways that subordinates try to persuade their superiors.[4] One therefore needs to learn the culture of a particular organization in order to be alert to acceptable and appropriate means for influencing superiors.

Language Barriers.   Problems of language and thought echo the discussion of the problems of intercultural communication in Chapter 4. Occasionally, management and the rest of an organization may seem to be operating in different subcultures. Recall that there may be significant gaps in education and status between some superiors and their subordinates. Also, the superiors in a relationship may be more aware of wider ramifications of various job-related issues than the people they directly supervise.

One summary of the research in this area concludes that there are numerous areas and topics in which large gaps in understanding exist between superiors and subordinates, including subordinates' basic job duties and supervisors' authority.[5] On the other hand, people may disagree on the very purpose or goals of the organization, depending upon where they are in the hierarchy. When a superior speaks of the firm's goals, for example, she may have in mind increasing market share, whereas a subordinate may have in mind maintaining a level of employment for him and his fellow townspeople.

Leadership and Management Style.   The discussion of various organizational theories in Chapter 2 noted the differences among the various management theories in regard to several communication issues. McGregor's distinction between Theory X and Theory Y management, or Likert's four systems, or the management grid of Blake and Mouton all point to differences in how managers can communicate with subordinates. Clearly, one's management orientation makes a difference for the perceived openness for superior–subordinate communication.

Intercultural factors may influence people's perceptions of a proper or appropriate style in superior–subordinate communication, as we saw in Chapter 4. Some people feel that people brought up in a culture in which Confucianism underlies the value system (say, people from Singapore, Japan, or Hong Kong) prefer a more formal, hierarchical relationship between superiors and subordinates. They may be rather uncomfortable with a style that people from the United States may see as more friendly and open. People from the Confucian cultures, such as Japan or Singapore, need to know where each person fits into a status structure. A firm that attempts to blend executives comfortable with the open American style and executives accustomed to the hierarchical style may therefore experience problems.

A recent focus on the variable of gender, as well as ethnic or cultural differences between superiors and subordinates, has highlighted potential differences in the communication styles of managers. While a survey of men and women managers conducted for the International Women's Forum found some unexpected similarities between men and women managers—their pay was similar, and they shared the same conflict in balancing work and family—they reported significant differences when describing men's and women's management styles. Male managers tended to describe their style in terms of a series of exchanges involving rewards or punishments for subordinates' actions. Female managers were more concerned to exhibit what Judy Roesner calls "interactive leadership." Such leadership encourages participation and emphasizes sharing power and decision-making.[6]

Other studies support the idea that women managers are seen as effective when they exhibit "sensitivity when dealing with others," and less effective when emulating the characteristics associated with more assertive male managers. Still, there are conflicting findings in this area, suggesting that context and differences in personal preferences and inclinations are significant.[7]

Feedback.   Feedback is a very important communication activity (see Figure 5-2). Certainly, much of what goes on in the superior–subordinate relationship relies on providing feedback, often in terms of evaluating another person's performance. Giving feedback, however, can be a problem, resulting in a situation in which people don't know where they stand or how they are doing.

Of course, there are several sources of feedback for a person regarding his or her performance in an organization. A lot of feedback is given outside the superior–subordinate relationship: Sales improve or go down, the new product works or it doesn't, one's group indicates approval or praise for what one has done, and so on.

Still, the feedback received from a superior is important in determining one's satisfaction and performance. Much of this feedback is provided in face-to-face, dyadic situations. An obvious barrier to such communication is that, at least in our society, an evaluative situation is often perceived as threatening. The perception leads naturally to a concern with defending oneself. Evaluative situations, therefore, can make the effective sending and receiving of feedback unlikely. Combine this tendency with the finding that supervisors are more likely to give negative rather than positive feedback, and one sees that providing feedback to improve a subordinate's performance can be tricky.[8]

A further complication in the matter of giving feedback is that one or both parties in the transaction may be concerned with establishing dominance or control in the relationship. Giving evaluative feedback, either positive or negative, may be used as a way of asserting one's superiority or control, and that purpose can take precedence over using the feedback for the purpose of improving performance or productiveness.

What do we know about how this feedback is typically handled? Some consistent findings from the research on performance feedback emphasize the importance of interpersonal communication. Most of the feedback tends to be oral and face-to-face. The nature of the interpersonal setting can lead to some distortion, because often the superior, when speaking directly to the other person, is reluctant to "come down hard" and so may soften or equivocate about a negative evaluation.

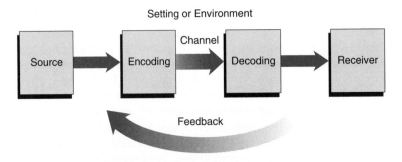

▶ **Figure 5-2**   *The feedback loop.*

Even though supervisors may be more prone to give negative feedback, they may not provide it in the clearest way. Feedback accompanied by vague suggestions about what to do to improve has been found to have little effect on improving the subordinate's motivation to do better (by "vague suggestions," we mean statements such as "Do the best you can," or "You'll have to straighten up and fly right").[9] More effective feedback includes specific descriptions of goals to achieve. In other words, an effective superior will prepare, in advance of a meeting with a subordinate, some specific actions that the subordinate can take to improve performance. This point is taken up in more detail in Chapter 7, which deals with interviewing, especially in the section on evaluation interviews.

Sexual Harassment.   Sexual harassment represents a negative form of interpersonal communication. While sexual harassment can occur between coworkers, it often involves the situation in which one person has power or control in the workplace over another person. For that reason, sexual harassment is a particular concern in the superior–subordinate relationship.

The Equal Employment Opportunity Commission (EEOC) is the major federal agency responsible for defining and enforcing regulations regarding sexual harassment in the workplace. The key to the definition of sexual harassment is that the aggrieved person is a victim of unwelcome sexual suggestions, requests, remarks, or actions by another person, typically someone perceived to have some power over the victim. As a result of such behavior, the person who is claiming harassment feels that there is an environment created that interferes with an employee's performance or that creates an intimidating or hostile work environment. The perception of sexual harassment in the workplace is widespread. A survey in 1986 found that 71% of business and professional women reported being sexually harassed on the job.[10] Another survey of federal employees indicates that sexual harassment continues to be a problem.[11]

At its most blatant, sexual harassment consists of a supervisor's demanding sexual favors from a subordinate in return for some reward or advancement on the job or in return for the supervisor's not carrying out some threat against the employee. The courts have generally held that the harassing behavior need not be as blatant as that to be in violation of the law. Physical contact is not a requirement; words construed as threats or repeated requests for sexual favors also constitute harassment.

The key is whether or not a so-called hostile or intimidating climate is created. One can be an indirect victim, for example. In one case, a woman complained that other women, who had submitted to sexual requests, were shown favoritism over her. Even though she herself had never been directly the target of such requests, she was held to be a victim of sexual harassment. In other cases, repeated use of sexually laden conversation, jokes, and pictures in the workplace have been found to create the kind of hostile environment defined as sexually harassing.

These cases are reminders of the importance of taking the perspective of the other person, an important skill of interpersonal communication. The central question must be how the other person perceives this communication. An organization needs to take steps to prevent this problem by developing a clearly written, specific

Dealing with Sexual Harassment

The federal guidelines define sexual harassment in the following way:

Guidelines in Discrimination Because of Sex, §1604, Sexual Harassment

Unwelcome sexual advances, requests for sexual favors, and other verbal or physical conduct of a sexual nature constitute sexual harassment when (1) submission to such conduct is made either explicitly or implicitly a term or condition of an individual's employment, (2) submission to or rejection of such conduct by an individual is used as the basis for employment decisions affecting such individuals, or (3) such conduct has the purpose or effect of unreasonably interfering with an individual's work performance or creating an intimidating, hostile, or offensive working environment (29 CFR Ch. XVI.)

The prevention of such harassment begins with communication that respects each person as a competent and professional individual, regardless of sex. The presence of a written policy against sexual harassment may or may not constitute compliance with the federal regulations, because the courts generally take into account the overall atmosphere or climate within the organization when a complaint is lodged. Because this is basically a communication problem, it requires a solution based on equitable and responsible interpersonal communication.

There are many sources in the business literature updating recommendations regarding the prevention of sexual harassment in the workplace. See R. T. Gray, (December 1991). "How to deal with sexual harassment," and D. H. Weiss (December 1991). "The principal ingredients of a sexual-harassment policy," *Nation's Business*, 79, 28–31, R. K. Robinson, D. J. Kirk & J. D. Powell (1987) Sexual harassment: New approaches for a changed environment. *Advanced management journal*, 52, 15–18, 47.

policy against sexual harassment, describing the kinds of communications and activities constituting the problem. In addition, the organization needs a written policy for spelling out procedures for investigating and dealing with such charges.

Highlights of Barriers to Superior–Subordinate Communication. This section considered the importance of communication in the superior–subordinate link in organizations. Some of the more important factors affecting communication in this dyad include perceptions of openness, tendencies toward upward distortions of messages, language problems or semantic information distance, differences in management style, and the problems with feedback. Many of the strains of the increasing diversity of organizations may be placing strains on the particular relationship between superiors and subordinates.

In many of the preceding problems, we note that the coded message itself is often not the real concern. Rather, many of the problems result from issues related to control within the relationship, attributions of intentions, or differing expectations related to the relationship. One method for improving this relationship and for overcoming some of these barriers is the process called "mentoring." The next section looks at this trend in contemporary organizations and examines how that trend can help deal with the barriers in superior–subordinate communication.

Mentoring

An important form of interpersonal communication on the job, often part of the superior–subordinate relationship, is mentoring. The term *mentor* means teacher or guide. A mentor is someone more senior in an organization, often in a position of higher status, who takes a younger, more junior person under his or her guidance and protection. One definition of the mentoring relationship emphasizes the purpose of "aiding in the organizational socialization of the less experienced individual and passing along knowledge gained through years of living within the organization."[12] The relationship between mentor and protege is often extended over time and may be somewhat confidential. Some authorities believe that mentors should have some distance from the protege, rather than being a direct superior.[13] Hence, at General Alum and Chemical, outside experts are matched with new managers.

Some organizations have developed formal mentoring programs, in which junior members are assigned to specified mentors to help them "learn the ropes." There is some disagreement concerning whether it is appropriate for firms to assign mentors or to simply let the relationship develop naturally. There are three possible ways that organizations can set up mentoring programs:

1. *Unguided.* A relationship simply evolves, in this type, as a result of contact or mutual attraction between the two parties involved. This situation was typical of traditional mentoring before recent attempts to foster mentoring in a more systematic way took hold.

2. *Encouraged but not forced.* In this situation, firms provide incentives for developing mentoring relationships. Not only are new members encouraged to seek out a mentor, but more experienced people are evaluated in terms of their ability to provide mentoring for younger people in the firm. At Honeywell, for example, the relationship between mentor and protege is recognized and publicly rewarded, but the development of the relationship is left to occur naturally.

3. *Systematic matching of mentors and proteges.* Here, specific people are matched with each other. Informal mentoring relationships may not be as available to women and to minorities as they are to white males; therefore, organizations

wishing to integrate women and minorities into management should consider these kinds of formal programs rather than leaving relationships to chance.[14]

Advantages.   Being a protege to an effective mentor has obvious benefits. Those who have received extensive mentoring report that they receive more promotions and were more satisfied with pay and benefits and their general position in an organization than those who did not receive mentoring. There appears to be a definite positive relationship between upward mobility in a firm and having a mentor.[15] These advantages derive from several functions that a mentor can perform. Kathy E. Kram has described these functions as either career-oriented or psychosocial. Career functions include sponsoring the protege for special assignments or positions, coaching the protege in specific activities, and providing protection for the protege's risk-taking. Psychosocial functions include providing a role model, counseling, and offering friendship with an "insider."[16] A mentor can teach a new executive or manager the organizational culture, the norms for behavior that are often not spelled out for newcomers. The mentor can serve as a sounding-board, allowing a new person to try out new ideas without the risk of presenting them cold to upper-level management.[17]

Mentoring also has benefits for the mentor. It helps mentors to stay in touch with the life of the organization, especially "in the trenches," at the lower level, thereby providing them a more accurate perspective. Upper management can avoid becoming isolated as a result of this information. The mentoring relationship also promotes teamwork throughout the organization, and to the extent the mentoring is successful, provides for a stable and predictable organizational culture. The mentor receives satisfaction and respect when a protege does well in the organization; the mentor is acknowledged as a leader with the ability to foster and develop good leadership in others.[18]

In short, mentoring has been shown to be advantageous for the organization as a whole because of its development of good leadership and teamwork, passing on the norms and cultural values of the organization. The development of mentoring programs, therefore, can operate to overcome some of the barriers in superior–subordinate communication discussed in the previous section.

About one third of major U.S. companies now have established a formal mentoring program. Some of these firms that have especially sophisticated programs include Schering-Plough, Colgate, Johnson and Johnson, AT&T, Pacific Bell, and Bellcore. Still, smaller firms report good success with mentoring as well as the larger firms.[19]

Potential Problems.   While mentoring is generally advantageous for people involved and the organization, there are some potential problems. First, mentors may be isolated from the day-to-day activities and problems of the proteges. There is the danger, then, that mentors will be passing on obsolete information. Mentors may also have the unintended consequence of stifling rather than encouraging new ideas.[20] Similarly, mentors can be overprotective and provide the continuation of an old boy network, with suggestions of freezing out new people who are too different. For such reasons, the organization should establish procedures for selecting and evaluating mentors. If effective mentoring is part of an executive's evaluation, these problems could be ameliorated.

Problems that could be trickier to deal with include those resulting from the socioeconomic, gender, and ethnic differences between senior and junior people in many organizations.

First, concerning socioeconomic differences, one study looked at managers and professionals in their early careers. While mentoring led to enhanced promotion and compensation for everyone, this positive relationship was noticeably better for proteges from the highest socioeconomic backgrounds. One explanation offered for this difference in outcome among proteges was that the higher-level managers who served as mentors were, at their career stage, more similar to the new managers from the higher socioeconomic class. This similarity could strengthen the relationship and facilitate communication.[21]

The second potential problem in the mentoring relationship—that of gender— receives much more attention in management literature. The facts of life in many firms mean that often the mentor is an older man and the one being mentored, a younger woman. Charges of tokenism, favoritism, or even office gossip suggesting sexual relationships can interfere with the development of a productive mentoring relationship.[22] Norms regarding male-female relationships in the workplace may place some unfortunate limits on the forming of male-female mentoring relationships. These problems may account for the fact that, so far, men report more satisfaction with mentoring than do women.[23] Suggestions for dealing with these gender problems include bringing the issue into the open, making it an item for discussion as part of the program for establishing a mentoring program. The establishment of a systematic program of matching mentors with proteges can also help alleviate such potential problems. With a systematic program, everyone knows what is going on, and there should be less opportunity for destructive gossip.[24]

The third potential barrier is that of racial or ethnic differences. Again, potential mentors, senior managers and executives, are generally white males. As a result, minority junior-level executives are unlikely to establish a mentor relationship with someone of their own ethnic background. As with cross-gender mentoring, there can be communication barriers in cross-racial mentor relationships. For example, one study found that white male mentors were unaware of or unwilling to discuss racial relations or the problems of racial discrimination with their proteges, even though African-American men and women felt that these were highly salient topics to be discussed within the mentoring relationship.[25]

Despite these potential problems, the advantages of mentoring usually far outweigh the pitfalls, especially for women and minorities. The key is to be aware of the potential problems and to deal with them openly in developing a mentoring relationship, for an individual, or a mentoring program, for an organization. The mentor-protege relationship allows for "wiring around" the distortions that are often present in the superior–subordinate relationship.

Highlights of Superior–Subordinate Communication.   This section focussed on the interpersonal communication between superior and subordinate, probably the most important dyad in many working situations. The discussion began with a troubleshooting section, bringing to awareness the typical problems or communication barriers present in this relationship. It is important to be alert to the trend in many organizations to develop systematically mentoring relationships designed to improve communication and to help integrate people in their early careers into a given organizational culture.

A positive communication climate between superior and subordinate can be fostered by developing the following characteristics:

1. Being communication-minded and letting others know that you enjoy communicating and are concerned about having good communication with others.

2. Making it clear that you are approachable and open, a willing listener.

3. Emphasizing in your messages persuading rather than demanding or telling; being willing to explain the "why" behind requests or orders.

◀▶ DYNAMICS OF INTERPERSONAL RELATIONSHIPS

It should now be clear that interpersonal communication and relationships are important on the job. Next is an explanation of how such relationships develop and change. Three areas of interpersonal communication theory seem especially important for helping to clarify the possible dynamics of these relationships:

1. Relational communication, which emphasizes the systemic nature of ongoing interpersonal relationships.

2. Impression formation, which clarifies ways that people develop perceptions of themselves and others and is the basis for the development of relationships.

3. Roles and rules in interpersonal communication, which provide people's expectations of each other as relationships grow and change.

▶ Relational Communication

The text so far has briefly referred to some general principles associated with the perspective of "relational communication." The part of Chapter 3 that dealt with empathic listening introduced some notions put forth by Watzlawick and his colleagues in the highly influential work, *The Pragmatics of Human Communication*.[26] ("Pragmatics" concerns the effects that symbols have on people.) These authors delineated five axioms that they felt underlay interpersonal communication; these axioms form much of the basis for later work in the area of relational communication and so are quickly summarized here.

Axioms.   The first axiom, mentioned in the introduction to Part 1, was that when two people are in each other's presence, it is impossible not to communicate.

It cannot be avoided that each person will read some behavior (or even the very presence) of the other person as having some message value.

The second axiom held that each message contains both some content (some meaning that could be phrased in a verbal code) and some statement about the relationship between the two people. "Hey—pass the salt," has the same basic content as "Please, pass the salt," but the relationship between the people involved is probably different. Bearing in mind that the sending and receiving of messages in this situation is inevitable, this axiom means that it is also inevitable that messages will deal with the personal relationship between people.

The third axiom stated that messages were either analogic or digital in their coding. This point may sound technical, but it becomes understandable if you think about how a compact disc player works versus how a record player worked. The term *digital coding* refers to those messages that are formulated in discrete, separable units, such as numbers, symbols, or words. The term *analogic coding* refers to continuous forms that lack separate units or symbols. The needle of an old record player, for example, followed the ups and downs of a groove cut into the record itself: that is, followed analogically the shape of the music that was to be produced. Usually, we think of nonverbal communication as being analogic: Gestures and movement shape or illustrate a message, the meanings are acted out. Verbal communication, on the other hand, is usually digital. In regard to the second axiom, content messages are typically digital in coding, with discrete meaning. Relationship messages are more typically contained in the less definite analogic medium of nonverbal communication. For example, the tone of voice (nonverbal and analogic) tells you what relationship exists between two people when one of them refers to the other as "you old snake in the grass" (digital and verbal).

Recall the distinction that Hall drew in intercultural communication between high-context and low-context cultures (as discussed in Chapter 4). High-context

▶ **Figure 5-3**   *Watches today can be digital or the traditional analog style.*

cultures could be said to pay more attention to the unstated, often analogic parts of communication, whereas low-context people pay more attention to those parts coded in digital form.

The fourth axiom maintained that in an ongoing relationship (a dyad), the participants would tend to punctuate the sequence of events or messages, each from his or her own perspective. In a long series of interactions, there is no definite beginning or end to sequences in the exchange of messages. One person may think that today she is beginning a new sequence, while her partner is still remembering and responding to some message that was received or sent the day before. Both people can always feel that they are simply responding to the other, or they can both feel that they are always the initiators of every transaction.

The fifth axiom has been the basis for much subsequent research and theorizing. It stated that all communication interchanges are either symmetrical or complementary, terms that require some explanation. A symmetrical interchange is said to be one in which both participants interact as equals; neither person is in control or superior to the other. A complementary interchange is one in which one participant is clearly seen as the superior and the other as the subordinate. For example, if George says, "Bring me that paper," and Ralph responds, "Certainly, here you are," that is a complementary exchange; the "one-up" order is complemented by the "one-down" compliance. On the other hand, if George says, "Bring me that paper," and Ralph responds, "Get it yourself," that is a symmetrical exchange (in fact, one of competitive symmetry), where the two statements are assertions of authority.

The Issue of Control.   Symmetrical exchanges can be competitive, in which both sides are striving to gain or maintain dominance or control in the relationship. Competitive symmetrical exchanges, such as that between George and Ralph in the previous example, may lead to a spiral in which matters escalate into a real conflict.

Often, such competitive symmetry results from unclear or ambiguous role definitions. They may also be the result of differing cultural expectations regarding the role positions of the two people. As noted earlier, one person's offer to let another person have something that both appear to want can be interpreted as a attempt at a "one-up" message. The implication is that by giving permission for the other to have something, the first person is in control.

There may, for example, be disagreements regarding the actual duties and authority of superiors in regard to subordinates, thereby leading to cases of competitive symmetry in relational communication. A manager giving feedback to a subordinate may be partly intending to remind the subordinate of the complementary nature of their relationship (having the right to criticize or evaluate another is seen as being "one-up"). Perhaps one of the reasons that supervisors may resist attempts to have subordinates participate in the supervisor's own evaluation is related to this view of the complementary relationship.

Imagine also the situation that could arise when a new worker does not realize that older workers see him or her in a subordinate position because of their seniority. The new worker may assume and communicate to others from the perspective that they are all equals because that is what the organization chart indicates (sending symmetrical messages). Meanwhile, the others persist in responding with one-up messages intended to establish a complementary relationship. The new person may not be able to figure out what is going wrong and may give interpretations to others' communication, such as, "They are all prejudiced against me." By being aware of the pattern, the new person can see that there is some disagreement or misunderstanding concerning status and hierarchy. Such awareness can lead to the possibility of bringing the real issue out into the open.

Now we can reinforce the claim that the meaning of a communication interaction may be more in the relationship than in the verbal messages. If each communication attempt does contain information about both content and the relationship between the people involved, the content may at times be less important than what is "said" about the relationship. That is the point Deborah Tannen makes when she states that what is said between a man and a women may not carry as much significant information as what the interchange means for the relationship.[27] For example, the content of a woman's message may be to solicit information about a man's plans, or to show interest or concern; the man may read that content in terms of someone trying to pry into his intentions, perhaps to get some control.

Metacommunication, or Breaking out of the Spiral.   Breaking out of some of the more destructive patterns of competitive symmetry or spirals may require the participants' shifting to so-called metacommunication. Metacommunication refers to the act of communicating *about* communicating. In other words, people break off from the normal development of their interaction to ask, "What is happening in our communication? How are we communicating with one another?" Often, this technique is a natural development. People need to have the possibility of metacommunicating brought to their attention. One function that a mediator can provide in helping people to resolve disputes is to provide the suggestion that people shift to metacommunication.

The basis for metacommunication can be the insights from the theory of relational communication. Look for the relationship as well as the content component in the messages that have been exchanged. Is there disagreement about the nature of the relationship? If so, why? Are messages being interpreted as complementary or symmetrical that were not intended that way? If so, why? Metacommunication, then, allows for people to do some troubleshooting when they sense that their communication attempts are not going well.

Highlights of Relational Communication.   Relational communication provides a perspective that allows analysis of some important issues and potential breakdowns in interpersonal communication. Some of the problems of superior–subordinate communication can be understood in terms of these insights.

It is very difficult to separate the relationship, with its implications for control and status, from the bare content of information that is exchanged in the interpersonal setting. This approach emphasizes the view that the system created by the interaction, the communication patterns in the dyad, should be the focus of

Three-Mile Island and Relational Communication

In March of 1979, the United States experienced its worst nuclear accident so far when a reactor at the electrical generating plant at Three-Mile Island (TMI) in Pennsylvania suffered a major failure in its cooling system. Some radiation was leaked into the atmosphere, and there was a great deal of fear and consternation. The Nuclear Regulatory Commission conducted an investigation of this accident and found that a "breakdown in communications" had been one of the significant "precursor events" to the disaster. The communication problem that the commission had in mind resulted from the fact that an engineer had recognized the possibility for the kind of accident that happened at TMI after a similar, earlier accident had taken place at a Toledo nuclear generating plant.

The response to the engineer's memo by a supervisor in the nuclear operations division of the company essentially rejected the recommendations for changed procedures. The engineer was in a delicate position in making his original recommendation because one interpretation could be that nuclear operations had been doing

our attention rather than the individuals who form the dyad. The purpose of relational communication has been to study the dyad as a unit.

The next section considers the issues involved in forming interpersonal relationships and how these factors affect the communication that occurs.

▶ ### Impression Formation

The dyad that is the basis for interpersonal communication on the job goes through stages of development. In the first place, one's whole view of what kind of communication behavior is appropriate in an organization develops over a lifetime.[30] Your first impression of what communication is like in the organization probably is formed during the initial interview with a recruiter or similar representative of the organization. Upon coming to work, you begin to form more impressions about the norms and expectations for communicating in that organization by observing coworkers, attending orientation and training sessions, meeting with one's supervisor, and possibly, reading organizational publications.

Uncertainty Reduction.   One way to begin to learn what another person is like is to use various communication strategies to learn about that other person. As-something wrong. In other words, the recommendation to change procedures can be interpreted as implying some criticism of the people responsible for those procedures. The supervisor responding to the original memo appeared to perceive the criticism and responded to it, according to one analysis of the incident.[28] The supervisor's response went to the issue of whether or not the engineer had the right to criticize the operations side of things. In defense of the supervisor, one should note that the engineer was relatively inexperienced and from outside the group that had been doing the actual work of running the reactors. The exchange became to some extent "part of a negotiation of their social status and their relative institutional positions."[29] In other words, the communication turned to the issue of relationship complementarity or symmetry.

See *Report of the President's Commission on the Accident at Three Mile Island* (1979). Washington, D.C.: U.S. Government Printing Office, esp. pp. 8–9; and *Staff Report to the President's Commission on the Accident at Three Mile Island: The role of the managing utility and its suppliers* (1979). Washington, D.C.: U.S. Government Printing Office, esp. pp. 119–130.

sume that we begin being uncertain about these other people; then we need to reduce that uncertainty in order to predict how they may behave. These others include those whom we perceive to have some role in meeting our own goals or needs; superiors, mentors, and coworkers obviously fall into this category of "significant others." Once we have determined that we need to gain more information about—that is, reduce our uncertainty about—these other people, we may proceed with any or all of several methods.[31] These methods are classified as three kinds of strategies: passive, active, and interactive.

As the name implies, *passive strategies* involve observing the other person. Two passive strategies may be used. First is the practice of observing how the person reacts to some situation. For example, you could observe the other person reacting to a special problem or crisis. Second is observing the other person in situations in which the person is unconcerned about the observations of others: lunching with friends without being aware of being observed, for example. The assumption is that in such a situation, the person will behave in a "natural" way and thereby provide you with more accurate information.

Active strategies involve efforts such as asking other people about the target person. When new on the job, one may ask another about what it's like to work for Smith or Jones, or what the other coworkers particularly like (or dislike) about

Smith or Jones. One may also attempt to set up situations, manipulate the environment, in order to observe directly how the other person would react to similar circumstances.

Interactive strategies involve direct communication with the target person. These strategies include direct questioning of the other person and self-disclosure, which is a more indirect strategy. The idea behind self-disclosure is that such an action may lead the other person to reciprocate by also self-disclosing. In this way, uncertainty about the other person is reduced because he or she provides some direct information that fosters an impression of him or her as a communication partner.

Strategies of uncertainty reduction include the following:

- Passive strategies
  —Observe reactions to events.
  —Observe actions when uninhibited.
- Active strategies
  —Ask others about the person.
  —Set up situations.
- Interactive strategies
  —Ask the person.
  —Self-disclosure.

The theory based on uncertainty reduction suggests that certain kinds of communication result from a person's efforts to reduce his or her uncertainty about another person. In other words, these kinds of communication strategies can be expected as part of the process of forming a relationship. The theory is intended to point toward how people process information in developing interpersonal relationships.

The most obvious applications of the uncertainty reduction techniques occur in interviewing situations. For that reason, the text refers to these ideas when discussing principles for interviewing in Chapter 7.

Attribution of Intentions and Motives.   How we will communicate with other people involves figuring out why they may do certain things. Attributing intentions to others is concerned with the everyday process that people go through in forming theories about the behavior of others. In other words, how does a nonpsychologist make these judgments without the benefit of scientific tools or observational methods (which is what people have to do everyday)?

First, we assume that we all have some need to make sense of other people's behavior. The text has already touched on a similar need in discussing the function of culture: providing the basis for our being able to make predictions in our lives. When we are going to have to work with another person for some time, we want to be able to predict how the person will react to various things that we might do. We can have a basis for making such predictions if we can explain the other person's behavior in reaction to other events. These explanations allow us to construct informal theories about the person's motives and intentions.

These explanations of the behaviors of others, therefore, are usually attempts to find causes for those behaviors. Most people think that if we know why someone did something, we will be able to predict their reactions better. In this search for causes, we can settle on internal or external causes. We attribute people's behavior to internal causes when we decide that they behaved as they did because of internal personality traits. If we hear that someone has cheated on an examination, we attribute the cheating to internal causes when we judge that he or she has some character flaw.

On the other hand, external causes are those that are seen as external to the person; they are present in the situation or environment and may not be under the control of the person at all. When we say that a person cheated on an exam because he or she was under extreme pressure, we are moving toward an attribution to external causes. When we say that people commit crimes because they are dishonest, we are attributing internal causation; when we say that people commit crimes because of their poverty and lack of opportunity, we are attributing external causes.

The fundamental attribution error is said to be the tendency of individuals to differentially assign internal and external causes, depending upon whether they are explaining others' or their own behaviors. If the action being explained is seen as negative (such as cheating on taxes or lying), this tendency means that we assign external causes when we are the perpetrator and internal causes when it is someone else. If one of us should lie, we would attribute it to causes beyond our control. If we hear someone else lie, we conclude that that is just the sort of person that he or she is (internal causation).

Conversely, when the action is positive, the fundamental attribution error is to attribute good internal motives to ourselves and external motivation to the other person. In everyday settings, the fundamental attribution error is seen in our tendency to attribute actions that we are not proud of to impersonal forces (my temper, my appetite, or some similar force).

Recall that in giving evaluative feedback, supervisors may tend to respond on the basis of the attribution processes described here. For example, negative behaviors or performance may be attributed to internal causes, such as lack of motivation or laziness rather than to external causes, such as inadequate training or instructions, lack of appropriate education, or skills. The fundamental attribution error, therefore, can be a basis for distortion in the communication between superior and subordinate. That is the reason the effective performance evaluation stresses descriptions of behaviors and actions rather than personality flaws. This point is further developed in Chapter 7, which discusses interviewing, especially evaluation interviews.

Highlights of Impression Formation. Psychologists and communication theorists have been concerned with explaining how people form the impressions of other people that lead to the kinds of communication they use. People proceed by trying to reduce uncertainty about those whom they believe will be significant others in their lives. People also try to develop their own theories to explain causes

Diversity in the Workplace

Impression Formation and Intercultural Communication: The Concept of Guanxi

Persons doing business in the new Pacific Rim economic powers of Taiwan and Hong Kong should be aware of the concept of *guanxi*, a special kind of relationship recognized in Chinese society. The word *guanxi* refers to a special relationship or bond that connects two people as a result of an exchange of favors. Although it can be based on friendship, "the relationship is basically utilitarian rather than emotional. The moral principle operating here is that a person who does not follow a rule of equity and refuses to return favor for favor loses face and becomes defined as untrustworthy."[32]

In contrast to the emphasis on groupness in Japan (the concept of *wa*), *guanxi* is individualistic. Also, *guanxi* must be maintained over time, or the relationship no longer holds. It is the emphasis on changeable relations between individuals that allows for Chinese workers to change employers often and easily. This idea is also in contrast to the Japanese tendency toward long-term (or life-long) employment with the same firm. These contrasts between Japanese and Chinese expectations means that it would be a mistake to consider all Asian cultures as the same.

A particularly Confucian aspect of *guanxi* is that the weaker or less-favored of the two individuals is considered to be in a position to demand special and greater favors from the more powerful. During negotiations, therefore, Chinese will often expect the stronger of the two parties to make concessions—often to the surprise of American negotiators—in view of this *guanxi* expectation. Another consequence of *guanxi* is that personal ties and relationships are necessary for accomplishing things in Chinese business cultures, such as Taiwan or Hong Kong. Also, business decisions tend to come slowly because of the necessity of working through each of the *guanxi* connections in the chain of command within various firms.

Based on J. P. Alston (1989, March–April). *Wa, Guanxi,* and *Inwha*: Managerial Principles in Japan, China, and Korea. *Business Horizons*, 32, 29–31.

for other people's behavior. One of the main contributions of uncertainty reduction theory has been to highlight the function of self-disclosure in learning about other people. Attribution theory reminds us that others have a basic need to create naive theories about why we and others do the things that we do. The fundamental attribution error alerts us to some of the typical pitfalls in that process.

Roles and Rules

This section points out that interpersonal communication is based upon the use of rules and norms. Rules and norms establish the expectations that are always present as we try to communicate with others. Chapter 4 on intercultural communication discussed the significance that such expectations can have on our behaviors.

Roles. A particular set of expectations are associated with the idea of a role. A role is an identifiable set of behaviors that usually can be labelled in a particular way. For example, one may enact the role of a father, mother, older sister, boss, or mentor. As Shakespeare put it, in our lives we are called upon to play many roles; our success in carrying out the expected behaviors associated with these roles probably determines in large measure our ultimate success.

The ability to take roles and to react to other people in their roles is an important aspect in allowing for even the possibility of communication between people. As we learn to talk and to communicate with other people, we have to be able to put ourselves in the position of, or in the role of, another person. Communication works because one person is able to think, "If I heard or saw someone saying or doing such and such, I would respond in this way—and so that is what I will do to get that response." By putting ourselves in the position of the other people, we are able to communicate with them.

Erving Goffman has been especially influential in exploring this role-playing aspect of human communication.[33] Like Shakespeare, Goffman sees much of the world as a stage and suggests that we are able to function and to communicate with others by knowing how to present ourselves in various roles. In his early work, Goffman described human conduct in terms of performances, in which groups work together as a cast, as performance teams, working on a stage, with backstage areas, scenery, and props. When we think of how a modern office may be arranged, with public, on-stage areas in the reception areas or in executive offices, and backstage areas for the break room, coffee-maker and microwave, and storage areas, the metaphor makes good sense. Hospitals, for example, clearly have on-stage and off-stage areas; and when nurses or physicians are off-stage they use a different language or jargon than they do when on-stage.

Rules. Knowing how to enact a particular role means knowing the rules that go with that role and others. Interacting successfully with other people means knowing the rules. "Miss Manners" continues to be a popular newspaper column around the country because people feel a need to have some guidance as to what the "rules" are in social settings.

The existence of rules provides people with the security of knowing how they and others are to act in various circumstances. Rules are not the same as laws in

The Shuttle Challenger and Role Theory

You may recall the disaster of the space shuttle, the Challenger, in January 1986. The ship exploded in mid-air within seconds of a launch from the Kennedy Space Center in Florida, killing all of the astronauts on board as well as the young school teacher who had been specially selected to accompany the mission. The Rogers Commission, which investigated this accident, found that communication problems were instrumental in the disaster.

In the Challenger case, a young program analyst, in a memo of July 1985, had pointed out the potential failure of the O-ring seals in the booster rocket that was to launch the shuttle. The commission found that, in fact, the O-ring seals did fail when the Challenger was launched, resulting in the explosion of the craft. The program analyst, who first sounded the alarm, was described by officials in NASA as "a young chap," and "not too knowledgeable."[35] The program analyst's role did not make him a highly credible source within the organization for providing this kind of information. His use of nontechnical language indicated his status as a newcomer.

A second aspect of the Challenger disaster came on the night before the launch, when the NASA and Morton Thiokol (the

that they are not strictly enforced. People can break the rules and suffer disapproval, although such disapproval may not always be obvious or immediate. Goffman defines communication itself in terms of such rules: "An act that is subject to a rule of conduct is, then, a communication, for it represents a way in which selves are confirmed."[34] Notice that he does not say that one must follow the rule to communicate, because either following or not following the rule will communicate something, just as it is impossible not to communicate, as we saw in the scheme of Watzlawick and his colleagues. It is the fact that the act itself is subject to being governed by rules that makes it a communication.

Rules are highly contextual. By this, we mean that the rules are different in different settings and circumstances. In some cases, such as wartime or playing poker, the rules permit or even expect people to be deceptive. So, we cannot always say that one should not deceive is a blanket rule for all times and places. As we mature, we learn many different sets of rules and, it is hoped, their appropriate contexts. Different rules apply in different settings.

Remember the mention of V. S. Naipaul's trying to determine whether he and his fellow passenger were going to have a Western or an Asian conversation so company that manufactured the booster rockets) people discussed by teleconference the potential effects of the unusually cold weather at the launch site in Florida and its effects on the O-rings. At one point, the senior Morton Thiolkol man told the head of engineering to "take off his engineering hat and put on his management hat."[36] The poll to decide whether to go ahead or not was limited to managers, since it was assumed that managers were able to make decisions. In other words, it was their role to make this kind of decision, and for an engineer to participate, he had to put off one role and take on another.

The Fall 1986 issue of the *Central States Speech Journal* (37:3) is devoted entirely to articles analyzing communication problems associated with the Challenger disaster; especially relevant to the interpersonal communication in the decision-making process are two of these articles: D. S. Gouran, R. Y. Hirokawa & A. E. Martz, A critical analysis of factors related to decisional processes involved in the challenger disaster, pp. 119–135; and R. C. Rowland, The relationship between the public and technical spheres of argument: A case study of the Challenger Seven disaster, pp. 136–145.

that they could coordinate the proper set of rules that were going to guide their discussion. It should be clear that another way of talking about the difficulties of intercultural communication is to discuss the different sets of communication rules being applied by the people trying to communicate with each other.

Highlights of Roles and Rules. Communication depends upon people's ability to take roles and to understand others' roles. This role-taking and communicative ability also depends upon people's being aware of the rules for interaction and how those rule systems change with the context and situation. As we become more skilled and mature in communication, we are (or should be) learning a wider variety of roles and becoming more and more sensitive to sets of rules operative in these different contexts.

SUMMARY

In your career, you will probably be immersed in interpersonal communication. For the purposes of this text, we have stressed interpersonal communication as face-to-face, usually one-on-one communication taking place within an ongoing relationship or a dyad.

One of the most studied and most significant of the settings for interpersonal communication is the superior–subordinate dyad. We have presented a basis for troubleshooting some typical problems of communication in this dyad and have discussed mentoring as a special form for dealing with some of these usual communication barriers. Pitfalls remain in the mentoring relationship as well.

These important work relationships, and the communication patterns that occur within them, can be further analyzed in terms of some general theories concerning interpersonal communication and relationships. Understanding some of the basic concepts of relational communication, impression formation, and roles and rules theories, can be especially useful in grasping how these relationship form and develop.

The following chapters begin to move from these more theoretical issues toward their applications in interviewing, group communication, making presentations, resolving conflict, and so on.

 **EXERCISES**   •

1. Make a list of significant dyads to which you belong. Do these dyads show features that differentiate them from casual conversation pairs? Can you describe how these dyads formed? What sort of communication patterns have developed over time? Can these patterns be improved? How?

2. Describe situations in which you feel that you and another person experienced the transactional nature of communication. Write a description of how a specific outcome was a transaction rather than an interaction in this relationship.

3. From your own observations or experiences, can you describe situations that illustrate the typical problems in superior–subordinate communication discussed in this chapter? Discuss methods that could be used to deal with specific problems.

4. Discuss the meaning of sexual harassment in contemporary organizations. Explain the role of perception and relational dynamics in this type of negative interpersonal communication. What concrete steps can be taken by organizations to minimize the possibilities of sexual harassment?

5. Select a major corporation or firm in your area, or consult information in your library in the business reference section. Does this firm have a formal mentoring program? If so, describe how it is set up. Have there been problems or special successes?

6. Describe situations in which the impossibility of not communicating has been particularly significant. How can this principle of communication cause misunderstandings in interpersonal communication?

7. Think of situations in which you have participated or ones that you have observed in which there has been disagreement deriving from mixed relational messages. Discuss these problems with others to see if you can come up with possible solutions.

8. List the important roles that you have to play in your everyday life. What are the roles that you most often encounter in your communication with others? Do you run into problems with people not seeming to know the rules for such encounters? What causes these problems? How can they be resolved?

9. Think of a place where you have worked or a work situation that you have observed. Describe the business in the dramatic terms used by Goffman. Is there a cast? An off-stage area? Costuming? Props? Examples of scripts? Who are the audiences?

Communication Problem: The "Mommy Track"

Mary is an audit manager for a major national accounting firm. She has a new baby and a two-year-old at home. Her husband is also a full-time professional. Mary wants to spend more time with her young children. But she fears being placed on the so-called mommy track, the term used for a career path laid out by an organization, usually with slower or fewer opportunities for advancement and leadership. There are other women in the organization in a similar situation. If you were Mary's mentor, what would you suggest for dealing with this issue? How would you deal with this issue if you were responsible for Mary's performance evaluation?

SELECTED SOURCES
FOR FURTHER READING

Alston, J. P. (1989, March–April). *Wa, Guanxi,* and *Inwha*: Managerial principles in Japan, China, and Korea. *Business Horizons, 32,* 26–31.

Bragg, A. (1989, September). Is a mentor program in your future? *Sales and Marketing Management, 141:*11, 54–63.

Burke, R. J., & McKeen, C. A. (1990, April–May). Mentoring in organizations: Implications for women. *Journal of Business Ethics, 9:*4, 317–332.

Condon, J. C. (1985). *Semantics and communication* (3rd ed.). New York: Macmillan.

Dreher, G. F., & Ash, R. A. (1990, October). A comparative study of mentoring among men and women in managerial, professional, and technical positions. *Journal of Applied Psychology, 75:*5, 539–546.

Fagenson, E. A. (1989, October). The mentor advantage: Perceived career/job experiences of proteges versus non-proteges. *Journal of Organizational Behavior 10:*4, 309–320.

Goffman, E. (1959). *The presentation of self in everyday life*. Garden City, NJ: Doubleday Anchor Books.

Goffman, E. (1967). *Interaction ritual: Essays on face-to-face behavior*. Garden City, NJ: Anchor Books.

Gouran, D., et al. (1986). A critical analysis of factors related to decisional processes involved in the Challenger disaster. *Central States Speech Journal, 37,* 119–135.

Greene, J. O., & Geddes, D. (1988). Representation and processing in the self-system: An action-oriented approach to self and self-relevent phenomena. *Communication Monographs, 55,* 287–314.

Hall, E. T. (1977). *Beyond culture*. Garden City, NJ: Anchor Press.

Jablin, F. M. (1981), An exploratory study of subordinates' perceptions of supervisory politics. *Communication Quarterly, 29,* 269–275.

Knapp, M. L., & Miller, G. R. (1985). *Handbook of interpersonal communication*. Newbury Park, CA: Sage Publications.

Kram, K. E. (1985). *Mentoring at work*. New York: University Press of America.

Littlejohn, S. W. (1989). *Theories of human communication* (3rd ed.). Belmont, CA: Wadsworth.

McKeen, C. A., & Burke, R. J. (1989). Mentor relationships in organizations: Issues, strategies and prospects for women. *Journal of Management Development, 8:*6, 33–42.

Miller, F. E. & Rogers, L. E. (1976). A relational approach to interpersonal communication. In G. R. Miller (Ed.), *Explorations in interpersonal communication*. Beverly Hills, CA: Sage Publications.

Noe, R. E. (1988, January). Women and mentoring: A review and research agenda. *Academy of Management Review, 13:*1, 65–78.

Parks, M. R. (1977). Relational communication: Theory and research. *Human Communication Research, 3,* 372–381.

Pearce, W. B., & Cronen, V. E. (1982). *Communication, action and meaning: The creation of social realities*. New York: Holt, Rinehart and Winston.

Pearson, J. C., Turner, L. H., & Todd-Mancillas, W. (1991). *Gender and communication* (2nd ed.). Dubuque: Wm. C. Brown.

Ragins, B. R. (1989, January). Barriers to mentoring: The female manager's dilemma. *Human Relations, 42:1,* 1–22.

Robinson, R. K., Kirk, D. J., & Powell, J. D. (1987). Sexual harassment: New approaches for a changed environment. *Advanced Management Journal, 52:4,* 15–18, 47.

Ruben, B. D. (1988). *Communication and human behavior* (2nd ed.). New York: Macmillan.

Shimanoff, S. B. (1980). *Communication rules: Theory and research*. Beverly Hills, CA: Sage Publications.

Stewart, J. (Ed.). (1990). *Bridges not walls: A book about interpersonal communication* (5th ed.). New York: McGraw-Hill.

Trenholm, S. (1991). *Human communication theory* (2nd ed.). Englewood Cliffs, NJ: Prentice-Hall.

van Dijk, T. A. (1989). Structures of discourse and structures of power. In J. A Anderson (Ed.), *Communication Yearbook 12*. Newbury Park, CA: Sage Publications.

Watzlawick, P., Beavin, J., & Jackson, D. (1967). *Pragmatics of human communication*. New York: W. W. Norton.

Whitely, W., Dougherty, T. W., & Dreher, G. F. (1991, June). Relationship of career mentoring and socioeconomic origin to managers' and professionals' early career programs. *Academy of Management Journal, 34:2,* 331–351.

Zey, M. G. (1988, January). A mentor for all reasons. *Personnel Journal, 67:1,* 46–51.

References

1. D. Tannen (1990). *You just don't understand: Women and men in conversation* (pp. 49–73). New York: William Morrow.

2. Jablin, F. M. (1985). Task/work relationships: A life-span perspective. In *Handbook of interpersonal communication* (p. 625). Newbury Park, CA: Sage Publications. Jablin is summarizing and updating research from a wide-ranging research review. This information is further updated and supported in F. Dansereau and S. E. Markham (1987), Superior–subordinate communication: Multiple levels of analysis. In *Handbook of organizational communication* (pp. 343–353). Newbury Park, CA: Sage Publications.

3. Jablin, F. M. (1981). An exploratory study of subordinates' perceptions of supervisory politics. *Communication Quarterly, 29,* 269–275.

4. Dansereau and Markham, p. 346.

5. Dansereau and Markham, p. 347.

6. Rosener, J. B. (1990, November–December). Ways women lead. *Harvard Business Review*, pp. 119–125.

7. Pearson, J. C., Turner, L. H., & Todd-Mancillas, W. (1991). *Gender and communication* (2nd ed.). Dubuque, IA: Wm. C. Brown.

8. Jablin, Task/work relationships, p. 631: "Supervisors tend to give negative feedback sooner to poorly-performing subordinates than they give positive feedback to well-performing subordinates."

9. This research is summarized in L. P. Cusella, Feedback, motivation, and performance. In *Handbook of organizational communication* (pp. 624–678).

10. Robinson, R. K., Kirk, D. J., & Powell, J. D. (1987). Sexual harassment: New approaches for a changed environment. *Advanced Management Journal*, *52*:4, 15–18, 47.

11. Kandell, W. L. (1988/1989). Sexual harassment: Persistent, prevalent, but preventable. *Employee Relations Law Journal*, *14*:3, 439–451.

12. Wilson, J. A., & Elman, N. S. (1990). Organizational benefits of mentoring. *Academy of Management Executive*, *4*:4, 88–94.

13. Brown, T. L. (1990). Match up with a mentor. *Industry Week*, *239*:19, 18.

14. McKeen, C. A., & Burke, R. J. (1989). Mentor relationships in organizations: Issues, strategies and prospects for women. *Journal of Management Development*, *8*:6, 33–42; Thomas, D. A. (1990). The impact of race on managers' experiences of developmental relationships (mentoring and sponsorship): An intra-organizational study. *Journal of Organizational Behavior*, *11*:6, 479–492.

15. See, for example, G. F. Dreher & R. A. Ash (1990), A comparative study among men and women in managerial, professional, and technical positions. *Journal of Applied Psychology*, *75*:5, 539–546; W. Whitely, T. W. Dougherty, & G. F. Dreher. (1991), Relationship of career mentoring and socioeconomic origin to managers' and professionals' early career progress. *Academy of Management Journal*, *34*:2, 331–351.

16. K. E. Kram. (1988). *Mentoring at work* (pp. 24–39). New York: University Press of America.

17. See J. Lawlor (1990, July 9). *Computerworld*, *24*:28, 106.

18. These benefits are supported by Kram, pp. 7–10; H. L. White (1990), The SELF method of mentoring. *Bureaucrat*, *19*:1, 45–48; B. Smith (1990), Mutual mentoring on projects: A proposal to combine the advantages of several established management development methods. *Journal of Management Development*, *9*:1, 51–57; Wilson and Elman, 88–94; D. Jacoby (1989), Rewards make the mentor. *Personnel*, *66*:12, 10–14.

19. Bragg, A. (1989, September). Is a mentor program in your future? *Sales & Marketing Management*, *141*:11, pp. 54–63.

20. See Wilson and Elman, pp. 88–94, for a discussion of these kinds of problems.

21. Whitely, Dougherty, and Dreher, pp. 331–351.

22. Lorinc, J. (1990). The mentor gap—Older men guiding younger women: Perils and payoffs. *Canadian Business*, *63*:9, 93–94; Noe, R. A. (1988). Women and mentoring: A review and research agenda. *Academy of Management Review*, *13*:1, 65–78.

23. See for example, Fagenson, E. A. (1989). The mentor advantage: Perceived career/job experiences of proteges versus non-proteges. *Journal of Organizational Behavior*, *10*:4, 309–320; still, one study reports no gender differences in regard to the frequency of mentoring activities nor their outcomes, contrary to the study's initial hypothesis. See Dreher and Ash, p. 544.

24. Burke, R. J., & McKeen, C. A. (1990). Mentoring in organizations: Implications for women. *Journal of Business Ethics*, *9*:4, 317–332; McKeen, C. A., & Burke, R. J. (1989). Mentor relationships in organizations: Issues, strategies and prospects for women. *Journal of Management Development*, *8*:6, 33–42.

25. Thomas, D. A. (1989). Mentoring and irrationality: The role of racial taboos. *Human Resource Management*, *28*:2, 279–290.

26. Watzlawick, P., Beavin, J. H., & Jackson, D. D. (1967). *Pragmatics of Human Communication*. New York: W. W. Norton.
27. Tannen, p. 50.
28. Herndle, C. G., Fennell, B. A., & Miller, C. (1991). Understanding failures in organizational discourse: The accident at Three Mile Island and the shuttle Challenger disaster. In C. Bazerman & J. Paradis (Eds.), *Textual dynamics of the professions* (pp. 279–305). Madison, WI: University of Wisconsin Press.
29. Herndle, Fennel, and Miller (1991).
30. See Jablin, Task/Work Relationships.
31. Uncertainty Reduction Theory has been advanced by C. Berger and his associates at Northwestern University; the three strategies described here are based upon Berger's classifications.
32. Alston, J. P. (1989, March–April). Wa, guanxi, and inwha: Managerial principles in Japan, China, and Korea. *Business Horizons, 32*, 28.
33. See Goffman, E. (1959). *The presentation of self in everyday life*. Garden City, NY: Doubleday Anchor, for his early presentation of the theatrical metaphor; Goffman, E. (1967). *Interaction ritual*, Garden City, NY: Doubleday Anchor, provides a good overview of his ideas of roles and rules for interaction; Goffman, E. (1974). *Frame analysis*, Cambridge, MA: Harvard University Press, is a good summary of his analysis of interpersonal interaction.
34. Goffman, E. *Interaction ritual*, p. 45.
35. Herndle, Fennel, and Miller, p. 299.
36. Gouran, D. S., Hirokawa, R. Y., & Martz, A. E. (1986). A critical analysis of factors related to decisional processes involved in the Challenger disaster. *Central States Speech Journal, 37*, 123.

Nonverbal Communication in Business and Professional Settings

6

CHAPTER

After studying this chapter, you should be able to:

1. Explain why nonverbal communication is important and yet difficult to interpret.

2. Describe the major functions of nonverbal communication.

3. Be aware of the various systems of nonverbal communication.

4. Be sensitive to facial expressions and eye contact in communication.

5. Explain the uses for the classification of gestures and touch as nonverbal signs.

6. Understand the importance of space and time as message-sending systems.

7. Describe the functions as objects and possessions as communication.

Overview

In discussing both intercultural and interpersonal communication, we touched on the important messages carried through nonverbal channels. The different inter- pretations of the use of eye contact referred to in the problem between a teacher and pupil in Chapter 1 is a reminder that people place great importance on such things and that they can change the meaning of messages. We are reminded that we receive the messages from others within a total context of sight, sounds, as well as smells, and other sensations. This total context determines the meaning of the whole experience.

The Importance of Nonverbal Communication

The last chapter noted how people form impressions of others and that each message in face-to-face communication carries both its content and something about the relationship between the two people involved. Nonverbal communication conveys most of this relationship information. The nonverbal messages are usually more ambiguous and less subject to definite translations because they use analogic rather than digital coding. We also saw that people have a need to attribute motives and intentions to the actions of others; often these actions are nonverbal. At least, the nonverbal behaviors of the other person provide information that we can use to help decide what the other's motives are. In short, nonverbal communication is extremely important to interpersonal communication.

These nonverbal messages consequently must play an important part in the effectiveness of communication on the job. There are several settings in which nonverbal cues are particularly important. We know that in interviews, especially selection interviews, the visual impression that the candidate makes upon the interviewer can become a central consideration. In everyday workplace communication, nonverbal cues alert others to status, roles, occupations, whether or not one is too busy to talk, and so on. Nonverbal cues can be important in dealing with conflict, in negotiating, and in bargaining. The arrangement or location of a room for negotiation sessions, for example, can go a long way toward determining the outcome.

A major problem with nonverbal communication on the job, however, is that there is a tendency to take them for granted. As with so many aspects of intercultural communication, nonverbal cues tend to operate at a level out of immediate consciousness.

Points to Cover

This chapter provides a summary of some of the major principles of nonverbal communication derived from theory and research. (There are whole courses and textbooks dealing with this subject, and we cannot here deal with this important subject to the depth or extent found in those sources.) The purpose here is to bring this often-subtle aspect of communication to awareness, especially in business and professional settings.

The first consideration is the nature of nonverbal communication, which usually operates in ways slightly different from the digital systems of verbal language. The text covers the particular functions of nonverbal communication, which grow out of its nature. Next, the section looks at various systems for nonverbal messages, because we send such messages through the use of the face, movement, our use of space and time, vocal characteristics (such as tone, rate, pitch), touching, and the use of objects, including clothing.

THE NATURE OF NONVERBAL COMMUNICATION

We begin with clarification of the term *nonverbal communication*. Nonverbal cues are those behaviors that we constantly emit to other people: our appearance, dress, facial expressions, eye gaze and direction, movements and gestures, and so on. These factors may or may not be noticed and interpreted by the other people. They have message value when other people attempt to place some meaning upon these behaviors: they then become signals to be interpreted as communication. This is not as simple as it may sound because we often send such messages without giving conscious attention to them, and we often receive and interpret such messages out of awareness as well.

Nonverbal communication is therefore concerned with interpreting the behaviors of other people, which behaviors do not include but often accompany language.

Ambiguity

All communication is in some sense ambiguous in that it is subject to differing interpretations and misunderstandings. Often, it is hard to pin down the exact meanings of words, and we can miss the connotations that words carry with them. While we can look up the meaning of an unfamiliar word in a dictionary, there is no dictionary that serves the same function for nonverbal signals.

Gestures, tone of voice, and movements can have a wide variety of easily misinterpreted meanings. A smile can mean that a person is happy, friendly, trying to be polite, trying to cover embarrassment, and so on. When our conversation partner stands with arms crossed in front of the body, does that mean that the other person is defensive, as some popular books on body language suggest, or just more comfortable that way?

One of the ambiguities of nonverbal communication is that there is no certainty that there was an intention to send a message. Did a person mean something by tilting her head back that way as she spoke to us? We cannot always be sure. The authors have a friend who claims to be sensitive to the eye drops used during an ophthalmologic examination. He always wears dark glasses, even indoors, all day

▶ *Smiles can be ambiguous.*

following such an examination. People may assign a meaning to the dark glasses (that is, trying to be cool), when in fact there is no such message intended; the glasses in this case are used for comfort and vision. We can be fairly sure that someone has spoken and said something, although what they say may not reflect their whole intentions either, but we are less certain whether someone has intentionally sent a nonverbal message or not.

Finally, there are many exceptions to this generalization. Many nonverbal signals have definite and fairly straightforward meanings for different communities of users. Certain gestures or movements have standard verbal definitions, such a two fingers as V for Victory, or the index finger in the air to mean, "We're number One," or the American sign for perfect with a circle formed by the index finger and thumb. When President Bush visited Australia, he inadvertently used the thumbs-up gesture to mean "Everything is OK," not realizing that this gesture has a vulgar meaning in that country. (We do not include systems such as American Sign Language [ASL] because it is a verbal rather than a nonverbal system of communication; verbal communication refers to language rather than to vocalized communication.)

▶ **Out-of-Awareness Aspect**

One confusing aspect of interpreting nonverbal communication is that some of the messages are sent and received without our *conscious* awareness. Recall that proximity, how close we stand or sit while conversing, is an important signalling system in interpersonal communication. An American may feel comfortable in conversation with someone with a separation of about 3 feet. Someone from the Caribbean may have learned to feel comfortable at about 18 inches. Neither partner in this conversation may be aware of why he or she is uncomfortable as each of them tries continually to establish the "proper" distance between them. The notion that distance for conversation can be based on the cultural system and, within a certain range dictated by the nature of conversational speech sound, largely arbitrary for each culture, has never been emphasized.

Again, people may be unaware of how different groups have developed systems of using eye contact to signal turn-taking in conversations. Generally, in the standard American culture, listeners give fairly continual eye contact to the person who "has the floor" in a conversation. When the listener wishes to say something, he or she will often break eye contact and glance away to signal an intention to talk. If one participant in the conversation is unaware of this convention or is from a region or culture that does not look directly at another person during conversation, mixed signals will result, but neither person may understand the problem. Instead, there may be some vague feeling of unease.

▶ **Powerful Effects**

By saying that nonverbal communication can have powerful effects, we mean that it can have the power to change or even overwhelm the verbal meaning of what is said. We have all heard the old saying that "what you do speaks so loudly that I cannot hear what you say." In our discussion of communication between superiors and subordinates, we noted that nonverbal elements can indicate a superior's actual openness (or lack of it) to being approached for communication, regardless of claims of the door being always open. For example, the boss can schedule meetings with subordinates late in the day or at incovenient times. Office furniture may be arranged so as to suggest the boss is barricaded against intrusions. A receptionist may be trained to make access difficult, and so on.

Nonverbal communication is especially powerful when it comes to communicating such things as warmth and trust or sincerity. People report that when a nonverbal cue seems to contradict the verbal message that it accompanies, they are much more likely to credit the nonverbal message as true. Nonverbal signals, therefore, can cancel what is being said in words.[1]

Whether or not a nonverbal cue contradicts a verbal message is, of course, in the eye of the one receiving the message. Someone who avoids looking us in the eye while claiming to be telling us the honest truth is perceived as sending such contradictory messages. As the interpretation of the verbal and nonverbal cues converge and become less contradictory, people in our culture seem to pay more attention to the verbal components of the message. In other words, nonverbal cues are especially powerful when they appear to be out of synch with the verbal component. This tendency may be due to our belief that it is harder to control our nonverbal messages than our verbal ones; we recognize that they may be encoded out of our direct awareness and control.

Obviously, there are cultural differences in what people look for and in the effect of nonverbal cues. Hall's distinction between high-context and low-context cultures is particularly important in this regard. In high-context cultures, people are more attuned to the nonverbal messages that make up the total context of a communication event than in low-context cultures. High-context people, therefore, may be even more aware of discrepancies between the verbal and nonverbal messages, while low-context people may give more credence to the verbal component and pay less attention to the nonverbal.

Nonverbal communication therefore can be seen as a powerful basis for determining speakers' credibility.

Multichannel Nature

So far the discussion has touched on the wide variety of behaviors that can be included under the rubric of nonverbal communication: facial expression, eye contact, dress, spatial arrangement of communicators, and so on. It is most unusual to employ just one of these types of behavior at a time. While we speak, we usually simultaneously display facial expressions, gestures, and movements. It is possible to send several messages at the same time, given the fact of this multichannel feature of nonverbal communication.

This multichannel capacity of nonverbal communication partly accounts for some of the other features already noted. The ambiguity of one's communication

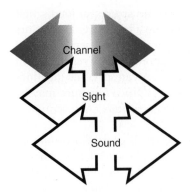

▶ **Figure 6-1**   *Several channels of communication.*

can be the result of competing messages sent by the same person through different channels. He may be communicating warmth by what he says, facial expression, eye contact, but he is standing or sitting too far away, and making no effort to establish closer proximity. The multichannel nature of nonverbal communication as represented in Fig. 6-1 also accounts for the importance that we attach to a lack of consistency in the various channels in judging truthfulness or sincerity.

The use of several channels at once also contributes to the notion that nonverbal cues are more spontaneous than verbal messages. It appears that there is just too much to plan and control in order to coordinate all these systems by conscious attention.

◀▶   # FUNCTIONS OF NONVERBAL COMMUNICATION

The nature of nonverbal communication suggests that it is better fitted for some purposes than others. As stated earlier, nonverbal communication often (but not always) serves to accompany verbal messages: it goes with the linguistic message and tells us how to interpret what is said. This section points out several functions of nonverbal communication.

▶ ### Expressive Functions

Nonverbal communication is especially suited for expressing emotions. Dale Leathers suggests that "nonverbal communication represents the primary medium for the expression of emotions."[2] Nonverbal cues act particularly to signal liking versus disliking, or immediacy, and the intensity, or the amount of emotional arousal. Within a given cultural group, people can closely assign emotional meanings to various nonverbal indicators of immediacy and intensity in the communication of others. In the U.S. culture, faces are especially important for indicating the kind,

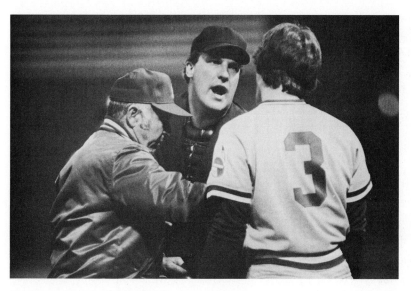

▶ *Proximity heightens the emotional message.*

or the name of, the emotion, whereas the state of bodily tension and movement indicates intensity. So, the face indicates that someone is angry; bodily tension and action tell the degree of the anger.

In addition to facial expressions and bodily movements, the most important nonverbal channels for expressing emotion appear to be vocal characteristics, touching, and proximity. Vocal characteristics refer to such aspects of speaking as the pitch (higher pitch typically indicates nervousness, anxiety, excitement, and the like); timbre or quality, or amount of tension in the vocal cords (a strained voice sounds tense, for example); or volume (loudness is associated with arousal, excitement, possibly anger, and so on).

Touching the other person can show higher levels of immediacy or intensity. If we grasp someone by the upper arm, while saying, "Now this is really important for you to remember," we have emphasized the importance by our nonverbal action. Proximity can also heighten the emotional message. When you see a baseball manager arguing with the umpire over a close call as in this picture, you probably notice that the manager really "gets in the face" of the umpire, thereby communicating the intensity of the manager's feelings. People communicate emotional detachment (low arousal or intensity) by physically creating or maintaining actual distance between themselves and the people with whom they are communicating.

Regulative Functions

We may be less aware of the regulative function of nonverbal cues than we are of the expressive function. We have already alluded to the use of eye contact in North American conversations as a regulator of turn-taking. Further, we noted that people

▶ *Hand raising can serve regulative functions.*

are often not consciously aware of how they are using eye contact in this way. In a one-on-one communication situation, nonverbal regulators play a variety of roles. When listening to another person, we signal that he or she should continue talking when we nod our heads, smile, and look interested. We may signal our displeasure with the course of the conversation by facial expressions, looking away, or seeming to focus on something or someone else.

Not only are nonverbal messages used to indicate turn-taking, as in the photo above, but to signal phases in the interaction, such as beginnings and endings. When you wish to break into a conversation, you usually do so by nonverbal means, such as "trying to catch the eye" of one of the participants, moving close to the participant you wish to communicate with, and so on. Picture this situation: You have just run into someone in the parking lot, and you have something that you wish to discuss. After initial greetings, you may touch the other person's arm, or raise your hand to indicate that you have something else to say.

Closing interactions may also be signaled by using nonverbal signals, such as looking away, moving sideways away from the other person in the general direction that you wish to be going, and so on. Such subtle cues are considered more polite than abruptly saying, "Look, I have to be going—can we finish this later?" Of course, one may use less subtle nonverbal methods (which may also be considered "less polite"), such as yawning, looking at one's watch, or purposely looking bored.

▶ ### Reinforcing Functions

One of the more obvious uses of nonverbal communication is to reinforce what is being said in the verbal stream of discourse. This function is often taught as an aspect of public speaking, in which gestures and movements are intended to support and reinforce what the speaker is saying. Observe other people at lunch or over coffee in deep or involving conversations. Chances are that you will observe some

▶ *Nonverbal messages reinforce the meaning.*

animated nonverbal behavior as people make their points to each other. Much of this movement is intended to strengthen or reinforce what people are saying, as when a speaker pounds the lectern.

Large, sweeping gestures, such as pounding one fist into the palm of the other hand, or, even more forceful, pounding a table, reinforce the idea and indicate force or determination. But nonverbal communication can reinforce messages in more subtle ways, as well. Some executives have been known to raise the level of their chairs in their offices higher than other seats in the office in order to reinforce their dominance. Of course, the furnishings and trappings of the office itself can be used to reinforce messages concerning that person's status or perhaps function within the organization.

Illustrator Functions

Similar to reinforcing, nonverbal signals are used to illustrate visually what one is saying in words. Verbal descriptions are often accompanied by hand movements that indicate the spatial relationships that are being described or the relationships in size among objects being described. Speakers can draw pictures or simplified representations in the air to illustrate our meaning. Giving directions is often accompanied by pointing and even some motions acting out how one should proceed.

Impression Management Functions

The nonverbal elements of an interaction may be significant in creating and maintaining a particular impression. Recall that people have a need to seek information

▶ *Gestures can illustrate a message.*

about communication partners, especially those in continuing dyadic relationships. Much of this information is obtained by observing the nonverbal behavior of the other person. When we enact a certain kind of role, we are aware of this surveillance aspect to the observations that others make of our role enactment. Goffman, you will recall, explicitly compared this day-to-day impression management to being on-stage.

When people present themselves as candidates in an employment interview, they are conscious (or should be) of the nonverbal signals that they are sending. They want to convey the impression that they are competent and self-assured. How is this done? The first nonverbal cues that are sent probably include direct eye contact with the interviewer combined with a firm handshake and a pleasant facial expression. The candidate also creates an impression by being neat and well-groomed, appropriately dressed, and speaking at a moderate rate that indicates confidence and energy.

▶ ### Metacommunication Functions

Related to many of these other functions is the use of nonverbal signals to indicate how a particular episode of communication is going: that is, communicating about the communication. A function of metacommunication is to give some indication of how the other person should understand or interpret the spoken message.

The metacommunication function of nonverbal signals is important in relational communication. As the text has pointed out earlier, the relationship aspect of relational communication is often carried by nonverbal channels. Relationship

▶ *Political candidates wish to appear approachable yet capable.*

messages that indicate liking and intimacy, similarity between the partners, and the amount of formality appropriate to the relationship can and often are communicated by nonverbal means. For example, Burgoon suggests that intimacy and similarity in the relationship are communicated by such nonverbal signs as "close proximity, forward body lean, relatively direct body orientation [face to face as opposed to side to side], frequent and longer mutual gaze, more gesturing, moderate relaxation, frequent touch . . ." and many others.[3]

On the other hand, certain nonverbal cues can help to maintain a more formal feel, as in a complementary relationship such as superior to subordinate. These cues include more distance between communicators, differences in apparel, fewer gestures, infrequent touch, and so on. Similarly, the trappings of the setting, such as an office, can reinforce the dominance or control of one person over the other. As we indicate later in discussing proxemics and chronemics, the higher-status person has more control over time and space than does the lower-status person. Consequently, the dominant person can enter the space of the other person more easily, more at will, than would be the case the other way around.

Note that nonverbal cues accompanying verbal messages can alter the verbal meaning or interpretation of intention. Whether a verbal message is meant to be taken at face value or to be interpreted as sarcasm or the like depends upon the tone of voice, inflection, gestures, possibly the bodily posture, and so on. Thus in the case of relational communication, whether a statement is "one-up" or "one-down" may be known only if one also knows the nonverbal cues made at the same time accompanying the statement.

▶ *Close proximity often communicates intimacy.*

Again, one must bear in mind that the relationship meanings associated with various nonverbal signals are often culture-bound. One cannot assume that the signals for relational closeness or difference are the same as one moves from culture to culture. Control over time, for example, is often not seen the same way in Latin America as it is in North America. People may often have different attitudes toward privacy, as well, which could lead to misunderstandings about the meaning of invading or controlling space.

Highlights of Functions of Nonverbal Communication

Nonverbal communication can convey a wide-ranging variety of messages and meanings. We have attempted to summarize some of the most important purposes for nonverbal communication. Most often, nonverbal communication serves to accompany verbal communication and functions to add expressive information, to reinforce or contradict the linguistic message, and to provide metacommunication, or indications of how the communication and the ongoing relationship is to be understood.

NONVERBAL COMMUNICATION SYSTEMS

The purpose of human sensory systems is to receive and begin to process information from the environment. These physical senses include sight, sound, touch, smell, and taste, the five senses. Some would add other senses that receive information from the environment, such as heat (and cold), pressure, and, perhaps, balance. Any inputs received through these various senses could be interpreted as having message value, that is, could be interpreted as incoming messages from another person.

The senses are a beginning point in thinking about the various systems that people typically employ for nonverbal communication. Some sensory data are not usually directly relevant in business and professional communication: Smell and taste, while important for some kinds of communication, can be set aside, for example. Also, relying strictly on physical senses overlooks the importance of culturally based communication systems represented by our uses of time, space, and objects.

For the purposes of this discussion, we will limit consideration of nonverbal communication systems to the following:

Facial expressions
Bodily movements and gestures
The use of space (proxemics)
The use of time (chronemics)
Vocal characteristics (vocalics)
The use of touch (haptics)
The use of objects

Facial Expressions

The face can be a particularly rich source for information. We have already pointed out that the face is especially used for expressing emotions. People are generally accurate in interpreting the meaning of facial cues in the following areas: in interpreting emotions expressed; and in determining whether a person being observed was subject to hostile or friendly treatment.[4]

A facial meaning sensitivity test has been developed that looks at people's ability to distinguish among a series of photographs intended to portray various emotional states.[5] The test first asks people to identify 10 general classes of facial representations of the following emotions (see Figure 6-2).

Disgust
Happiness
Interest
Sadness
Bewilderment
Contempt
Surprise
Anger
Determination
Fear

The test proceeds by requiring the test-takers to make increasingly finer distinctions among more specific expressions and emotions. The use of such a test allows a

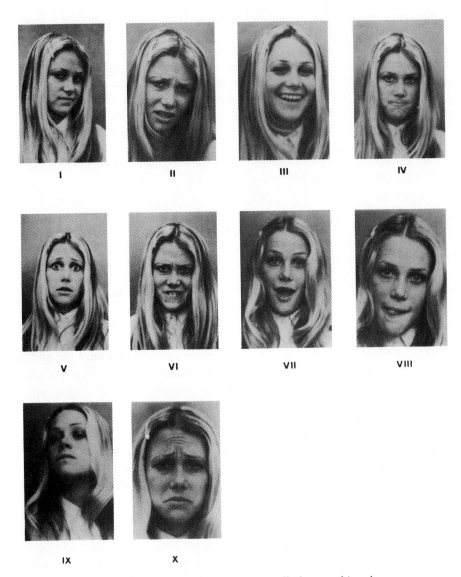

▶ **Figure 6-2**   *The Facial Meaning Sensitivity Test calls for matching the emotion with the facial expression. (Reprinted with the permission of Macmillan Publishing Company from Successful Nonverbal Communication by Leathers. Copyright © 1991 by Dale E. Leathers.)*

person to determine how sensitive he or she is to the meanings of facial expressions. Such testing can be the basis for heightening sensitivity or for practice in developing such sensitivity.

Intercultural Considerations.   One question that has intrigued scholars of nonverbal communication is whether or not certain of these expressions are similar regardless of culture. In other words, could they be inherent in human nature, rather than culture-bound)? Charles Darwin first looked at this question in 1872 following the publication of his work on evolution.[6] The research of two psychologists, Paul Ekman and Wallace Friesen, has led them to conclude that a certain small range of emotions is connected with a fairly universal set of facial signs (see Fig. 6-2).[7] These similarities are usually exhibited in cases in which there are sudden changes of emotion such as fear, surprise, anger, distrust, sadness, and happiness. In working with those expressions that "flash on and off" the face in a few seconds, Ekman and Friesen found agreement across cultures in matching these five or six emotions with standard expressions. The two psychologists believe that these similarities indicate that these expressions have evolved with the human species and are therefore universal. All other expressions of emotions are no doubt mostly or entirely culture-bound.

Cultural similarities, however, cannot be used with great confidence in intercultural communication. One problem is that there are differences between cultures concerning what events inspire these emotions themselves. A second problem is that very similar facial expressions may be used for other communication purposes, as well. So, while smiling may universally indicate happiness and friendliness, it may also be used in one culture to indicate some other message (such as embarrassment, in certain Asian cultures). Third, there may be cultural norms that determine how these emotions should be controlled, meaning that the facial display may be too brief or may be masked by other nonverbal cues that limit the ability of those from outside the culture to detect the emotion.

The Eyes in Facial Communication.   For most people, the most important element in acquiring information from the human face is the eyes. We even have sayings about how the eyes can talk and that you can tell someone's character by "looking deep into their eyes." There is a scene in the movie, *The Year of Living Dangerously*, in which the main character, a news reporter, must enter the palace of a Southeast Asian president for an interview. The guards require the character to remove his sunglasses so that they can inspect his eyes; they believe that they can spot an assassin by looking into his eyes. Also, some research backs up the notion that most people find the eyes the most important part of the face for communication purposes. This study reported that most of the time listening to another person talk is spent looking at the eyes (43.3% of the time), considerably more than that spent on looking at the second most frequently observed region, the mouth (12.6% of the time).[8]

We have already seen that eye contact plays an important role in regulating face-to-face communication. In addition, the eyes seem to be important in people's determination of the other person's honesty and sincerity. When people are asked how they can discover whether another person is telling the truth or not, they often report that they watch the other person's eyes. They are watching for the avoiding of direct eye contact, looking away or looking down, or "shifty" eyes. In addition, people believe that competence and confidence are often communicated by the direct eye gaze of the other person. We speak of people's eyes' "glazing over" when they are bored or disinterested.

Besides eye contact, the other information that people can get from the eyes involves pupil dilation and the region around the eyes. Pupil dilation refers to the opening or closing of the iris (the black spot) to let in more or to restrict the amount of light that enters the eye. In general, we believe that we open up the iris, dilate the pupils when we see something or someone we like, and that we close down the iris when we see something or someone we don't like. There are reports of salespeople, particularly in the Middle East, who watch specifically for such pupil dilation when showing a customer various objects. Presumably, when the customer sees something that he or she really likes, there is involuntary pupil dilation; such involuntary nonverbal signs are felt to be more authentic or accurate because they are not directly under the control of the person sending them.

Highlights of Facial Expressions.   The face is very important in nonverbal communication, especially for expressing emotions. People can generally discern different emotions depicted by facial expressions. There are cultural differences, however, that make even the interpretation of fairly universal facial signs difficult. The eyes are probably the most important region of the face for providing nonverbal communication.

Bodily Movement and Gestures

It is a little difficult, at first, to separate movements of the rest of the body from the movements associated with facial expressions. In fact, one can refer to expressions as facial gestures. A major difference, however, is that the face is better for indicating specific emotions, whereas the use of arms, hands, and shoulder, for example, are less useful for indicating the content of the emotion. They are better for indicating the intensity and force of emotions and for a wide range of other informational purposes.

An early researcher in the field on nonverbal communication, Ray Birdwhistell, attempted to delineate the important units for nonverbal displays, on the analogy of the linguistic units that linguists use for describing and analyzing natural languages.[9] The smallest unit of linguistic speech that differentiates meaning is the phoneme (for example, the sounds /p/ and /b/ differentiate the words "pan" and "ban," and so are phonemes). Birdwhistell tried to identify similar units of nonverbal communication, which would be "kinemes," within a larger system that he termed *kinesics*. As we have seen, however, the range of bodily movements and nonverbal communication is more of an analogic system than the digital system of ordinary language.

In a country as diverse as the United States, cultural differences in the use of nonverbal gestures can make a difference. A consultant in a northern New England town, near the Canadian border, found that long-time inhabitants were complaining about a younger coworker from "down country" (New York City). The problem was that the newcomer gestured and talked with his hands. The older townspeople found this habit disconcerting. The advice to be expressive and to use gestures to reinforce your message must be qualified by an awareness of local cultural norms.

One of the most often used methods for categorizing and analyzing the various kinds of gestures and movements for communication has been advocated by Ekman and Friesen.[10] This system is useful for sensitizing us to the various meanings that can be communicated by such bodily movements and sensitize us to the messages we are sending. The five classes of bodily signals are the following:

Emblems
Illustrators
Affect displays
Regulators
Adaptors

Emblems.   Emblems are the physical cues that have some direct verbal translation; they are closest to verbal language of the nonverbal communication devices. We have alluded already to the familiar "O.K." or "perfect" signs used by North Americans. There are emblems that we use for greeting, such as waving, shaking hands, and nodding heads. There is a wide and rich set of emblems that are used for insults, especially in certain cultures.

Because these emblems are tied directly to verbal translations, they are usually arbitrary in form and meaning. This means that one cannot always interpret the gestures from one language or from one culture to another. Showing someone the soles of one's shoes has little meaning in Great Britain or in Germany (probably it would be met with bewilderment), whereas in many parts of the Middle East, such as Egypt, such an action is a serious insult.

▶ *Emblems have specific meanings.*

Obviously, when one uses emblems, one cannot say that they are employed out-of-awareness, as with certain other kinds of nonverbal communication. While using them may be second nature, one must be aware that they convey an intention.

Illustrators.   Recall that one of the functions of nonverbal communication is to illustrate what one is talking about. Illustrators are used to "draw pictures in the air," that is, when we try to show, usually with hand movements, what we are saying in words. Again, the use of illustrators becomes second nature. We have observed people giving elaborate hand directions while explaining to someone how to find a particular place, even as the photo shows while speaking on the phone!

Ekman and Friesen subdivided illustrators into several kinds. For example, some illustrators do not represent anything in a pictographic (or iconic) way. When we shake our fist or pound the table, we are demonstrating the intensity of our feeling or the strength of our determination. Some illustrators are used to point to objects or people, whereas others are used to emphasize the rhythmic movement of something we are talking about. In other words, illustrators refer to all those signs that we use to both reinforce and illustrate what is being communicated in discourse. They are useful in aiding the listener to understand what meaning is intended by the speaker.

Affect Displays.   Affect displays are nonverbal signals that indicate the sender's emotional state. Since the most important carrier of affect displays is the face, much of the discussion of affect displays has already been covered in that section. In addition to the face, however, liking or not liking (typical affect display purposes)

▶ *Some people even use illustrators while speaking on the phone.*

▶ *Smiling is an obvious affect display.*

can be indicated by other nonverbal signs as well: proximity (closer for liking, further for disliking); bodily orientation to the other person; forward or backward lean of the body; and so on. We may also look to other kinds of nonverbal communication for indicators of affect, such as the pressure of the hand in a handshake or incidental touching on the arm or shoulder.

In comparison to emblems and illustrators, we generally believe that affect displays are less under the conscious control of the person sending them. There is therefore some tendency to give such affect displays more credence when they betray what we feel is an unintended emotional response on the part of the other person.

Regulators. Another function noted for nonverbal communication is to regulate the flow of communication. Regulators are gestures or movements people use to indicate beginning or ending encounters, turn-taking during the encounter, and the like. Knapp has further differentiated turn-regulation cues as used by speakers vs. listeners.[11] For example, we signal to the other person that, as speaker, we wish to continue to hold the floor by glancing away at regular intervals and maintaining the continual use of illustrators. When we are ready to relinquish the floor to the next participant, we look at the other(s) and stop the flow of illustrators. To indicate a desire to say something, the listener can also use the glance-away signal and accompany it with head nodding, leaning forward, and even raising an index finger.

The appropriate use of regulators often marks a person as knowledgeable and competent in interpersonal communication. People who do not follow the rules that are generally in force within their culture or subculture regarding the use of these regulators will probably be judged negatively. For example, in the middle-class culture of much of U.S. business, inappropriate signals to end a conversation are movements such as beginning to rise and walk away, and other rather abrupt gestures.[12] Of course, these signals are largely culture-bound and must be learned as one begins to operate in a culture different from one's home culture.

Adaptors.   Notice that the categories of nonverbal signals developed by Ekman and Friesen move from those under the greatest conscious control to those that are less under such control. The fifth category, adaptors, refer to nonverbal signals that are assumed not to be under the conscious control of the sender. Here again the axiom of Watzlawick et al.—that it is impossible not to communicate and that people can and will assign meaning to our behaviors whether we intend them to be read as messages or not—is relevant. Occasionally, these adaptors are interpreted as nervous mannerisms or habits, such as smoothing back the hair or playing with a button on a shirt while talking.

Adaptors may be important sources for information about the internal or psychological state of the other person precisely because of the assumption that they are not done consciously or intentionally.

Ekman and Friesen distinguished between two kinds of adaptors: self-adaptors and object-adaptors.[13] The first kind refers to movements that involve doing something to oneself, such as scratching, touching the hand to the mouth or face, rubbing the neck, and so on. Object-adaptors refer to the manipulation of some object,

▶ *Adaptors are gestures that usually occur out of conscious awareness.*

such as playing with a pencil, absently pulling apart a paper clip, or wadding up a piece of paper or tearing paper.

People often look to these out-of-awareness adaptors as signs of some internal state. For example, someone may think that an increase in self-adaptors indicates

Problem-Solution

Nonverbal Cues for Deception

Most people believe that they can tell when someone is lying to them. They often depend upon nonverbal signs, such as lack of eye contact, what appear to be forced smiles, excessive finger tapping, and the like. Paul Ekman, who, along with Wallace Friesen, has pioneered much of the research into nonverbal communication, believes that people's confidence in their ability to detect deception exceeds their abilities. On the basis of twenty years of research, Ekman concludes that not much reliance should be placed on such judgments. Mark Knapp, another expert on nonverbal communication, reports that researchers have found some support for nonverbal cues indicating deception, such as higher voice pitch, an increase in the number of adaptors (such as rubbing hands or the face), slower rate of speech, more speech errors, and fewer use of illustrating gestures (see citation below).

Still, Knapp reports, the findings are inconsistent. Most people do no better than chance in detecting other's deception from nonverbal indicators alone. Ekman and others have found that even people trained and experienced in detecting lying, people such as policemen, judges, customs agents, or psychiatrists, do no better than average when put to the test. In one recent study, which is cited below, Ekman found that only Secret Service agents, as a group, displayed accuracy beyond mere chance in detecting deception on the basis of nonverbal cues. The cues that we may look for to determine whether another person is lying are simply too ambiguous and too complex for us to make really good judgments. Do not be too sure, therefore, that you can tell when another person is lying or trying to deceive you based upon your evaluation of his or her nonverbal behavior.

There has been a lot of interest in this aspect of nonverbal communication. A good summary of the problem can be found in Knapp, M. L. (1978). *Nonverbal communication in human interaction* (2nd ed.). New York: Holt, Rinehart & Winston; a useful summary of the recent research and a report on the study of professionals' abilities at detecting deception can be found in Ekman, P. & O'Sullivan, M. (1991). Who can catch a liar? *American Psychologist, 46,* 913–920.

nervousness, lack of self-confidence, or some kind of uncertainty. Some people may interpret the use of object-adaptors as indicating a lack of interest in the communication. Leathers reports that some police investigators claim that suspects often begin playing with objects such as pencils or pieces of paper at the exact moment when they are attempting deception.[14]

Posture and Stance

In addition to the messages that we can send intentionally or unintentionally by movement, we also communicate by the general posture and orientation of our bodies. Postures are not as easily classified as are gestures and movements. Remember that your mothers may have thought it was important for you to stand up straight. At some point in growing up, people may have told you that it was not polite to slouch or lounge around in the presence of certain people.

Posture can be described as upright and alert, tense or relaxed. Some would say that posture is an important channel for indicating respect or disrespect. During an interview, a candidate will often want to sit up alertly, slightly leaning forward, while avoiding looking tense and uncomfortable. Status and power are often conveyed by differences in posture between people in communication. A person of higher status can lean back and look more relaxed and open than the person of lower status or power can. In fact, one of the markers of disrespect is to assume a relaxed posture in the presence of a person who believes that he or she is of higher status or power. Notice how posture, then, can be a method for sending a relationship message in relational communication that may contradict the verbal messages.

The Use of Space (Proxemics)

As noted before in the discussion of intercultural communication, the use of spacing during communication sends messages and is interpreted as messages by others. As Edward T. Hall said, "Space speaks."[15] The term *proxemics* has been formed on the analogy with phonemics, in the way that Birdwhistell coined the term *kinesics*. Hall means to suggest by the use of this term that there are units of space or distance that can be meaningful. Our awareness that such norms can be violated is shown in standard phrases such as, "Get out of my space," or "He was in my face." We are conscious of an invisible "bubble" of space around us, and we are uncomfortable when others intrude into this.

As we move from this personal bubble (which is different in size depending upon one's culture), we feel that certain kinds of communication transactions should be enacted within certain distance limits. As indicated, standard casual conversation distance is about 3 to 5 feet, although this distance varies by region of the United States and contextual factors such as crowding, noise, and so on. Japanese expect to maintain distances somewhat greater than this and so may feel that Americans are standing too close for comfort. Farther distances appear to be more formal, appropriate for public speaking or similar public performances. The standard U.S. distances are illustrated in Figure 6-3.

When these spatial expectations are violated by a partner in communication, we may have a vague sense that there is something wrong with the other person. Recall that the so-called standard attribution error may operate to cause us to impute bad motives to the other person, without realizing that the other person may come from a culture in which distances for various interactions are different from our own. Of course, we compensate for obvious outside factors that require the rules to be broken, such as in a crowded elevator for instance.

Besides communicating with others by the distance that separates us during communication episodes, we also communicate by the use of space: that is, how we break it up, organize it, and what we put in it. The amount of space that one controls is often a good indicator of status or position in a hierarchy. Those higher in the pecking order are assigned more space than those lower. The location of the space one receives can also communicate status or power. The "room with a view," say, at or near the top of the corporate tower, is clearly a significant status marker. Sharing space, on the other hand, is usually a sign of lower status in an organization.

Similarly, the control over one's space and that of others is a mark of status and power. In general, those higher in status have barriers, such as reception-

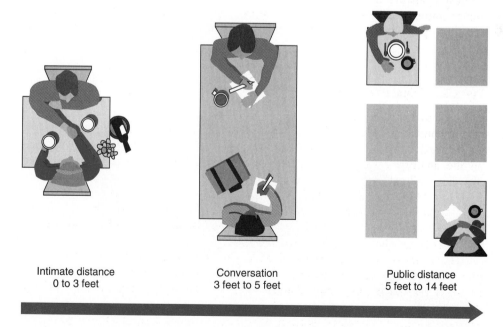

| Intimate distance | Conversation | Public distance |
| 0 to 3 feet | 3 feet to 5 feet | 5 feet to 14 feet |

▶ **Figure 6-3**   *Standard U.S. distances for intimate conversation, casual conversation, and public distance.*

ists or secretaries, who can prevent direct intrusions by others into that person's space. The higher-status person, on the other hand, can often enter the space of a lower-status person without going through such barriers and may be allowed to walk right in.

There are also differences in regard to what kind of space one can have control over: differences in what is private space and what is public space. In Medieval Europe, bedrooms, especially those of high nobility and royalty, were considered public spaces for many purposes. Nobles would vie for the honor of dressing or undressing the king or queen, for example, or for assisting in other events that most of us today would consider private. There may also be differences in whether one's work space is considered to be public or private. Some people may resent intrusions into the area of their laboratory stations, personal computer stations, offices, and the like.

The way that a person or organization organizes space can also constitute communication, that is, send messages. Architects and their clients have long understood that space can be a powerful method in setting a tone or establishing a particular image for an organization. Are the more favored executives and departments placed in the newer facilities, located in more attractive parts of a town or nation? Does everyone have a separate office or work space, or are desks spread out over a floor without separators or walls, as in the old city rooms of newspapers?

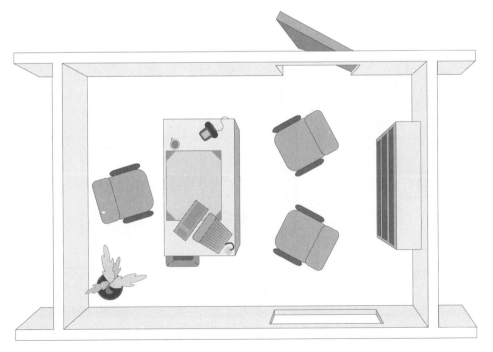

▶ **Figure 6-4**   *Typical office arrangement.*

The arrangement of spaces within a building can provide clues to how the organization assigns priorities to various parts of the operation.

The arrangement of an office, as in Fig. 6-4, can be significant, also. Is the desk or table placed in such a way so as to serve as a barrier between anyone entering the office and its occupant? When a person enters the office, does the occupant (a) rise, go around the desk, and personally greet the visitor or (b) wave the person to have a seat in front of the desk while staying behind his or her desk? If (a), one would assume that the visitor is of equal or higher status than the occupant; if (b), that the visitor is probably of lower status. Notice how the use of space can be used to send relationship messages.

The Use of Time (Chronemics)

Hall has reminded us that if "space speaks, time talks," meaning that our use of time (how we segment it, what we do during it) communicates messages.[16] A standard illustration from the business world is the premium placed on promptness and on not wasting time. In other words, in Western cultures, there is a tendency to think of time as a commodity, or a currency, that can be spent or wasted. We have a definite sense of what it means to be late or how late is too late. If someone has a job interview, that person should know that being even 5 minutes late is going to send a negative message to the interviewer.

▶ *Monochronic time systems emphasize serving customers in order.*

Hall was one of the first anthropologists to note that time can be segmented arbitrarily just as can space (or the color spectrum). How late is "too late," in other words, depends upon the culture in which one is operating. In some places, 20 minutes late is approximately the same as being 2 minutes late in the United States. A person from such a culture may wonder what the problem is if the English or American person with whom he or she had the appointment is upset over the 20-minute lateness. Again, because of the out-of-awareness nature of this aspect of culture and nonverbal communication, the misunderstanding could conceivably never be worked out, with neither side knowing what code was violated.

Hall has gone on to distinguish cultural attitudes toward time in terms of what he calls "monochronic" systems and "polychronic" systems. In monochronic systems, such as those found in Western Europe and the United States, things are usually done one thing at a time, and there is a great deal of concern with scheduling. In polychronic systems, there is less concern with doing things in sequence. Rather than lining up and serving people on a first-come, first-served basis, people may crowd around, in no particular order. There is less concern with schedules, and people may often engage in several events at once. Monochronic people are easily bewildered in polychronic settings.

Like other cultural systems, our sense of time and how it should be used is built into our second natures. When others do not conform to our sense of time, the messages tend to be negative until we become sensitized to other ways of looking at time.

Vocal Characteristics (Vocalics)

When we use our voices, listeners discern two aspects of the vocal sound: the linguistic content (the words) and the accompanying features of the vocal sound itself. These vocal features, also known as paralinguistic cues, include tone, pitch, volume, rate, and vocal quality (such as tense, strained, or breathy, for example). As noted in the discussion of the expressive function of nonverbal communication, these vocal characteristics are important in signalling one's emotional state. A fast rate, spoken in a high pitch, for instance, is often interpreted as excited or apprehensive. Increased volume can accompany excitement or anger or similar strong emotions. Tension or apprehensiveness can be indicated by a tight or tense sound to the voice.

The vocal features are also used to punctuate the spoken discourse. This aspect of paralinguistics is closely associated with learning the language itself. We learn that by emphasizing different words in a sentence, we can shade the meaning of that sentence: *I* thought you were in Kansas, for example, means something different than, I thought *you* were in Kansas. The second sentence, with the emphasis on "you" implies that actually someone other than the person in question was in Kansas.

Different languages usually develop different tonal cues and patterns of vocal emphasis. Some languages, such as Chinese or many African languages, are known as "tonal" languages, which means that a change in the tone or pitch in pronouncing a syllable changes the entire meaning of the word as much as changing a letter in a word in English. People who speak a second language, other than their own home language, may not be attuned to the emphasis and tonal meanings of the new language, and they may miss the paralinguistic cues.

The Use of Touch (Haptics)

In Chapter 4, we referred to one dimension that seems to differentiate some cultures from others: low-contact and high-contact cultures. Touching has different meanings as one moves from one culture to another. There are certain ritualized touching activities that are expected and common in business settings: The handshake is the most obvious of these ritualistic touchings. Within the culture, certain conventions develop around the use and manner of enacting such rituals. In the United States, it is customary to shake hands upon meeting someone for the first time or, for friends and acquaintances, after some period of time between encounters. In certain European cultures, friends are expected to shake hands at each meeting and departure.

In Japanese business circles, the bow replaces the handshake, although when working with Westerners, Japanese will often enact both bowing and handshaking. There is a set of norms accompanying bowing in Japan, just as there is for shaking hands. The more junior of the two people greeting is expected to bow slightly lower than the senior person, for example. Reportedly, the Japanese are uncomfortable with the American handshake, but are so accustomed to it that they may be even more uncomfortable should the American fail to shake hands.[11] At any rate, the firm handshake, so often favored by Americans to show warmth or

▶ *Shaking hands is a familiar use of haptics.*

strength, really is disliked by the Japanese, who much prefer a more relaxed grip. Beyond that, Japanese are much more uncomfortable with touching, such as touching the arm or patting on the back, than are Americans.

As noted in the previous chapter, there is growing concern in the United States over the problem of sexual harassment. Such concerns mean that touching between those of the opposite sex is approached more carefully. Studies have indicated that in public or business settings men tend to touch women more than vice versa, but that in same-sex pairs, women do more touching than men in the U.S. culture. In parts of Asia and Africa, it is not considered unusual for male friends to walk along hand in hand, an action that would signal an intimate relation in the United States.

Touch often has an expressive function in nonverbal communication, and it is often used to communicate warmth, friendliness, or reassurance. Touches have been found to be effective communicators. People who were "inadvertently" touched on the hands or arms while checking out of a library or a business establishment have reported having a more favorable impression of the service they received than people who were not touched. Part of the picture here seems to be the attribution that the receiver gives to the intentions of the person doing the touching. When the touching is perceived as inadvertent, appropriate, or professional, there is generally little negative association with the action. Touching that is seen as unwanted or intentional receives more mixed reactions, including the extreme discomfort related to sexual harassment.

▶ ### The Use of Objects

A final area of nonverbal communication that can be highly relevant in professional settings in the use of objects or artifacts to communicate. This system is sometimes referred to as "objectics," following the analogy of proxemics, chronemics, and so on.

Certainly, the trappings or furnishings of a building or office usually communicate some message. Attorney's offices, for example, are often furnished in a classic and traditional style to communicate success and competence. The leather upholstery and panelled wall is meant to indicate that the firm is successful (and therefore should handle your case well) and shows refinement and taste. Medical offices, on the other hand, often show a different style. Many physician's offices are decorated in muted styles in the outer area or reception area to convey a feeling of reassurance. In the examining rooms, there is an emphasis on scientific and technical equipment. In other work areas, one may find that the latest in hardware is displayed in order to indicate that the occupants are up on the latest technology.

Objects as communication include one's clothing. Different organizational cultures often are marked by different styles in dressing; some are formal, some are "breezy," and some are utilitarian. Scientists or physicians often wear white lab coats, as a mark of their expertise. Those in sales often make an effort to appear as conventional as possible in their dress. Musicians effect a different style of dress, and so on. The clothes that we wear can be important elements in impression management. For a time, there were a series of self-help books and articles concerned with telling Americans how to "dress for success."

Diversity in the Workplace

Meishi: *The Japanese etiquette of business cards*

Business cards, or *meishi*, are ubiquitous in Japan, and there are some specific rules regarding their use. Someone doing business in Japan is well advised to bring a large supply of these objects. It is inexcusable to be without one's cards at any time. The cards should be well printed, with English on one side and Japanese on the other (see Fig. 6-5). One of the main purposes of the *meishi* is to indicate the rank and function of the person presenting the card within his or her organization, so this information should be explicitly and accurately given on the card. Remember that small details of rank are important to the Japanese.

When presenting your card, hold it outstretched toward the recipient, with the writing facing the other person: This should be the side of the card with the Japanese writing, of course, if the recipient is Japanese. Remember to have a logo printed at the top of the card on the Japanese side so that you can be sure you are not presenting that card with the writing upside down. Holding the card as you present it in both hands indicates that the other person is of very high status. The other person accepts the card, with a slight bow, in his or her right hand; you should also bow slightly as the card is taken. The recipient then studies the material on the card carefully; simply putting the card away in a folder or a pocket would be considered rude.

The cards you receive, in fact, should be maintained for later reference, because you will be expected to know all this information about the other person when you do business again. There is also a prescribed order for presenting *meishi* depending upon rank. If you are the visitor, though, this is less complicated, because hosts present their cards first.

An especially useful source is D. Rowland (1985). *Japanese business etiquette*. New York: Warner Books.

Objects can be used, then, to send messages about one's occupation or function, one's status within an organization (or in society), and one's interest in or knowledge of certain kinds of expertise. Clothes or styles of dress are often specific to certain occupations and corporate cultures.

インディアナ日米協会

テレッサ A. コザック
専務理事

ファースト・インディアナ・プラザ ＃1570
米国インディアナ州インディアナポリス市 (〒46204-2491)
電話：(317) 635-0123

**Japan-America
Society of
Indiana, Inc.**

Theresa A. Kulczak
Executive Director

First Indiana Plaza, Suite 1570
135 North Pennsylvania St.
Indianapolis, IN 46204-2491

317-635-0123
Fax 317-635-1452

▶ **Figure 6-5**   *Front and back of business card to be used in Japan. (Used by permission of Theresa Kulczak, Executive Director and Japan-America Society of Indiana, Inc.)*

◆▶ SUMMARY

A major feature of nonverbal communication is that it uses several different channels. This chapter has reviewed important channels, or systems, of nonverbal communication. When we engage in face-to-face communication, we can employ a wide range of message-sending behaviors and objects. Some of these channels are more suited for certain kinds of messages rather than others: For example, facial expressions are especially useful for communicating emotional states. We believe that the system used by Ekman and Friesen for classifying types of nonverbal signals provides a useful way of conceiving the various visual messages we send and receive.

In addition to the usual nonverbal channels associated with the face, gestures, and vocal characteristics, it is important for people in business or professions to be aware of the out-of-awareness systems of space use, time, and object, especially as they may have intercultural dimensions.

EXERCISES

1. Arrange to form a pair with another person in your class; face each other and try to send a series of messages nonverbally. Alternate taking turns as sender and receiver. How well did you do in understanding the messages? What aspects of the situation accounted for successes or failures? Are some types of messages more easily decoded from nonverbal communication than others?

2. Explain why nonverbal communication is often ambiguous. What are the reasons for this ambiguity?

3. What problems are encountered in conversations when people are not aware of the rules of nonverbal communication? What may account for these problems? How can they be overcome?

4. Describe examples that show each of the different functions of nonverbal communication discussed in this chapter. Can other functions be added to the list? What might they be? Can you identify nonverbal cues that you tend to miss, such as regulative?

5. Write a definition of nonverbal communication that includes what you believe all the important elements are; compare this definition with others in your class or group. Can the different definitions be combined in a complete definition? What problems may there be in developing a complete definition of this phenomenon?

6. Make an inventory of the facilities of a building on campus or at work. Does the reception area indicate the type of work that is done there? Write down features that suggest the feelings or values of the people who work in or use the building. Be explicit about what features communicate the feelings and values.

Communication Problem: Interior Design

Imagine you are the manager for a team of seven professionals who all work together on the same (third) floor of a four-story building. You want to arrange the work stations of all seven people plus yourself to enhance the sense of team-building but allow for sufficient privacy for each to concentrate on research or report writing. You also wish to provide for some spaces for confidential conferences and interviews with team members.

Describe a layout of furniture, work stations, and so on to meet your major objectives. Be sure to allow for an attractive atmosphere and the possibility for people to personalize their own spaces.

SELECTED SOURCES FOR FURTHER READING

Birdwhistell, R. L. (1970). *Kinesics and context*. Philadelphia: University of Pennsylvania Press.

Burgoon, J. K. (1985). Nonverbal signals. In Knapp, M. L. & Miller, G. R. (Eds.), *Handbook of interpersonal communication*. Newbury Park CA: Sage Publications.

Efron, D. (1972). *Gesture, race, and culture*. The Hague: Mouton.

Ekman, P., & Friesen, W. V. (1977). Nonverbal behavior. In P. F. Ostwald (Ed.), *Communication and social interaction*. New York: Grune and Stratton.

Janik, J. W., Wellens, A. R., Goldberg, M. L., & Dell'oso, L. F. (1978). Eyes as the center of focus in the visual examination of faces. *Perceptual and Motor Skills*, *47*, 857–858.

Knapp, M. L. (1980). *Essentials of nonverbal communication*. New York: Holt, Rinehart, and Winston.

Knapp, M. L. (1978). *Nonverbal communication in human interaction* (2nd ed.). New York: Holt, Rinehart and Winston.

Knapp, M. L., Hart, R. P., and Friedrich, G. W. (1973). Verbal and nonverbal correlates of human leave-taking. *Communication Monographs*, *40*, 182–198.

Leathers, D. G. (1986). *Successful nonverbal communication: Principles and applications*. New York: Macmillan.

Leathers, D. G., & Emigh, T. H. (1980). Decoding facial expressions: A new test with decoding norms. *Quarterly Journal of Speech*, *66*, 418–436.

References

1. This generalization applies particularly to adults; children tend to rely more on verbal cues. See J. K. Burgoon (1985), Nonverbal signals. In M. L. Knapp & G. R. Miller, Eds. *Handbook of interpersonal communication.* (p. 347). Newbury Park, CA: Sage Publications.

2. Leathers, D. G. (1986). *Successful nonverbal communication: Principles and applications.* New York: Macmillan.

3. Burgoon, p. 375.

4. Ekman, P., & Friesen, W. V. (1977). Nonverbal behavior. In P. F. Ostwald (Ed.), *Communication and social interaction,* (pp. 37–46). New York: Grune and Stratton.

5. See Leathers D. G., & Emigh, T. H. (1980). Decoding facial expressions: A new test with decoding norms. *Quarterly Journal of Speech, 66,* 418–436.

6. Darwin, C. (1872). *The expression of emotions in man and animals.* London: Murray.

7. Ekman, P., & Friesen, W. (1971). Constants across cultures in the face and emotions. *Journal of Personality and Social Psychology, 17,* 124–129; and Ekman and Friesen, (1977). Nonverbal behavior, pp. 37–46.

8. Janik, J. W., Wellens, A. R., Goldberg, M. L., and L. F. Dell'oso, (1978). Eyes as the center of focus in the visual examination of faces. *Perceptual and Motor Skills, 47,* 857–858.

9. Birdwhistell, R. (1970). *Kinesics and context.* Philadelphia: University of Pennsylvania Press.

10. Ekman, P., & Friesen, W. (1972). Hand movements. *Journal of Communication, 22,*353–374

11. See Knapp, M. L. (1978). *Nonverbal communication in human interation* (2nd ed.), p. 298.

12. Knapp, M. L., Hart, R. P., Friedrich, G. W., & Shulman, G. M. (1973). The rhetoric of goodbye: Verbal and nonverbal correlates of human leave-taking. *Speech Monographs, 40,* 182–198.

13. Ekman, P., & Friesen, W. (1972), p. 362.

14. Hall, E. T. (1959). *The silent language.* New York: Doubleday; see esp. Ch. 10, "Space speaks," pp. 146–164; Hall's views on proxemics are developed more fully in E. T. Hall (1966). *The hidden dimension.* Garden City, NY: Doubleday.

15. Hall, E. T. (1959), see Ch. 9, "Time talks, American accents," pp. 128–145.

16. Zimmerman, M. (1985). *How to do business with the Japanese* (p. 27). New York: Random House.

Interviewing

7

CHAPTER

After studying this chapter, you should be able to:

1. Describe the communication characteristics of interviews.

2. Understand problems of communication in interviews.

3. Understand the principles of preparing for conducting interviews.

4. Prepare for organizing parts of interviews, wording questions, and recording information.

5. Prepare for specific types of interviews, such as information-gathering interviews, selection interviews, and appraisal interviews.

6. Understand how to avoid legal entanglements in interviewing.

Overview

Thousands of interviews are conducted in businesses everyday. For example, corporations and other organizations select their employees and associates on the basis of interviews. Candidates may be from outside or inside the company and may have to face a panel of interviewers or survive a series of interviews. Once the successful candidate enters the corporation, she or he enters a world in which interviews are conducted constantly: Informational interviews convey corporate policies and procedures; review and appraisal interviews assess progress at regular intervals; information-gathering interviews, sales interviews, and even exit interviews serve other purposes.

As people climb the corporate ladder and become supervisors or managers, they begin conducting interviews: hiring or selection interviews, grievance interviews, reprimand interviews, exit interviews and, perhaps, even dismissal interviews. Add specialized interviews such as those conducted by newspaper, radio, and television news organizations to the number of interviews regularly conducted in businesses, and it becomes clear that the total is astronomical. Interviews go on all around us on an ongoing basis. One popular textbook in the field of communication argues that interviews are the most "common form of purposeful, planned communication."[1]

▶ *Interviews are widespread settings for communication in most organizations.*

Another measure of the interview's importance is the effect on the individual. Interviews are vital to the individual's career success. Selection interviews, after all, are at the heart of the hiring process. Moreover, many corporations use selection-type interviews for internal placement and advancement. Employees are evaluated and rated for a variety of reasons including salary and promotions, based on information from regular appraisal interviews. In many ways, interviews have a pervasive effect on one's career.

This chapter covers the main steps in the process of preparing for interviews. In so doing, we discuss the following aspects of interviewing:

Characteristics
Problems
General preparation
Specific preparation

◀▶ CHARACTERISTICS OF INTERVIEWING

Broadly speaking, interviews involve the exchange of information in order to accomplish some task or purpose. Sometimes, information gathering is the major purpose of one of the participants in an interview: for example, when getting information about the qualifications of a potential employee, information to make a decision, or information to construct a presentation. Conversely, some interviews are aimed to convey information. Informing employees about new procedures or policies may be accomplished through an interview form.

An interview is defined as "a semistructured, purposeful communication activity, usually involving two parties, who exchange ideas and information while focusing on a preconceived and specific topic."[2] The interview is a purposeful and planned communication event in which two people talk and listen. Interviews are said to be "purposeful" to distinguish them from casual conversation. Typically, they are subject to more careful planning than conversations, as well.

Although interviews are purposeful, or task oriented, they have much in common with conversation as well as with more structured communication activities, such as decision-making groups, presentations, and speeches. Many characteristics of the verbal and nonverbal communication in interviews reflect their interpersonal nature. Usually, two people sit closer together and more senses come into play than would be the case for speaker and audience at a formal presentation. Facial expression is more easily perceived and responded to at the typical interviewing distance.

The interpersonal nature of the interview situation can be further explained by describing several important characteristics of the communication in interviews:

1. *Interviews involve dyads.* An interview almost always involves two participants. Although some selection interviews may involve a panel of interviewers, these situations are relatively infrequent. This dyadic nature of the interview is one of the most obvious differences between the interview and other structured forms of business or professional communication.

Since the number of individuals in a communication situation is reduced to two, the factors that influence the success or failure increase. In a speech, the speaker can aim at the average of an audience and not worry too much about the individuals who might be missed. In an interview, however, there is an audience of one, so the audience analysis must be very specific. As the number of participants decreases, moreover, ability to analyze the audience and predict specific behaviors or reactions decreases. Compared with more informal or casual conversations, involvement obligations are high for participants. The interview requires the active and effective participation of both participants for it to succeed.

2. *Communication in interviews is transactional* (see Fig. 7-1). The nature of an interview stresses simultaneous rather than linear communication. As the questions are asked, the interviewee's nonverbal response may be nearly instantaneous. A smile may indicate pleasure or agreement. A nod of the head may indicate understanding. A raise of the eyebrow may indicate confusion.

Roles in this situation change continually. The two individuals talk and listen alternately. The expectation is that each individual in the process will both ask questions and answer questions. Information is given by answering; information is gathered by asking questions. In an interview, feedback is instantaneous. In the public speech, the speaker receives some feedback from the audience. Unless the

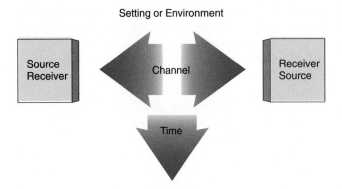

▶ **Figure 7-1**   *A transactional model of the elements and relationships in communication.*

audience reacts very strongly, the effects of the feedback may be minor. Few audiences expect immediate responses to feedback. In the interview, however, feedback is instantaneous and a response is expected. The typical pattern is circular. Source becomes listener and then goes back to source.

3. *Communication is both structured (planned) and spontaneous.* An interview agenda as well as questions and possible responses are planned and often rehearsed. Unpredictable questions and unanticipated responses are possible and even likely. Less planning magnifies the potential for vagueness or confusion, which increases the necessity for clarifying questions. In such a freewheeling atmosphere, an interview cannot be as carefully organized as a formal presentation.

On the other hand, communication in interviews has the advantage of spontaneity. In many interviews, digressions are necessary and even planned. Instead of a question and answer sequence in which one person consistently asks questions from a prepared list and the other person answers those questions, many interviews take the form of response followed by response.

4. *Nonverbal messages are magnified.* In the interview situation, proximity heightens the importance of nonverbal communication and increases the number of messages being conveyed. In an interview, two individuals talk and listen alternately, while nonverbal messages are exchanged simultaneously.

Proximity also means that socioemotional cues are highly evident. Interviews are useful in discovering participants' attitudes and feelings. Consequently, interviews allow us to address personal needs or problems effectively and allow for social support to be established and developed. The socioemotional nature of interviews can have negative effects, though. The personal nature of the communication increases the potential for risk. The interview may be seen as more threatening by one or both of the participants and thus more defensive communication may result.

In summary, these characteristics of the interview situation derive from the nature of human communication, as described in Chapter 1 and from the special one-on-one nature of the interview. Interestingly, communication with one person often may be more difficult than that with an audience.

PROBLEMS OF INTERVIEWING

Obviously, communication in an interview can break down just as can any other kind of interpersonal communication. Some of the typical causes of communication breakdown were already discussed in Chapter 3. This section, however, brings to attention some problems specific to interviewing.

Lack of Empathy

Empathy, or its absence, is important in all forms of interpersonal communication. For example, one common purpose of communication is therapeutic, in which people tell each other their problems. In many cases, counselors are expected to do more than just listen; they are expected to give advice, as described in the section on empathic listening in Chapter 3.

As long as people have problems, managers, supervisors, and coworkers will find themselves in counseling-like situations. One of the key attributes needed by people in such counseling settings is empathy. When the nonempathetic listeners confront another person's problem, they might respond with "Oh, don't worry. You're exaggerating."

A simple classroom exercise illustrates both the cues that communicate lack of empathy and the effects of lack of empathy. Two students are paired off for a conversation. One is instructed to discuss a personally important topic; the other individual is instructed to convey disinterest. Usually, the receiver knows how to signal apathy, such as by gazing off into space, folding the arms, rolling the eyes, and even yawning. Even in such an artificial situation, the first speaker usually feels disheartened, frustrated, threatened, and angry.

Although the classroom exercise artificially creates a feeling of indifference, in many cases, lack of empathy is not calculated nor malicious. Lack of empathy springs from a variety of related characteristics connected with how information is processed by human beings. First, lack of accurate knowledge or ignorance of the facts or the reasons behind certain behavior can cause lack of empathy. If we miss an appointment with our supervisor because we forget, we are judged to be more "at fault" than if we missed it because of our mother's illness. Facts about the context make empathy more likely. Second, we can lack empathy because our experiences are not similar to the other person's. Cultural differences are an obvious example of dissimilar experiences that impede empathy. Third, perception of status and power differences can make empathetic relations more difficult. It is sometimes hard for people to put themselves in the place of someone of far higher or lower status or power. Characteristically, nonempathic listeners evaluate a problem or situation only from their own perspective.

▶ **Defensiveness**

A defensive climate is one in which one of the participants in the communication feels threatened by the proceedings. As just indicated, a lack of empathy on the part of the interviewer can lead to the interviewee's feeling defensive. This is more likely to be the case when the interviewee perceives as a potential outcome of the interview some kind of action that will be detrimental to him or her. Often, such a perception is present in those cases in which the interviewee feels that he or she is being evaluated or judged. We all tend to experience evaluative situations as threatening to some extent. A defensive interviewee, one who feels threatened, will often become uncooperative or unusually argumentative and may even refuse to participate in the interview.

Frequently, a lack of empathy evokes defensive behaviors by the respondent or interviewee. When dealing with high-status or high-power individuals, a subordinate may adapt strategies designed to please the superior. When the respondent feels manipulated, trapped, or threatened, he or she becomes more defensive or argumentative. One manifestation of defensive communication is an over-willingness to satisfy the interviewer. Some people do not like to disappoint or to confront conflict. The true "yes-sayer" assumes that the only appropriate answer to any question is "yes." Of course, the high-power individual can be defensive also and exhibit defensive communication. A supervisor, for example, who is forced to convey bad news concerning a layoff or other cutbacks represents such a case.

▶ **Bias and Premature Judgment**

Related to a lack of empathy is the problem of bias. Bias is any unreasoned prejudice or opposition based on arbitrary judgment or choice. Unrecognized bias is dangerous. For example, individuals are attracted to those who are like themselves or whom they perceive to share similar key values or characteristics; this factor is termed *homophily*. Interviewers are no exception to this tendency. Interviewers tend to evaluate or rate those whom they perceive to be like themselves more highly than those whom they perceive as dissimilar.

If uncorrected, this tendency to select candidates based on similarity could have serious consequences. In the evaluation interview, unrecognized bias could result in different evaluations (and raises) for individuals whose work-related performance is similar. In selection or employment interviews, the interviewer may subconsciously evaluate one candidate as better than another based, not on potential performance or competence, but on compatibility. Frequently, biases proceed from the way that humans process information. We tend to form impressions of others on the basis of very limited information.

In addition, humans are quick to evaluate. When we meet people for the first time, we form impressions based on their physical appearance and their apparent character. Based upon those preliminary impressions, we evaluate them as well. We may decide whether they are competent or not, nice, and likable. We use incomplete impressions to form judgments that are complete: that is, whole or entire individual profiles.

When we reason and make judgments based on a few examples or little information, we commit the error known as hasty generalization or premature judgment. Further, the problem of premature evaluation is compounded by another problem: Once we form impressions, those impressions are resistant to change. All of the problems connected with premature evaluation would not be a problem if humans reasoned well and their first impressions were accurate. Unfortunately, first impressions are often wrong.

Employment or selection interviews exemplify the tendency of communicators to make dangerous "snap" judgments. Selection interviewers frequently make decisions based upon impressions formed in the first few minutes of an interview. This judgment then becomes the basis for processing and interpreting other information gathered during the interview. Information that supports the first impression, for example, is interpreted by the interviewer as "the rule"; information that questions the interviewer's previous (or biased) impression is dismissed as "the exception."

Inadequate Planning

Effective communication usually requires planning. While most communicators assume that giving a major speech or presentation requires planning, few consider that the audience spends a great deal of time preparing. At most, audience members might review writings or other information about the speaker or topic. As communicators, we must, however, take care to avoid approaching an interview in the same way that we might approach being a part of an audience for a speech.

In some cases, inadequate planning for an interview results from inadequate training, and many interviewers have no formal training. Many corporations also lack rigorous procedures or guidelines for conducting interviews. In other cases, inadequate planning springs from overconfidence on the part of the interviewers or interviewees concerning their ability to communicate. The interviewer might argue, "I talk with people all the time. After all, an interview is just talking. Besides, I know who would fit in at this company." Or the interviewee might rationalize, "Hey, I'm good at shooting the bull. I've been talking all my life." As noted earlier, an interview is semistructured. An interviewer has to balance spontaneity and structure or to go from conversation to the carefully planned interview structure.

Whatever reason for the lack of it, interview preparation is in some ways harder than that for a public speech because the situation is less predictable. Recall the earlier mention of this in regard to interview characteristics. In a presentation, the roles are clear: One individual is the speaker who stands up and provides information; the rest of the participants are audience members, who sit quietly and listen. Remember that predicting the response of one specific individual is trickier than predicting the average or general response of a group.

A complex activity, such as communication during an interview, works best if both parties understand the expected purpose and processes so that they can adopt the appropriate strategies and techniques. Potential confusion over purpose is especially likely if there are several purposes for the interview. A selection interview, for example, contains a variety of purposes for both the interviewer and the interviewee. The interviewee may think that his or her main goal is to get the job and may lose sight of a preliminary question: Do I want a job in this particular corporation? If the interviewee concentrates on getting the job or getting the second interview, opportunities to ask questions about the organizational climate and the corporate culture could be lost. The person may get the job and only too late discover that there were some important questions that should have been asked.

Confusion over the goals and purposes of communication are a constant source of communication problems. In an interview, both the interviewer and the interviewee must be aware of the purposes of the interview. Once both know the purposes, then both can organize their answers and questions.

Lack of Adequate Feedback

In any interpersonal communication, feedback is a defining characteristic. Feedback serves a variety of functions. In an interview, verbal and nonverbal feedback is vital in the question and answer format. After all, many of the questions that one decides to ask depend on answers previously received. Limited feedback restricts gaining the information needed to allow for effective communication.

Feedback may be restricted because of a lack of empathy or interest on the part of one participant. For example, one person may perceive some threat in the situation and so not really think about providing the necessary kind of feedback. You may recall the example of the bank manager, in the discussion of listening barriers in Chapter 3, who felt that his people did not really listen to any part of their work evaluations until he got to the "bottom line." The text discussion has already noted that the nonverbal feedback in a face-to-face interview may be misleading for cultural or related reasons.

Highlights of Interviewing Problems.   In summary, then, problems in interviewing can result from some of the following conditions: (1) lack of empathy, (2) defensiveness, (3) bias or premature judgment, (4) lack of adequate planning, or (5) lack of appropriate feedback. In order to overcome or at least ameliorate some of these problems, one needs to understand some of the principles of preparing for interviews, which is taken up in the next section. Preparation helps to ensure proper planning and helps participants to put themselves in the frame of mind to avoid some of the pitfalls noted here.

PRINCIPLES OF PREPARING FOR INTERVIEWS

When preparing for and participating in interviews, the special characteristics and problems of the interview should be kept in mind. Recall that an interview is less structured than a formal presentation but more structured than simple conversation.

Planning, as mentioned earlier, is vital to success of the interview. Although neither participant in the interview has complete control of the success or failure of the interview, both participants must analyze their roles and prepare as much as possible. The following principles of planning apply specifically to the interviewing process:

- Establish goals and purposes.
- Analyze the other person in the interview.
- Analyze the climate, or psychological setting.
- Analyze the physical setting.
- Gather and select information.
- Determine the amount of structure for the interview.
- Consider potential problems.

1. *Establish goals and purposes.* Planning for any communication should start with a consideration of goals and purposes. Ask yourself what are the goals and possible outcomes of the interview. Each participant needs to determine what is to be accomplished. Essentially, what information do you need as an interviewer or as an interviewee to make a decision or accomplish your goal?

If possible, the objectives should be specified in such a way that they can be observed or measured as objectively as possible. In the employment interview, the interviewer's first purpose is to find a candidate qualified for the position. For the salesperson, the first purpose of a persuasive interview is to make a sale. For a selection interviewer, the first purpose is to find the best available person for a particular opening.

The interviewer should consider what constraints are placed upon his or her ability to gather information. What legal or ethical constraints apply? How is the data to be used, recorded, tabulated, or analyzed? In thinking about interview outcomes, the interviewer needs to think in terms of how the results or the answers will be recorded or presented later. If the information is to be presented as statistical data, the questions need to be framed especially carefully to allow for putting the answers into tabular or statistical form.

Once a primary purpose for the interview has been established and some of these preliminary concerns have been considered, the participants should consider additional goals. For example, the persuasive or sales interviewer and employment interviewer want to create good will for themselves and their corporation in addition to accomplishing the primary goal of persuading, selling, or hiring.

Determining goals and purposes suggests what topics will be covered, what questions will be asked, and even the chosen environment. Considering the purpose allows both interviewer and interviewee to do everything possible to maximize the chances for success and minimize the opportunities for failure. For the interviewer, this part of planning should suggest the line of questions to be followed, and the interviewer should write out a list of topics to be covered.

2. *Analyze the other person in the interview (audience analysis).* In an interview, one other person usually constitutes our audience. Each participant should learn as much as possible about the other, within reasonable limits. Consider such elements as the other's motives for the interview, perspectives, and, when possible,

something of his or her background and reference groups: that is, the groups or organizations that inform his or her beliefs, attitudes, or values, to the extent that they might have a bearing on the interview.

In the employment interview, the interviewer usually has a resume which provides information about the candidate. The candidate or interviewee can find information about the corporation, if not the interviewer, from a variety of sources. At a minimum, such preparation provides knowledge about the other's frame of reference and can create understanding empathy for the other participant.

3. *Analyze the climate or psychological setting.* The communication climate refers to the subjective perceptions that each participant has regarding the atmosphere for the interview, for example, tense or relaxed, tightly controlled or free-wheeling, friendly or hostile, warm or cold, and so on. Both the selection and the appraisal interview can produce stress or defensive communication. Dealing with personal problems of the interviewee is stressful. Dismissal interviews or disciplinary interviews can obviously be high-stress situations, as well.

4. *Analyze the physical setting.* If you, as the interviewer, have control over the environment, you can select a room or environment to enhance the communication effectiveness in the interview. The location, size and shape of the room, or its design can suggest a formal or informal setting. In an office setting, ask yourself how the room is laid out. Is there a desk or table between the participants, and, if so, how far apart are they? If there is a physical barrier, the communication situation is seen as more formal, or as more distant and potentially threatening. Be especially aware of potential distractions. In one reported situation, for example, a supervisor oriented his desk with his back to a western-facing window. Late in the day, any interviewee is forced to stare into the sun, with the result that employees used any excuse to avoid later afternoon interviews.

Time and social setting can indicate appropriate behaviors, including dress and formality or informality. Is the interview connected with a social event such as lunch or cocktails? Is it in a restaurant or at the corporate headquarters? Is it held late or early in the day? Such information provides nonverbal cues about the appropriate messages and potential barriers or problems.

Sensitivity to these factors of the setting could be particularly important for intercultural settings. Chapter 1 indicated that in different cultures there may be different perceptions of what is appropriate or fitting for a particular kind of setting. Chapter 1 also outlined the problem of the person who wanted to talk business with his Japanese colleagues at the dinner they had arranged to welcome him. Outright discussions of business would be seen as inappropriate for this kind of occasion from the Japanese point of view.

Finally, consider how much time is available for the interview. If you have a short period, how can you cover the questions and topics efficiently? Do you need to limit the topics to be covered?

5. *Gather and select information needed for conducting the interview.* The purpose of the interview should suggest the kind of information that you need to gather in advance. If it is to be a selection interview, you need to review the requirements for the position and the resumes of the candidates. If you are the candidate in a selection interview, recall that you need to review information about the organization and the position sought.

After you have reviewed your goals, decide what specific information you need to accomplish the purpose. If you need to do some research, how and when can you do that? Prior to the interview? Through reviewing a resume? Or would this step be accomplished most efficiently by asking and answering questions? Perhaps other people have recently interacted with the other participant in another interview or relevant setting. Could you talk with these people to get a better feel for what you might expect in your interview?

6. *Determine the amount of structure for the interview.* The next question to be answered concerns the level of structure for the interview. Structure can be thought of as high, moderate, or low. In the highly scheduled, or structured, interview, all questions are planned in advance and carefully worded and organized. Such planning is appropriate when there is a need for comparability across several interviews.

Certain interview situations demand high scheduling in order to establish validity and reliability: The data gathered must effectively measure what it claims to measure and the data from several interviews must be comparable. Opinion polling (such as the famous Gallup Poll) represents this kind of situation. Certain types of specialized information gathering interviews also fall into this category: health information collected by the pharmaceutical industry as part of drug-testing processes, for instance. Highly scheduled interviews are also good for selection interviews when specific comparisons of candidates are desirable. Problem-solving or persuasive interviews or counseling interviews, on the other hand, typically have less need for so much structure.

Another way to think of structure is how directed or controlled the interview should be. The directive versus nondirective dimension stresses the level of control exercised by the interviewer. Directive is highly controlled; nondirective is less controlled. The most common technique for exercising control is exhibited in the type of question used: Open-ended questions are associated with a nondirective approach and closed questions with a directive approach. When we discuss open-ended versus closed questions below, criteria for using one or the other approach are covered there as well.

Organization and structure in an interview depend on the needs of the situation. Interviews that have high needs for validity and reliability such as selection, appraisal, and certain information-gathering interviews require more control and structure than others.

7. *Consider potential problems.* Obviously, the general problems of all interviews discussed in the previous section should be considered. In addition, each specific interview type has problems particular to that type. We have seen, for example, that appraisal interviews (such as one's annual performance review) are prone to defensiveness and restricted feedback. The selection interview seems

Interview Planning Form

1. What type of interview (selection, disciplinary, exit or other) is it?
2. What are your objective(s) for this interview?
   A. Primary objective.
   B. Secondary objective.
   C. Other secondary objective.
   (For example, in a selection interview, my primary objective is to hire the best candidate for the job. One secondary objective is to leave all candidates with a favorable impression of the organization.)
3. What do you know about the interviewee?
   A. What are his or her objectives?
   B. What other factors may be important?
      1. (Education, experience, or training)
      2. (Recommendations and references)
      3. (Communication and interpersonal skills)
4. What will be the setting or environment for the interview?
   A. When? In relation to what other relevant activities?
   B. Where?
   C. Who should be present?
   D. What climate and tone should you set?
5. What information do you need?
   A. About the situation?
   B. About the process or procedure (including legal questions)?
6. What is your opening?
   A. Greeting and placing at ease
   B. Orientation, motivation
   C. Purposes, benefits, outcomes of the interview
7. What is your general approach?
   A. Question areas?
      1. Topic one.
      2. Topic two.
      3. Topic three.
   B. Organization (such as funnel, problem-solution)?
8. What is your closing?
   A. Summary
   B. What happens next, outcomes, reporting

prone to problems of bias and premature judgment. Solutions to the problems of interviewing will be discussed under the discussion of types of interviews later in this chapter. Increasingly, interviewers need to be aware of certain legal requirements deriving from Equal Employment Opportunity legislation and from Civil Rights legislation and regulations. An interviewer should be familiar with the law and how it applies to specific questions that can and cannot be asked.

As an aid to planning for interviews, consider using a planning form such as the one reproduced on page 212:

Highlights of Principles of Preparing for Interviews. As we suggest throughout the book, planning is vital to communication, and the interview is no exception. Systematic preparation for an interview begins with goals and purposes. Then analyze the other person, the climate, and the physical setting to determine the other person's point of view or expectations and how the setting can contribute to your goals. After careful analysis, information relevant to the purposes of the interview should be selected and organized. Finally, consider any problems that could arise.

ORGANIZING FOR THE INTERVIEW

Now let us turn to a discussion of the parts of a typical interview. As the diagram on page 214 shows (see Figure 7.2), each interview consists of an introduction, body, and conclusion. Some feedback or followup should normally occur relatively soon after the end of the interview.

Opening the Interview

The first part of the interview, which can be thought of as equivalent to the introduction of a speech, is calculated to introduce the structure and procedure for the interview. Normally, this part performs the following functions:

1. *Establish a relationship or rapport.* In general, when we meet people for the first time, we attempt to break the ice and put them at ease. A handshake, greeting, and appropriate small talk about such things as the weather, mutual friends or hobbies, indicate an interest in the other person as an individual.

2. *Introduce the purpose and organization to be followed in the interview.* Appropriately, the interviewer should provide an overview of purpose, organization, expectations, and procedures that will be followed. In any interview, such goals and expectations can be the subject of discussion or negotiation between interviewer and interviewee. Communication in a persuasive interview (such as in sales, for example) may be more relevant if the salesperson understands potential opposition or concerns of the client, which can be brought out in these preliminary stages.

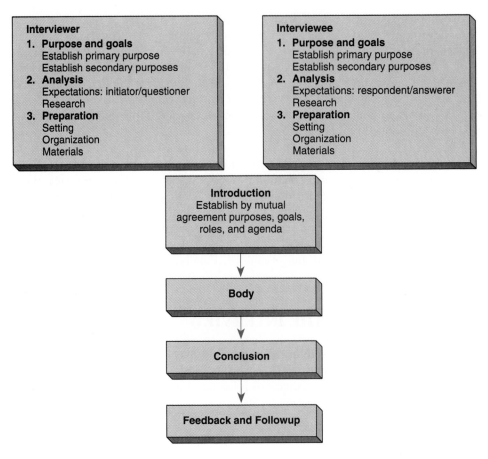

▶ **Figure 7-2**   *The overall plan for an interview.*

3. *Provide orientation and motivation for participation in the interview.* Basically, one needs to be sure that both individuals know what's in it for them. When conducting information-gathering interviews, it may be especially important to provide some incentive for the interviewee to provide the information sought. In addition, as mentioned earlier, communication may be facilitated if participants know important related information, such as how the information derived from the interview will be used to help either or both participants reach certain goals.

The interviewer is mainly responsible for seeing that the opening meets these needs: that is, establishes appropriate rapport, introduces the topics and procedures for the interview, and provides some orientation and motivation to achieve the best level of participation from the interviewee.

Body of the Interview

Once the preliminaries are accomplished, the body of the interview begins. Here, the questions and answers constitute the critical part of the communication process. The text begins by briefly indicating different ways to provide overall structure to the interview and then turns to the process of selecting and wording questions.

Organizing the Body of the Interview.   Most interviews can be thought of as following no more than five organizational patterns, or question sequences, for the body of an interview.

   1. *Funnel, or general to specific.* In the funnel sequence, the interviewer asks a series of open-ended or general questions and then proceeds to the closed or more specific questions. (The distinctions between these types of questions are further discussed in the next section.) Such a sequence allows the interviewee more freedom of expression at the beginning of the situation.

   2. *Inverted funnel, or specific to general.* The inverted funnel sequence is the reverse of the funnel sequence. The interviewer asks a series of closed or specific questions followed by open-ended or general questions later in the interview. At the start of the interview, the interviewer exercises tight control. As the interview develops, the respondent is allowed more freedom of expression.

   3. *The tunnel, or string.* The tunnel sequence uses all open-ended or all closed questions, or, in other words, all questions of the same type. When interviewee

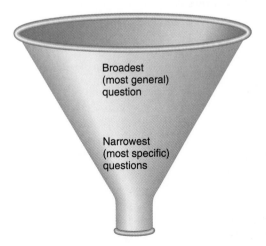

▶ **Figure 7-3**   *Drawing of funnel organization for an interview: general questions to more specific questions.*

▶ **Figure 7-4**   *Drawing of inverted funnel organization for an interview: specific questions to general questions.*

openness and freedom is appropriate and sought by the interviewer, such as in a counselling situation, the open-ended sequence is used. When control is desired, such as in an information-gathering interview, then a sequence consisting of all closed questions might be desirable.

4. *Topical.* When the interviewer has a list of points or topics to be covered, frequently organization of the question sequence is determined by topics rather than by question type. For example, in a marketing survey, you may wish to discuss

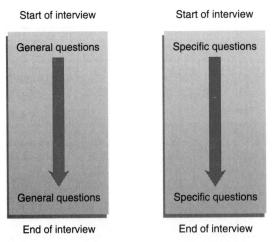

▶ **Figure 7-5**   *Examples of tunnel organizational format.*

the topics of price, convenience of use, comparison with other products, and so on. A list of topics is thus covered by the interviewer; each topic is completed before proceeding to the next.

5. *Problem solution.* In problem solving, or in some persuasive interviews, the problem solution format may be appropriate. The question sequence, therefore, aims at taking the interviewee through a full consideration of the problems and its ramifications before taking up a consideration of the possible solutions and their various advantages and disadvantages.

Types of Questions in the Body of the Interview.   This section considers each type of question typical of different interview situations and discusses the uses and limitations of each.

1. *Closed questions versus open questions.* Closed questions are used when a specific and limited answer is required. For example, what is your current address? How many years have you been at WeWA, Limited? Open questions, on the other hand, allow the interviewee to choose what kind and how much information to provide. An open question would be, "Tell me about your last job."
Closed questions are best to accomplish certain goals:

- Classify. For example, are you a member of a professional association?
- Determine agreement or disagreement. For example, do you find it inconvenient to have both PCs and Macintoshes in the workplace?

Other benefits of closed questions include their perceived lower threat level. Closed questions require less effort to answer: "Yes" or "no" is easy. More importantly, closed questions decrease the level of threat by keeping the amount of personal revelation low. Finally, a series of closed questions allows control for the interviewer since a large number of questions can be asked in a short period of time, and answers can be tabulated easily and quickly.
The benefits of closed questions are similar to their weaknesses, however. If a series of close-ended questions are asked, the respondent talks very little. Closed questions usually provide less information than open-ended questions do. Consequently, the open-ended question is more appropriate in those cases in which the interviewer seeks more insight into the person of the interviewee. The open-ended question can provide a lot of information and, especially, a lot of personal information about the interviewee. Of course, open-ended questions have limitations as well: The answers may be relatively hard to record, to compare with other answers, or to analyze in statistical or tabular form.
The following table suggests the appropriate uses for open and closed questions in interviews.
Other question types can be selected for other purposes.

2. *Primary versus secondary questions.* This dimension distinguishes between questions that introduce new areas or topics and questions that ask for further

▶ **Table 7-1**   *When to Use Open-Ended and Closed Questions*

Use Open-Ended Questions When:	*Use Closed Questions When:*
• Goal is to discover feelings.	• Goal is to discover specific facts.
• Rapport and trust are low.	• Rapport and trust are high.
• Ideas of respondent seem unclear.	• Ideas seem clear.
• Positions of respondent are unclear.	• Positions of respondent are clear.
• Interviewer is unsure of type information respondent has.	• Interviewer is sure of information.
• There is no time limit.	• There is a time limit.
• Interviewer is skilled.	• Interviewer is unskilled.
• Respondent talks freely.	• Respondent does not talk freely.
• Strength of emotion is important.	• Strength of emotion is unimportant.
• Recording of answers is unimportant.	• Recording is less important.
• Comparison with other interviews is not important.	• Comparison is more important.

information or followup. Secondary or followup questions are also called probes. Probes can be hypothetical: "What would you do if the product were not available?" Hypothetical probes are designed to discover how the respondent would respond to different circumstances. Probes can also be confrontational: "Doesn't that seem inconsistent with what you said earlier about down-time?" Confrontational probes should probably be avoided in situations in which the interviewer is trying to develop openness or build trust, because they can seem argumentative and may provoke defensiveness. Reactive probes, the third type, are simple requests for the respondent's response to an existing state of affairs: "How do you feel about this situation?" They are more neutral in tone than confrontational probes.

    3. *Direct questions versus indirect questions.* There is a distinction between questions whose point is apparent and questions not obviously on the specific point or for which the use of the answer is not straightforward. The distinction may be important if a direct question could threaten the respondent. If the threat is potentially high and could result in defensive behavior, the indirect question might be successful where the direct question would not be. Indirect questions may often take the form of asking for more information or clarification. "What do you see as your options in this situation?" (indirect) versus "Are you planning to resign now?" (direct).

    4. *Restatements.* Restatements may not necessarily be in the form of a question. They rephrase or echo an answer to clarify that answer or to check the accuracy of the interviewer's listening or understanding. Such questions are frequently phrased as follows: "Can we summarize this point in this way . . . ?", or, "Am I correct to understand that you mean . . . ?"

Wording Questions.   The next concern is wording of interview questions: that is, the language to be used. Not all questions, of course, can be planned out in detail. Still, it is useful to work out some specific questions that deal with the main topics or introduce the main subjects that you wish to cover.

The following are criteria for effective questions:

1. *Clarity.* To gather accurate and complete information, questions should be clear. Word choice influences clarity. For example, concrete and specific language evokes a more specific response than general and vague language does. Contrast these questions: "Are these your things?" versus "Who is the owner of the contents of this suitcase?" The second question is more likely to provide the specific information sought; the vague reference to "things" in the first question could refer to "things" in your pocket, handbag, and so on.

Appropriateness of vocabulary is also important to clarity. Analyze the participant in an interview. What level of vocabulary is appropriate for the respondent? Is the language you might use with a professional colleague too complex or too technical?

2. *Answerability and relevance.* Questions should be phrased so that they can be answered by the respondent. Effective audience analysis is important. For example, does the interviewee have access to the information required to answer the question? If not, the question is a waste of time. Moreover, the questioner should consider whether or not the answerer can ethically speak about the matter. Questions that violate legal or ethical codes should be avoided. A candidate for employment should not be asked questions that would not be legitimate employment requirements (concerning, say, physical differences between the sexes when there is no relevant job requirement).

The last section of this chapter focuses on the legal requirements regarding interviewing. Refer to that section for principles about wording questions in order to avoid charges of discrimination on the basis of sex, age, physical disability, national origin, race, or religion.

3. *Emotional climate.* Questions should create the proper tone or atmosphere for the interview. In most cases, the climate should encourage free and open responses. Effective questions should be nonthreatening and supportive. Loaded questions such as, "How could you make such a stupid decision?" are calculated to bring out a defensive response.

On the other hand, questions can help to create a supportive environment. Questions that indicate a willingness to listen or a concern for the interviewee could increase the effectiveness of the interaction. "I would be very interested in hearing more about how you have handled similar problems in the past," for example, could indicate such a willingness to listen.

4. *Simplicity.* Questions should be brief and simple to the extent possible and reasonable, given the subject matter. Long, complex, questions should be avoided if an accurate, clear answer is desired. "Should we close the Akron plant?" versus "In view of the economic conditions and prospects for international negotiations pending in the coming fiscal year, should there be some consideration to downward revision in the number of plants in our corporation, such as the one in Akron?" The second question could lead the answerer off on a number of tangential directions, if not just confuse the respondent.

Recording Information.   A final concern is how best to record the information gathered during the interview. The most common type of recording devices are pencil and paper. Other alternatives are memory and electronic recording devices such as video or audio tapes. Each method has advantages and disadvantages.

Paper and pencil methods are widely used because summary and followup are facilitated by written notes. Pencil and paper can interfere with spontaneity in the interview, especially in counseling, in which openness and acceptance are encouraged. Moreover, interviewers may be forced to ask for repetition or to spend their time and concentration writing rather than listening and responding.

Memory can be very useful in situations where recording equipment or pen and paper are inappropriate or unavailable. Counseling settings are excellent examples of such situations. Relying on memory also has problems, however. Detail and facts are likely lost. If the interviewer has to wait before recording the interview or if the material is complex, memory will not work as well.

Finally, the interview can be recorded electronically. Electronic recording is the most accurate and, if video tape is used, both verbal and nonverbal communication can be retained and later evaluated. Of course, electronic materials are costly to transcribe accurately. Pencil and paper allows for a running commentary on the interview that could only be provided retroactively with a recording. Of course, it is possible to combine both electronic and written recordings of the interview.

Bear in mind that written comments may be used as evidence in proceedings dealing with charges of discrimination. On the positive side, written notes may support the interviewer's claim that only legitimate concerns were discussed or considered in the interview. On the negative side, written notes can be used to imply discriminatory actions. For example, one plaintiff successfully showed that he had been the victim of age discrimination. Written interview summaries included notation of each applicant's age and references to other candidates' "high energy level." The court found these comments suggested that age was a factor in the selection process.[3] Written notes, therefore, should be stated in neutral and objective terms and should relate to actual job criteria.

▶ ## Closing the Interview

The final portion of the interview consists of the closing, in which the interviewer hopes to wrap up the interview and leave the interviewee in a proper frame of mind. The closing normally comprises the following parts:

1. *Summary*. The summary consists of a review of the major points and a review of what was decided, including additional topics and information. This process should allow for feedback from either participant. The format is still question and answer, but the purpose is to correct or add to the material that was discussed. In some cases, additional information or even additional significant topics will be discovered in the closing.

2. *Arrangement for followup*. The conclusion of an interview should clarify what will happen next and what is expected of each participant after the interview is completed. Usually an interview will be followed by three other events: The information and data should be analyzed; some decision is made; and some feedback is provided for the interviewee. (At a minimum, the concerned individuals should be notified about what happened.)

3. *Formal conclusion*. In its simplest form, this part of the closing consists of simple ritual. The participants rise, shake hands, thank each other for participating, and wish each other "good bye" or "good day."

PREPARING FOR SPECIFIC TYPES OF INTERVIEWS

This section describes specific types of interviews in more detail. For each type, information is provided about goals (for interviewer and interviewee, where appropriate), problems, and techniques that should be used. The types of interviews covered include:

- Information-gathering
- Selection, or employment
- Evaluation, or work appraisal
- Counseling
- Disciplinary
- Grievance
- Exit
- Dismissal

Information Gathering

As suggested before, all interviews involve the giving or gathering of information, but in some cases the exchange of information is the main purpose for the interview. Journalists interview eyewitnesses, experts, public officials, and celebrities to gain information in order to prepare news stories, articles, and reports. Technical specialists, researchers, and polling organizations collect data for politicians, local, state, and national government or government agencies, retailers, advertisers, and scholars.

Although such specialized interviewing techniques, such as those used for scientific research or polling, are beyond the scope of this book, many business and professional people will on occasion have to gather information through an interview.

When gathering information in any interview setting, there are certain key factors that the interviewer should remember. Many of these factors involve listening techniques that were described in detail in Chapter 3.

1. *Collect the facts.* Whatever type of interview is being conducted, it is useful to collect data concerning the topic during the interview. The most basic type of data derived from such an interview is the descriptive observation.

2. *Separate facts from inferences.* Because of the various problems that occur when humans process information, the interviewer should separate observations and objective materials from reasoning about those observations (as reasonable and appropriate).

3. *Isolate interpretation or evaluation.* The same behavior or action can be evaluated in a variety of ways, depending on the frame of reference of the interviewee.

4. *Compare and contrast with other similar data.* Frequently, information is compiled and sorted into categories. Scientific surveys stress collecting data so that statistical inferences can be made. These needs require standardization, including standard questions and a uniform recording format. People who do polling (political or market research) use highly scheduled question forms, in which the questions must be asked the same way every time for each interviewee; the form usually includes a space or expected response to be circled or marked as the interviewer listens to the interviewee's responses.

5. *Be flexible.* As explained above, one must be prepared to be flexible in recording answers in interviews. Too much emphasis on note-taking could inhibit the free flow of information in an interview. Consider carefully the principles related to recording discussed above.

An important twist regarding informative interviews is that occasionally the interviewer's purpose is to provide information for the interviewee. For example, a manager is called upon to describe to a new employee how to run a turret lathe; a supervisor has to explain his department's computer requirements to the purchasing officer; new company policy has to be explained; or a personnel officer needs to explain steps in filing a claim for sick leave. Every day, interviews are used to convey information, orient new employees, explain steps in a process or task, and describe criteria or job requirements. The techniques for presenting information in this setting are very much like those for making public presentations. These techniques are described in detail in Chapters 10 and 11.

Selection, or Employment

The selection or employment interview is at the center of the selection process. There are some variations of selection interviews, such as screening interviews, hiring interviews, and placement interviews. A screening interview, which can eliminate the clearly unqualified candidates from the pool or select the best, is intended to specify a pool of the most qualified candidates; the hiring interview aims at selecting and employing one acceptable candidate; and the placement interview may be used within the corporation to pick good internal candidates for new positions. These variations are sufficiently similar to allow for discussion of all these forms under the rubric of the employment interview.

The interviewer has a number of purposes:

Discover candidates(s) who are suitable for a job.
Provide the candidates with an accurate picture of job and corporate expectations.
Introduce successful candidates to the corporate culture and climate.
Create good will for the company.
Protect yourself and the corporation from litigation.
Get the best fit between employee and organization.

From the perspective of the interviewee, the purposes include the following:

Determine if you want the job.
Determine if you want to work for this organization.
Discover the corporate expectations and culture.
Discover salary, benefits, and other information.
Present a professional image.
Secure the job.

The importance of communication during the interview seems obvious, for after all, interviewers are being told constantly to look for the ability to communicate well.[4]

As indicated earlier, there are problems specific to the selection interview. The major problems include the tendency toward hasty generalization or judgment, interviewer bias, and potential legal difficulties.

First, there may be a tendency toward hasty generalization on the part of the interviewer. Studies of selection interviews conclude that interviewers often make hiring decisions based on a stereotype of the ideal candidate. Moreover, hiring decisions are made during the first 4 to 7 minutes of the interview. To compensate for potential stereotyping, the interviewer could use the open-question, funnel pattern. The funnel pattern allows the respondents to talk more and to present themselves more fully early in the interview. Applicants who are allowed to talk more and who spend more time in their responses, rather than in answering closed questions, are more successful in making a good impression.[5]

A second and related problem is that of interviewer bias. Interviewer bias is especially significant for evaluating those candidates of average or middle-range ability. Candidates who show very high and very low ability are easily and accurately evaluated, but for candidates in the middle range (usually a majority of the candidates), distinctions are more difficult. The problem of bias is greater and individual perception is more substantially affected, because the differences among these middle-range candidates are less obvious. For evaluating these candidates, similarity of attitudes between interviewer and interviewee, even if not relevant to the job, becomes an important factor in interviewers' evaluation of "average" candidates.[6]

A third kind of problem that can be even more difficult to deal with is the case of the illegal question. Despite Equal Opportunity Act guidelines, questions that have nothing to do with bona fide employment qualifications are still a recurring problem. Studies support the notion that the problem is greater for female than

Diversity in the Workplace

Culture Clashes and Interviewing

Japanese businesses are accustomed to selecting people on the basis of interpersonal knowledge and trust. It is not unusual to probe into a prospective employee's personal background in order to determine whether or not the right personal chemistry exists between the organization and the applicant. As one might expect, these tendencies have clashed with U.S. legal restrictions on what can be asked in employment interviews. Consequently, there have been many lawsuits brought against Japanese companies operating in the United States, alleging sexual or ethnic discrimination because of what appeared to be improper interviewing techniques.

As a result of these kinds of problems, several consulting firms have appeared to help sensitize Japanese doing business in the United States to the interpersonal and legal issues of interviewing in this country.

See, for example, an article by D. L. Jacobs in the business section of the *New York Times*. (1990, September 9). Japanese-American cultural clash, (p. 25) and D. Rowland (1985). *Japanese business etiquette*. New York: Warner Books, esp. Chs. 19 and 20 dealing with working for a Japanese firm.

for male candidates. One recommended solution is for both participants in the interview to try to get beyond "gamesmanship" and stress the optimum fit between job and person.[7]

Keeping in mind the communication setting and the typical problems encountered in employment interviews, consider guidelines for preparing for participation in this kind of interview. The steps in preparing for an employment interview differ for the interviewer and the candidate, or the interviewee.

For the interviewer, preparation includes the following steps:

1. Prepare or review the position's description.
   Preparation of the job description is a critical part of overall preparation. The interviewer should concentrate on the four to six key characteristics of the position including the following:

   - Title, or position.
   - Job requirements, especially in terms of education and experience.
   - Specific description, including duties, schedule, and supervision.
   - Compensation.

2. Prepare or review a description of the organization and benefits.
3. Review selection interview guidelines.

   - Company guidelines.
   - Legal guidelines.

4. Review candidate resumes.
5. Plan schedule of questions and the physical setting.

For the interviewee, preparation includes the following steps:

1. Research the corporation; see the most recent annual report, if available; look up the company in standard references, such as *Standard and Poor's*.
2. Analyze or review your own strengths and weaknesses.
3. Consider your own professional and individual goals.
4. Research and review typical questions. What are you likely to be asked?
5. Prepare questions you should ask about the corporation and job.
6. Practice asking and answering questions.

Obviously, one of the first steps for the interviewee, for the candidate for a position, is the preparation of an effective resume.

Evaluation or Work Appraisal

Sometimes called the performance evaluation, the work appraisal interview provides employees with feedback concerning their job performance. The work appraisal interview can help to communicate organizational policy and aid the interviewee to meet the goals of that policy.

The Resume

A resume is a written summary of personal data, educational qualifications, and experiences designed to demonstrate an applicant's professional qualifications or ability to fill a particular position. There is no one accepted format for a resume. There are as many preferences as there are personnel officers. Even general recommendations such as white 8-1/2 × 11-inch bond or no more than 1 page are not hard and fast rules. Analysis of the corporation and what is acceptable to them is suggested. Basically, the resume should be free of spelling and grammatical errors plus be geared toward a particular position.

Parts of the Resume. Identification includes permanent address and phone number at the top of the resume.

Professional objective(s) should be stated to catch the employer's attention.

Education begins with the highest degree earned. Include the degree, graduation date, major subjects, and honors. High school can be omitted unless it shows academic honors or leadership.

Experience should stress your most important skills and your performance. Indicate your highest position and your success at that position. Be sure to describe how well you performed on the job as you describe your work experience.

Additional information might be important. This might include specific background, professional associations, community or volunteer activities, outside interests, etc.

The problems associated with performance appraisal interviews are often related to feelings of threat and resultant defensiveness. Even under the best of circumstances, defensive reactions are likely because evaluative situations seem inherently threatening. This tendency to feel threatened by evaluations works both ways. For example, many managers accept criticism from those that they manage only with difficulty.[8]

The solution to problems of this sort appears to be to place emphasis on the opportunities for learning or growth as a result of the appraisal: that is, to attempt to remove the punitive emphasis and to stress, instead, the behaviors that can result in positive outcomes.

In view of these principles, we now take a look at the goals that the interviewer (that is, the supervisor or evaluator) should have for the performance appraisal interview:

Interviewer

1. Communicate criteria for performance to interviewee.
2. Communicate other corporate expectations.
3. Set performance standards or criteria.

   - Mutual goal-setting (employee and supervisor).
   - Be as specific as possible.
   - Concentrate on observable, measurable standards.

4. Discuss variance between standards and employee's performance.

   - Provide feedback in a supportive manner.
   - Stress opportunities for education and training.

5. Coach the employee on how to improve performance.

if they do this then they won't feel threatened

Interviewee

   Since most of us will also find ourselves in the situation of the person being evaluated, we should also consider the goals of the interviewee in a performance evaluation situation:

1. Share successes over the past reporting period.

   - Communicate development of skills.
   - Indicate successes in achieving goals.

2. Seek help for future success.

   - Discuss and help set future objectives.
   - Discuss opportunities for training and development of abilities.

3. Discuss dissatisfaction or satisfaction with job-related activities.

   In order to attain these goals, we recommend certain steps in preparing for participation in an appraisal interview. First, the interviewer or supervisor should do the following:

1. Select or review appropriate data regarding performance.

   - Review past performance interviews with the employee.
   - Review mutually set goals.

2. Gather data concerning performance from a variety of sources including the following:

   - Evaluation by clients, customers, or other groups served by the person being evaluated.
   - Evaluation by peers, those who may be in a position to understand the technical requirements of the position.
   - Evaluation reports from the person's own subordinates.
   - Objective measures of performance, such as number of clients served, billable hours, revenue generated, etc.

3. Review employee needs and motivation as previously discussed or determined.

The interviewee should prepare for the evaluation interview by following these procedures:

1. Review the evaluation material to be used.
2. Prepare to supply data on performance.
3. Prepare to participate in setting performance criteria by working out the following:

   - Personal goals.
   - Relationship of personal goals to work needs.

4. Prepare to discuss developmental (or training) needs.
5. Prepare to share knowledge about the job.

To summarize, appraisal interviews should be based on these guidelines:

- Objective standards should focus on observable behaviors.
- Ratings should be ongoing and recorded.
- The climate should be positive and supportive.
- Coaching should emphasize continuous feedback.
- Feedback should be nonconfrontational.
- Development or training should be stressed.

To allow for focus on improving performance, wage and salary should be separated from the appraisal. Ongoing appraisals are often the norm in many organizations, especially in those where mentoring programs have been instituted. At any rate, at least two or more interviews should be held each year. In sum, the intent should be to stress process more than outcome and reward more than punishment.

▶ **Counseling**

As discussed earlier, an interview can be a forum for discussing and discovering emotions and feelings. Such discussion is the essence of the counseling interview: to discuss feelings and emotions in order to define and solve individual problems. In the counseling interview, the interviewer takes the role of a counselor. The basic role of the counselor is that of a facilitator attempting to help the interviewee.

The counselor is a facilitator whose function is to help the counselee to: (1) define a problem; (2) gain insight into the problem, including causes and consequences; and (3) discover some ways to deal with the problem. To achieve these primary goals, the interviewer or the counselor uses an approach that will create trust and therefore create a permissive climate for discussion.

Frequently, the approach that is recommended for counseling type situations is the nondirective and supportive approach. The nondirective approach assumes that the counselor does not have all or even the best answers. The aim of the nondirective approach is to concentrate on the interviewee and the interviewee's perceptions of her or his needs. The interviewer-counselor serves to help the interviewee explore feelings and emotions. The interviewee, not the interviewer, defines the problem and its causes, proposes solutions, and evaluates them.

The basic need in the counseling interview is to develop and maintain the trust essential for the interview's effectiveness. The counselee should be encouraged to speak openly. This permissive climate and the associated trust can be created by an effective counselor.

In summary, the supportive behaviors, such as a problem-solving orientation, spontaneity, and empathy create the trust that is vital to an effective counseling interview. The supportive behaviors are, in turn, communicated by using certain verbal and nonverbal cues and avoiding others. The counselor avoids nonsupportive verbal responses such as tangents, irrelevancies, and interruptions. Verbally, the effective counselor engages in clarification, explicit acknowledgment of what the interviewee says, and agreement. Physically, the counselor leans forward, nods, uses a variety of eye contact and facial expressions, all to communicate a depth of concern and feeling that echoes the counselee's own. Recall that these techniques are described more fully in the section dealing with Empathic Listening in Chapter 3.

Disciplinary

The disciplinary interview is directed toward dealing with perceived errors or wrong-doing. The disciplinary interview informs the interviewee about and attempts to correct nonstandard behavior or violation of expectations. The secondary goals concern the future behavior of the individual and other employees.

The climate for the disciplinary interview is particularly important. Basically, the disciplinary interview is effective if the climate exhibits both seriousness and fairness. Seriousness is expressed by formality of the communication and setting. Fairness has to be established, in part, before the interview takes place. Specifically, the interviewee should know what the policy is, what punishments are associated with violations, and that punishment is certain.

During the interview, the interviewer should concentrate on facts and documentation. The best material on which to base a disciplinary interview is behavior that can be observed. In many ways, the techniques of the counseling and the appraisal interviews should be applied. For example, the interviewer should use descriptive language and avoid inflammatory accusation or evaluation: terms such as *liar*, *thief*, etc., increase the defensiveness of the employee and can lead to serious legal problems.

Problems unique to disciplinary interviews include timing and associated anger on the part of the interviewer. Timing must be considered carefully. To be effective, discipline should not be delayed; still, the interviewer should investigate the situation carefully before conducting the interview. The interviewer should strive to keep the situation under control. Finally, the interview should be conducted in private. Because the disciplinary interview creates defensiveness, only those individuals who need to be present should be included.

A last major consideration for conducting the disciplinary interview is the question of equity and legality. Although privacy facilitates more openness, there may be legal reasons to have a witness present, such as the union steward or even an attorney. Whoever is present, careful records should be kept. Lawyers, unions, and the Equal Employment Opportunity Commission (EEOC) as well as the organization itself may require accuracy and completeness including date, time, and a record of what was discussed.

In the interview, the interviewer needs to discover what happened, what caused the problem, or why the problem occurred. Some parts of the disciplinary interview may resemble the counseling interview. In many cases, the interviewer needs to discover all sides of the story. The interviewee should be allowed to express feelings and emotions. By the end of the interview, the interviewee should know where he or she stands specifically and individually.

▶

Grievance

The grievance interview emphasizes "What's wrong?" Unlike the disciplinary interview, however, the grievance interview is initiated by the employee rather than by the interviewer, who is usually a supervisor or manager. The primary goal of the grievance interview is to discover what is bothering the employee and to take steps to solve the problem.

In the grievance interview, a clear and accurate record is important. At the end of the interview, the record, including topics discussed and essential facts, should be summarized and reviewed by both interviewer and interviewee. Additionally, a written record should receive the same treatment and be reviewed by both participants.

Although each corporation's procedure for investigating grievances might be slightly different, the steps in the process could be generally summarized as follows:

1. Listen and record the complaint.
2. Get additional information.
3. Explore all sides of the story.
4. Record and document.
5. Take action as needed.
6. Report back to the employee.

▶

Exit

The exit interview is a relatively inexpensive way to gain information about a variety of organizational programs, policies, and procedures. An exit interview is not the same as a dismissal interview in that the person may be leaving for a variety of reasons: for example, has a new position elsewhere, has been transferred, or is retiring or resigning. Specifically, the exit interview can provide information covering such areas as the following:

- Reasons for leaving.
- Employee's position and job description.
- Evaluation and appraisal of various aspects of the organization.
- Views on salary.
- Views on corporate policy.
- Evaluation of training and development programs.

The exit interview could be the first step in a problem-solving process. The primary purpose is to provide information about what the corporation does well or does ineffectively. In addition, the interview can be used to create goodwill for the organization by providing a good lasting impression for the person leaving the organization.

The problems of the exit interview are fairly obvious and straightforward. For one thing, the employee may be suspicious about the intent. The employee may fear that information may be used against coworkers or friends. Also, the employee may be reluctant to give information, especially if it is negative.

Even if the exit interview is mandatory, the information gathered may not be useful if the requisite trust is lacking. Lack of trust can be a problem if the interview is conducted by an immediate supervisor or some other individual who has a perceived interest in the outcome of the interview. The exit interview should usually be conducted by a perceived neutral party, and assurances of impartiality or confidentiality are important.

Specific preparation before the interview may increase the usefulness of the information. The interviewer should prepare by checking supervisor's evaluations and assessments and collecting independent information from other employees, including supervisors. If possible, the employee's supervisor should prepare a formal report when the exit is to occur.

Frequently, the exit interview is the last part of the termination process. The exit interviewer needs to have information about a variety of details. The employee may ask about insurance, pension programs, benefits, references, and similar matters. Even if the exit interviewer is not the main source of this information, he or she should know whom the employee should contact and be able to detail the general steps in the termination process.

Dismissal

The dismissal interview is one that most people would like to avoid. Whether for cause or due to no fault of their own, interviewees are being terminated by the organization. Even if the interviewer has training in termination interviews, the natural reaction on the part of the interviewee is often guilt and avoidance. If the interview is to be as positive as possible, the interviewer should provide four types of information:

- The decision.
- The reasons for the decision.
- The steps in the process leading up to the decision.
- The effects of termination, including potential for reemployment, references, and other factors such as insurance, placement services, and the like.

LEGAL REQUIREMENTS IN INTERVIEWS

Discrimination on the basis of race, sex, national origin, age, or physical disability is not legal. Equal opportunity is enforced by a number of government agencies, chief among these being the Equal Employment Opportunity Commission (EEOC). Basically, an employer, including the employer's representatives such as recruiters, supervisors, and managers, cannot discriminate in conditions of employment on the basis of certain attributes. The following federal laws are most applicable in business and professional interviews:

- Title VII of the Civil Rights Act of 1964, as Amended.
- The Age Discrimination in Employment Act of 1967, as Amended.
- The Equal Pay Act of 1963.
- Sections 501 and 505, Rehabilitation Act of 1973 as Amended (prohibitions against discrimination in federal sectors).
- Americans with Disabilities Act of 1990.
- The Pregnancy Discrimination Act of 1978.

Conditions of employment include, but are not limited to, hiring or selection, promotion, compensation, benefits, or training. Any of the interview types—selection, appraisal, counseling, disciplinary, etc.—discussed above could fall under EEOC or other regulations or guidelines.[9]

Although the basic rule of thumb in employment interviewing or appraisal interviewing is that questions that ask for information dealing with a bona fide job criterion are legitimate, questions should be worded carefully. In many cases, ill-chosen words are likely to be a source of problems and potential discrimination suits. Mentioning or inquiring about possible causes of employee problems in appraisal, disciplinary, or counseling interviews could provide the basis of a suit. For example, a manager notices that Roy, who is 60 years of age, is not performing up to his usual level. If the manager, no matter how sympathetically, says, "Roy, you're not doing as good a job as you used to. You know, this work is pretty tough on someone your age. Could I find an easier job for you?" that might be a discrimination case in the making, because the manager's casual remark mentioned age.[10]

Because the federal regulations prohibit discrimination on the basis of national origin, asking matters such as the following could cause problems and should be avoided:

- Citizenship
- Height or weight
- Fluency in English
- The candidate's training or education in a foreign country

Of course, these are not absolute prohibitions, but an interviewer needs to be sure that asking questions in such areas must be justified by a bona fide need of the specific occupation. For example, news readers for television or radio need to be fluent in English. While you should not ask for citizenship, you can usually inquire about whether the person is prevented from working in this country because of immigration or visa problems. Consequently, questions such as, "That sounds like an Italian (or Polish, or whatever) name; is it?" or, "Where did you learn to speak Turkish (or whatever)?" place the interviewer on dangerous ground. The issue is whether the person speaks Turkish or Italian (if that is needed for the job), not where he or she learned it.

Also, questions that may be seen as probing into a candidate's age, religious preferences, or possible physical disabilities may be red flags. To avoid charges of ageism, an interviewer should avoid questions such as, "When did you graduate from high school?" or, "How old are your children?" or, "How far are you from retirement?" A question such as, "What religious holidays do you observe?" could open one to charges of discriminating against certain religious groups. The straightforward question, "Are you handicapped?" would be unwise in view of the Americans with Disabilities Act.

Obviously, questions of women candidates that seem to probe their marital status or to ask about pregnancy, plans to have children, and the like are out of bounds. Therefore, inquiries such as, "Who will take care of the children while you are at work?" or, "Will you follow your husband if he is transferred to another city?" should be avoided. Similarly, one should not ask a woman about plans for a family, what she might do if she has a baby, and the like.[11]

Since discrimination is such an important area, you should keep up to date with company policy documents and appropriate company officials about the general requirements of fairness, equity, and legality. Since this is a changing area, anyone involved in interviewing should keep up to date regarding current guidelines and requirements. (These should be available by contacting the appropriate agency or governmental office in your area.)

Moreover, be careful about wording questions and choosing language. Be specific and objective, and avoid areas that are not connected to bona fide job qualifications. Finally, a general principle is to keep good records. Interviews and decisions based on interviews should be recorded. The information should be specific, accurate, and as complete as possible. Finally, decisions should be consistent. Employees with similar qualifications and in similar situations should receive similar treatment.

Problem-Solution

Guidelines for avoiding charges of discrimination in interviewing include the following:

- Ask everyone the same questions, especially in areas that might be related to the dangers just mentioned. For example, instead of asking a woman candidate how she would handle child care in order to meet some odd hours at the job, ask *all* candidates whether they can deal with unusual working hours or conditions. After all, the real question is whether the candidates can do the job, if that involves odd hours, rather than whether they are mothers or fathers.
- Review job descriptions to ensure that they reflect the actual necessities for carrying out the task. Under the Americans with Disabilities Act, an organization must be prepared to provide justification for any requirements that would limit access of persons with disabilities.

The work appraisal interview is often the basis for discrimination suits. It therefore becomes vital for you and the organization to regard the appraisal as a potentially key piece of evidence in a lawsuit or government investigation. The following guidelines might be useful for such situations:[12]

- Keep written records.
- Let employees review their records.
- Let employees submit comments on their appraisal.
- Do not discuss the appraisal with anyone and everyone.
- Keep the appraisal objective and based on measurable criteria.

 SUMMARY

Interviewing is an important and recurring activity in many businesses and professions. Obviously, there are professions or careers that are built around interviewing: journalism, personnel work, certain market research agencies, social service agencies, and the like. Even beyond these careers, however, most people will find themselves in many situations in which they are interviewing or being interviewed. Almost everyone will have to go through employment and placement interviews and do some of that kind of interviewing later on in their careers; and most people will have to participate in performance evaluation interviews on a fairly regular basis.

There are some standard principles that apply in interview settings. Interviews should be planned as carefully as possible. Interviews share some characteristics of conversation and some characteristics of presentations; they are planned but still spontaneous, allowing for the give and take of questions and answers. Recall that the reactions of one person can be more complex to predict than the general or average response of a larger audience. Nonverbal cues are more evident, and emotional states can be more readily observed because of the proximity and involvement obligations of the participants.

The major problems encountered in interviewing are lack of empathy, defensiveness, bias and premature judgment, inadequate planning, and inadequate feedback during the interview. In the first place, interviewers and interviewees should be clear about the purposes and objectives of an interview. One should be aware of the basic structure to most interviews and the need to have an opening and a closing as well as a body of the interview. Each part of the interview should accomplish its purpose. Also, note the effects and purposes for different kinds of questions that can be employed.

In this chapter, we looked at eight different kinds of interviews, discussing the special problems that are often encountered with each type:

- Information-gathering interview.
- Selection or employment interview.
- Evaluation, or performance-appraisal interview.
- Counseling interview.
- Disciplinary interview.
- Grievance interview.
- Exit interview.
- Dismissal interview.

SAMPLE EMPLOYMENT INTERVIEW

Interviewer: Ralph G., personnel executive with a large marketing firm in Cleveland, Ohio.
Candidate: Karen H., recent graduate with a B. S. degree in business administration from a state university in Ohio.

Karen has been invited to the firm's main building in downtown Cleveland for an interview in an office in the personnel department. A receptionist has announced her arrival, and Ralph greets her at the door of the office, inviting her in.

Ralph: Good morning, Karen. I'm very pleased that you could arrange to meet with me this morning. Please have a seat right over here in front of the desk. Would you like some coffee or tea?
Karen: Oh, no thank you, Mr. G., I'm fine.
Ralph: I hope you didn't have too much trouble getting here. I forgot that they

still had the street torn up—the construction never stops in the summers around here.

Karen: Oh, no—no problem—I'm used to the city—and a friend had warned me about the construction. The people down front were really nice about directing me to your place here.

Ralph: Ah, good. Well, I think you know that we have screened several candidates for the positions that we have this year. Your record looked like one that we wanted to follow up on. This is our first opportunity to get to know each other. After a short talk here, we want you to take a tour of our shop here, and you'll have a chance to meet some of the department heads. If we both are interested in following this up, we'll arrange for an interview later with the head of marketing research.

Karen: That sounds fine.

Ralph: Well, O.K. Let me get your resume here—ah, here we are—now let's see. Why don't you begin by telling me a little bit about yourself—why you chose State University, your major, and something about your time there at the school.

Karen: Sure . . . let me see. Well, first, I was pretty active in band and music activities in high school in Warren, and I had the opportunity to try out for marching band at the university. That led me to look into some of their . . . uh . . . programs, their courses, things like that. I wasn't really sure what to major in, at first—you know, a lot of kids are like that—but . . . uh . . . I took an accounting class in my first year. My dad thought it would be a useful thing to have no matter what. I sort of enjoyed the class—a surprise to me. I started looking at some of the other courses in business—and well, things sort of followed after that . . .

Ralph: I see—did you stay with the band, with your music activities there at the university?

Karen: Oh, yeah, for a while. I really enjoyed that because of the friends, the trips to away games, things like that. But in the last year or so, I felt I needed to help out with money and stuff—and so I got a job on campus—between that and classes, I really didn't have time, I didn't think I had time, to keep up the band.

Ralph: Uh-huh. Did you get involved in other activities on campus?

Karen: Uh . . . yes—I was on the dorm council; we were sort of in charge of getting entertainment, bands or concerts, for the hall—and I wrote some pieces for the hall's little newspaper we put out.

Ralph: I forgot to ask—what sort of job was it you had on campus?

Karen: It was with the . . . um . . . food service; taking food coupons, IDs, cleaning up, setting up, things like that.

Ralph: What about summer jobs?

Karen: Oh, sure—I always had something in the summers back at home. I did some waitressing and worked as a temp for one of those services.

Ralph: You mean temporary office work, that sort of thing?

Karen: Yeah, that was basically it.

Ralph: I see—well, I wonder now if you could tell me something about your interest in marketing. Did that come from some of the courses that you had at the university?

Karen: Oh, yes. My first course in it—I mean, introductory marketing—was really . . . uh . . . interesting. You know, when I first started, freshman year and all that, I wasn't sure what it was—thought it was just selling or sales—like that. I think I might have said, I kind of like math and stats, so the marketing course was, well, more interesting than I was thinking it would be.

Ralph: I don't think that you did mention your interest in math, but I see on your transcript that you did have several math and two stats courses. Is that right?

Karen: Yes, that sounds right.

Ralph: Well, tell me, what sort of work do you see yourself doing in a firm such as ours?

Karen: Well, you may have seen on my resume that I had an internship one semester—part-time with a marketing and public relations firm in Dayton—well, I worked on helping set up some campaigns and doing some market research. That was great—I really learned a lot about what they did. Anyway, I feel that that's the sort of thing I would be involved with here.

Ralph: Do you know much about what we do here?

Karen: Yes—sort of. I contacted my supervising instructor from the internship—she gave me some good information that sounded really impressive—the volume, a ball-park figure on the number of accounts, things like that. I looked up some recent figures from your annual report—although I didn't find this year's.

Ralph: Oh—here I can see that you get one when you leave.

Karen: Oh, thanks—that would be nice.

Ralph: Are there some questions that you have—some things you feel like we should cover at this time?

Karen: Well, I was wondering about location—don't you have several sites with openings?

Ralph: Yes, that's right, Karen. We are looking to fill some openings in several locations—Pittsburgh, Lima, Fort Wayne, and some others. Is location important to you?

Karen: Well, not terribly important, but I would like to stay in the Midwest. I think that . . . uh . . . another question I would have concerns your . . . development programs. Do you have some training or educational programs?

Ralph: Do you have something specific in mind?

Karen: I would hope to go on for an MBA or another master's degree. Is that sort of thing given much support?

Ralph: Oh, I see. Why, yes, we do have a program of helping you with support for tuition, things like that. We are interested in encouraging that sort of thing.

Karen: Ah . . . well, that's good to know. I'm . . . sure that other things will come up during the day.

Ralph: Oh, yes, this first meeting is somewhat preliminary—there's plenty of time to discuss some of our other personnel policies. Oh—I see that it's time for your first tour. Let me take you to where that all starts. Now, I will be in touch with you later in the day and I will send you a followup letter within the week letting you know how things seem to be going. Okay?

Karen: Sure, and thanks so much for your meeting with me this morning. I enjoyed our talk.

Ralph: Yes, me, too. Thanks for coming in and for thinking about us here at Marketing. Now, let me give you some more material on the company, and that annual report . . .

EXERCISES •

The first three questions refer to the sample interview.

1. How would you assess Ralph G.'s performance in this interview? Did he seem well prepared? Did he do a good job of putting the candidate at ease? How did he handle probes and followup questions? What suggestions would you make for improving his performance?

2. Do you feel that Karen H. was well prepared for the interview? Why or why not? How would you assess her communication in the interview? What suggestions would you make for her to improve her performance on subsequent interviews?

3. Looking over the transcript of the interview, do you think that sufficient and effective use was made of open-ended and closed questions? Were there enough probes? What other questions should have been asked that were not at this point?

4. Describe interviews that you have participated in. Were they similar to this particular employment interview? Can you think of aspects of your interviews that were especially effective or ineffective?

5. If you were a candidate for a position, how would you handle a question that you feel is inappropriate or possibly illegal, such as a woman being asked about plans for having children?

6. Prepare to interview an expert on campus: a professor of astronomy regarding space exploration, an economics professor on the national budget deficit, or the like. Formulate some specific questions that would give you the kind of information that you wish; prepare to present your information to the class. After the interview, discuss the special problems that you ran into. What surprised you or caught you off-guard in your interview?

SELECTED SOURCES FOR FURTHER READING

Barnlund, D. C. (1962). Toward a meaning-centered philosophy of communication. *Journal of Communication, 2,* 40.

Donaghy, W. C. (1990). *The interview, skills and applications* (rev. ed.). Salem, WI: Sheffield.

Berkeley, A. E. (1989, February 20). Job interviewers' dirty little secrets. *Wall Street Journal*, p. A4.

Gibb, J. R. (1961). Defensive communication. *Journal of Communication, 11*, 141–148.

Jablin, F. M. (1985). Task/work relationships: A life-span perspective. In *Handbook of interpersonal communication* (pp. 615–654). M. L. Knapp & G. R. Miller (Eds.), Beverly Hills, CA: Sage Publications.

Kleiman, C. (1990, October 2). Art of communication becoming more important in search for job (p. E.2). *Chicago Tribune*. Reprinted in the *Indianapolis Star*.

Nelson-Horchler, J. (1988, September 19). Performance appraisals (pp. 61–63). *Industry Week*.

Panaro, G. P. (1990). *Employment law manual*. Boston: Warren, Gorham & Lamont.

Public Service Indiana. (1982, July). *Supervisory EEO Bulletin, no. 16*.

Public Service Indiana. (1982, January). *Supervisory EEO Bulletin, no. 14*.

Sincoff, M. Z., & Goyer, R. S. (1984). *Interviewing*. New York: Macmillan.

Stewart, C., & Cash, Jr., W. B. (1991). *Interviewing: Principles and practices* (6th ed.). Dubuque, IA: Wm. C. Brown.

Tengler, C., & Jablin, F. M. (1983, September). Effects of question type, orientation, and sequencing in the employment screening interview. *Communication Monographs, 50*, 261–262.

References

1. Stewart, C. J., & Cash, Jr., W. B. (1991). *Interviewing: Principles and practices* (6th ed.). (p. 1). Dubuque, IA: Wm. C. Brown.
2. Samovar, L. S., & Hellweg, S. (1982). *Interviewing: A communicative approach*. Dubuque, IA: Gorsuch Scarisbrick, p. 4.
3. Panaro, G. P. (1990). *Employment law manual* (p. 43). Boston: Warren, Gorham & Lamont.
4. Kleiman, C. (1990, October 2). Art of communication becoming more important in search for job (p. E.2). *Chicago Tribune*. Reprinted in the *Indianapolis Star*.
5. Tengler, C., & Jablin, F. M. (1983, September). Effects of question type, orientation, and sequencing in the employment screening interview. *Communication Monographs, 50*, 261–262.
6. Samovar and Hellweq, p. 20.
7. Berkeley, A. E. (1989, February 20). Job interviewers' dirty little secrets. *Wall Street Journal*, p. A4.
8. Nelson-Horchler, J. (1988, September 19). Performance appraisals (pp. 61–63). *Industry Week*.
9. See, for example, Public Service Indiana, (1982, July), *Supervisory EEO Bulletin, no. 16*, p. 2.
10. Public Service Indiana, (1981, July), *Supervisory EEO Bulletin, no. 12*, p. 4.
11. See Panaro, *Employment Law Manual*, pp. 28–43, for these and similar examples.
12. Public Service Indiana, (1982, January), *Supervisory EEO Bulletin, No. 14*, p. 2.

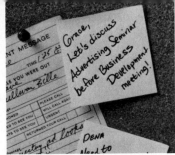

Problem-Solving Groups

CHAPTER

After studying this chapter, you should be able to:

1. Identify those situations in which groups are especially useful.

2. Describe the main characteristics of problem-solving groups.

3. Explain three main functions for the communication that occurs in small groups.

4. Explain the major variables usually present in small group communication.

5. Show the effects of typical problems of small group communication: group myths and so-called groupthink.

Overview

Groups are everywhere. Most of us belong to many groups, including family, school, church, work, recreational, social, volunteer, and so on. Our memberships in these formal and informal groups have a variety of purposes. Groups vary from formal ones with constitutions, paid staff, and regular meetings to the informal types with few written rules and no appointed or elected leader. Some are social groups, such as fraternities and sororities; some are occupational and job-related groups, such as professional associations; some are short-lived and task directed, such as study groups; some are recreational, such as hobby groups; some are personal interest groups such as political parties; and some are problem-solving groups.

Group communication is as important to corporations and other formal organizations as it is to people in their everyday lives. Organizations use group communication to meet a variety of functions. Executives, managers, supervisors, and others spend a great deal of time talking and listening in a variety of groups, including team sessions, meetings, conferences, staff meetings, etc. Much of the work of many organizations gets done in these groups.

Although small groups fulfill particular functions and do some jobs better than individuals working alone, there is no guarantee that groups will work effectively or efficiently. Participants must understand the problems inherent in small group problem solving and decision making and work to overcome them, if the small

▶ *Much business is accomplished in meetings and committees.*

groups are to succeed. This chapter stresses the nature of small group interaction and the innate problems of small groups. Chapter topics include the following:

Nature of problem-solving groups.
Communication in small groups.
Problems of decision-making and problem-solving groups.

NATURE OF PROBLEM-SOLVING GROUPS

Problem solving and decision making are essential to organizations. A good deal has been written about these issues, so there is a lot of good information available on these functions (see Selected Sources for Further Reading at the end of this chapter).

Why Groups Are Good for Problem Solving

Organizations use problem-solving and decision-making groups because generally they can perform better than a single individual and even better than the collective but separate work of many individuals. The synergy, or the effect of group interaction, produces a better product than individuals do. In other words, the sum of group interaction is often greater than the total of contributions of the individuals that make up a group.

Groups can be more effective than individuals under the following conditions or circumstances:

1. *Idea creation is important.* In any situation in which the quantity of ideas is important, groups are effective. Stimulated by interaction, groups tend to produce more ideas than individuals working alone. An idea, a word, or a phrase may trigger new ideas and responses. Such synergy increases the number and quality of ideas that would be produced by a single individual working alone. Moreover, a sharing of many ideas within a group allows comparison that should lead to superior choices.

2. *Division of labor is appropriate.* Groups tend to be effective when the task allows some division of that task into component activities. Such a division of tasks is called the "assembly effect." Based on analogies to the assembly line in automobile production, the term *assembly effect* as used here suggests that each group member complete some parts of the task, all of which are put together to produce a final product. The analogy also suggests that the contributions of the individuals need to be somewhat standardized so that the final product is seamless, that is, avoids jolting differences in style, format, etc. Moreover, the assembly effect requires that the group trust each individual's judgment. If any one individual in the group fails to perform, the results, or the end product, could be harmed.

3. *Redundancy is needed.* Redundancy acts as a way of checking for and minimizing errors. Recall from our earlier discussions of redundancy that it involves

▶ *Groups can divide labor to achieve an assembly effect similar to assembly lines in manufacturing.*

both duplication and feedback. The most obvious redundancy system is language. An individual says the word, "Stop!" and holds up a hand. The word and action reinforce one another. The manager who hands a report to a colleague for her opinions or corrections is seeking redundancy. Groups tend to be able to detect problems or mistakes that an individual misses, especially in complex problems that consist of a number of steps. There is truth in the old saying, "More heads are better than one."

4. *Understanding is essential.* Complex solutions are easy to criticize when all the facts are not known. Interaction in a group may lead individuals to accept unpopular solutions as the best of a bad lot. A situation that was particularly meaningful for one of the authors was a case of annual tuition increases at a small university. Traditionally, feeling ran high among the student body and the faculty that tuition increases were ill-considered and unnecessary. One year, the president created a committee composed of students, faculty, and administrators to consider all relevant data. After several months of careful study, the group concluded unanimously that the tuition increase proposed by the administration was the most reasonable alternative. In this case, discussion created understanding.

5. *Solution implementation is needed.* If shared decision making can create better understanding of the problem and the solutions, shared decision making can also enhance implementation. Individuals who take part in making a decision have a vested interest in defending that decision and in putting that decision into effect. Identification with the group and the decision that the group made ("ownership") can motivate the individual. Consequently, as long as people are convinced that they had a part in making the decision, participation in that decision making can be used as a motivator.

▶ **Definitions and Types of Groups**

Classifying groups is a useful way of organizing our thinking about small groups and small group communication. For our purposes, small groups consist of from three to fewer than a dozen people interacting in face-to-face communication for some specified purpose. Another way of clarifying what we mean by a group is to enumerate the various types of groups. In modern organizations, small groups can be categorized in a number of different ways. Several different methods that are useful to the student of business communication are discussed next.

Presence of an Audience.   The first perspective for categorizing groups takes into account the presence or absence of an audience. Groups can be differentiated by whether or not an audience is present. This factor suggests two general types of group situations: (1) meetings of problem-solving and decision-making groups whose activities, in most cases, are not open to an audience; and (2) public discussion groups that perform primarily for an audience.

The presence or absence of an audience makes a difference since observers affect the nature of the communication within a group. In the discussion of how to prepare for public discussion later in this chapter, we will analyze those differences in detail.

Types of public discussions (groups with audiences) can be panel discussions, symposia, or conferences.

A panel discussion is composed of experts or knowledgeable individuals who discuss a topic among themselves for the benefit of an audience who watches but does not participate during the main part of the discussion. At the end of the discussion, the panel usually entertains questions from the audience. In the panel discussion, the emphasis is on the exchange of ideas rather than prepared speeches. Frequently, an effective panel discussion centers around a controversial topic on which a number of different positions can be taken. The audience has enough prior information to be able to listen effectively.

A symposium is a collection of individual presentations or speeches meant to stimulate audience interest, enthusiasm, questions, and participation. The symposium should be thought of as individual presentations. It can be used effectively to inform or persuade. At a sales meeting, for example, a company will introduce a new product line by calling upon a series of speakers who make individual presentations. One presentation might focus on product research; another might give marketing research; a third might present the sales campaign. Overall, the symposium is more formal than the panel discussion. In the symposium, one unprepared participant can damage the program significantly since each speaker will talk for 10 or 20 minutes apiece.

A conference is the largest type of public discussion; it encompasses a variety of presentational methods to (1) provide the audience with new information and

▶ *The public discussion has special characteristics.*

technique and (2) enable the audience to practice or evaluate the new information and technique. This is the most formal of the public discussions in that it requires the most careful planning, organization, and control.

As noted, these public groups will be considered in a separate section later in the chapter.

Group Tasks.   A second perspective for categorizing groups considers specific group tasks. Groups can be divided into three categories according to their primary task or job:

The first is the *fact-finding group*, whose major purpose is to determine what is true or to answer questions of fact. The fact-finding group can be simple, such as three electricians who are trying to discover if an electrical circuit can carry the increased load of your new computer system or as complex as the team of accountants who are closing out the financial books for the previous year. In either case, the group's main purpose is to organize data and facts.

A second type is an *evaluation group*, which has as its primary aim determining what something is worth or answering questions of value. After the facts have been collected, we want to know what they mean. Groups may be organized to consider, for example, whether or not the sales staff is doing a good job. External consultants may be brought in to evaluate the work on the factory production floor. An evaluation group primarily determines worth, excellence, value, etc.

The third type of group is the *decision-making or problem-solving group*, whose major goal is to determine what should or should not be done or to answer questions of policy. Technically, there is a difference between decision making and problem solving. Decision making focuses on selecting alternatives. For example, the decision-making group might be faced with the question of whether training should be handled internally or through outside consultants. Problem solving, on the other hand, focuses on identifying a need or reason to change and outlines the advantages of changing. A problem-solving group might ask, for example, what, if anything, is wrong with the allocation of office space. The problem-solving group is the most complex type of group. By complex we mean that problem solving involves gathering information, evaluating it, and making decisions.

Formal versus Informal Groups.   The *formal group*, characterized by structure and legitimacy, includes work units, work teams, and departments that interact more or less constantly and are recognized within the organizational hierarchy. The organization of a department is typical of the nature of a formal group. There is a specific hierarchy, each member knows the roles that they play and that others play, and many of the norms (rules of procedure, such as dress or other expectations) are stated explicitly in writing.

The *informal group* is not officially recognized in the corporate hierarchy or organizational chart. An informal group may be a group of individuals who interact because of proximity, common need, interest, or friendship. Through interaction, the individuals begin meeting and a common purpose begins to evolve. Informal groups lack the explicit structures of the formal groups, of course.

Highlights of Definitions and Types of Groups.   There are three ways to classify or define groups:

- The presence or absence of an audience.
- Task of the group, including fact-finding, evaluation, and decision making.
- Formally constituted versus informal groups.

Public groups can be further classified as panel discussions, symposia, or conferences.

SMALL GROUP COMMUNICATION

Groups exist in organizations to perform some function or to fulfill some purpose. For that reason, the first part of the discussion is on the purposes of the communication in the small group. From there, we move to a consideration of the various aspects of group interaction that influence group communication and its effectiveness. Communication in small groups has been subject to systematic research. Therefore, there is a lot of good information regarding the effects of certain communication variables in groups. This research has indicated that communication in the group context does have some unique characteristics. We can improve participation and productiveness working in and with groups by being aware of these findings.

Purposes of Communication in Small Groups

This section looks at the purposes of the communication in any group. (Do not confuse purpose here with the purpose of the group itself, such as fact-finding or decision making, as purposes of groups, referred to above in regard to classifying types of groups.) Regardless of the nature of the groups itself, the communication occurring within that group will be directed toward fulfilling one or more of the following four purposes.

1. *Task.* By the term *task*, we mean the job that has been assigned to the group. The group may have been assigned, for example, to develop a fund-raising campaign meeting; coming up with the specifics of this plan is the task. The task is not the only reason for the existence of a group, especially to the members of that group. The task is imposed by the expectations, commands, or other pressures that exist outside the group. In fact, the need to produce some product within a given time frame frequently leads to tension, anxiety, and conflict within each group member, among the group members, and with groups and individuals outside the group itself. Task purposes are often referred to as "concern for productivity."

2. *Social and emotional interaction.* If the outside pressure to produce some finished product (the task) were removed, social interaction and attempts to

increase group cohesion might become the primary group goal. Consequently, tension always exists between the desire to successfully complete the task and the desire to socialize. Groups that spend too much time on the task while ignoring the social and emotional needs of the group may end in disaster. The social and emotional purpose of group communication is often referred to as "fulfilling a cohesion function."

The desire to accomplish the task and the wish to socialize and increase group cohesion are not mutually exclusive. Cohesiveness, or the combination of forces that makes a group attractive to an individual, is directly related to productivity. As cohesiveness increases, productivity also increases. Consequently, as the group produces, the more attractive it becomes and the more cohesive it becomes. Thus, cohesiveness and productivity tend to reinforce one another, with one important reservation: If groups become too concerned with socioemotional interaction, then productivity begins to decline.

3. *Personal satisfaction.* Individual rewards are one of the main reasons why individuals join groups and continue to attend meetings or participate. Each individual must receive some satisfaction from the group. In other words, we gain identity or status from the group. The greater this satisfaction or the attractiveness of the group, the greater the power that the group has over the individual. The less satisfaction the individual receives, the more likely the individual is to be dissatisfied with the group and to consider leaving it. Remember that people can receive satisfaction in any number of ways: from a sense of belonging, a sense of mutual purpose or interest, and a sense of achievement, to name just a few. As long as the pressures to remain are greater than the pressures to leave, the individual will remain in the group. One purpose of group communication, therefore, is to enhance the satisfaction that the individual feels in membership. Such satisfaction leads, as well, to the fourth purpose.

4. *Group survival.* Groups are more than the sum of their parts or members. Once in existence, they continue even when the original purpose has faded and even when some or all of the original members have departed. A group can become a source of individual identity and pride. Groups tend to emphasize their own value and accomplishments and devalue the ideas of those outside the group. Given that groups are a source of esprit de corps for the individual, attempts to disband them could meet with resistance. In fact, successful groups can be reluctant to admit that they have achieved their goal or that their reason for existence is gone. Therefore, a final purpose of group communication can be to maintain the existence of the group itself.

An effective group leader or participant needs to recognize that all four of these goals need to be served. While they cannot always be satisfied simultaneously, the goals have to be served at some point during the group's collective existence. Once we understand these natural goals of small group communication, we describe some of the other factors involved in the following sections. First, we note that groups seem to grow through a fairly predictable life-cycle. Next, one of the most important findings regarding communication in small groups is the importance of the development of group norms and roles. These factors are related to the development of status and power within the group, which leads to a discussion of the important subject of leadership in a group. An important variable relating to norms, roles, status, and leadership expectations is the appearance of deviance. We then consider some environmental factors that affect the nature of communication within a group: physical setting, group size, and the presence of an audience.

Stages or Group Life-Cycles

Characteristically, during the completion of their tasks the communication in small groups develops in stages. These stages do not represent logical stages of analyzing the task itself: These logical stages are called agenda systems and are discussed in the next chapter. The communication stages discussed here represent how group communication develops over time. Although the number of stages described may vary, the following stages are typical (see Figure 8-1):

1. *Orientation.* When individuals meet for the first time or begin a new project, communication is tentative. This represents initial uncertainty or primary tension, such as the tension that we feel when entering a new situation or meeting for the first time. Situations such as a first date or a first day at school are associated with feelings of primary tension. When a group meets for the first time, conversation frequently turns to trivial matters. Individuals feel ill at ease, and speakers appear uncertain. Statements are qualified with frequent reservations: "This may sound stupid but . . . ;" "If no one objects, we could . . . ." Overall, the orientation is characterized by probing to feel out how others see the situation.

2. *Conflict or period of tension.* Once individuals and the group as a whole feel more secure, they begin to experience conflict. This conflict represents an attempt to sort out relations in both interpersonal and authority relationships. Even when the group has an appointed leader, group members may still try to gain authority and status. Ideas are advanced and opposed as a way of enhancing one's power or status as well as a way of accomplishing the group task. We can all remember times when an idea advanced by one member of a group is rejected, while a similar idea advanced by another member of the group is accepted. In such cases, conflict serves to test not only the value of the idea but also the authority and status of the idea's advocate.

3. *Resolution.* A final stage is resolution, in which individuals establish relationships and an informal group hierarchy. At this point, the productivity of the group normally increases. More time is spent on the task than before. Although

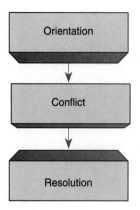

▶ **Figure 8-1** *Stages in the life cycle of a group.*

relationships may still be developing and group rules may still be undergoing testing, conflict concerning these matters decreases. Cooperation becomes more apparent as the group organizes itself to get the job completed.

Obviously, these three stages of orientation, conflict, and resolution are the average. Some groups may disband before coming to the third stage; for others, one of the stages may last an extended time. Typically, however, these stages can be experienced by most groups as they work through a task.

▶ Variables Affecting Communication in Groups

The stages of development are one way of seeing what is going on in group communication. Another way is to look at factors that influence small group communication. The following factors have been found to influence both the amount and structure of communication within the small group: norms, roles, status and power, leaders and leadership, and deviance. Physical setting, group size, and audience also have an impact on the communication in groups. We consider each of these factors in turn.

1. *Norms.* Norms are rules of behavior, standards of procedure, or rules of etiquette that determine what is allowed or appropriate and what is not allowed or is inappropriate in a group. Some principles that characterize group norms follow.

Norms differ among groups. One group may severely limit the amount of interpersonal criticism or conflict that is allowed in the group. Other groups may allow relatively free rein, providing that the negative comments are made in the prescribed time when the group is not working on the task. In other words, what is constant about norms is their presence, not their content. Group communication, like all human communication, is rule-governed. The organizational culture often determines such rules, hence the importance of learning the local organization culture ("the way things are done around here"). The point is that each culture will develop its own rules, different in many respects from the rules adopted somewhere else. Moreover, members are expected to follow the norms of the groups. For the individual, consequently, realization that each group has different norms will serve as a warning to adapt to the norms of each group.

Norms can be formal or informal. Within some groups, the standards of behavior are very strict but unwritten and, therefore, considered informal. For example, certain organizations have strict dress codes that are communicated to new members of the group by the fact that most members (including the most influential and powerful) wear similar clothes, but nowhere is a dress code written out. We are reminded of a *New Yorker* cartoon of a few years ago which showed several people working on a task. The men are in white short sleeves and ties; one says to another, who has loosened his tie, "In this outfit, Smith, we take off our jackets but we do not loosen our ties." On the other hand, some organizations require members to wear certain types of clothing by written directive. Sometimes this is done for reasons of health and safety, but frequently the reasons are less apparent and involve, for example, public image. The fact that a norm is written does not mean that it is more important or stronger than unwritten rules. Often, the greatest taboos are the unspoken ones.

Norms tend to produce conformity. The reason for the existence of norms is to produce individual compliance with rules that the group feels are important. The rules may be positive (what you can or should do) or negative (what you should or cannot do). Likewise, their effects may be positive or negative, depending on the specific norm and how it is enforced. A norm that requires a group to give all sides a fair hearing may help the group in the long run; it might be a hindrance in the short run, or when the group is under time pressures to complete a task. Most norms might be considered good or bad, depending on the situation. For example, a dress code could be important to a group of salespeople or to any group that needs to present a positive image toward the outside world. On the other hand, a norm could stifle creativity and productivity. In other words, does the norm facilitate communication and productiveness or restrict them?

The more attractive the group, the greater the strength of the norms. This strong finding comes from a great amount of research in group behavior. When an individual is attracted to a group, the group has great influence over the individual's opinions and behavior. This factor explains the strength that adolescent peer groups have over their members. Teenagers particularly need a sense of belonging, and rejection by peers is much feared. On the other hand, a weak culture is one in which the members may not feel strongly enough attracted to the organization to bother with holding up the established norms; people seem to ignore the rules and get away with it.

Norms are dynamic. By this, we mean that norms change over time. Group norms undergo a continual process of modification and change. Even norms that have been perceived as essential to the group's identity or existence can be constantly challenged and tested, if not changed or modified. One cannot assume, therefore, that norms observed at one stage in the operation of the group will be in force when one returns to the group after an absence.

Norms apply to different individuals differently. Although this may seem unfair, norms are not always applied to all individuals within the group equitably. Persons of middle power and middle status within the group are expected to conform to the norms more closely than individuals (such as leaders) who have high power and high status, or individuals who have low power and low status. Leaders can set new norms and violate old ones, providing that these norms are relatively unimportant. This practice is part of what it means to be a leader, of course. Yet, concerning norms that are fundamental to the group's identity or the group's existence, even the leader has less leeway and is expected to exemplify the behavior of the group. An interesting finding in the research is that low-status, or marginal, members of the group also seem to experience less pressure to conform. Presumably, the actions of these people are not considered to be threatening, or their violations are not seen as unexpected, which may partly explain their low status. Norms therefore have the greatest force for the majority of those group members in the middle of the hierarchy.

Norms play an important part in small group interaction; specifically, they determine standards of correct and incorrect interaction. The six important attributes of norms are:

1. Norms differ among groups.
2. Norms can be formal or informal.
3. Norms tend to produce conformity.
4. The more attractive the group, the greater the strength of the norms.
5. Norms are dynamic.
6. Norms apply to different individual differently.

2. *Roles*. Roles are a set of behaviors that are given a name, for example, the "leader," the "secretary," or the "recorder." With each role come two sets of expectations. The first set includes the expectations of others about what the role involves. To the members of a decision-making group, being a leader entails certain specific behaviors plus more responsibility than the other members of the group. Second, the leader has expectations about the role and what type of behaviors are essential to being a leader. In addition to the expected role (that is, what the members want) and the perceived role (that is, what the person who occupies the role expects), there is the enacted role (that is, what the person actually does).

Obviously, the potential for role conflict is great. The leader thinks that she is required to perform in a certain manner; the members may think otherwise. Moreover, the discrepancy between what is expected and what is actually done can cause tension for the members and for the leader. If an individual belongs to several groups, the demands of a role in one group may conflict with the demands of a role in another group. A manager who acquires information in confidence from a superior that is essential to the decision being considered by another group to which she belongs is caught in role conflict, if not an ethical dilemma. Finally, strict performance of the role itself may prevent effective communication. If the expected role of a group member is loyalty to the group's leader, what happens when the leader makes an inferior decision?

3. *Status and power.* As might be expected, status, or a person's standing within a group, and power or his ability to reward and punish influences the amount of communication that the individual initiates and receives. Status is often based on perceptions of the person's rank or standing within some larger organization. When a mayor is appointed to a task force of community leaders, the mayor can be expected, at least initially, to be accorded fairly high status on the basis of the elected political position.

Diversity in the Workplace

Wa: *Japanese group consensus*

The Japanese place a great deal of importance on group membership and group loyalty. The concept of *wa* suggests a search for mutual cooperation that allows for a total effort toward achieving group goals. Group harmony takes precedence. An illusion of group harmony must be maintained while the group works toward real consensus. Generally, nothing will be done until the real consensus has been achieved. Discussion and compromise will therefore continue until unanimity has been reached.

The Japanese decision-making process is usually a careful effort to achieve consensus of everyone who may be affected by the decision. The process, known as *ringi-seido*, involves circulating a document, the *ringi-sho*, which various people can revise and sign on. Often the process is not even begun until unofficial support for the proposal has been obtained from many of the people involved. This process is obviously time-consuming but results in thoroughly developed group decisions.

See J. P. Alston. (1989, March–April). *Wa, guanxi,* and *inwha*: Managerial principles in Japan, China, and Korea. *Business Horizons, 32,* 26–27. The ringi system of decision-making is described in most works dealing with Japanese managerial practices; see B. M. Richardson & T. Ueda (1981). *Business and society in Japan.* New York: Praeger; M. Zimmerman (1985). *How to do business with the Japanese.* New York: Random House.

Status can be based upon expertise or performance. If a person appointed to a group is known to have been highly successful and competent, that person will be accorded high status. Assume that an environmental group includes an outstanding chemist who has a well-known record of research. The chemist will no doubt be a high-status person in that group.

Power, similarly, can be derived from several different attributes of the individual. One's power in the group can be based on the position that one holds in a bureaucracy, for example. Or power can also be derived from competence or expertise: If you know how to fix the machine, you have power compared to those people who don't know how it works. In group communication, power can also come from one's attractiveness: A well-liked, popular person has power, for example.

High-status, high-power individuals tend to speak more and their communication tends to be more favorably received than that of a low-status, low-power person. Moreover, an idea presented by a high-status, high-power individual will usually be more favorably received than the same or similar idea from a lower-power, lower-status individual. Finally, high-power, high-status individuals will receive more communication from other members of the group than will lower-power, lower-status individuals. Both leaders and participants need to guard against these tendencies because overemphasis on status and power can deprive a group of valuable contributions and participants.

4. *Leaders and leadership*. Despite the frequent use of the terms *leaders* and *leadership* interchangeably, the concepts are not synonymous. This distinction is important in understanding what goes on in groups. A leader is a person who occupies a central position in the group; for example, the chair of a committee is a leader. Leadership, on the other hand, is vested in anyone in the group who performs certain specific leadership behaviors. While only one person is the designated leader, every member of the group can exercise some leadership. Leadership therefore refers to a set of behaviors, whereas leader refers to an individual.

The behaviors associated with leadership include those which contribute to completing the group's task behaviors, socioemotional behaviors, and procedural behaviors. In other words, in order to complete the task, certain direction must be exercised that moves along the business or task at hand, keeps the group communicating in a friendly or productive manner, and enacts certain procedures of group activities, such as setting an agenda for future meetings. Any member of the group, in addition to the designated leader, can perform activities that perform these kinds of leadership functions. These task, socioemotional, and procedural functions will be discussed in fuller detail in Chapter 9.

5. *Deviance*. A deviant is a person who noticeably departs from the norms or role expectations of the group. As might be expected, individuals who dissent from an apparent group consensus find themselves the sudden recipients of and the source of more communication than the other members of the group. Through various persuasive techniques, a great deal of pressure will be brought to bear on the deviant individual. If the dissenting individual is a valued member, dissenting on an issue vital to the group, the group might spend a major amount of time trying to win over the dissenter.

If the matter is important—if there is pressure to resolve the problem occasioned by the deviance before moving on—the group may turn to various conflict resolution strategies (as further described in Chapter 13). Strategies can range from forcing or coercing conformity through some power or enforcement mechanism, to negotiation with the deviant, to mediation or arbitration, which involves bringing in a third party to assist in resolving the matter.

ENVIRONMENTAL VARIABLES IN GROUP COMMUNICATION

The discussion has outlined the factors that have been found to have significant effects on how communication proceeds within small groups: norms, roles, status and power, leaders and leadership, and deviance. In addition, there are characteristics of the environment in which the discussions occur that have been found to have a bearing on the nature of communication.

Physical Setting

Physical setting can influence the communication in a small group in the same way that scenery and props can affect a play. As in any other communication situation, the physical setting can influence the communication that occurs.

The physical relationship among group members most commonly noted is seating (see Figure 8-2). For the small group, the most efficient and effective seating arrangement is the roundtable or circle. This maximizes the ability of each group member to see and to speak to every other member of the group with ease. Although the closest members of the group are those sitting on either side, the individual may find it easier to speak to those directly across the table in a small five- or six-person group. Other seating arrangements may isolate members of the group and lead to subgrouping or fragmentation. For example, a long, rectangular table will isolate members at the corners; the people at either end can easily break off into their own discussions as well. Fewer comments are directed to the group as a whole, and more are directed to a fraction of the participants.

Group Size

The optimum size for a productive group is open to question. Somewhere between five and eight members is the most common range authorities give for effective small groups. In the smallest groups of from three to five members, there is more opportunity for each participant to express views, explain, and comment on all facets of the topic under discussion. Larger groups encourage less individual participation. As the group becomes larger and takes on the characteristics of an

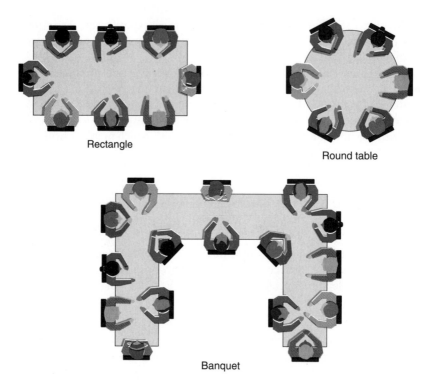

Rectangle

Round table

Banquet

▶ **Figure 8-2** *Group organization: physical layout.*

audience (from each speaker's point of view), some individuals develop stage fright, and their inhibitions restrict their contributions. Within the large group, moreover, more people are competing for the same limited amount of time. Large groups, we can say, seem more like an audience and require more overt controls; more formal communication thus is required. The total effect of large groups is less spontaneity and less give and take.

Large groups are harder to control. The larger the group, the more likely that subgroups will arise. A group of five might form subgroups of three and two members each; a group of eleven could form three groups of three and a group of two. Large groups are less cohesive, less orderly, and more subject to fragmentation or subgrouping. The results may be more conflict of a kind that allows issues to be freely discussed (positive) or conflict of a kind that would splinter the group (negative).

There are advantages to larger groups, however; for example, larger groups have more resources. If one of the values of a group is the sharing of diverse opinions, the larger group has more people available to express opinions. Of course, groups may be large in order to bring into the discussion several different perspectives. Membership may be expanded to bring in different powerful or important constituencies that might be excluded from a small group of three to five members. There may be political reasons, therefore, for using a large versus a small group.

The size of the group also is related to pressures to conform within the group. Smaller groups usually produce more pressures to conform, which gives the group more power over the individual. The pressure to conform may result in less independence for each member and may limit the introduction of radical or unusual opinions. Thus, small groups may have two disadvantages compared to larger groups: fewer opinions from fewer members.

Group size has a profound influence on communication. Optimum size ranges from five to eight in many cases, but the ultimate choice depends upon contingencies of the situation. Small groups allow easier interaction, have more cohesion, give greater member satisfaction, and allow each member to discuss the topic more fully. Large groups have more resources, allow more opinions to be expressed, and exert fewer pressures to conform. The needs of the task could therefore determine the optimum size.

Audiences

All groups are similarly affected by the preceding factors, but public groups experience another series of dynamics that result from the presence of an audience. The presence of an audience can make the public discussion more difficult to organize and manage effectively than the group that meets in private. Once the organizers, leaders, and participants understand what will happen, however, the difficulties can be minimized.

The presence of an audience has several effects, as discussed next. First, discussions are more formal. Just as a speaker before any new audience tries to make a good impression, group members see the panel, symposium, or conference as a kind of formal speaking situation. Consequently, group participants tend to dress, sit, and speak more formally than they would if the audience were not present.

Second, discussions are more cautious. Uncertainty in a new situation, such as the presence of the audience, tends to produce more caution. Speakers fear being misunderstood, corrected, or challenged to prove a point. Consequently, they tend to avoid conflict, be more courteous, and be more compliant. In other words, audience awareness tends to moderate the positions that a member may take in private. This may not necessarily result in a friendly or conflict-free situation, however. In fact, it is possible that conflict may be exacerbated as participants play to an audience or wish to appear strong. As Chapter 13 outlines, an audience may complicate conflict resolution.

Third, discussions are less productive. Concern with the audience will result in more reception of old points of view, old arguments, and fewer attempts to break new ground. Moreover, the fear of being misunderstood will result in greater amplification of the points being made; therefore, the presentation of positions will probably take longer than would be the case if the group were operating in private.

Fourth, discussions are prone to disorganization. In a public discussion, the statements of each participant, as well as the goals of the discussion, should be clear to everyone concerned. One good way to do this is to provide more structure in each participant's statements. Remember, the audience members may be confused early in a presentation and have to wait to ask for clarification.

▶ ### Highlights of Factors Affecting Communication in Groups

Most people know quite a lot about the nature of communication that usually occurs in small group settings. Being aware of these factors allows us to predict the way that communication will go in given groups. In preparing for leading or participating in a group task, one should review these factors as a way of thinking through what may happen in the group and a way to avoid some problems that can be related to these factors. The next section turns to some of the major reasons that group communication can break down.

◀▶ ## PROBLEMS IN SMALL GROUP COMMUNICATION

The most important problems of groups fall into two categories: myths, or unrealistic expectations about groups; and groupthink, which leads to poor decisions. We will take these two problems in turn. Myths stress the expectations of group members, such as avoidance of conflict, which inhibit effective group performance. Poor decision making stresses problems such as groupthink that arise from the nature of groups. Groupthink reflects an unthinking tendency to go along with the group and its decisions.

▶ ### Group Myths

Group myths arise from people's unrealistic expectations about groups. Whether a leader or a participant, each individual enters a group situation with certain expectations. If these expectations are not met, then the individual may feel bewildered, frustrated, angry, or sullen. B. Aubrey Fisher has listed some of the common expectations under the label of "conventional wisdom" about group interaction.[1] These myths or conventional wisdom about what a group should be or should do can cause problems. A few of the myths, and discussion of them, that you may encounter follow.

1. *Objective discussants have no preconceived opinions.* If the participants in a discussion are interested in the topic and have been exposed to the various issues prior to the discussion, they will have formed some opinions concerning the topic. If an attempt is made to suppress these attitudes, the biases become a hidden agenda, or an undercurrent that influences the discussion but is never revealed. In most cases, it is wiser to put feelings on the table. It is better to reveal attitudes so that they can be discussed and analyzed by our fellow discussers. Given that interest is a precondition for most discussions and that this interest will lead to a search for opinion and information prior to the discussion, the probability that most group members have previously formed opinions is high.

2. *Conflict should be avoided.* Conflict is not harmful to a group if the group can handle it or if the conflict sharpens the quality of the final product. Moreover, interpersonal conflict or conflict involving personalities should not be avoided if the avoidance would inhibit the group's productivity. Although there are distinctions made between conflict over issues and conflict over personality, the distinction may be more apparent than real. In most cases, individuals are unable to separate one from the other. An attack on my idea becomes an attack on me. Frequently, the suppression of conflict will lead to worse consequences for the group than if the conflict had been brought to the surface.

3. *Groups should proceed in a logical and orderly fashion,* or *There is a right way and a wrong way to conduct discussion.* Each group should be allowed to develop its own rules of procedure and techniques for solving problems, as long as those methods satisfy the group and produce effective results. The imposition of a particular agenda could stifle creativity and discourage innovation. Moreover, this approach may increase individual frustration. All in all, the tendency to regard one pattern of problem solving as superior is a potential communication problem. Groups may spend valuable time arguing over how they should conduct the discussion rather than on the task.

One potentially damaging assumption is that groups should always follow an agenda in an orderly manner. Frequently, groups discuss issues and topics in a disjointed fashion, moving from one aspect of the question to another. In each case, the group moves on before the issue is completely resolved to everyone's satisfaction. This type of procedure will become a problem if the group is using it to avoid conflict or a particularly divisive issue.

Conversely, changing the subject of the discussion, or taking things out of order, can allow reflection, encourage creativity and flexibility, and allow tempers to cool. The important consideration is the accomplishment of a task and the satisfaction of the group. If individuals will not discuss the topic in an orderly manner, it can be more disruptive to the group to force them into an overly strict agenda rather than allowing the group to move from topic to topic.

4. *A single set of rules will apply to all groups.* Groups are like people in that each is unique. Groups result from the collective behaviors, beliefs, attitudes, and intentions of each member plus the result of their interactions. As a result, a change in one member of the group will affect the entire group. Even the occasion and physical environment of the group meeting place will alter the group's behavior patterns. The number of different group patterns is very large, then, if not infinite.

The first set of problems considered result from the nature of the individuals' expectations about the group. These expectations affect how people communicate in groups. Consequently, knowing our expectations and knowing that they are unrealistic is a major start toward solving these problems.

▶ ### Groupthink

The second set of problems—related to poor decisions—requires more complex and formal corrective measures and is discussed in this section. Chapter 9 discusses the solutions, that is, agenda systems and leadership.

Theoretically, the goal of decision making and problem solving is to produce optimal decisions by considering all the alternatives and selecting the best one. This is impossible, of course, because individuals and groups are unable to consider all the available alternatives because there are too many. Consequently, suboptimal decisions are made; one of the most common types of suboptimal decisions is satisficing. Satisficing involves selecting the first solution that is advantageous over what was being done rather than selecting the optimal solution.

Some researchers such as Irving Janis start with the question: why do groups produce bad decisions? The answer in recent years centers on the nature of groups and group interaction. Janis calls the phenomenon "groupthink."[2]

Irving Janis uses the term *groupthink* to describe the dynamics that cause poor decisions.[3] Janis suggests that groups contain many pressures to conform, such as the attractiveness or cohesiveness of the group, as indicated earlier. As the group becomes more cohesive, conflict and criticism become negative behavior, and the careful evaluation of ideas can suffer as a result.

In addition, cohesive groups may exaggerate the worth of their own ideas and ignore or denigrate the ideas of other groups. Alternative perspectives are lost as a result. If membership in the group is based on similar frames of reference (for example, all engineers or all public relations specialists), moreover, then the advantage of different perspectives or competing ideas is lost. Groupthink is the unwillingness or inability of a group to critically evaluate its own ideas.

Symptoms of groupthink are easy to spot. For example, students are assigned to work in groups to accomplish some graded task. The individuals begin discussing the assignment. Within 10 minutes, someone suggests a topic, arguing, "I did a paper for an accounting class last semester on this topic. There's a lot of material available. Let's do it." Another member responds, "Yeah, let's get going." Several others nod. If the group accepts this first suggestion, they might be making a mistake because there might be other topics that would be better suited to the group. Idea creation or brainstorming takes at least 15 minutes or, perhaps, several hours.[4]

As this hypothetical discussion proceeds, moreover, other problems develop. On hearing the topic suggested, several other members of the group have negative reactions. One doesn't have any interest in the topic; another thinks that the information available may be limited; a third feels that the topic may not meet the requirements of the assignment. Each of the three have important reservations, and each fails to speak out of a desire to avoid conflict.

Highlights of Groupthink. This chapter discussed the nature of groups and group communication as well as the problems associated with group expectations

Problem-Solution   **?** . . . **!**

Groupthink, Problem Solving, and the Corporate Culture: The Problem of Innovation

Problem. In some corporate cultures, change becomes institutionalized as so-called innovation. Such cultures see that change is both inevitable and positive. Those proposing change are seen as missionaries. A corporation in such a state is labeled as bad or old fashioned. The air is full of statements such as "The need for change is obvious," or "Surely, no one could defend our present approaches." Those who oppose such change are seen as disloyal. Irving Janis argues that such institutionalized thinking is just one form of groupthink. An example is found in *Macworld* columnist Steven Levy's review of *West of Eden* (Viking, 1989) by Frank Rose:

> "Rose suggests that the Mac team went too close to the edge. This is reflected by a scene in which a marketing person tells the computer's designers that Apple has a challenge ahead of it in selling the Mac. Everybody jumps on this poor fish: What do you mean? they retort. All we have to do is make them and everybody will want to buy them!"

Such defensive reactions can undermine a group's ability to evaluate its decision-making process and result in less than optimal decisions. All questions that indicate that the group decision is not intuitively workable or may cause other problems are greeted by hostility and incredulity.

Solution. Analyze your audience. Regard true believers as a hostile audience and proceed accordingly, stressing common ground and good evidence (see Chapter 10).

S. Levy. (1989, February). Throwing the book at Apple (p. 61). *Macworld*.

and decision making. Groups have a specific nature that separates them from other forms of interaction. The dimensions explained under the nature of groups include synergy, or ways in which groups are effective, definitions, and types of groups. The nature of group communication includes purposes of group communication, the stages or life styles of groups, factors in group communication, and the group environment. Finally, the chapter concludes with a discussion of problems, including myths and groupthink.

Overall, the nature of groups and group communication contributes to problems and potentially inferior decision making. We are often confounded by our own expectations about groups, and the nature of group interaction increases the opportunity for making inferior decisions, as in groupthink. Cohesiveness has been noted as a positive attribute because it contributes to productivity. Cohesiveness, though, can inhibit communication, if it contributes to groupthink.

EXERCISES

1. Why do discussions break down? List as many reasons as you can for why discussion fails to adequately solve problems or make decisions. Describe specific discussions you have participated in that exhibited such problems. How could they have been corrected?

2. All of us are part of ongoing groups. a. What factors seem to influence the group and its communication? Consider group pressure, physical environment, groupthink, or time pressures. b. What are the patterns of interaction? Which members seem to talk most? Whom do they talk to? c. What are the norms of the group? Who seems to have the most status and power?

3. How do groups develop cohesiveness? Consider social as well as work groups, housing units, and even families. For example, the company picnic or banquet is a traditional way for corporations to develop cohesiveness. Drawing upon your own experiences, describe other methods companies or organizations use to develop cohesiveness. How do high schools develop school spirit? How do fraternities and sororities develop cohesiveness?

SELECTED SOURCES FOR FURTHER READING

Barker, L. L., Wahlers, K. J., Watson, K. W., & Kibler, R. J. (1987). *Groups in process*. Boston: Prentice-Hall.

Bormann, E. G. (1969). *Discussion and group methods*. New York: Harper & Row.

Brilhart, J. K., & Gloria, G. J. (1967). *Effective group discussion*. Dubuque: Wm. C. Brown.

Fisher, A. B., & Ellis, D. G. (1990). *Small group decision making, communication and the group process.* New York: McGraw-Hill.

Goodall, L. H. (1990). *Small group communication in organizations* (2nd ed.). Dubuque: Wm. C. Brown.

Gouran, D. S. (1990). *Making decisions in groups* (rev. ed.). Prospect Heights, IL: Waveland Press.

Janis, I. L. (1972). *Victims of groupthink.* New York: Houghton Mifflin.

Scheidel, T. M., & Crowell, L. (1979). *Discussing and deciding.* New York: Macmillan.

Shaw, M. E., & Gouran, D. S. (1990). Group dynamics and communication. In G. L. Dahnke & G. W. Clatterbuck (Eds.), *Human communication theory and research.* Hastings, CA: Wadsworth.

Tubbs, S. L. (1978). *A systems approach to small group interaction.* New York: Addison-Wesley.

Weick, K. E. (1969). *The social psychology of organizing.* New York: Addison-Wesley.

Weick, K. E. (1979). *The social psychology of organizing* (2nd ed.). New York: Addison-Wesley.

Wilson, G. L., & Hanna, M. S. (1990). *Groups in context.* New York: McGraw-Hill.

References

1. Fisher, A. B., & Ellis, D. G. (1990). *Small group decision making, communication and the group process* (pp. 6–7). New York: McGraw-Hill.
2. Janis, I. (1972). *Victims of groupthink.* Boston, MA: Houghton Mifflin.
3. Janis, pp. 3–9.
4. Scheidel, T. M., & Crowell, L. (1979). *Discussing and deciding* (p. 257). New York: Macmillan.

Group Leadership

CHAPTER

After studying this chapter, you should be able to:

1. Define the importance of vigilance for effective group decision making.

2. Identify the major functions of group leadership.

3. Understand the importance of effective agenda systems for conducting productive group meetings.

4. Plan effectively for fact-finding, evaluative, and problem-solving groups.

5. Recognize the special conditions for organizing and conducting public group meetings.

Overview

The previous chapter considered problems that small groups face, such as myths and groupthink; this chapter considers the solutions. In proposing solutions, we follow Dennis Gouran of Pennsylvania State University and others, who argue that "vigilance" over attitude and good process are necessary to combat "groupthink."[1] The solutions that we propose to the major problems of groups are divided as follows: leadership functions, and effective agenda systems.

EFFECTIVE LEADERSHIP FUNCTIONS

Definitions

Leadership represents a role, as indicated earlier. The distinction between leader and leadership highlights a person's position on the one hand and a role or set of behaviors on the other. A leader is the person or the position; leadership is the role or behavior that contributes to the group's meeting its purpose. An overarching concern of effective leaders is to ensure that groups practice effective vigilance over their processes.

Vigilance over group processes means systematic thinking that allows identification of hidden assumptions, prejudices, and information gaps that would impede effective decision making. Recall that groupthink can impose a mind-set on group members that leads to inferior group decisions. The purpose of vigilance is to guard

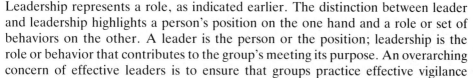

▶ *Group leadership is essential in modern organizations.*

against groupthink as well as the group myths discussed in Chapter 8. There are additional benefits to following systematic group processes. For example, processes can provide an effective format for presenting group findings and decisions to others. In other words, the agenda followed by a group can provide the outline for the group's final report. The agenda can check on whether the group has a well-developed rationale for its recommendations. The steps followed by the group in its deliberations could also provide a guide to follow in implementing its proposals.

▶ **Theories of Leadership**

The questions of who leaders are and where they come from are significant in themselves and of interest of those who would hope for eventually attaining a leadership role. Group communication research has devoted some attention to these issues (see references at end of chapter).

There are a number of possible approaches to analyze group leadership. At one time, leaders were assumed to have certain traits. If you were asked to describe "a great leader," you might mention characteristics such as tall, attractive, forceful, etc. The so-called trait theories of leaders stress that individuals possessing certain innate attributes make them leaders. In other words, leaders are born, not made.

In reaction against the trait or great man theories, researchers began to stress that leaders could be trained in effective leadership. One group of researchers focused on styles of leadership that could be taught. Styles of leadership were seen as placed on a continuum from the authoritarian leader, who controlled the communication and discussion directly, to the laissez-faire leader, who exercised little or no control over the flow of the discussion. With an authoritarian leader, everyone knows who is in charge and what is expected. For some groups, this directiveness or control is very comfortable. The laissez-faire leader, on the other hand, encourages maximum group determination of matters in the group and actively shuns involvement. On the continuum between the authoritarian leader and the laissez-faire leader is the democratic leader, who consults widely and stresses shared decision making. The democratic leader participates actively in the group's deliberations but stresses that the group needs to develop its own policy and procedure.

A third set of theories stress the situational or task environment in the development of leaders. According to these theories, individuals who can adapt to various types of situations, environments, or demands of the group make effective leaders. In other words, various contingencies determine how effective the leader will be, or even who the leader will be. Faced with a new or unanticipated situation, the individual who can explain and suggest a way of dealing with the situation will be perceived as the successful leader. Consequently, an individual might evolve as a leader in one situation and not in another. Especially when leaders can emerge during group interaction, leaders are linked to the requirements of the situation. In other words, such contingency theories envision a situation in which the designation of leader changes with the nature of the task or environment. If there is a medical emergency on an airline flight, a physician on board will suddenly assume a leadership position, shifting from the role of ordinary passenger. If you are the expert on a certain topic that a group takes up, you may suddenly find yourself a leader of that group.

Overall, the theories of leaders share an emphasis on people's perception and communication. Leaders depend on followers to recognize them as leaders. Such recognition comes from interaction and, therefore, communication with and among the members of the group. You are a leader not only because of your position but also since you are regarded by the members of the group as a leader. The relationship between the leader's performance and perceptions of group members concerning that performance stresses the interactive nature of communication and leadership in small groups.

Leadership Roles

The roles delineated below can be performed by any member of a group. Generally, effective groups are those in which these roles are shared rather than left to any one individual, such as a chair or designated leader, to perform. Leadership can be classified in three areas:

1. Procedural roles.
2. Interpersonal roles.
3. Task, or problem-solving roles.

Procedural Roles.   Procedural roles deal with the mechanics of planning, organizing, and otherwise mobilizing the group's resources to accomplish the task. As you look over the roles that follow, you will note that any member of the group could perform some of them. For example, any member, not necessarily the leader, can summarize what has been said about a certain issue. On the other hand, some of these functions typically are duties of a group leader, such as opening a discussion, preparing the physical setting, calling the meeting, and so on (see Figure 9-1). Specific procedural roles include the following:

    1. *Planning or preparing for the discussion to take place.* This role is usually assumed by the leader or delegated to another. The planner(s) should do several things.

First, know the participants. Analyze the strengths and weaknesses of the participants. The leader should know who the participants are, what qualifications they have in the topic area, and what specific opinions they hold. Leaders should attempt to assess the possibility of personality clashes between members. They need to ensure that there is a variety of points of view and that participants bring a wide range of knowledge and expertise to the group.

Second, direct any preliminary research. The leader should be prepared to guide members who need to do further study, share any important references with members of the group, and add any individuals to the group if that would help the group accomplish its goal, by bringing a needed viewpoint or knowledge base into the group.

Third, arrange the physical setting. The leader should arrange for a place to meet, complete with necessary furnishings and other comforts. A round table with room to take notes, chairs that are not too comfortable, and an absence of distractions such as noise or excessive heat or cold are important factors.

Fourth, provide any necessary materials. Any syllabi, agenda, or other material that is going to be or has the potential to be an important part of the meeting

---

Leadership: Procedural Roles

- Introducing the topic for discussion
- Clarifying contributions
- Ensuring thoroughness
- Summarizing
- Closing the discussion

▶ **Figure 9-1**   *Procedural leadership roles.*

should be provided to the group members before the meeting, so that they will have a chance to study it. Moreover, extra copies should be available for those who misplace their material prior to the meeting.

Fifth, arrange for a time for the first meeting. Even if you carefully arrange schedules, some individuals will be unable to make the meeting; therefore, try to make it as easy as possible for people to attend, but do not expect all to attend.

In sum, the purpose of planning is to ensure that physical and intellectual conditions have been prepared to allow for effective decision making.

2. *Introducing the topic for discussion.* Again, this task is typically assumed by the leader and consists of two possible steps.

First, a prediscussion meeting can be useful when the topic is complex, when the participants are unfamiliar with one another, or when the discussion will be in front of an audience.

Second, a concise but detailed introduction of the topic at the group's first formal meeting is essential. The leader should stress the purpose of the discussion as specifically as possible; emphasize the importance of the discussion; and attempt to stimulate the participants to be in the discussion. For example, at a meeting to begin preparations for company expansion, the leader would want to place the proposed expansion in terms of the organization's overall goals and purposes, potential effects of the expansion on internal and external constituencies (how it will affect their community, for instance), as well as practical considerations to guide the group's planning. The purpose is to set the stage and to encourage constructive thinking. Therefore, the leader may want to delineate specific issues and topics to be discussed as part of the process.

3. *Clarifying contributions.* Because of differences in perception, language choice, and a variety of other factors, the precise meaning of a member's statement may be unclear. When you are unsure of the message or when the message is ambiguous, be sure to ask for clarification. Obviously, any member can perform this leadership task, as well as the next two.

First, if the contribution is too general, ask for specifics. Second, if the contribution is too specific, ask for the general import of the example or incident.

The purpose of clarifying is to ensure that everyone understands the material and how it fits into the discussion. For example, if a member comments that the plans for expansion seem threatening to people in her department, ask for more specific information: What aspect of the plans are threatening and in what way? Are people concerned that hiring new people could be upsetting to a well-functioning work team? Are they concerned the new people would receive more status or resources than they have been getting? Are they worried that the new positions would leave their current needs unfulfilled?

4. *Ensuring thoroughness.* One advantage of a group is its sharing of distinct viewpoints, information, and other resources. This can occur only if all sides of a question are discussed openly and frankly. If you are unsure that the topic has been covered, be sure to probe for more.

First, ask for other possible opinions. Second, ask for opinions of other experts or authorities that members have found in their research. Third, play devil's advocate and articulate the opposing opinion yourself. Fourth, ask the group to role play a situation in which they attack their own position, information, arguments, or ideas.

5. *Summarizing the discussion at appropriate points.* At certain points, clarify what has come before by stating what members of the group seem to agree upon, what issues are unresolved, and what remains to be done. Be sure to avoid summarizing too frequently, though.

First, summarize when asked to summarize. Second, summarize after a major issue has been resolved. Third, summarize to clarify where the group stands during the middle of a prolonged argument. Fourth, if you are unsure of what has happened, ask the group or another member for a summary.

6. *Closing the discussion.* This is a procedural function that usually will be performed by the group's designated leader. A good conclusion or summary should contain certain elements:

First, a final summary emphasizing what has been accomplished, what remains to be done, agreement and disagreement, and possible future plans should be included.

Second, agreement on needed material that should be secured before the discussion can continue should be included. A discussion of how the material can be secured or collected should occur as well.

Third, understanding about what will be done after the discussion to prepare for the next step in the process—whether another meeting, action to implement the suggestions of the group, or some other appropriate followup—should be included. As soon as possible, the leader or the recorder should reinforce the oral summary with a written memo or report.

Interpersonal Roles.   Interpersonal roles of leadership refer to functions that aid people's feelings of satisfaction with the group, with the other members of the group, and with their role in the discussion (see Figure 9-2). All members can enact leadership roles. For example, any member could encourage others to participate in the discussion, drawing out reticent members. Designated leaders usually perform the functions of regulating participation, but others can as well. Some of the major interpersonal functions involve reducing tension, helping to manage conflict, and producing and maintaining a positive climate (that is, one of openness, low threat, and high trust). These last few functions require the cooperation of several people in the group.

1. *Encouraging participation.* In order for members to contribute freely to the discussion, they need to feel that their participation is important. The extreme is the individual who refuses to participate. Techniques for drawing out a reticent individual include the following:

First, ask that person for an opinion. Second, encourage the individual's con-

---

Leadership: Interpersonal Roles

- Encouraging participation
- Regulating participation
- Controlling conflict
- Reducing tension
- Promoting a positive climate

▶ **Figure 9-2** *Interpersonal leadership roles.*

tributions by nodding your head or using other forms of nonverbal reinforcing behavior. Third, ask the person questions that only that individual can answer. Fourth, protect the individual from negative comments that could inhibit further contributions. Be especially willing to agree with the quiet individual. Even if you disagree with part of what the person said, seek something that you do agree with. Always start with agreement. Fifth, outside the discussion, ask the individual why no contribution is being made. When you understand the cause, you can then work to eliminate or modify its effects. Sixth, outside the discussion, ask other members to help you encourage the reticent member to speak.

2. *Regulating participation.* Sometimes a few members will dominate the group, or hidden communication networks (cliques) will be established among a few members. There are several ways to reduce the impact of these problems. First, you can direct questions to all members of the group or members who are not part of the subgroup. You can set time limits for how long anyone can speak, although this tactic should be used sparingly due to the desire to encourage thorough discussions. Also, you can talk to the individual who is causing the problem outside the group. Tactfully suggest that the subgroup or domination is hindering the group and causing tension. If faced with one individual who is dominating the group, you can suggest that he or she become the group's recorder. Above all, combat hidden communication networks or cliques by encouraging contributions from everyone.

3. *Controlling conflict.* Conflict is frequent, especially in larger groups or in groups dealing with controversial issues. While some conflict can be energizing, at times it may be necessary to take steps to prevent conflict from threatening the group or individuals within it. Several techniques can be used to channel conflict in a positive direction. You can direct attention to issues (rather than personalities). Although this may not be possible, the attempt may reassure some members. Focus on facts, evidence, and objective material. Also, you can make sure that the points

Diversity in the Workplace

Gender Differences in Leadership Style

A recent article in *Nation's Business* highlighted the trend for companies to encourage diversity of leadership styles in management, especially the differing styles of men and women, which can be "complementary, producing a synergism that gives the company benefits it would not receive if two men or two women were in those jobs."[2] One reason for such benefits is that today's better educated work force expects more openness and interaction in discussing decisions, traits of the new generation of women managers.

Maureen Dowd, in an article in *Working Woman*, reports studies that indicate a first and second wave of women managers. The first wave usually tried to emulate the leadership style of male colleagues, while the second wave does not. Dowd characterizes women of the second wave as "less dependent on formal authority and believing more in power of personality."[3] These characteristics are shown in tendencies to share power and decision making and to motivate others by building their self-respect.

See S. Nelton (1991) Men, women & leadership. *Nation's Business*, *79*, 16–22; M. Dowd (1991) Power: Are women afraid of it—or beyond it? *Working Woman*, November 1991, pp. 98–99 and J. B. Rosener (1990) Ways women lead. *Harvard Business Review*, November–December, 1990, pp. 119–125.

of difference are clear. Ask for specifics, as in clarifying the procedural roles. Make sure that all areas of disagreement are located (it may be very hard to get at personality conflict). Finally, resolve the least difficult problem first. Having resolved the least intense or least explosive issue, the group will have the confidence to tackle the harder issues.

4. *Reducing tension.* While conflict is being faced and managed, action needs to be taken to reduce group tension, to reduce anxiety, and to build cohesion. You can do this by first calling attention to the group's progress. Also, praise other members and their contributions, including the members of your opposition. Remain friendly with everyone within the group. Explicitly compare the progress of your group with the progress of other groups, if it is favorable. Use humor whenever possible or, at least, be willing to find the humor in the situation. Recess the meeting to allow tempers to cool. Verbalize your feelings. If you attempt to restrain your feelings too long, the explosion may become more tense and more divisive.

5. *Promoting a positive climate.* The emphasis on accomplishing a task and the importance of the matter under discussion may threaten the informality, security, and cooperativeness of the group. To keep the climate positive, protect the ability and the right to express all opinions. Allow the group to relax or engage in a nontask activity. Don't put too much pressure on an individual to talk. Don't put too much time pressure on the group to make a decision. Finally, avoid obvious uses of power, status, or other arbitrary behavior.

Task and Problem-Solving Roles of Leadership. The third area associated with group leadership involves the use of materials directly concerned with the task at hand: specific goals, information, analysis, logic and solutions, including action (see Figure 9-3). These functions include keeping focus on the goal, encouraging critical thinking, and especially evaluating proposals and reasoning.

Problem-solving functions will be accomplished if the following principles are observed:

1. *Focusing on the goal.* The idea is to remind the group of its overall picture and purpose. These reminders should help to provide a context and meaning for the group's deliberations.

First, make sure that everyone understands the goal early in the discussion. Second, ensure that information is tied to other pieces of related information. Look for explanations of how contributions relate to the overall purpose.

2. *Promoting evaluative and critical thinking.* Critical thinking is at the center of promoting group vigilance. The major task function is to ensure high-quality decision making in the group. The purpose of leadership, therefore, is to promote good critical thinking. Critical thinking requires that the group is working with

---

Leadership: Task and Problem-Solving Roles

- Focusing on the goal
- Promoting evaluative and critical thinking
- Critically evaluating solutions

▶ **Figure 9-3** *Task and problem-solving roles of leadership.*

sound evidence as well as sound reasoning. Hence, good leadership should ensure that enough information is available; information is up to date; and information is used in a logically consistent manner.

Any member of the group can ask questions intended to promote good critical thinking. For example, someone can ask about the sources for information being used. Where did these figures come from? Are they up to date? Are we working with the most recent statistics? A member should also question the relevance of the facts and figures that are being used in the discussion. (Chapter 3 covers this in detail.) The techniques of effective critical listening should be applied here in the group setting.

Note also that asking for sound critical thinking should be consistent with the interpersonal roles above. As much as possible, you should avoid sounding too threatening when challenging other member's facts and figures. Emphasize that you are asking for clarification and for using the best possible data.

3. *Critically evaluating solutions.* This idea is covered in more detail later in this chapter. The essence is to use appropriate criteria and standards for evaluating solutions.

First, make sure that all possible solutions are considered. Groups should avoid simply satisficing (as introduced in Chapter 2). One technique is to brainstorm to come up with as many solutions as possible without allowing criticism until you have a long list.

Second, help the group develop criteria for evaluating solutions. For example, cost-effectiveness is a typical criterion. Others might include quality of the product or service, effects on health, and so on.

Third, make sure that each solution is evaluated consistently. This means, do we ask the same questions about all solutions that are proposed? The criteria should be applied consistently.

Fourth, point out the consequences of decisions and solutions. Consider unintended effects or by-products. Try to visualize situations that would result from the implementation of the proposal.

Highlights of Effective Leadership Functions. The various functions just listed—interpersonal, task, and procedural—encompass only the most obvious positive roles that contribute directly and indirectly to accomplishing the task. Although some of these functions are usually performed by group-appointed or elected leaders, most can and should be performed by anyone in the group. Effective leadership is the first step to improving performance in groups. The second way to improve group performance is to proceed systematically, or to use an agenda system. Our assumption is that better processes will lead to better decisions.

EFFECTIVE AGENDA SYSTEMS

Within an organization, teams and groups are set up to make and implement decisions. Agenda provide a systematic approach to questions such as what, if anything, can be done to reduce absenteeism, or how four new accountants can fit into the same amount of physical space or which computer, if any, should a company purchase.

At times, the group or team may be presented with simpler tasks such as fact-finding or evaluation. For example, "What are our space needs for the next 5 years?" or "Which computer best meets our graphic needs?" Each of these cases (fact-finding, evaluation, problem solving, and decision making) requires a systematic approach. First, we consider the purposes for all agenda and, second, considerations for wording a good question for discussion. Then we will take up in turn each of the three types: fact-finding, evaluative, and problem solving.

Purposes of an Agenda

In some cases, a great deal of thought and analysis has been done about a problem even before the group meets. A discussion outline circulated to the group members prior to a meeting can provide a starting point when the group meets and stimulate each member to analyze and expand the original outline. As the discussion proceeds, groups need some way of keeping track of whether or not the topic has been sufficiently developed. A carefully prepared outline, or agenda, should serve as an aid to this process, as long as it is carefully revised as the situation warrants.

Many groups have to produce some final written report. The outline, carefully constructed and revised during the discussion, makes the final report much easier to produce. The discussion outline is not a straitjacket. Do not expect the discussion to always proceed logically from premise to evidence to argument to decision. Outside the classroom, in the so-called real world, people do not always think in this fashion. More importantly, there is no evidence that attempts to proceed through an outline from start to finish while avoiding tangents significantly improve the group's productivity. Using the outline aggressively can cause resentment, increase frustration and tension, and stifle creativity. The organizational patterns should serve as guides only to whether or not the topic has been covered adequately.

Questions for Discussion

Good analysis can come only after the group has an exact goal in mind. This goal, or the question for discussion, limits and guides everything else that happens in the discussion. Preparing a good question, or statement for discussion, involves (1) wording a good question, (2) limiting it in terms of what is to be covered, and, sometimes, (3) defining important terms and (4) revising it when necessary.

Wording the Question. A good question for discussion has certain characteristics.

1. *It is worded as a question*. Questions tend to be more open-ended than statements and allow more alternatives to be discussed: "Will this insurance plan meet our company's needs?" versus "We should adopt Mutual of Idaho's plan." A statement tends to suggest what should be done and thus shapes thinking. At times, however, when a statement may be preferred; for example, when a decision is being reviewed or reconsidered, a statement of that decision may be better than a question.

2. *It is worded simply.* The rule is to keep the question as short as possible. Unnecessary words, long and complex clauses, or other items that increase sentence length should be edited out. Do not try to put all aspects of the problem into the wording of the question: "Should we close the Akron plant?" versus "In view of the economic conditions and prospects for international negotiations pending in the coming fiscal year, should there be some consideration to downward revision in the number of plants in our corporation, such as the one in Akron?"

3. *It is worded specifically.* You should try to say precisely what you want to say—nothing more and nothing less. In your choice of words, use specific terms or phrases, including proper nouns, whenever possible. The Akron plant example could be more specific, as in: "Should we close all operations at the Akron plant by 1994?"

4. *It is worded neutrally.* As much as possible, try to avoid words or phrases that load the question. For example, words and phrases such "free enterprise," "bureaucracy," or "politically correct" tend to cloud questions with emotion. The wording should also avoid no-win assumptions. A typical problem can consist of assuming a problem. Before a problem can be solved, you have to decide whether a problem actually exists, and the wording of the question could assume that a problem exists before that has been actually determined. For example, is foreign investment in the United States a problem to be solved, or is it a source for capital that provides jobs? A group beginning with the notion that there is a problem may not look at the issue of whether it is a real problem or not.

Limiting the Topic.   Limiting the question for discussion becomes necessary because of limitations on resources.

1. *Consider the time available.* If the topic is too broad, really successfully study and completion of task may take longer than the group's available time. If the deadline cannot or should not be changed, then the extent of the topic will have to be limited.

2. *Think about the group's power or authority.* In most situations, the realities of what you can do and cannot do are unfortunate but real. If the group confronts a "sacred cow," or has limited ability to implement a decision, or discovers that the solution lies outside its area of decision making, the topic must be redefined or limited.

3. *Consider the group's level of expertise.* Members should be knowledgeable in the areas that they are discussing. If they are not, then they should have the time and other resources available to become comfortable with the area. If they lack this, the question should be limited, rephrased, or abandoned.

4. *Analyze the need for research.* Closely connected with the area of expertise is the area of available research. If no available material exists, the group can either commission new research or redefine the question.

An example of attempts at limiting a problem-solving question might go as follows:

- "What should be done about this country's economic problems?" seems broad.
- "What should be done about this country's unemployment problems?" is a little more specific by focusing our attention on the employment issue.
- "What should be done about this country's structural unemployment problems?" further restricts attention to a type of unemployment.
- "What should be done about the structural unemployment problems of American youth?" turns attention to a specific group of people affected by this problem.
- "Should a program of manpower training be implemented to solve the unemployment problems of American youth?" This attempt is even more specific in that it focuses on a definite plan of action to solve the problem.

Defining Important Terms.   Once you have a well-worded, limited question for discussion, you need to define important terms in and related to the question. For example, if we are discussing unemployment, we need to be certain that all members understand the kind of unemployment in question. Frequently, groups and individuals are confronted by petty haggling over definitions. Therefore, groups should be careful to define specialized terms or words that appear in the question or that are used in the course of the discussion. Being clear about definitions is an aspect of practicing good group vigilance.

This section reviews systematic methods that can be used to define such critical terms.

1. *Logical definition.* Logical definition consists of three steps: naming the term to be defined; putting that term into a class; and separating that term from all other members of that class.

For example, "persuasion" (the term to be defined) is the communication process (the class) of changing beliefs, attitudes, or behavior and/or of reinforcing beliefs, attitudes, or behavior (separating the term from the other members of the class).

2. *Definition by example.* Through specificity and detail, the exact image evokes a more vivid understanding: "Persuasion is the process of selling an air conditioner to a resident of Point Barrow, Alaska."

3. *Definition by comparison or contrast (or negation).* In comparison, we define by saying that the unfamiliar word to be defined is similar to a more familiar word whereas contrast emphasizes the differences. For example, field hockey is like ice hockey (comparison) without the violence or the skates (contrast). Negation is similar to contrast except that all alternatives are eliminated.

4. *Definition by synonym.* In many cases, a word or phrase that means approximately the same thing will suffice: "Persuasion is political advertising."

5. *Definition by division.* In some instances, it is more meaningful to define a word or concept by listing its various parts or components. For example, it is frequently more meaningful to list the various companies that make up a conglomerate rather than to give the name of the parent corporation. PepsiCo is the corporation that includes Frito-Lay, Kentucky Fried Chicken (KFC), Pizza Hut, and Pepsi-Cola.

6. *Definition by authority.* When all else fails, we can use a dictionary or some other special authority in a given field. For legal terms, *Black's Law Dictionary* is cited frequently. For less technical terms, a standard dictionary will suffice. In some cases, we have to track down the expert or group of experts who coined the word in order to understand the correct meaning.

Revising the Question during Discussion.   Most questions will be revised during the course of the discussion. As problems with the topic become apparent, the group should feel free to revise and refine the question; it may turn out that there is not enough time or resources after all to deal with the full scope of the original question, for example. Momentary agreement that the group has arrived at a question should not lock the group in to that specific wording.

Agenda for Fact-Finding Groups

Fact-finding groups attempt to prove or disprove something ("There has been an increase in foreclosures in this district over previous years," for example) or the existence of some state of affairs ("We are in a state of recession or not"). Common types of questions of fact involve causal arguments: Something is the cause of something else: "Is program trading the cause of instability in stock markets?" These causal questions of fact can be subdivided into two types: those dealing with current or past causes, and those concerned with the future: "Will the development of market economies in Eastern Europe result in increased prosperity?"

A fact-finding discussion agenda consists of three major parts:

1. *A well-worded question of fact.* This includes definition of all terms in the question and definition of all other important terms that will be used in the course of the discussion.
2. *Careful analysis of the question of fact.* This involves breaking down the question of fact into its component parts; using the tests for valid evidence and attempting to verify each of the parts of the argument; and attempting to verify any special relationships among the various parts of the argument.
3. *Report on findings and implications.*

For example, imagine you have been asked to chair a committee to determine whether the use of program trading leads to instability in the stock market. In the beginning, you may know very little about this topic, but the agenda ought to point you and your group in the right direction for discovering the information that you need. Program trading refers to the use of computerized programs for determining when to buy or sell stocks based on a range of high and low prices. When the stock market index, such as the Dow Jones, falls below a certain point, such as 3200, the program would automatically call for selling a block of stock. Such an automatic decision could depress prices further, triggering other programs to do the same thing. You would prepare an agenda by following the preceding steps, elaborated here.

1. *Formulate a well-worded question for discussion*: "Does program-trading lead to instability in the New York Stock Exchange?" (Notice that the original question has been refined somewhat in line with the directions for wording questions. It is now a little more specific by focusing on a specific stock market. It could be even more specific by concentrating on fluctuations in the Dow Jones Industrial Average.)
   a. Define the term *program trading*. (Do you want to include all kinds of computerized buy and sell programs for stock investors, or only certain kinds of automatic programs?)
   b. Define the term *instability*. (This term is particularly unclear, and instability may be a loaded term. You may need to refine this concept during the discussion: Do you mean erratic fluctuations of prices or the index by a certain amount?)
2. *Analyze the question*.
   a. Component parts: Is program trading widespread? Are there fluctuations? Are they major? Are they harmful?
   b. Test evidence for validity. Is the data recent? Current? Has a scientific study been made of this issue?
   c. Determine the relationship between program trading and stock market fluctuations. Is it a causal relationship? The main cause? Are there other causes? What factors are necessary for the cause to work?
3. *Report on findings and implications*. To what extent did we verify that program trading causes stock market instability?

Agenda for Evaluative Groups

Questions of value involve judgments concerning the worth of a person, place, thing, event, organization, or idea. While a question of fact concerns a state of affairs, a question of value asks about justice, fairness, beauty, ethics, and the like.

An outline for an evaluation uses the criteria-satisfaction method, in which criteria are developed for judging the worth of the thing in question. Criteria are any standards that can be used to determine the value of something. Arriving at these criteria or standards for judgment is often the hardest part of any discussion.

There are several principles of well-worded criteria for judgments.

First, they are complete sentences stating the principle involved. They are worded as general principles. Criteria should not deal with the specific person, place, or thing that you are going to evaluate. A principle seems more defensible in theory than it may seem in a specific instance. A more objective decision will come if the group works from general to specific. In the trial example, any person deserves the right to confront accusers.

Well-worded criteria are objective. Observables are easier to verify than values. Consequently, attempt to make the criteria as close to factual questions as possible. The test is whether or not someone who did not take part in your deliberations would answer the questions in the same way that you did. In the trial example, whether or not a person is represented by an attorney is clearly verifiable.

Sound criteria are exhaustive. The group must uncover all important aspects of the situation.

In order to use criteria for setting agendas, we recommend ranking the criteria in order of importance. In some situations, one criterion for decision may be absolutely essential; that is, the criterion is a defining characteristic. For example, cost may become such a defining criterion: any solution costing over $500,000

Criteria for Fair Trial

Some good examples of what we mean by criteria are principles that courts evolve to evaluate whether or not an individual received a fair trial. A brief list of some of these criteria of fair trials include the following:

1. The person should be represented by legal counsel.
2. The person should be allowed to present witnesses on his or her own behalf.
3. The person should be allowed to know and confront accusers.
4. The jury sitting in judgment must be unbiased and impartial.

In a specific case, these criteria are applied as questions: "Did Ralph receive a fair trial?"

1. Was Ralph represented by an attorney?
2. Was Ralph allowed to present witnesses on his behalf?
3. Was Ralph permitted to confront accusers?
4. Was Ralph's jury unbiased and impartial?

will be unacceptable. In other situations, meeting several criteria taken together may be more important than meeting any one. In deciding whether a certain computer best meets our graphic needs, we probably would take into account several factors, such as cost, compatibility with other equipment, learning curve for staff, and so on.

Use the criteria reasonably as a general rule. In situations in which you and your group have no vested interests, you can decide on the criteria and apply them to the specific situation. When you might have a specific ax to grind, criteria can become even more important in order to prevent your preconceptions from getting in the way. In other words, the criteria reinforce vigilance in the group process. They allow you to see if you can defend your decision in principle as well as specifically. If someone asks you what principles were the basis for your group's decision, you will have a good answer.

Evaluative groups, then, should organize their discussion around comparing the thing at issue with some objective, reasonable, and agreed-upon criteria.

Agenda for Problem-Solving Groups

The problem-solution approach is a systematic method of decision making. Specifically, a problem-solving approach allows you to make choices and defend them using meaningful justifications.

Developing agenda for problem-solution discussions involves several important steps. These steps are presented in outline form, because agenda should be prepared in outline form. Agenda in outline form are easier to follow during a discussion.

1. A well-worded question of policy.
   a. Definition of all terms in the question.
   b. Definition of all other important terms that will be used in the course of the discussion.
2. What is the nature of the problem?
   a. Is there a problem?
   b. What is the extent of the problem?
      (1) What is the harm?
      (2) Is the harm widespread?
   c. What are the causes of the problem?
3. What is the best solution?
   a. What solutions are available?
   b. How should we judge those solutions?
   c. Which solution or combination of solutions should we pick?
   d. What are the effects of the solution? Advantages and disadvantages?
4. Report on findings and implications.

For example, you must draw up the agenda for a group set up to study the problem of falling enrollment at your institution. Follow the steps in the suggested outline above.

Problem-Solution

> ### The Problem-Solution Approach—Performance Excellence at Eli Lilly
>
> Eli Lilly and Company of Indianapolis uses a *Performance Excellence Guidebook*, developed by the Florida Power & Light Company. One aspect of this guidebook is "The PE Problem-Solving Process."
> The PE problem-solving approach consists of seven steps:
>
> 1. Reason for improvement, or what is the problem?
> 2. Current situation or what is the harm?
> 3. Analysis or what are causes of the problem?
> 4. Countermeasures or plan and implement a solution to remove the causes of the problem.
> 5. Results or measure the effect of the plan.
> 6. Standardization or implementation in other areas.
> 7. Future plans or other problems and how well did the team work?
>
> The Lilly *Performance Excellence Guidebook* concludes:"The seven-step Performance Excellence Story is a powerful, systematic method of problem solving used to improve the quality of products and services and the workplace itself."
>
> Eli Lilly and Company (1989). *Performance excellence guidebook* (p. 27). Copyright 1989 Florida Power & Light Company. Used by permission of the Florida Power & Light Co.

1. What, if anything, should be done to reverse falling enrollment at Winsocki?
   a. Define or explain "enrollment." Do we mean full-time students only? Or do we include part-time students? Are only undergraduates to be included?
   b. Define falling enrollment. Do we mean declines of a significant amount? For a certain period of time?
   c. Define other terms that may be important: full-time equivalents, part-time student, undergraduate, and so on.
2. What is the nature of the problem?
   a. Is enrollment declining?
   b. What is the extent of the problem? What is the harm from falling enrollment? Decreased financial resources? How significant is the loss?
   c. What are the causes for declining enrollment, such as, increasing tuition, declining student age population, recession, and so on?
3. What is the best solution?

      a. What are available solutions? Expand recruiting area? More financial aid? Lower tuition?

      b. What are the criteria for judging the solutions? Cost? Personnel and faculty effects?

      c. Which solution best meets the criteria?

      d. What are the effects of the solution? Advantages? Disadvantages?

   4. Report on findings and implications.

Highlights of Effective Agenda Systems

After reading through these checklists for preparing agenda for different types of discussions, you should have a fair idea of what type of preparation you will need to become an effective discussion participant. Leaders or chairpersons have special responsibilities, of course. Leaders should make the following types of information available before the group has even met. For example, what topic will be discussed? If a question has been worded, what is it? If just a potential problem has been isolated, what is it?

Also, what resources does the group have? Is there any preliminary information that could be made available? How much time and power does the group have? How many members and who?

With this information in hand, the individual participant can begin constructing an outline and gather information about the topic in order to prepare the kinds of agendas indicated earlier. In the real world, there is often neither the time nor the necessity to cover every agenda item or question included in the checklists. They are there to help make sure that you have covered all the bases that you need to for this particular discussion.

ORGANIZING AND CONDUCTING PUBLIC DISCUSSIONS

On special occasions, you may be called upon to conduct public discussions, that is, discussions before an audience. We have suggested that there are three kinds of public discussion groups: the panel discussion, symposium, and conference. A panel discussion is composed of experts or knowledgeable individuals who discuss a topic among themselves for the benefit of an audience who watches but does not participate during the main part of the discussion. A symposium is a collection of individual presentations or speeches meant to stimulate audience interest, enthusiasm, questions, and participation. The symposium should be thought of as individual presentations. A conference is the largest type of public discussion encompassing a variety of presentational methods to (a) provide the audience with new information and techniques and (b) enable the audience to practice or evaluate the new information and technique. This is the most formal of the public discussions requiring the most careful planning, organization, and control.

Preparations for public discussions are typically divided into certain major stages:

▶   **Preparation for the Public Discussion**

Preparation includes the following steps:

1. Analyze the audience for the discussion.
2. Prepare the question for discussion.
3. Analyze the participants.
4. Arrange physical facilities.
5. Hold a prediscussion meeting with the participants.

Before the public discussion can occur, the organizer needs to consider several important problems. First, the organizer should analyze the audience in the same manner that a public speaker would analyze the audience before a speech.

Next, the specific question for discussion and all subsequent decisions must be made with an audience in mind. The organizer has to adapt to the audience needs, interests, attitudes, and knowledge level. Then a specific question for discussion has to be worded taking all these elements into account. Moreover, the organizer has to be concerned with balancing time versus the need to cover the topic. Once the question has been formulated, the organizer needs to ensure that all important aspects of the topic will be covered. The most embarrassing public discussion situation is to violate audience expectations by announcing that a group will address a specific question and then failing to cover some important aspect of the topic. The problem of time restraint influences the breadth of the question to be covered and the number of panelists or participants. More than an hour of discussion without a break may tax an audience.

Once the topic and question have been selected, the organizer considers the discussants. The individuals who agree to take part should be articulate experts of a particular position or point of view. They should be skilled in oral presentation as well as knowledgeable on the subject. Even the most authoritative expert needs to present his or her knowledge in a stimulating and entertaining as well as informative or persuasive fashion.

Also, the organizer plans the physical arrangements. This includes being sure to consider the size of the auditorium or hall, based on the size of the expected audience as well as ensuring that the seating is arranged so that the audience can see the speaker. In the panel discussion, speakers should be arranged in a semicircle or some other formation that allows them to see one another and still be able to address the audience. A raised platform or podium and proper lighting are all important. Most of all, make sure that everyone can hear, and, if necessary, have a public address system available. (Test the system before the discussion is to begin and have an alternative plan if it should fail.)

Finally, prior to the actual public discussion, there should be at least one meeting of the principal participants so that they can meet one another. Such a meeting allows the participants to exchange opinions, information, and the subject of their presentation.

Although participants in panel discussions are not making a speech, they should be prepared to talk in a stimulating manner. One unprepared group member who does not speak will not harm the discussion, whereas a prepared speaker who talks constantly will hurt the discussion. Characteristically, discussants will not give long speeches; instead, participants might make a point and give one or two examples or pieces of evidence, listen for a while, and make another point. The prediscussion meeting should be used to talk about what topics will be introduced and some of what will be said about each topic, as well as to accustom the participants to the physical surroundings and the moderator or leader.

Conducting the Public Meeting

Opening and Closing the Discussion.   The moderator is responsible for opening and closing the discussion. To open any public discussion, the moderator introduces the specific question for discussion. Also, the moderator provides the general and specific reasons for the discussion, such as why the topic is important, why this audience should be concerned about the topic, or why it is of current interest. Another "opening" responsibility includes explaining any rules or procedures that will govern the discussion. Finally, the moderator introduces the members of the group or panel.

In the panel discussion, the members are introduced before the moderator's first question. In the symposium, each speaker is introduced just prior to his or her presentation. Finally, in the conference, since too many participants may be present to be able to introduce each, the moderator may simply introduce the keynote speaker and subsequent speakers when they first contribute.

▶ *A meeting room set up for a panel discussion.*

The introduction of the participants should include information that will help the audience to determine the speaker's competence and biases. Information might reasonably include the speaker's area of expertise, degrees held, unique experiences, publications, or other reasons why these individuals were chosen to take part. The moderator should consult with the participants and avoid showing any prejudice for or against a particular discusser.

Closing the discussion is simpler. The moderator should spend 2 or 3 minutes summarizing the major points that were made in the discussion, thank the participants, and thank the audience for taking part.

The Body of the Discussion.   Each of the three major forms of public discussion are analyzed separately to avoid confusion.

In the panel discussion, attention is focused on the participants whose discussion proceeds from point to point with as little direction from the moderator as possible. However, the moderator should be prepared to perform the following functions:

- *Maintaining order* by ensuring that only one speaker has the floor at any one time, allowing opinions to be made fully with a minimum of interruptions and, in other ways, controlling the orderliness of the discussion.
- *Maintaining fairness* by making sure that the participants are protected from personal attack and that all views are expressed as completely as possible, even if they are unpopular. In extreme cases, the moderator should become the devil's advocate.
- *Clarifying meaning* by restating, summarizing, providing transitions, and questioning. This may include keeping an eye on the panel's involvement in the discussion. If the panel becomes too involved, they might forget the audience. The moderator should keep placing himself in the shoes of an intelligent but relatively uninformed member of the audience.
- *Encouraging participation* by directing questions at silent members, by politely interrupting members who dominate the discussion, and by asking provocative questions when the discussion falters.

In the symposium, the moderator plays a more restrained role. Specific functions include the following:

- *Introducing each speaker* and the particular topic that the speaker will discuss.
- *Providing a transition* between each speaker and topic so that a coherent and organized whole is maintained. This is done in the same manner as an individual speaker would provide transitions throughout a speech.

The symposium moderator introduces the first speaker, indicating the subject of the presentation. After the first speaker has finished, the moderator provides a transition to the next speaker's topic and introduces the next speaker. This continues until all speakers are finished.

In the conference, the moderator may become a presiding officer if the conference is large enough. Consequently, the moderator may be called upon to perform the following functions:

- *Ruling on procedure*, as would any parliamentary chairperson. This requires a working knowledge of parliamentary procedure, specifically *Robert's Rules of Order, Newly Revised*, although a parliamentarian may be essential. Specific attributes for a presiding officer are knowledge of the group's specific rules of procedure as well as general parliamentary rules. In addition, the leader should analyze her audience to know how rigid or how lax she can be in enforcing these rules. Moreover, the chairperson must be fair to all sides and maintain order. Unpopular opinions must be respected and protected. Finally, the parliamentary leader should be prepared to be confident and authoritative. Especially in large, controversy-ridden conferences, the presiding officer must be strongly and firmly in control of the situation.

Question and Answer Period. Many public discussions include a format for questions from the audience. If this is done, the discussion leader is responsible for the following:

- *Stating the rules.* If situations, such as time limits, call for it or if the panel members request it, the moderator may state some specific rules, such as only one question per individual. If not, there are still certain standards of conduct that will facilitate the question and answer period. Request that each question be short. Suggest that each question be written out before it is asked. Some moderators prefer to handle only written questions.
- *Clarifying the questions.* Some of the questions are bound to be unclear; if that happens, try to clarify what the questioner is asking. Attempt to get the questioner to use specifics such as names, events, and situations. If there are few alternatives, ask the questioner, for example, "Do you mean full-time enrollment or full-time equivalent enrollment?" Make sure that you, the panel member, and the audience understand the question.
- *Stimulating the audience.* Sometimes an audience is reluctant to ask questions. The moderator can handle this situation by asking the first question, by using a method such as buzz groups (see the box), or by planting one or two questioners in the audience who will ask the first question. If the panel or symposium members have done their job, then only one or two questions will be needed to get the discussion going.
- *Protecting the panel.* Panel members or other public discussants are not there to be insulted or personally attacked. A good moderator will protect panel members by intercepting personal attacks. Techniques include ruling the question out of order or using humor to lessen the impact of the question.
- *Providing audio facilities.* Both the question and the answer need to be heard. In a room large enough to hold 50 or 60 people, a public address system may be necessary, as stated earlier. If the panel is seated at the same table, they can be served by one microphone; the moderator should have one. Finally, the

Buzz Groups

One way of maximizing participation at conferences is by using buzz, or breakout, groups. These subgroups allow for personal involvement and stimulate the cohesion that comes from small groups.

Format. The audience at a conference listens to a speaker or other presentation. Then the members are grouped into committees of five or six individuals and asked to discuss some aspect of the presentation for 5 to 10 minutes. After the discussion, the groups can be asked to report or respond to the participants in some way. This method can be used to generate questions, responses, and encourage discussion as well as give the audience members a feeling of participation.

Listening groups. Five or six individuals are assigned to listen to a presentation and to focus on some specific aspect of what is said. The group is expected to respond or evaluate the presentation. If the groups are formed on the basis of meaningful differences such as occupation or technical speciality, then the critique can be especially valuable.

Subcommittees. These are more formal smaller groups and are frequently used at large conferences to generate interest and involvement. They meet at the same time, and each discusses similar or distinct questions, hears reports, or uses some other method to share information. Subcommittees may or may not report back to the conference as a whole. If subcommittees are used, two other types of people become important: discussion leaders who serve to work with each of the subcommittees and resource-persons who can provide the subcommittees with information, opinion, and other stimuli.

audience should have access to one or two microphones; questioners step to the microphone and ask their questions.

▶ Highlights of Public Discussions

This section detailed some of the issues specific to public discussion with an audience: the panel discussion, symposium, and conference. These public discussions require some special considerations and preparations. Public discussions of this sort must take account of the role of the audience and the public roles of the participants.

SUMMARY

This chapter covered small group communication, stressing solutions to problems of group myths and groupthink. All members of the group should be prepared to

---

Meeting Checklist

A list of suggestions for preparing to run a meeting follows.
1. What is the purpose of the meeting?
    Whom do I report to?
    What is expected of our group?
    What can we reasonably accomplish?
    What do I need for the final report?

2. Who should attend? Be sure to consider including individuals who would not ordinarily attend.

3. Have I analyzed and consulted with the individuals in the group?
    What is each person's interest in the topic?
    Experience?
    Knowledge?
    Attitude?

4. How will I organize the meeting?
    Is there an agenda or organized list of topics?
    Have I prepared a detailed outline for my own use in leading the meeting?

5. Special preparations
    Has an announcement of the meeting and the agenda been distributed?
    Do I have the necessary materials? Room?
    Related information and references?
    Audiovisual equipment?
    Writing pads and paper?
    How should I arrange the physical facilities?

exercise leadership functions. Each member should be prepared to ensure that task, interpersonal, and procedural roles are performed. In addition, groups need to be concerned with effective logical development of their ideas.

Specifically, the group should use an agenda system that covers these important points: purposes of the agenda; wording effective questions for discussion; and preparing agendas for fact-finding, evaluative, and problem-solution (or policy) groups.

EXERCISES

1. How many groups do you hold membership in? Make as complete a list as possible. What kind of groups are these: fact-finding, social, work, etc.? Write out a description of your role in some of these groups. Who is responsible for leadership functions in these groups?

2. Observe a public meeting of a group. Analyze how well the moderator performs leadership functions. What suggestions would you make to improve his or her performance?

3. Prepare well-worded questions for discussion on the following topics (or others that are relevant to local circumstances or interests): tuition increases at colleges and universities; the reform of the American educational system; dealing with local crime; fairness in grading.

4. Observe a regular meeting of some organization to which you belong. Is there a published agenda? Is it complete? Is it always followed?

5. Prepare an agenda for a committee meeting to select a class gift to the university. What considerations might be especially important for this discussion? Who should be present? What information is needed prior to the meeting itself?

6. Prepare a list of criteria for the class gift referred to in question 5. Arrange the list in order of priority.

SELECTED SOURCES
FOR FURTHER READING

Barker, L. L., Wahlers, K. J., Watson, K. W., & Kibler, R. J. (1987). *Groups in process*. Boston: Prentice-Hall.

Bormann, E. G. (1969). *Discussion and group methods*. New York: Harper & Row.

Brilhart, J. K., & Galanes, G. J. (1967). *Effective group discussion*. Dubuque: Wm. C. Brown.

Fisher, A. B., & Ellis, D. G. (1990). *Small group decision making, communication and the group process*. New York: McGraw-Hill.

Goodall, L. H. (1990). *Small group communication in organizations* (2nd ed.). Dubuque: Wm. C. Brown.

Gouran, D. S. (1990). *Making decisions in groups* (rev. ed.). Prospects Hts., IL. Waveland Press.

Janis, I. L. (1972). *Victims of group think*. New York: Houghton Mifflin.

Scheidel, T. M., & Crowell, L. (1979). *Discussing and deciding*. New York: Macmillan.

Shaw, M. E., & Gouran, D. S. (1990). Group dynamics and communication. In G. L. Dahnke & G. W. Clatterbuck (Eds.), *Human communication theory and research*. Hastings, CA: Wadsworth.

Tubbs, S. L. (1978). *A systems approach to small group interaction*. New York: Addison-Wesley.

Weick, K. E. (1969). *The social psychology of organizing*. New York: Addison-Wesley.

Weick, K. E. (1979). *The social psychology of organizing* (2nd ed.). New York: Addison-Wesley.

Wilson, G. L., & Hanna, M. S. (1990). *Groups in context*. New York: McGraw-Hill.

References

1. Gouran, D. (1990). *Making decisions in groups, choices and consequences*. Prospects Hts., IL: Waveland Press.
2. Nelton, S. (1991). Men, women & leadership. *Nation's Business*, 79, 16.
3. Dowd, M. (1991). Power: Are women afraid of it—or beyond it? *Working Woman*, November 1991, p. 99.

Sexual Harassment: Problems of Interpersonal Communication on the Job

The October 20, 1991 edition of *Inside Business* addresses the question: "Is sexual harassment a problem in the workplace?" The opening segment introduces the problem of sexual harassment, discusses the relevant legislation, and defines the two major types of sexual harassment.

Broadcast soon after the widely televised confrontation between Supreme Court nominee Clarence Thomas and Anita Hill, the program begins with data concerning the amount of sexual harassment in the workplace. In 1991, the Senate hearings on the confirmation of Justice Clarence Thomas for the Supreme Court raised questions concerning sexual harassment when Anita Hill, a law professor at the University of Oklahoma, claimed that Thomas had sexually harassed her while she was an assistant of his at the EEOC.

Sexual harassment represents a serious problem of face-to-face communication on the job today. While it typically affects superior-subordinate communication, it can also hinder effective interviewing and even group communications. This problem touches on several elements of interpersonal communication, such as the attributions people place on other people's behavior, the interpretation of the roles and rules of communication, and the meanings that can be assigned to different nonverbal communication cues.

The opening video clips indicate that claims of sexual harassment in the workplace are on the rise. In an interview, Barbara Rogers, formerly an executive with a Wall Street firm and now the President of Financial Women's Association, explains that she left Wall Street because she found the climate there to be intimidating for women because of sexual harassment. Judy Vladeck, who assists people making claims concerning sexual harassment, explains some of the difficulties that these people can face when making such charges.

The video reminds you that sexual harassment can take two forms. The first can be called the quid pro quo form. It describes those cases in which a person is requested to trade sexual favors for some job-related benefit. In these cases the harassment usually involves one person having a supervisory role or some other form of power over another. The second can be called the environmental form. This form involves cases in which a person feels that an intimidating work atmosphere or climate is created by the sexual jokes, remarks, or tone of other people's conversations or actions. In these cases the person perceived to be the harasser need not be in a position of authority over the person who feels victimized. Consider what kinds of communications would indicate each of the two types. Is one type more difficult to substantiate than the other?

A case study is presented in which you hear, first, a supervisor describing a case involving his secretary. You then hear the story from the secretary's point of view.

After viewing the case, two guests in the CNN studio discuss whether or not it illustrates sexual harassment. Terrence Simmons, who represents a consulting firm that deals with cases of sexual harassment, and Sharon Kalin, who represents a Wall Street firm, do not agree on this particular case. What do you think? Recall the two different foms that sexual harassment can take. Dating another member of an organization is a concern. In what ways could such dating lead to sexual harassment? Should a supervisor date a subordinate? Should a professor or a high school teacher date a student? Under what circumstances, if any, would this be appropriate? What are the policies in regard to sexual harassment at your school or place of work? How were these policies communicated to you?

Discuss the arguments that are presented by the two people in the fictitious example and the issues raised by Simmons and Kalin. In your consideration of this case, take special note of the communication elements that are involved. Note that there are two important dyadic relationships: the one between the secretary and her boss, and the one between the secretary and the co-worker. What are the effects of the nonverbal elements in cases of this sort? For example, discuss the chronemics in this case; what are the effects of when things are done? Note how the secretary segments the time sequence in the relationship into a definite before, during, and after. What are the effects of the proxemics in this case, that is, where things are done? Note especially the different ways that roles are defined by the people involved in this case. How can you distinguish public and private roles in a situation of this sort? At what point does a private matter become one affecting one's professional role? What should the supervisor do in this case? Discuss how to handle a counseling or work-appraisal interview with the secretary in this case.

Presentations

This part of the book considers the special case of making presentations, that is, well-prepared oral performances by one source (a speaker) before a number of receivers (an audience). Presentations include lectures, oral reports, briefings, and ceremonial remarks, such as introductions, presentation and acceptance of honors and awards, and public speeches.

Chapter 10 covers the principles of and steps in selecting the best materials for a presentation, in view of the presenter's purpose and an analysis of the audience and occasion.

Chapter 11 is concerned with the steps of putting the materials into shape and delivering and evaluating the presentation itself.

Chapter 12 considers the use of both presentational and interactive media, particularly the effects that the use of different media can have on the interpretation of the message being presented.

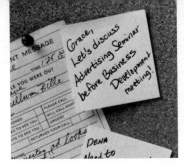  

Preparing Presentations

10

CHAPTER

After studying this chapter, you will be able to:

1. Determine and "word" the main points of your presentation.

2. Analyze the intended audience and occasion.

3. Select the best verbal materials for a presentation to achieve your purposes.

4. Understand the principles for using various kinds of visual supporting materials.

Overview

As people move up in an organization and gain more responsibility, typically they are more often in situations that require the ability to make good oral presentations. An article in an airline in-flight magazine, intended especially for business travellers, made this point forcefully, in contending that people "cannot possibly rise through the ranks without the ability to persuade, inform, and inspire others with their business speeches."[1]

A sales presentation to a client or a customer or a budget request before upper management are examples of occasions when you must give an oral presentation.

For many years, one of the authors sat on a budget allocation committee for local charities. Each year, the charitable agencies were required to come before a formal meeting of this committee and explain in 15 or 20 minutes their needs for the coming fiscal year. The skill of the presenters was extremely important in the final determination of the committee. Groups that seemed disorganized or even a bit unprofessional in these presentations were often seen as not well prepared and not deserving of the full amount of their requests. A smooth, well-planned presentation was just as often rewarded. The members of the committee formed a definite impression regarding the level of competence of the presenters and made related assumptions about how well they were running their agencies and overseeing the use of the money.

▶ *Professionals are often called upon to make formal presentations.*

This committee typifies situations in the business world. Usually a customer or management team or committee sits in judgment on proposals for sales, funding, or resources. The presentation is a structured activity in which you must sell your competence as well as your product.

Not all presentations are strictly persuasive situations: oral reports, briefings, or training lectures are all common examples of formal presentations in organizations. For example, new employees of a corporation are first introduced to the company and its policies by attending an orientation or training session. These sessions often consist of a series of structured presentations. Presentations are also used for such purposes as explaining new work rules, procedures, benefit packages, new programs, reorganizations, and so on. Training of all sorts in corporations is frequently accomplished through presentations.

Nor do these examples include the many times that you have to deliver a formal speech to stockholders, management, employees, community organizations, or the general public.

This chapter deals with the first three steps in the process of making presentations.

1. Determining the main objectives of the presentation.
2. Analyzing the intended audience in order to effect the desired outcome.
3. Selecting the best materials to achieve this outcome.

Chapter 11 presents methods for organizing and delivering the presentation most effectively.

CHARACTERISTICS OF PRESENTATIONS

A presentation is a *structured, prepared, oral performance by one source before a number of receivers.* Presentations include lectures, oral reports, briefings, ceremonial remarks (such as introductions, presentation and acceptance of honors and awards), and public speeches. A presentation can be performed by a team (each responsible for a part of the presentation) as well as by an individual; in other words, the one source can be a group or a team.

Structured Nature

Both dyads and small groups, subjects of the preceding chapters, are marked by a degree of informality and spontaneity not typical of presentations. As we noted, turn-taking and role interchange occur frequently in these interpersonal settings. Giving a presentation or a public speech implies more structure and, usually, more formality. Roles are not interchanged as frequently; one person usually holds the floor while audience members remain listeners during the presentation.

Presentations require careful and thorough planning; in fact, some performances can be highly scripted and rehearsed with complex audiovisual aids. There is less opportunity for immediate feedback during a presentation than in a conversation, interview, or group discussion. Still, a good presenter watches for nonverbal clues of feedback, but these clues are ambiguous and less clear cut than feedback in discussions.

▶ *Presentational speaking permits less direct interaction than interpersonal communication.*

▶

Problem-Solution Nature

Usually, a presentation is given in response to some felt need as a solution for some perceived problem. Therefore, we suggest that preparing for a presentation is the same as dealing with any problem-solution situation. The problem is the need to make the presentation; the solution is the presentation prepared and delivered.

The Need: Determining the Purpose.   First, consider the need: Why is a presentation called for? Analyze thoroughly the problem to be addressed by this presentation. Assume that you have been asked to give a presentation to senior management on the progress your team has made over the past quarter on a special project. You would begin by considering all the ramifications of the reasons for this presentation. Partly, the need is to keep management informed of progress on the project itself, but there are probably other considerations as well. A good presentation may indicate that your team is effective and should be entrusted with similar projects; it may show need for further budgetary support; it may show that you are capable of taking on more responsibility; and so on. Faced with this kind of assignment, you would probably want to confer with other team members to get their views regarding the needs to be met by the presentation. You would have to determine a major, overriding goal. There will probably be subsidiary goals and specific objectives that will lead toward the meeting of this goal, also. This process should result in wording a useful statement of specific purpose, together with a list of main points to be covered.

Analyzing the Audience and Occasion in View of Purpose.   Next, look at the criteria for a successful presentation. What will a good solution—that is, a good presentation—look like? How will you determine whether or not you have met the need that called for this presentation in the first place? Will there be increased funding, responsibility, or respect? In other words, exactly what is the response that you desire from your immediate audience? In the example above, the senior management team is obviously the immediate audience, the group whose response is most important. Have in mind for each presentation some specific kind of observable reaction, such as a question and answer period, to gauge audience feedback.

At this point in your preparation, you should begin to analyze the people who will constitute the audience for this presentation. Do important members of the audience emphasize bottom-line issues? Are some especially interested in the development of people in the corporation, listening for development of skills or knowledge on the part of the team members? Are some focused on productivity and competitive advantages in the marketplace? These questions should suggest specific ways to approach the preparation of the presentation.

Selecting and Organizing the Best Material to Meet the Need.   Now you can start to develop possible solutions. In this case, that means choosing the methods for putting together the presentation and gathering and assembling the information, the material that comprises the presentation. In addition to selecting the material for your presentation, you should also decide how best to arrange this material.

Ask what sort of organization would be most effective, given the nature of this material and the kinds of answers that you have made to the questions concerning purposes and audience. What should go first, and what should be given last? How should this information be introduced to the audience? What is the best way to conclude to leave the listeners in the best frame of mind?

Implementing the Presentation.   Next, select the best solution and implement it. Bring together the verbal and visual materials that will best make your point, and prepare the text or notes, visual aids, and any other supporting documents or materials. Rehearse and prepare for the actual delivery of the presentation itself.

Evaluating the Effects.   Evaluate the presentation's effectiveness next. Did you get the expected response? Did you get unexpected responses? How can you seek out feedback from your immediate audience? Of course, sometimes the feedback is instantaneous: You got the contract, the raise, the sale, or the approval. Often, though, the response is more delayed: You have to wait for later to see whether you got a promotion, more responsibility, additional business later on, and so forth.

Highlights of Steps in Preparing Presentations.   Preparing a presentation follows these steps:

1. Determine the primary purpose and the exact response desired.
2. Analyze the audience and occasion.
3. Choose the materials that are best for your purpose and for this audience and occasion.
4. Implement the presentation by organizing and preparing text, notes, rehearsing, and delivering the presentation.
5. Evaluate the effectiveness of the presentation.

The first three steps are covered in this chapter; the remaining two, in Chapter 11.

PREPARATION OF PRESENTATIONS

Determining the Purpose

We begin with the question of why a presentation is called for. What is the need to be met by this presentation? For example, if you have been asked to explain a new budgeting procedure to the members of your department, the need is to provide instruction in this procedure: The purpose is primarily informative, to give this instruction. If you have been asked to brief upper management on the design of a new product, again the purpose is primarily to provide information. On the other hand, if you have been requested to make a presentation to a grants committee of a foundation in order to win funding for your organization, the purpose is primarily persuasive. Finally, there are needs that fall under the category of fulfilling ceremonial functions: to give awards at the annual dinner or to honor retiring executives. Each presentation should have only one primary purpose.

Of course, oftentimes you will have to combine information with persuasion to be successful. To motivate people to buy your widgets, you have to give them basic information about the widget, its competitors, and so on. To provide information to others—say, about the new budgeting procedure—you will find it necessary to persuade people that it is in their interest to learn this information. Still, there is just one primary purpose that is the overriding reason for the presentation. Persuading people to pay attention and to retain the material paves the way for the major purpose: to teach them how to carry out the new budgeting procedure, or whatever. (By the way, entertaining is an important element in teaching or in persuading, facilitating both teaching and persuading.)

Confusion about the primary purpose can lead to a confused presentation, as well as some churning in the preparation stages. The first step of analysis, therefore, is to decide whether the presentation is primarily aimed at informing or persuading. Subsequent strategies derive from this determination.

How do effective presenters avoid awkward and divided statements of general purpose? First, try to avoid certain constructions: For example, avoid compound sentences such as, "To inform the audience about the types of Smythe Widgets and to persuade them to buy Smythe Widgets exclusively." The bottom-line purpose here is to get the receivers to buy the widgets; giving information is subsidiary to that purpose. This statement is therefore primarily persuasive and should be worded as follows: "To motivate people to buy Smythe Widgets."

Complex sentences can also be a problem: "Although the Smythe Widget is more expensive, it outperforms any other widget in the field." The main idea is in the second clause: that is, to convince people that the Smythe Widget is more reliable than its competitors. The "although . . ." clause introduces a negative concept that should be dealt with in a later part of the presentation, and it obscures the presentation's main goal. The simpler and more straightforward the general purpose, the more you will keep your thinking straight during the preparation and the more likely that the audience will stay with you.

There are, then, two types of general purpose: to inform and to persuade.

Informative messages provide information that could be of use to the receiver: the need is to find the best way to communicate this information to the specific audience. Informative presentations have the following purposes:

- To describe
- To demonstrate
- To define
- To teach
- To explain

To persuade is to be more directive. Persuasion aims to change or reinforce belief or action. A saleswoman selling automobiles, a politician canvassing for votes, or an employee asking for a raise are all engaged in persuasion.

Persuasive presentations should be worded as follows:

- To convince
- To refute
- To redefine
- To sell
- To motivate

The distinction between informative and persuasive speeches is sometimes hard to determine and lies on a continuum between a clear example of persuasion (a salesperson's pitch) and a clear example of information (how to write a computer program). Between the two extremes, the line between information and persuasion is less certain. Still, making the distinction is worthwhile because it will clarify for you the kinds of material that will best meet your needs.

Wording a Statement of Specific Purpose. Your analysis of the need for the presentation should provide a fuller understanding of the ends to be fulfilled. A successful statement of specific purpose answers at least three of the one-word questions associated with good newspaper leads: Who? What? and Why? The other two well-known "W" questions may also be included: When? and Where? The question of "How" may also be answered, but the specific purpose should not get too complex.

First, then, who should carry out the action or exhibit the belief or skill or knowledge?

Second, what is to be done, to be understood, to be believed?

Third, why should this thing be done or learned or believed?

Good specific statements of purpose, therefore, should be worded as follows: "Office personnel (who) will learn the new accounting procedure (what) in order to save time inputting invoices (why)." Or, "Upper management (who) should grant increased budget to our product development (what) in order to enhance competitive market position (why)."

It is no accident that the wordings of these specific purposes resemble exercises in Management by Objective (MBO), because the idea is the same. Formulate an overall objective for the presentation that includes a summary of the agent (who), action or belief desired (what), and the reason (why). An important reason for working this out is so that listeners can have a quick and simple statement that covers your main purpose completely; it is, of course, useful for you as well. When people are given a memorable and specific statement, they are more likely to remember and to act upon it.

At times, it is desirable to be even more precise concerning the specific objective. For example, in the case of seeking increased budget, you could develop a specific purpose as follows: "Upper management (who) will increase budget for our product development by $750,000 (what and a specific target) in the next fiscal year (when) to enhance competitive market position (why) in the Pacific Rim (where)."

Sharpening and limiting a statement of specific purpose can follow much the same process that was used for limited the topics for group discussions, as described in Chapter 9.

Carefully wording a specific statement of purpose is well worth the trouble. The best presentations are those in which presenters are clear about their goals.

▶ ### Analyzing the Audience and Occasion

Effective communication is, as already stressed, audience-centered. In determining what a successful presentation should accomplish, you must first consider the receivers and their points of view, beliefs, needs, and attitudes. How will they perceive and understand your purpose? How will audience characteristics affect your attempt to meet the goals of your presentation?

Determining success or failure depends upon a thorough understanding of where your audience is in their understanding or abilities prior to your presentation. The presentation is designed to adapt to their current position and bring them to the desired level of understanding or ability. In addition, the setting or occasion, where the presentation will occur, when, and under what circumstances can influence how the audience receives your message. Therefore, following an analysis of your audience, you then should consider factors of the occasion.

Analysis of the Audience.   The first part of this text discussed elements of communication that determine the ways receivers decode and process incoming messages. Many of these factors are critical in determining the audience response to a presentation.

Before analyzing in detail the characteristics of your audience, you should consider whether there may be more than just one target audience. First, there is an immediate audience made up of people directly present with you during your performance; in many instances, this is the only audience with which you need be concerned. But there may be secondary audiences at other times. When the president of the United States delivers the State of the Union message, his immediate audience is the Congress of the United States. The secondary audience—and the one that the president may consider more important—is the general public and the press, who will explain and disseminate the address to the general public. Similarly, you may have an immediate audience for a presentation, such as a committee. But you may hope to influence a superior who will receive a copy or hear reports of your presentation. Other secondary audiences include reporters from trade journals and the regular media, and indirectly, competitors and the general public. Also, there may be individuals who will report via the company grapevine to your superiors and subordinates.

Although all audiences share certain characteristics, essential differences exist among various audiences and even within the same audience. If the audience is favorable or hostile to your message, you want to know that; or an audience may be split between supporters and the hostile. Whatever type of audience you face, you will feel more confident if you know who they are and how they feel about you and your message. Moreover, understanding some of their major characteristics will allow you to adapt to your audience's interest, comprehension, and understanding. Your job as a presenter is to analyze the potential audience(s) to determine ways to develop your message to take advantage of the unique characteristics of the audience.

There are three general questions about an audience that should always serve as the beginning of this analysis:

- What is the audience interest?
- What is the audience knowledge?
- What is the audience attitude?

For an informative presentation, the first two questions are obviously important. For the persuasive presentation, the last question is vital.

1. *Audience interest.* Is the audience interested in your subject? Are they very interested to start with, or can they be made more interested? The answer to these questions determines the amount of attention that the audience will probably give you and your subject. Initially, audience interest can range from very interested to equally uninterested.

If they are interested from the start, ask why they are so interested and how you can maintain their interest. If they are uninterested, how can you win and maintain their interest? You must tell them why they should be interested in your subject. Of course, if you cannot give a good reason for their being interested at this point, you may have solved the problem of this particular presentation: Don't give it!

The level of initial audience interest depends upon the situation, the occasion, and the people who make up the audience. For example, if people have made a special effort to come to hear your presentation, this signifies a fairly high level of interest. If you are making your presentation as part of a routine meeting—the people were going to be there anyway, whether you spoke or not—and if there are many other items on the agenda, assume they have less interest and attention.

How do you get information about how interested this audience may be? Other presenters they have heard may be useful sources. Ask them what sort of response they seemed to get on similar topics. What kind of issues were these people especially interested in? At times, you may be sufficiently familiar with the audience to know things such as whether some are interested in product development, some in short-term profits only, some in long-range, strategic planning, and so on.

In conclusion, it is essential to write out an answer to questions of this sort whenever you are planning a presentation: especially, How interested is the audience in my presentation? Why should this audience be interested in this presentation?

2. *Audience knowledge.* What is the audience's knowledge about the subject? The question concerns what they already know about the subject before you start presenting. You can think about their knowledge in the following areas: knowledge level, comprehension level, and source of information. Let's take each of these areas in turn to show how you can carry out a systematic analysis of audience knowledge.

The level of the audience's knowledge can be visualized as a range in terms of quantity, quality, breadth, and currency.

In some cases, your audience will have a great deal of information about your subject; at other times, very little. For audiences with a lot of information, you should be able to skip over or briefly mention basic concepts and principles. A speaker could mention material already familiar to the audience to avoid boring them with too much they already know. When audiences know quite a lot about your subject, you can concentrate on a solution or on giving new information.

On the other hand, when your audience is unfamiliar with the subject or the specific material being presented, obviously you will have to take more time filling background for them. You may find that with these kinds of audiences, the presentation may have to be spread over two or three sessions in order to fill the audience in on the necessary information.

Audiences may consist of experts or professionals in the field who understand the theory and implications of your topic. If your topic were acid rain, the expert audience (such as chemists with this topic) could understand and appreciate the importance of pH levels and chemical complexities. Conversely, the lay audience would be more interested in a discussion of effects: Is it harmful? How much will it cost?

With expert audiences, you may wish to concentrate on the broader implications of your topic, which may not be as immediately obvious to the experts. Taking the acid rain example as a case in point, the chemists may not have considered the social or political implications involved, although they may be very familiar with the chemistry of the problem. With lay audiences, you must decide how much technical information is necessary for them to understand your point. You can lose your audience if you pitch your information at a technical level without explaining the meaning in lay terms. Again, you must carefully analyze exactly how much technical information is essential.

In the previous example, the chemists may be very knowledgeable about the chemical process that creates acid rain and less knowledgeable about biological implications or public policy. Similarly, other audiences may concentrate in a specialized field without having to consider broader implications of a related topic. Construction engineers may not be involved in negotiations with construction unions, and so may not have a broad understanding of the entire field of construction. People in marketing positions for a public electric utility may not be expected to understand power production.

In some fields, information changes rapidly; in others, not so quickly. If the audience has outdated information, the speaker must spend more time bringing them up to date. You may need to determine how recently the members of the audience have dealt with the material in your presentation. Did they have a few courses back in high school or college but no real involvement with your topic since then? Some audience members may think they know a lot about your subject, but their knowledge may not be current.

The next section includes questions about the understanding audiences have of their available information.

The most dangerous information is that which we are sure we know that is not true. Does your audience hold any important misconceptions? Stereotypes? A speaker may need to spend time debunking myths that people hold about a topic.

Misinformation may be related to the question of currency of information, when audience members remember one form of a product or process from earlier times without knowing about significant changes since an earlier, perhaps unfortunate, experience. For example, they may believe that high-sulfur coal is unusable for producing electricity without realizing that advances in scrubbers or forms of combustion processes have been made to alleviate the problem of sulfur emissions from smokestacks. Or, they may believe that certain kinds of electronic equipment are very expensive without knowing that recent advances have greatly reduced the prices.

Comparisons, analogies, and similarities shape much of our thinking. How information is organized or defined determines what arguments are reasonable or unreasonable. If you represent AT&T, for example, does the audience see your corporation as a utility, such as water or power, or do they see you as just another corporation? The advantage of knowing this kind of information about your audience is that it allows you to show relationships between your information and other information that may be more familiar to your audience. Look for connections between your topic and subjects with which this audience may be familiar.

Finally, you need to consider where the people in the audience get their information and whether you are the sole source of information on the topic or not. Two dimensions relate to the question of audience sources:

If the audience will receive information from sources in addition to your presentation, this must be taken into consideration. It is usually wise to indicate to the audience you are aware of other points of view. Several studies in the field of persuasion reveal that when audiences have other sources of information on your topic, they expect you to show familiarity with this other information. If the other sources disagree with the point that you make, it is very important to understand that disagreement and to be able to explain why you hold your position. Otherwise, audiences may discount your presentation.

The audience may be confused about the information that they do have because their sources are in conflict with each other. You may need to spend more time than usual in careful explanation of the facts when there is this kind of confusion.

There have been conflicting reports in the media, for example, on various health matters. Some studies suggest that foods such as oat bran reduce cholesterol significantly, whereas other reports suggest the effects of oat bran are not significant. Experts seem to disagree on whether coffee is harmful or not. On these kinds of questions, it is important to carefully develop the reasons for your position.

Therefore, you need to be aware of the exposure that the audience has had to conflicting or confusing information related to your topic.

3. *Audience attitudes.* This area of audience analysis concerns audience attitudes that determine their reactions to your message. By attitudes, we mean the evaluative responses that people have to objects, ideas, people, or activities that predispose them to react positively or negatively toward those things.

Several aspects of audience attitudes that may be relevant to your preparation— their attitudes toward you as a person, their attitudes toward the organization you represent, and their attitudes toward your subject and your purpose—are delineated next.

Audience attitudes toward you make up their assessment of your credibility. Your ability to inform or to persuade an audience is based on who you are (how you appear to them) and what you are (what you have achieved).

How credible or believable speakers appear depends upon at least three judgments made by the audience: your competence, your goodwill or trustworthiness, and your fairness. Some authorities prefer to reduce these judgments to two: your competence and your likability (combining the second and third factors). Audience judgments about your competence and trustworthiness are often based upon the following characteristics: appearance, reputation or credentials, and memberships in organizations or groups.

Competence refers to the audience's perception of your training and knowledge. When they first see you, the audience members make inferences about who you are and your competence. Such inferences are based on your appearance and what they know or find out about you, frequently, what you tell them about yourself.

In making determinations about your credibility, the audience first looks at your dress and general appearance. Do they suggest that you are a professional? Many professions carry expectations about dress; some may expect an accountant or banker to be more conservative in dress than an artist or public relations director, for example. Do your dress and manner suggest that you are similar to the audience in your attitudes and values? People tend to trust those who are like themselves. Verbal assurances that you are like the audience, or understand and respect them and their values, are important for identification between speaker and audience.

This consideration suggests that it is important to give some thought to matters of dress and appearance. One general rule is to determine the practice of the group that you will be addressing. Do they usually wear business suits or casual wear at their meetings? Do you want to establish some level of authority by dressing slightly more formally? Audiences may consider it a sign of respect for them or their group if a speaker dresses more formally than they do; it can suggest that you take your speaking before them seriously.

Reputation, rank, and title also indicate your credibility. The earliest scientific studies on audiences' perceptions of a speaker's credibility involved announcing to an audience that a particular speech was written by a certain kind of person: an important official, in one case, or an uninformed student, on the other. The responses to the same speech content varied significantly depending upon the credentials ascribed to the alleged speaker in each case. Audiences base evaluations on credentials such as degrees earned, profession, and official rank, or designation such as CEO, senior vice president, or attorney. Individuals who have training, experience, or are in a position to know are considered to be more credible than those who lack these identifiers or titles.

It may be useful to have the audience know that you have made a special study of the issue under discussion, written a book on it, gotten a degree in the requisite subject matter, have had so many years of experience in this business, etc. If this

Executive Credibility and the Corporate Culture

In his fourth century B.C. *Rhetoric*, Aristotle divided presentations into three parts: *logos* or logic, *pathos* or emotional appeals, and credibility or *ethos*. Aristotle argued that credibility that resided in the communicator was "almost" the most important part of a presentation. Today, credibility is still important to the corporate communicator.

> Becoming a charismatic communicator, the kind that builds commitment, seems not beyond the ability of the typical managerial mortal. Consider the research findings of Charles O'Reilly, a professor at the University of California's graduate school of business at Berkeley. Expert after expert has noted the importance of a strong corporate culture if a company is to be a winner. O'Reilly studied how workers at Silicon Valley companies with strong cultures perceived their corporate leaders. A credible leader, he found, had three principal attributes. He or she was perceived to be trustworthy—from seeing him in action, workers judged that he had their interests at heart as well as his own. He was thought to be an expert. And he was seen to be dynamic and attractive, by which workers meant not much more than they could see him in motion—walking around, talking about the company, working on projects with them.

W. Kiechel III. (1986, January 6). No word from on high. (pp. 125–126). *Fortune*. Used by permission of *Fortune Magazine* (C) 1986 Time Inc. All rights reserved.

Problem-Solution

The Business You Love to Hate

Traditionally, some businesses and industries are seen in a less than favorable light. People selling used cars have often been unfairly put down because of their occupation. Other industries that have felt defensive lately include the insurance and the oil industries. Insurance executives report being cornered at parties and having to defend themselves and their professions—possibly because people usually deal with insurance companies only under negative circumstances, say, following an auto accident or a break-in.[2]

Utilities, especially electrical companies and phone companies, seem to feel the same kind of defensiveness. Speakers representing utilities have told the authors that they often fear audience hostility based on negative attitudes toward electric rates, phone service, or utility companies in general.

Solutions lie in personalizing the organization and establishing common ground with audience members. People tend to be more negative toward abstract institutions than toward individuals representing them. Speakers need to establish that they and the audience members share many of the same values, needs, and problems. For example, representatives of utilities could point out that they live in the same community, pay the same rates, and have the same needs for energy or phone service or whatever.

information cannot be worked comfortably into the presentation itself, you may wish to see that it is included in an introduction.

Audience perception of you can be affected by knowledge that you are a member of certain organizations, such as a political party or professional society, as well. Membership is taken as an indication of interest in the goals of the society and adherence to certain key values of the organization. Of course, one type of membership that may be important in determining audience perceptions is the group or organization you represent. If you are speaking to the downtown Kiwanis Club as a representative of the telephone company, attitudes toward your employer will influence their judgments about you, which leads into the next area of concern: audience attitudes toward the group that you represent.

Goodwill or trustworthiness is largely communicated through your manner and style of delivery during the presentation. Principles for effective delivery and emphasizing establishing good rapport with your audience are discussed in Chapter 11. Basically, we trust speakers who maintain eye contact with us, seem interested in us as listeners, and seem to take our point of view seriously.

The audience members may have feelings not only about you as a person, but you as a representative of some institution or industry. When one of the authors speaks to a group, some people may groan, "Not another college professor." They are responding to what they think we represent, rather than to us as individuals. When giving training to speakers in industry, we often find that speakers are afraid of the audience's response to them as representatives of the "phone company," or "city government," or "the police," or whatever.

Attitudes toward an organization result from several factors: the audience's familiarity with it, the organization's image, and similarities between it and the audience's organization.

If your firm or organization is known to the audience, you should be concerned with their previous experiences. Have they been good or bad? Good experiences with your organization may provide you with initial goodwill. Negative experiences, hostility, and suspicion are potential barriers. If your firm is unknown to your audience, you may have to explain its purpose.

Besides experience with your firm, audiences may have images of it. Organizations' images are created by their own efforts and their histories and are related to long-term relationships, current events, or even local situations. Organizations, like individuals, are seen as competent or incompetent, fair or unfair, and trustworthy or untrustworthy. A large, respected organization may have a strong positive image. An organization that is in receivership (bankrupt) or whose officials are under indictment will not have a good image. A positive image can help, whereas a negative one can be a hindrance. Exxon Oil, following the Alaskan oil spill, found that it had an "image problem." Speakers representing that firm had to expect and to cope with this image. People who work for certain governmental agencies, such as the Internal Revenue Service, find that they must also be aware of the associations people hold for their organizations.

If the interests of your organization coincide with the interests of your audience, then your job should be much easier. Often, though, the interests of your firm may differ from audience interests. The worst situation would be that of direct competition, in which your firm is seen as an adversary. In many cases, the interests of your organization and of the audience are complementary or coordinate, meaning that their relationship to the organization is, for example, that of consumers or customers, employees, creditors, associates, stockholders, or contributers. It may be helpful to point out such complementary relationships when they may not be immediately obvious to the audience. Employees of your firm, for example, could be customers of businesses represented in the audience. These audience members, then, would have an interest in the well-being of your organization.

Once you have determined audience attitude toward you and your organization, you need to consider how the audience will respond to your topic and purpose. Although subject and purpose are related, your audience may respond favorably to your topic but not your specific purpose. For instance, the audience may like the idea of cheap power but not the idea of a nuclear power plant in their backyard to produce that power.

You need to know if the audience is for or against your point, and whether they are active or passive in the expression of that attitude, and how strongly held is their attitude about your topic. The possibilities can be seen as lying along a continuum that runs through five points, as shown in Figure 10-1. Determining where an audience, on average, falls on the continuum can be predicted by analyzing the audience's perception of the topic.

If you feel that your audience is actively opposed to what you propose, then you may find your best hope is to gain a favorable hearing and begin a process of winning them over. In this case, emphasize the interests that you and audience members have in common, rather than the specific proposals that may divide you. Point out, for example, that you both want to improve productivity and cut costs, but that you differ on the best way to achieve the result.

Passively opposed audience members are not strongly in opposition to your position. They may not be deeply concerned about the subject; perhaps they don't have much information about it. In that case, the careful laying out of more information may help win a more favorable response. Emphasize verifiable facts and information and avoid heavy doses of emotional persuasion.

Neutral audiences should be easier to win over than those who are opposed, but you may need to overcome apathy or lack of interest in the topic. If so, demonstrate that your issue is vitally important. Specific examples or cases that show how the audience is directly affected would be useful. For example, many people may not be concerned about the price of Japanese stocks in Japan, on the Nikkei Index. Still, one could show that declining prices there could cause Japanese investors to pull out of American investments and buy the relatively cheaper Japanese stocks. Explain that eventually, such action could have an impact on American interest rates, bond prices, employment, and other parts of the economy that could directly affect audience members.

With audiences favorably disposed toward your position, your job is to reinforce that attitude or to get some kind of action or immediate response from the audience. Again, you may need to overcome some apathy and to show that the subject has definite consequences for them as individuals. Emphasize not just winning the audience over but strengthening their resolve to take some action.

The following specific factors help determine how audiences perceive your subject and your proposal.

Practical, beneficial information increases an audience's attention and interest. Explicit assurances, early in the presentation, that the information is useful and beneficial makes a speaker's job easier. The presenter should show exactly how the audience can use the information or can benefit from what is proposed. Point

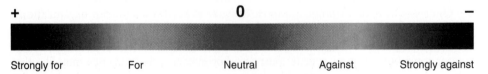

▶ **Figure 10-1**   *Continuum of audience attitudes. Audience attitudes may cluster at more than one point, for example, neutral and strongly against.*

out that with your information—say, how to use a new computer program—they will become more productive and thereby earn so much more profit. With the new product line, they will increase sales a significant amount, and so on.

Significant issues that involve the audience directly and that are near in time and place are given priority over issues that seem insignificant. With the political and social changes that have occurred in Eastern Europe, people may feel that foreign aid is no longer as important as it was once; they may assume that it is no longer necessary to compete with the "Soviets."

Audiences give more attention to programs or plans that appear feasibile. You need to show that what you are proposing is a practical solution to some problem. Otherwise, the audience may turn you off.

While you speak, people in the audience may be weighing what you say against other proposals or messages they have heard on this topic. Therefore, try to determine what kind of information the audience has about the general subject before beginning the presentation. In our discussion concerning the information available to the audience, recall that you should discover what other sources of information the audience has on your subject. Then you can show how your proposal is better than others they have heard about; this is what is meant by showing a comparative advantage.

Gathering Data for Audience Analysis

How does one go about gathering all this information about the audiences or potential audiences? Fortunately, many presentations are delivered before groups already known to the speaker. In these instances, the speaker is more likely to have the answers. Still, it is always useful to make yourself go through this analysis to ensure that all bases have been touched. When the audience is less familiar or unknown, there are three standard procedures:

1. *Observation.* It may be possible to attend meetings of the group that will compose the audience or to observe potential audience members in other settings or meetings.

2. *Interview.* If possible, meet with listeners in advance, and try to discover what their special interests are.

3. *Research.* There may be reference works or similar information about these people. Look for indications of goals or objectives of the group, special projects in which they are involved, accomplishments, statements of purpose, and the like. The following is a sample worksheet to be used for preparing an audience analysis.

Analysis of the Occasion and Setting. The occasion and setting for the performance can influence the effectiveness of your presentation. The nature of the occasion or meeting determines what is appropriate in style and method of pre-

---

Audience Analysis Worksheet

Title or subject of the presentation:

Approximate date, time, and place of the presentation:

Presentation requestor:

Your objectives for this presentation:

1.

2.

3.

4.

Audience Characteristics (if relevant to your presentation):
Age (range) ___   Sex ___   Hometown ___
Education level ___   Economic condition ___
Profession(s) or Job(s) _____   Political affiliation _____
Religion(s) _____   Ethnic background _____
Reference groups _____   Other _____

Audience interest in the subject:
High ___   Moderate ___   Low ___

Audience knowledge of the subject:
High ___   General ___   Limited ___   None ___
Accurate ___   or ___ Inaccurate
Expert ___   or ___ Lay
Broad ___   or ___ Narrow
Current ___   or ___ Dated

Audience sources of information about topic:

Audience perception of you:
Expert ___   or ___ Nonexpert

---

sentation. The informality or formality of the occasion can be determined by considering the time of day, size of gathering, dress of participants, and nature of the message. An awards banquet at a prominent downtown hotel requires a different style of presentation from a talk made at the annual corporation outing or picnic.

How do we interpret the nature of the occasion? Is the meeting formal or

Audience relationship to speaker:
Peer ___ Supervisor ___ Top management ___
Subordinate ___
Other _____

Audience relationship to organization:
Customer ___ Competitor ___ Public ___ Employee ___
Other _____

Audience attitude toward organization:
Familiarity _____
Image _____
Similarity of interests _____

Audience attitude toward your proposition:
For ___ Neutral ___ Against ___
Audience attitude intensity:
Strong ___ Moderate ___ Weak ___
Audience involvement in issue (if any):
Active ___ Somewhat active ___ Inactive ___

Summary of important aspects of audience analysis.

Audience interest:
How interested is the audience in this subject?
Why should this audience be interested in this subject?

Audience knowledge:
How much does this audience know about my subject?
What do they need to know?

Audience attitudes:
Audience is (circle one)
Actively opposed   Passively opposed   Apathetic
Indifferent   Unaware of topic
Passively for   Actively for

informal? Is it an important meeting? Have people been called together especially to hear your presentation, or is it part of a routine program? The following factors are clearly indicators that you can use to infer what the occasion may call for.

It is important to know how much time you will have to make your presentation. You may need to redo your plans should it appear that there will not be time to accomplish all you wanted. If your audience analysis indicates that you must provide a great deal of background information, you may have to adjust your presentation, as well, by shortening some parts in order to give more time for background. The time of day may also be a factor in your planning. Business people may feel more rushed at a noon meeting than at an evening meeting. Some meetings are held at or before breakfast; how would that affect your condition or your audience's?

The size and shape of the room may determine what kind of visual materials you can or cannot use. For example, if people are seated at round tables, scattered throughout the room, poster-board visuals, such as charts and drawings, may be less effective than if people are arranged in classroom style. The size of the room and the number in the audience may determine whether you need amplifying equipment or not. Will your movements be restricted behind a lectern with a microphone, or can you move around more freely and get closer to your audience?

It may be important for you to discover that there are certain expectations or norms for this audience. Perhaps they always expect a lengthy question and answer period, for example; or they may have a rule that the meeting ends punctually at a certain time, whether the speaker is finished or not. You may wish to know what precedes or follows your presentation, since this could shape the frame of mind in which you find your audience. After a solemn tribute or ceremony, you may feel that your humorous opening is less appropriate, for example; or if the proceedings have been mostly lighthearted, you may be concerned about how you will introduce what you consider a very serious subject.

Assembling Materials for Presentation

Verbal Materials.   The essence of the presentation is the material that comprises it: the facts and figures, reasons and arguments that explain and justify the point you are making. In gathering materials, bear in mind the different kinds of verbal supporting materials. A presentation is enhanced by varying the types of supporting material used. First of all, such variety is more stimulating to the audience: People become tired of just all statistics or all quotations from authorities. In addition, using a variety of supporting material suggests that there is a lot of backing for your position. The following categories can be used as a checklist to help ensure that you do not overlook potentially useful materials.

Types of Verbal Materials.   There are many different ways to categorize verbal materials useful for speeches and presentations. The following categories make sense in business and professional presentations:

1. Quantitative materials (numbers, statistics, percentages, etc.).
2. Factual materials (laws, geographic facts, historical information, etc.).
3. Illustrative materials (stories, anecdotes, analogies, case studies, etc.).
4. Authoritative materials (quotations, citations of authorities, laws, regulations, etc.).
5. Logical materials (reasoning, arguments).

1. *Quantitative materials.* People, especially in the corporate world, are influenced by quantitative data and by statistics, such as corporate earnings for a quarter, interest rates, costs, income, market shares, prices, as well as general descriptive statistics. Statistical data presents material in a way that allows for direct or simple comparison. The use of quantitative data also suggests concreteness and assurance. When people ask for the bottom line, they are hoping to hear something concrete indicating an improvement in profits, a definite reduction in costs of a certain amount or certain percent, or the like. People often believe that if you can count it, it is real.

This book is not intended to provide training in the field of statistics; our main concern, rather, is with communicating statistics effectively when they have been derived or already discovered. Nevertheless, a quick review of the types of statistics generally used for presentations may be helpful.

Statistics can represent an entire range or distribution of values with a single number, such as the arithmetical mean when we say that the average household income for a town is $23,100. The median falls in the middle of a range of values, and a mode is the value that occurs most often in a distribution. The range of incomes in our town may be from $4300 to $123,000, but the income in the middle of all the individual incomes, the median, is $26,000, whereas the income that occurs most often, the mode, is $22,500. Features of a distribution are shown by grouping data within a certain range or group. For example, it may be useful to know that 70% of the unemployed in a city are 15–23 years old.

Statistics requiring more complicated calculations can be used to show the relationship between one variable and another. For instance, does the use of computers vary with the age of people in an organization? To arrive at this, we ask when we change the value of one factor whether that results in a change in the value of some other factor.

Statistics can be computed about events not directly observable, as when pollsters rely on responses of a relatively small number of people to predict accurately the responses of a much larger group. Because these statistics are concerned with making inferences rather than describing an existing state of affairs, they are called inferential statistics.

The following principles are useful for handling quantitative data in oral presentations:

- Make statistics meaningful to audiences.
- Be consistent in the use of statistics.
- Keep the base or unit of comparison clear.
- Present statistics visually whenever possible.

Make statistics meaningful to intended audiences. Audience analysis should indicate whether the audience is conversant with the kind of data you intend to use. Should the audience have mixed statistical expertise, take special care in dealing with numerical data. Relate the data to something meaningful to them by using comparisons or illustrations. For example, if you say that there were 237 new businesses opened in the state during the last calendar year, indicate how that number compares to other years or compares with the rate in similar states. A comparison of this sort gives the audience a better idea of what your number means.

To help your audience understand large numbers, such as the federal deficit in a fiscal year, illustrate what the amount means in terms of specific products that could be purchased with that much money. Simply giving the total values of products lost by retail stores to shoplifting in a given year lacks any real meaning for most people until you indicate the extra amount they must themselves spend for products in order to cover this loss.

Be consistent in the use of statistics. Numerical data can be difficult to follow if the basis for computing varies from example to example. Audiences will have difficulty following percentages of percentages and the like. For instance, it is always hard to make clear increases or decreases in the *rate* of change. If you say that the rate of increase in violent crime is declining by 5% a year, many people will think you said the number of crimes is declining, when in fact that is not true.

Avoid confusing estimates with actual facts or conditions. For example, a speaker may claim that the acidity of rain has gone up 500% over the last 40 years. This sounds convincing unless you clarify that there were no measurements actually taken of rainfall acidity in the 1950s in the United States. The original base upon which the percentage increase is calculated is an estimate, not a real measurement.

Keep the base or unit of comparison clear. Are you really comparing statistical apples and oranges? Obviously, 10% of the gross national product (GNP) of a country like Kenya is different from 10% of the GNP of Japan. Kenya is predominantly an agricultural economy while Japan is predominantly industrial. The percentages cannot be percents of the same products or services.

Be careful when statistics or percentages are computed over different units of time, as, for example, when the rate of increase in divorces from 1950 to 1983 is compared to the rate of increase from 1984 to 1987. Without carefully holding constant the unit of time (per year) and the unit of comparison (say per thousand marriages), the resulting statistic is not clear.

Present statistics visually whenever possible. People are more likely to grasp complex material that is both seen and heard. For examples of visual presentations of data, see the various tables and graphs that are used for presenting statistics on pp. 325–329.

To assist you in gathering statistical information, some standard sources for statistical information are indicated in the list of sources at the end of this chapter on pp. 330–331.

2. *Factual materials.* In this category are items treated as facts that are not necessarily expressed in numerical or statistical form. The type of labor contract in force at a plant, for example, is a factual matter. The competitors in a particular field and their products are facts. The legal and regulatory requirements or restraints in some industries are facts. Other types of facts are scientific (the chemical com-

position of a toxic substance), historical (the dates or sequence of events in the growth of an industry), or journalistic (reports that appear in the news media).

Facts should be distinguished from inferences, in that inferences are derived from facts. Inferences refer to ways that we think about facts, how they might be related to each other, or what they might mean. As an illustration of this distinction, notice that when we see a car weaving down the road and assume that the driver is drunk, we are not stating a fact, but an inference. This inference is based upon the combination of our actual observations of the car on the road and past associations between such observations and the state of the driver. In fact, the driver could be ill, distracted by a wasp that has flown in the window, learning to drive, and so on. Recall that this distinction between facts and inferences was explained in Chapter 3, in the discussion of critical listening.

Facts can be differentiated by the strength with which we hold them to be true. When facts are established by rigorous scientific observation, for example, we accept them as strongly based. Other facts may be less strongly held because of their uncertain or controversial nature. For example, there is disagreement among medical authorities concerning the facts regarding the causes of certain cancers. The facts of global warming seem clouded, because of disagreements among different scientists. Some information may be inappropriately presented as fact. For example, a statement that a certain chemical is safe to drink is based on what one defines as "safe." Terms such as *safe*, *dangerous*, *healthy*, *risky*, and the like are really value judgments.

Finding facts for your presentation depends upon the domain of your topic and the nature of your subject. At the simplest level, facts are found in basic reference works that can provide you with existing regulations or laws; with names, dates, or events of history; with scientific information; with news events, personalities, and the like. Some typical reference works and data banks are provided at the end of this chapter.

3. *Illustrative materials.* This category of supporting material refers to examples, case studies, and specific instances. Examples can immediately direct your audience to a real-life event or case that clarifies your point. Examples can be drawn from history, personal experience, or reports in the press. Typically, case studies are extended examples in which a great deal of detail is presented to show the operation of various factors in a process. When we refer to ecological disasters, we give examples, such as the oil spill in Alaska caused by the wreck of the *Exxon Valdez* in 1989, or the horrible explosion at the nuclear plant at Chernobyl in the former Soviet Union. These are examples of factual instances; examples, of course, can be hypothetical, intended to illustrate a general point.

Hypothetical examples are especially useful when you are trying to show how a process works. You could show the workings of intermittent reinforcement (a concept from behavioral psychology) by using the example of gambling in Las Vegas or New Jersey. This principle holds that positive reinforcement after some, but not all, performances of a desired response are better at causing a respondent to maintain that response than reinforcing the response every time it occurs.

Stories, anecdotes, or narratives can be useful for illustrating a point. In using stories, the intent is to awaken audience interest by the personalizing of an event or phenomenon. For example, Abraham Lincoln, exasperated in an argument with a young law client finally tried this tack. "OK," he said, "how many legs does a cow have?" "Why, four," the man answered, somewhat bewildered. "Well," said Abe, "what if we called the tail a leg, too. Then how many legs would a cow have?" "Five," the other responded. "Now that's where you're wrong," Abe concluded. "There are still four. Calling a tail a leg doesn't make it a leg." Stories do not have to be humorous to make a point; too many people believe that telling a joke, probably off-color and unrelated to the topic of the presentation, typifies public speaking.

Comparison and contrast are also good devices for illustration. Take a process well known to the audience and then show how your new process is similar to or different from the familiar one. For example, in trying to explain a new expense form, show how it is the same as or different from some other more familiar reporting form. The comparison is said to be literal when the two things being compared are actually alike in most respects, such as two cities, two automobile manufacturers, two pharmaceutical companies, and so on. When the comparison is based on only one central point of comparison, the comparison is said to be figurative. For example, we call a poorly running car a "lemon" because the two things share the characteristic of being sour.

4. *Authoritative materials.* Research often turns up opinions and testimony of experts and other authorities that can support a presentation. For example, you may wish to cite conclusions of university researchers who have been studying your issue. Or you may wish to quote from a speech by a widely respected leader in the field. The followers of the corporate culture school of organizational theory remind us that there are are so-called founding heroes and priests who could be good sources for useful quotations in some organizations.

External authorities are often used in a presentation to lend weight or believability to information or claims. In dealing with environmental issues, for example, independent scientists are the most credible sources or authorities for most people, whereas company representatives are seen as the least credible. Determining which authorities or experts to use is based on your analysis of the audience: What authorities are they likely to accept as most credible? For most audiences, to continue the example, scientists should be used for claims about environmental matters, rather than company spokespersons.

Internal authorities are people cited because they are particularly respected inside the organization, perhaps heroes in the organization. For example, the statements of a revered founder, such as Thomas Watson at IBM, may be used to justify a conclusion or proposed course of action. There may be heroes who are respected because of their performance, such as outstanding fundraisers or salespeople. Their word on issues related to their expertise should be especially effective. There are internal authorities who have a reputation for being up on the history or tradition of the organization, and who would be good authorities for precedents or lessons from the past.

To use authoritative materials effectively, explain to your audience who the authority is and why he or she is an authority on the subject, unless the name is so well known that people will instantly accept the authority without your giving the qualifications.

5. *Logical materials.* Logical materials refer to the use of reasoning or logic as support for your conclusions. The important point about the use of such materials is that you have to be able to explain the logical force of your argument to the target audience.

At this point, you may find it useful to review the material in Chapter 3 concerning critical listening, the definitions of and types of arguments are explained there. Also, you should review the distinctions between arguments and assertions as well as the uses of facts, inferences, and judgments, which are also in that section.

Logical materials are derived from the facts or figures upon which they are based. You therefore must base your logic on the facts or statistics that you have already gathered. When presenting logical arguments, be sure to explain how your data justifies your conclusion. Why are these examples being used to draw this inference? Can you use the airline industry as a case to prove that deregulation can be harmful? Are there examples of industries in which deregulation has been beneficial? How do you deal with these counterexamples?

Logical arguments are of two basic kinds: deductive and inductive. Deductive arguments try to show that an item is the member of a general class of similar items. What is true of the members of the general class should also be accepted as true concerning the individual item. All software written in a particular language is compatible with a certain computer, one could argue. This piece of software is written in that language; therefore, it should run on this computer. Arguments of this sort are based on the application of a definition or a general rule. If smoke is always a sign of fire, then where there is smoke, there is fire. The usefulness of the sign or indicator is based on the general rule that this thing is always a sign of something else.

Inductive arguments attempt to show that because there are so many examples of an event happening in a special way, there must be a general rule or generalization that covers all similar cases. For example, a piece of software may work on this computer, and this piece, and this piece and so on, all written in this one language. We can therefore conclude that all software written in this language will run on this computer.

Audience analysis should alert you to the objections that your audience can or will make to your specific reasoning. When using deductive arguments, for example, you should be sure that your audience will accept the generalization that is the basis for the deduction. Let's say that you argue that all trade barriers are ineffective and counterproductive; therefore, a restriction on the import of, say, figs into the United States would not be good policy. But if your audience does not accept the generalization that all trade barriers are ineffective and counter- productive, your argument loses its force. Similarly, if you are arguing inductively, using examples to prove your case, your audience may be aware of counter examples that could undermine your claims. These situations reinforce the importance of analyzing your audience in terms of their knowledge and attitudes prior to your presentation.

Highlights of Verbal Materials.   Verbal material that can be used to support presentations include five types:

    1. Quantitative material, especially statistics. You must be careful to make statistics meaningful and clear to your audience.

    2. Factual materials, such as scientific, historical, legal, and journalistic facts.

    3. Illustrative materials, which are used to clarify or explain points for the audience. Examples, illustrations, stories, comparisons are especially useful.

    4. Authoritative materials, quotations or citations of authorities, experts, her- oes, successful people, and so on.

    5. Logical materials and the use of reasoning from evidence to convince your audience.

    The use of all of these materials should be based upon information from your audience analysis indicating which materials are especially respected by or con- vincing to your audience.

Visual Supporting Materials

Visual material enhances an audience's attention, understanding, and retention. Attention is enhanced when visual material is colorful or attractive. Understanding and retention are enhanced because the use of the visual channel reinforces infor- mation being presented orally. We are more likely to remember material that we both see and hear. In fact, the more senses involved in communicating a message, the more reinforcement there is. This is why active training sessions are effective.
    Visual material is also important for dealing with two potential problems of presentations: length of time and complexity of material. During a long presen- tation, say a half-hour or more, listeners' minds can wander. Short multimedia segments in the presentation can reawaken or refocus listening. Complex material is more easily understood when it can be seen. Regarding statistics, we have already pointed out the importance of visually presenting quantitative data. As a general rule, numbers and unfamiliar material should be seen as well as heard, which means

that unfamiliar words, terms, concepts, products, or the like should be presented visually as well as orally.

Factors in Using Visual Material.   Although visual material is almost always a plus for presentations, their effectiveness depends upon several factors. Certain kinds of topics lend themselves better to visual presentation than others. The speaker and the audience can make a difference as well. The following points

Diversity in the Workplace

The Presentation in the Pacific Rim

Visual aids are especially helpful when making presentations to Asian business audiences.

- Visuals are often expected. Japanese business people especially prefer to see charts and graphs showing detail and effort because they indicate the presenter's seriousness and professionalism.

- Because of communication in a foreign language, the written and visual cues can be especially helpful. Many executives in Korea, Japan, and other parts of Asia read English better than they understand spoken English. The visuals will help to ensure your message is getting across.

- Written handouts are also very useful. Especially useful are articles from trade journals or technical sources that make positive references to your company or your product.

- In countries where Confucianism is important, the spoken language is often considered to be suspect. Pictures and written material are felt to be more credible.

See C. Engholm. (1991). *When business East meets business West: The guide to practice and protocol in the Pacific Rim.* New York: John Wiley & Sons; and D. Rowland. (1985). *Japanese business etiquette.* New York: Warner Books.

indicate factors that you need to take into consideration when deciding what kind of visual materials to prepare:

1. *Subject matter of the presentation*. Some material is well presented visually, such as numbers or statistics, or unfamiliar or foreign terms. Other kinds of material that should be presented visually include charts of organizations or networks, summaries of points that you wish to make, diagrams or plans for structures, and key terms.

2. *The presenter*. A dynamic speaker who understands the material well probably has less need for visual aids than another speaker, who may be less experienced or dynamic. The use of visual material and multimedia techniques, however, can help an ordinary speaker seem more exciting and can boost the speaker's confidence.

3. *Audience size*. The smaller the audience, the easier it is to adapt your information to individuals and to respond to individual's questions. A speaker cannot respond to larger audiences in such individualized ways, however, and the use of visual materials can help clarify information for a larger number. Of course, the smaller group can more easily see some kinds of visual aids than can larger ones. Larger audiences require larger and bolder visual aids.

4. *The occasion, including time, place, and setting*. Some settings are better for using visual materials than others. For example, a room equipped with overhead projectors and the right kind of screens would be a good site for showing overhead transparencies. The seating arrangement in the room can be an important consideration. As mentioned before, meal setups are often difficult because people do not have clear lines of sight for charts or tables. Slides or film projected onto a large screen, however, may be quite effective for a banquet.

5. *Audience expectations*. Most people now are accustomed to extremely slick and professional performances on television. When you try to use similar techniques, remember that your low-budget effort may suffer from comparison. Also, bear in mind that the audience may be expecting entertainment along with a substantive presentation. Their expectations may be that speakers always use visual aids.

6. *Money and other resources*. Of course, the extent to which you can produce and use media techniques may be restricted by budget and by the skills of the people producing the visual aids. A poorly done visual presentation may be more harmful than a presentation without visual material.

Types of Visual Material.   Just as a variety of verbal materials can stimulate your audience and enhance your presentation, variety in the use of visual materials can be stimulating and especially help maintain audience interest. The types of visual material you can use include objects (the actual thing itself or a model), charts or illustrations, projected still images, and projected moving images, such as videotape. In addition, there are several interactive devices available that enable you to combine and coordinate the various types.

- *Real objects or models of objects.* If the object itself or a model of it is small enough to handle, this can be an effective visual aid. The use of objects is subject to the certain restraints. First, the object and any important components must be clearly visible at about 30 to 35 feet. Ideally, the main parts of the object should be visible from the worst seat in the room. The object's visibility can be enhanced by highlighting parts with chalk dust or brightly coloring certain components. The object could be shown both assembled and disassembled.

- *Charts or illustrations.* Graphs, charts, diagrams, maps, cartoons, and drawings are examples of this type; these are two-dimensional representations of items. The impact of these visual aids depends upon essentializing, or representing the part of the information that is vital to your purpose. This means that you need to pull out for your audience the important elements and highlight them in your illustration. Samples of various kinds of charts or illustrations follow.

The principle of maximizing visibility for all the people in the audience means that all charts, drawings, and the like must be large enough to be seen by everyone in the room; 3 feet by 3 feet is a good size. Keep charts as simple as possible for instant clarity. Use solid lines and contrasting colors for easy visibility. Present only one major idea or table per each visual aid. Don't scrimp on the chart paper or transparencies by crowding too much information on each chart.

Explain the visual aid as you present it to the listeners. What do the scales mean? What is the source for the information? How was the material collected? In order to maintain eye contact with the audience, be sure that you are familiar with the visual aid or chart, so that you can talk about it without losing direct contact with your audience.

Product	Year			
	1960	1970	1980	1990
Horses	103	127	130	147
Eggs	579	568	881	834
Chickens	602	896	1,245	2,065

Sales growth in thousands of dollars for selected products 1960 to 1990

▶ **Figure 10-2** *Statistical table.*

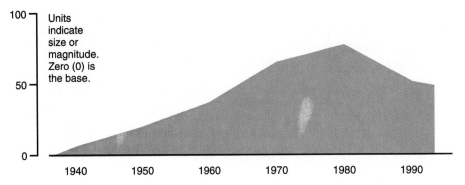

Single line graph with shading.

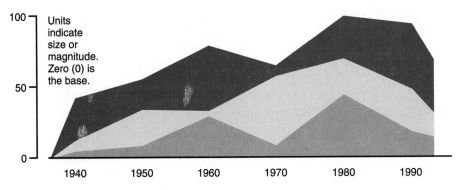

Multiline graph with shading.

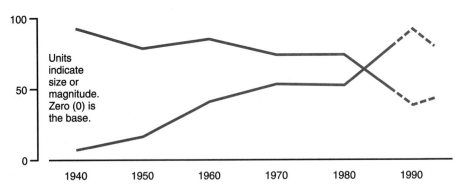

Multiline graph without shading.

▶ **Figure 10-3**   *Various types of line graphs. Top is a single-line graph. Center is a multiline graph. Below is a multiline graph showing converging trends.*

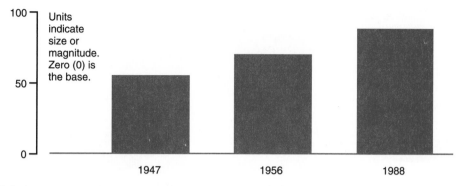

Units for each bar could compare years: for example, 1947, 1956, 1988.
Units for each bar could compare products: for example, wheat, barley, rye.

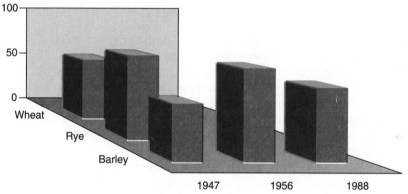

Three-dimensional bar graph. One dimension could equal years. One dimension could equal product:
for example, wheat, barley, and rye. One dimension could equal amount sold.

▶ **Figure 10-4**   *Two-dimensional bar graph and three-dimensional bar graph.*

• *Projected images*. Projected images include overhead transparencies and slides. An advantage of the overhead projector is that you can maintain your orientation to the audience without turning around or looking back at the visual; what you see on the projector is exactly what the audience sees. You can point to parts of the transparency on the projector with a pencil or pen, and it will be seen on the screen by the audience. Prepared transparencies guarantee a neater and more polished look.

Possible disadvantages are that the room may have to be partially darkened to allow good vision, and the screen may not be properly oriented for best viewing by all in the audience. The best screens are tilted overhead to eliminate visual distortion and to place the image above the speaker, so that you do not block the line of sight of people in the room. They can see both you and the screen overhead.

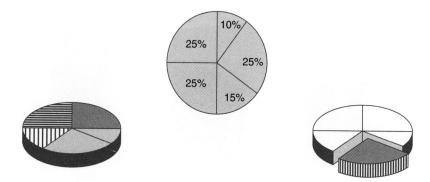

▶ **Figure 10-5**   *Pie graphs show proportion or relative size through percentages. The three-dimensional pie graphs allow dramatic emphasis through shading and "exploding" one slice of the pie.*

Often, you have to work with slide screens, flat against a wall behind you. Then you must be careful about blocking people's view of the screen.

Slides can be polished and professional in appearance, but they cut down the direct interaction between speaker and audience. Usually, the room must be completely dark, and the presenter becomes more of a narrator rather than a public speaker. Slide shows can be coordinated with computers and audiotapes for a very slick performance, if desired, but such performances are getting away from the main focus of this chapter, the spoken presentation.

Videotapes and films can also be used to supplement oral presentations, but again, they are outside the scope of the kind of presentations that we are talking

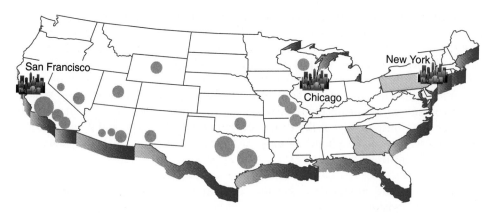

▶ **Figure 10-6**   *A map. Information can be indicated by colors, dots, shading, labels, or even perspective.*

1950

1980

2000
(est.)

▶ **Figure 10-7**   *A pictograph. A pictograph could be used to compare growth in chicken consumption in the United States. Each unit represents a number (perhaps millions) of pounds of chicken consumed. Units are grouped in three's for ease of comparison.*

about in this section. Chapter 12 returns to the use of presentation media and their effects.

SUMMARY

This chapter provided steps for preparing the materials for a presentation. First, we emphasized the importance of determining a specific purpose for the presentation. If you are clear about what you are doing, it is more likely that your audience will also understand. If you are confused, there is little hope that your listeners will have a good idea of what you are trying to accomplish. The problem is that most people rush into preparation without sufficient attention to this first step.

Second, we presented a methodical system for analyzing your intended audience. We believe that careful adaptation to the specific audience goes a long way toward ensuring success. The analysis of the audience includes their attention level, knowledge level, and their probable attitudes toward you, your organization, your subject, and your purpose. If you cannot answer the question, "Why should these people be interested?" satisfactorily, then you should probably reconsider giving the presentation. We have provided an audience analysis worksheet as a guide to use for gathering information about your proposed audiences.

Third, we reviewed the kind of supporting material that you can use in the development of the presentation. We categorized the possible material into five groups: quantitative (mainly statistics); factual (facts presented in a nonquantitative fashion); illustrative (examples, illustrations, stories, comparisons); authoritative (quotations, testimony of experts); and logical (reasoning based upon inductive or deductive approaches).

The next chapter turns to the matter of taking this material and organizing and presenting it to audiences.

EXERCISES   ●

1. Using the Audience Analysis Worksheet, write a complete audience analysis of the following:

   a. A downtown service club in your community, such as the Optimists or Kiwanis.
   b. A local chapter of the League of Women Voters.
   c. A meeting of a local neighborhood association.
   d. One of your classes.

2. If you were to prepare a speech advocating the buying of American products versus imported products, what features of these audiences would be important to know? Explain your reasoning.

3. Indicate the best sources of information for gathering materials on the following topics:

   a. A local school board referendum on a bond issue to raise money for the local schools.
   b. Programmed trading in the stock market.
   c. The meaning of the global warming problem.
   d. American competitiveness in international manufacturing markets.

4. After researching these topics in the sources indicated, write out specific purposes for presentations on each of the above topics, applying the principles explained in the chapter.

5. In a source such as *Vital Speeches*, find a speech by a business executive or CEO. Describe the uses of quantitative, factual, illustrative, authoritative, and logical materials. Does one type of use seem more common than others? If so, why do you think the speaker has made these decisions? What visual materials would enhance these speeches?

◀▶ **SELECTED SOURCES FOR FURTHER READING**

Statistical Abstract of the United States, U.S. Department of Commerce, Bureau of Census. A list of sources at the end makes this a good source for finding other statistics published by the government. There is a paperback version,

American Almanac: U.S. Book of Facts, Statistics, and Information, published by Grosset and Dunlap each year.

Handbook of Labor Statistics, published by the U.S. Bureau of Labor Statistics, Department of Labor. *The Monthly Labor Review*, published by the same source, provides timely employment data.

American Statistics Index, published by the Congressional Information Service, Washington, D.C. Again, this deals with statistics produced by the federal government.

Almanacs can also be good sources of statistical information: *World Almanac— Book of Facts*, Newspaper Enterprise Association, Inc., has been published since 1868. *Information Please Almanac* is published by Simon & Schuster.

The H. W. Wilson Company publishes several indexes to various kinds of literature; their most famous index is in the *Readers' Guide to Periodical Literature*. For business interests, they provide the following indexes: *Business Periodicals Index*, H. W. Wilson Co., New York; *Applied Science and Technology Index*, H. W. Wilson Co., New York.

There is an ever-expanding list of on-line computer data services. See the following updated directories: *Directory of Online Databases*, Cuadra, Santa Monica, CA; *Datapro Directory of On-line Services*, Datapro Research, Delran, NJ.

References

1. Kaplan, B. (1990, January). Speaking successfully. *USAir Magazine*, p. 86.
2. See, for example, Fanning, D. (1990, August 19). If people hate your industry, parties are tough. (p. B13). *Indianapolis Star*.

Organizing and Delivering Presentations

11
CHAPTER

After studying this chapter, you should be able to:

1. Understand the principles of effective organization.

2. Select patterns of organization appropriate for presentations.

3. Explain the major principles of effective delivery.

4. Rehearse and present effective presentations, including dealing with questions and answers.

Overview

Now that you have gathered the best material for a presentation, you have to put it all together and present it in the most effective way possible. This chapter goes through the steps of taking materials, putting them in shape for presentation, and revising and modifying them until you have an outline or manuscript for presentation. Then you rehearse for the actual presentation itself, make any last-minute changes including preparing for possible audience questions, and deliver the finished product to your audience.

This chapter covers two main topics: organizing your materials for the most effective presentation; and preparing to deliver your presentation.

ORGANIZING MATERIALS FOR PRESENTATION

Purposes of Organization

As indicated at several points in this book, effective communication depends upon the audience. Audiences respond to messages in four stages: (1) They must give attention to the incoming signals and recognize that it is a message; (2) they must understand the meaning of the message; (3) they need to remember or retain the

▶ *Many presentations involve small groups or committees.*

information; and (4) they need to take some action to respond to the message (see Figure 11-1). Haphazard material is harder to understand and harder to remember. People will lose interest in things that are presented in no particular order, and they probably will have trouble figuring out what they are supposed to do.

There is no question that organized or patterned material is easier to comprehend and retain. In business it is important to present material concisely, with all reasons and options clearly set out. Otherwise, audiences have difficulty understanding and recalling complex material. Even when you present a lot of detailed information, it will be easier to follow if the overall pattern of organization is simple and clear.

Patterns for Organizing Materials in the Body

Since patterning information is so important, this section provides several templates for organizing materials for the presentation. These patterns represent the end-product of the process of organizing your materials; in other words, they describe what the final outline should look like.

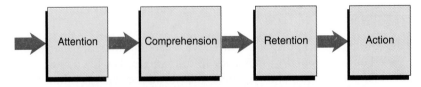

▶ **Figure 11-1** *Diagram showing the stages in the active reception of messages.*

All presentations are generally divided into the three parts used to organize any effective communication, whether written or oral: introduction, body, and conclusion. Despite the temptation to start with the introduction in preparing, the authors recommend that you start with the core of the presentation, that is, the body. After you have the body properly developed, then you can attend to the introduction and the conclusion.

To organize the body of the presentation, you should begin with the presentation goal. First, rough out or sketch various ideas; then develop an initial statement that seems comfortable. As you do your research, however, you will discover examples, quotations, and facts. This new information will lead you to revise your goal statement or some of your main headings. Figure 11-2 suggests the process of revision that goes on while you are at this stage of preparation.

At this point, you can go back to formulating the specific purpose that you used in gathering your materials, as Chapter 10 described. Remember that to formulate a statement of purpose, you begin by answering at least three of the "w" questions: who? what? and why? (You may wish to review the section in Chapter 10 that deals with wording and limiting the statement of specific purpose.)

After working out the statement of specific purpose, several additional ideas should come to mind that clarify, explain, or prove this statement. For example, you have been invited to explain to a high school economics class what it means to be a public utility. Since you represent the phone company, you can take your own business as an example to illustrate the defining characteristics of a utility.

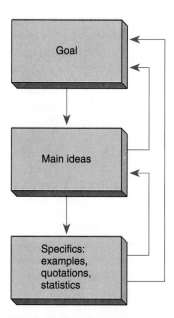

▶ **Figure 11-2**   *The process of revising your organization of material. As the speaker discovers new information, the new ideas and goal are altered.*

Problem-Solution

Writing a Specific Purpose Statement

To write a statement of specific purpose, you can fill in answers to questions of this sort:

First, then, *who* should carry out the action or exhibit the belief or skill or knowledge? _____.

Second, *what* is to be done, to be understood, to be believed? _____.

Third, *why* should this thing be done or understood or believed? _____.

Good specific statements of purpose, therefore, should be worded as follows:
"Office personnel (who) will learn the new accounting procedure (what) in order to save time inputting invoices (why)."
Or, "Upper management (who) should grant increased budget to our product development (what) in order to enhance competitive market position (why)."

So, you begin by making a rough list of the differences between a private corporation and a publicly regulated utility. You come up with ideas such as your prices are regulated by a public commission, on the basis of laws made by the legislature; you are a monopoly; stockholders in your company are guaranteed a reasonable return on their investment; and so on. Perhaps other ideas come to mind, as well. At any rate, you look at this list and begin to put them into a reasonable form.

These major ideas that clarify, explain, or prove your statement of specific purpose become the main points for the body of your presentation. The next section shows how these main points can be organized into logical patterns, depending upon whether you have an informative or a persuasive purpose.

Types of Presentations.   As indicated before, business and the professions are usually concerned with either informative or persuasive presentations. For that reason, the discussion here looks at standard formats for these two kinds of presentations. Here, we are talking about the way to organize the main points that constitute the body of your presentation. Once you have written out a specific statement of your purpose, you should try to write down the major ideas that explain or prove this specific purpose statement. Keep revising this rough draft of ideas until they work into a logical order or pattern.

Informative presentations usually take the form of defining something, explaining a cause-effect relationship, or explaining a process. Examples of informative purposes include the following:

- "Indiana Bell is a public utility." (a definition)
- "Direct contact with the CEO increased worker satisfaction." (cause-to-effect)
- "Creating a presentation is divided into five parts." (a process)

Persuasive presentations typically take two forms: calling for the audience to make some judgment (for example, this thing is good or worthy or dangerous or unethical or whatever), or calling upon the audience to take some action (or approve of taking some action). Examples of persuasive presentations would be:

- "Telephone interviews are the best way to check references." (a value judgment)
- "WAWE, Inc. should build a new corporate headquarters." (calling for some specific action)

Informative Presentations.   Informative presentations are usually concerned with defining something, establishing that something is a cause or effect of something else, or describing or explaining a process.

In defining something, we establish criteria for the general category and then apply the criteria to the term to be defined. That is, we try to show that the thing we are talking about has the characteristics that define it as one thing or another. Often, the purpose of such a presentation is to explain a term or concept. In the following example, the presenters are trying to explain to an audience what it means for a corporation to be defined as a public utility.

This results in the organizational pattern outlined below.

Specific purpose: To show that Indiana Bell is a public utility.
   (First, we state the criteria for a public utility):

I. A public utility meets three criteria.
   A. A public utility's rates are set by government.
   B. A public utility's service is regulated by government.
   C. A public utility enjoys a monopoly in a territory.

(Once we have established the criteria for a public utility, then we apply them to AT&T.)

II. Indiana Bell's local phone service makes it a utility.
   A. Indiana Bell's local phone rates are set by government.
   B. Indiana Bell's local phone service is regulated by law.
   C. Indiana Bell enjoys a monopoly of local services.

Another type of informative presentation could be based on defining the object in question by its parts or divisions.

Specific purpose: Buggywhips Inc. Corporation has three divisions (based on the parts of the whole).

    I. Buggywhips contains a product division.
    II. Buggywhips contains a service division.
   III. Buggywhips contains a sales division.

A second typical type of informative presentation is based on a cause(s)-to-effect(s) relationship. A cause-effect relationship simply means that one situation has the power, means, or facility to create another. For example, consider this example of a purpose for an informative presentation:

Specific purpose: Direct contact with the CEO can increase worker satisfaction.

    I. The CEO made direct contact with the workers. (cause)
       A. The CEO visited the production floor.
       B. The CEO ate in the general cafeteria.
       C. The CEO visited disabled workers.
    II. Worker satisfaction increased. (effect)
       A. General productivity increased.
       B. Workers contacted by the CEO expressed increased
         feelings of loyalty.

The third kind of informative presentation describes a process, or a way of doing something. For these kinds of presentation, the material is usually organized in a time sequence or chronological order, that is, from first step to last step. For example, we have suggested the following process for developing business presentations:

Specific purpose: Creating a presentation consists of five parts.

    I. Analyze the reason for the presentation.
    II. Determine the response desired from a specific audience.
   III. Gather and assemble materials.
   IV. Prepare and rehearse.
    V. Evaluate the effects of the presentation.

Persuasive Presentations.   Recall that there are two kinds of persuasive presentations: asking for value judgments and asking for action or policy. The first kind of persuasive presentation involves an evaluation of worth or benefit. Claiming that something is the best implies it is the best in comparison with other, lesser alternatives. The following is an example of an evaluation presentation:

Specific purpose: Telephone interviews are a good way to check references.

  I. Effective checking of references should meet four standards.
    A. A good reference provides positive characteristics of the candidate.
    B. A good reference provides negative characteristics of the candidate.
    C. A good reference gives specific examples about the candidate.
    D. A good reference is candid.
 II. Telephone interviews meet the criteria for good references.
    A. Telephone interviews provide positive information about the candidate.
    B. Telephone interviews provide negative information about the candidate.
    C. Telephone interviews provide specific information about the candidate.
    D. Telephone interviews are candid.

The second type of persuasive presentation emphasizes the action to be taken. In most cases, speakers show how the solution solves the problem and additional benefits for taking the action. The organizational pattern therefore is divided into three parts: problem, solution, and advantages. The standard format would be as follows:

Specific Purpose

  I. The problem
    A. What is wrong with our present approach?
      1. How significant is the problem?
      2. How widespread is the problem?
    B. What are the causes of the problem?
 II. The solution
    A. Will the solution solve the problem?
    B. Is the solution workable?
    C. Is the solution free from objection?
III. The advantages of the solution
    A. What are the benefits over the present system?
    B. What additional benefits result?

The following sample outline illustrates how a typical persuasive presentation should be developed following this format:

Specific purpose: WEWA, Inc. should build a new corporate headquarters.

  I. WEWA, Inc. lacks adequate office space. (problem)
    A. WEWA now occupies three office buildings.
      1. Departments are split among buildings.
      2. Communications among buildings are awkward.
      3. Customer service has suffered.
    B. WEWA's rapid expansion has caused the problem.

  II. A new building would solve WEWA's problems. (solution)
      A. One building would solve the problem.
         1. Departments will no longer be split.
         2. Communications will be easier.
         3. Customer service will be improved.
      B. We can build one building.
         1. We have the necessary land.
         2. We have the money.
      C. The program lacks serious disadvantages.
         1. Neighbors are not against it.
         2. Employees are not against it.
 III. A new building is advantageous. (additional benefits)
      A. Morale will be improved.
      B. Internal communications will be simplified.
      C. The corporate image will be enhanced.

These examples follow a logical pattern and have a small number of main points, usually two or three. Three principles should guide effective organization in oral presentations. First, try to use a logical pattern that your audience can easily grasp and follow. Second, keep the number of main points to a minimum. In the outlines above, Roman numerals indicate the main points in the body of the speech; at most, three main points have been used. Third, word the main headings simply and clearly; the sample outlines avoid specialized or technical jargon and keep the points worded as simple, complete thoughts.

When wording the main points of an outline, watch out for phrases or terms that are habitual within your organization that may be unknown outside that group. For example, people who work for the Disney corporation refer to "good mickey" or "bad mickey," or to meals being "on the mouse." The phrase "bad mickey" describes anything seen as negative, while positive things, such as praise for a job well-done is a "good mickey." At IBM, a "hipo" is someone on the fast track toward upper-management (from high-potential). The "violin" at *Newsweek* magazine, is the lead or top national story, because it is supposed to set the tone for the rest of the issue, as a violin sets the tone for an orchestra.[1] You may become so accustomed to using your organization's own language that you may have to catch yourself using such terms when speaking to external audiences.

Principles of Emphasis.   One other matter to consider in working out the best pattern for presenting your material is that you can emphasize points by the way you organize your main points. You place emphasis on points by where you place the idea, how much time you give to it, and the transitions you use. The principles of emphasis, therefore, are: placement, proportion; and power.

    Placement. Audiences are usually most attentive to the first and last parts of a presentation. Ask yourself which are the first and last main points in the body of the speech. Place the most important ideas, therefore, either first or last in the body of the presentation.

    Proportion. Receivers give importance to points on which you spend a lot of time. Your listeners will say to themselves, "She spent a lot of time on the regulated monopoly idea; it must really be important." Or, they might say, "She spent very little time on the Federal Power Commission; it must be insignificant."

Power. When you expressly tell the audience that something is important, you say, "Write this down," or "If you remember nothing else, remember this," or "This is important." Each of these phrases emphasizes your most important ideas. Finally, what you repeat is given emphasis. Even if we do not like the slogan, we remember advertising jingles and slogans because they are repetitious.

Highlights of Organizing Materials in the Body of the Presentation. Organization helps get and hold your audience's attention and enhances their comprehension and retention of your message. Clearly organized material is easier to follow, understand, and remember than randomly presented information. Therefore, we suggest ways to pattern material for both informative and persuasive presentations.

Introductions

Once the body of the presentation has been prepared, the introduction and the conclusion should be added. After all, you don't know all of what you are introducing until you have prepared the body of the presentation. Introductions serve to lay the groundwork for the main purpose of the presentation. Effective introductions do four things:

1. Gain the attention of the audience.
2. Show how your topic is related to the audience.
3. Announce your specific purpose.
4. Preview the main points to be covered.

1. *Gain the attention of the audience.* Your first obligation as a speaker is to get the audience interested in your subject. It is effective to begin with an attention-getting device, which can be a humorous story, a famous quotation, or an illustration, specific case, or example that deals with the main topic. Rather than beginning starkly with, say, "My subject is lasers. They are concentrated beams of light," it may be more effective to begin with "Remember Star Wars, when R2D2 and C3PO were running down the corridor of a space ship with light beams all around them? This was science fiction, but in 10 years such a scene might be possible. Laser technology has come a long way."

Audiences also respond readily to things that are familiar to them. Events in their hometown, individuals they know, and problems faced by their company attract their attention. From your audience analysis, you may be able to make a specific reference to an event or person familiar to this particular audience.

Also, audiences react to the new, the unusual, or the exotic. A promise of new information or knowledge or the description of something beyond their experience will hold their attention. In other words, show them how they will learn something new as a result of your presentation.

Audiences are attracted by competition between principles, organizations, or individuals. The rivalry between corporate products can be as dramatic as the competition between baseball teams such as the Red Sox and the Yankees.

You can catch the audience's attention by a short but compelling story that allows them to visualize some of the main ideas that you will be discussing. Often, such stories play upon humor, but this is not required. In fact, there is no worse way to begin your presentation than with a joke that falls flat.

2. *Show how the topic is relevant to the audience.* Audiences will listen more attentively if you explain what is in it for them. The relationship of your purpose to them and their interests is an important consideration. They will listen more attentively if the topic is vital to them and if it is near in time and in place. The professor who announces, "I am giving a quiz on this material tomorrow," focuses attention better than one who says, "This information is interesting." Once you have analyzed your audience, you should be able to answer the question, "Why should you be interested in this topic?"

3. *Announce your specific purpose.* You should announce your purpose concisely. The easiest way to accomplish this is to use your specific purpose statement. Remember your purpose is to gain understanding and retention; be sure the audience knows what you want from them.

4. *Preview your main points.* Give the main points of your presentation. Audiences will listen more attentively if they know where you are going; the appearance of organization will increase your credibility; and, like an advertising slogan, the repetition of the main ideas will increase the likelihood that it will be remembered.

Introductions can be long or short, depending on the topic and the time available. The following sample introduction includes a review of the past and a compliment to the audience to spur them on. Notice the statement of major purpose followed by a preview of the main points of the body of the presentation.

Thank you, Bill. And greetings!
The last time we met, you had a tough job to do: Introduce and establish a totally new line with superb styling and performance but with higher prices. And, rekindle dealer interest in a product most dealers had almost forgotten.
Well, you did both.
You met and surpassed our June objectives. You sold a display package to the broadest selection of independent dealers we've enjoyed in years. And you turned the "big guys" on, the keys where we had some concern over import price competition. Polk Brothers bought. Jordan Marsh bought. Korvettes bought. Rich's bought. J. L. Hudson bought.

You got the line exposed at retail. And you have our most enthusiastic "thank you!"

But most of that is last week's news.

The early part of the race is ours.

Now there's a new challenge: Making the new products the demand line at retail this fall. That's the primary objective of our August program. And I'm going to outline a three-part plan to meet that objective. A plan that includes an exciting new ingredient to the industry's biggest ad campaign . . . a plan that puts dollars where you need them most now.

This introduction begins with past success and an appeal to the pride of the audience for their part in that success: attention and relation to the audience. Then the speaker turns to the future. The goal for the future is the specific purpose and the three-part plan is the forewarning of the main points of the body of the presentation.

Conclusions

◀

Conclusions are as important as the introduction. You have probably heard presentations that lacked a real conclusion. The speaker may have looked at his watch and announced, "Well, I guess my time is up—that's about all." Since you want your audience to understand something or to take some action, use your conclusion to make a final effort at pushing your main point. Leave the audience with a sense of closure, or completion, that lets them see what you have accomplished and what is to happen next.

A good conclusion should accomplish two purposes: The audience should know what is expected of them; they should be in a proper frame of mind to carry it out. To accomplish these goals, the conclusion should consist of two parts: a summary of the main points and a final appeal that creates an appropriate ending point.

The following example of a conclusion lays out a step-by-step advertising campaign and ends with a strong call for success:

Now let's put it all together on the calendar to get an idea of just how much we really do have going for us in the next four months, including the national advertising support.

First, September, when we kick off the new line. Our big week gets underway, and leads us into October, with local advertising support and the continuation on network TV of the new "Claimboard" commercials up through every game of the World Series.

Then, starting the last week of October and continuing to build through November—the announcement of our new product, on network television, major magazines, and in high impact advertising at retail—a

SAMPLE OUTLINE FOR A PRESENTATION

Briefing on Department of Corporate Communication's goals and objectives for the communication policy of this firm (30 minutes).

Proposition: The function of each part of the departments fulfills the goals and policies of corporate communications.

Introduction.

I. (Attention step) Management has determined that communication is the most important function at this time in our history.
   A. Quotation from CEO.
   B. Reminder of departmental reorganization.

II. (Importance to audience) These new goals and objectives will be the basis for your operations and evaluations this year.

III. (Specific purpose) Therefore, I am going to explain the goals and objectives of the communication policy of our corporation.

IV. (Preview of briefing) I will cover in this briefing the following three points:
   A. The goals of the firm, showing the importance of communication in the meeting of the corporate goals.
   B. The process of carrying out communication policy.
   C. The specific objectives of each part of the department in carrying out the goals and policy.

Body of the Briefing.

I. There are four corporate goals of special interest to this department.
   A. To provide quality of service.
      1. This goal requires that we listen to customers.
      2. We must recruit and train employees who listen and respond to customer needs.
      3. We must promote wise and safe use of the product.
   B. To attract and develop qualified people for present and future corporate need.
      1. This goal includes training in seeking and giving feedback.
      2. The internal communication system is important to meeting this goal.
   C. To maintain a safe working environment.
      1. This goal involves both health and safety.
      2. Internal communication must promote safety consciousness.
   D. To create general understanding and support for positions and policies essential to corporate success.
      1. Internal and external audiences are stressed.
      2. This goal depends upon the credibility of the firm with its audiences.
         a. Open and candid statements.
         b. Responsible and timely disclosures.
         c. Policies perceived to be fair and reasonable.
         d. Day-to-day actions and decisions of employees.

II. Communication policy is enacted in a five-step process.
   A. We must monitor the environment.
      1. We should be aware of significant public issues in the service area.
      2. We should monitor both media and opinion leaders in the community.
   B. The issues are researched and shown in relationship to corporate operations.
      1. Concern over gas pipeline proposal is a good example.
      2. Environmental issues are important all over the service area.
   C. Based upon this research, public positions are formulated.
      1. Our statement on the Clean Air Act is an example.
      2. Our recent concern over PCBs indicates an area where we have had a problem.
   D. These positions are then communicated.
      1. Internal audiences are important.
         a. Employee communications.
         b. Communication with stockholders.
      2. External audiences are multidimensional.
         a. General public.   b. Legislative bodies.
         c. Regulatory agencies.   d. Special interest groups.
   E. Responses are evaluated for effectiveness.
      1. Direct responses may be received.
      2. Monitor media for responses.
III. The department is organized in four sections to carry out this process.
   A. The public information section is concerned with the public.
      1. Advertising.   2. Media relations.
      3. Educational services.   4. Speakers' bureaus.
   B. Employee information section deals with internal messages.
      1. Internal newsletters.   2. Video productions for internal release.
      3. Bulletin boards.   4. New employee orientation.
   C. Administrative section provides overall direction.
      1. Relations with upper management.
      2. Communications with other departments.
   D. Communication services section supports the other sections.
      1. Graphics and art services. 2. Speech writing.
      3. Communication training.   4. Video and technical services.

Summary and closing of the briefing.
   I. (Summary) The specific functions of each section of the department are designed to carry out communication policy in meeting corporate goals.
   II. (Reinforcement) Communication is a critical function in corporate success.
   A. Quotation from chairman of the board on the importance of communication.
   B. This department is of central importance to the corporation.

real barrage that will impact the consumer at the peak of the selling season and carry us into December, along with a continuation of the black and white campaign in national magazines.

I'm sure you'll agree that the program we have mapped out for the next four months is a powerful one—one that will make your dealers and their customers and competition sit up and take notice now—for it will not only put us *on track* for what could turn out to be the best four months in our history: It could be our launching pad into the next four years in which our preeminence in the industry becomes and remains undisputed.

In summary, introductions and conclusions should be developed after the body of the presentation has been outlined. A good introduction gains audience attention, relates the topic to their needs, states the specific purpose, and previews the organization of the body of the presentation. The conclusion summarizes the main points in the body and provides closure. A good conclusion should leave the audience well disposed to the speaker's purpose.

▶ ### Internal Organization: Transitions and Internal Summaries

Because the audience is listening rather than reading what you are saying, you need to provide ample transitions and internal summaries. Keep your audience apprised of where you are in the presentation of your material. Listeners do not have the luxury of glancing ahead on a page to see what is coming next; they have to wait for you to say something. Therefore, it is necessary to provide previews to reinforce what is coming next.

Internal summaries are another type of internal organization. Stop at the end of major sections of your presentation to review the main points in that section. This should help the audience retain the main points.

▶ ### Highlights of Organizing Materials for Presentation

Pages 344 through 345 contain a sample outline for a presentation.

◀▶ ## PREPARING TO DELIVER YOUR PRESENTATION

Once the materials for the presentation have been organized and placed in final outline form, it is time to begin preparing for delivering the presentation. Considerations include choice of manner of delivery and awareness of characteristics of good delivery, especially in the use of voice and body. You will also want to give attention to building confidence, rehearsing, and preparing notes.

Manner of Delivery

There are four choices for the manner of delivery:

- Impromptu
- Extemporaneous
- Manuscript
- Memorized

The first choice, impromptu, is usually ruled out by all that has gone before in the various stages of development of the presentation, because such a presentation lacks specific preparation. In the give-and-take of discussion or debate, one must often present coherent speeches that have not been prepared in advance. Such speeches grow out of past training, experience, reading, discussion, education, and so on.

The second choice, extemporaneous, is usually selected for presentations in the businesses and professions. Extemporaneous delivery is used when the presentation has been researched, organized, and otherwise prepared in advance, but has not been written out word for word. This style allows for more flexibility and adaptability during the presentation. There may be questions and interruptions, so trying to stick to a prepared script would not only be difficult but, possibly, foolish. An extemporaneous presentation can be rehearsed, but the rehearsal is used to work out the flow of the ideas and to familiarize oneself with the general contours of the material.

The third choice, manuscript, is preferable when getting the wording exactly right is important. Such situations include speaking before a very formal gathering, and when the presentation will become part of an official record. Or, there may be situations in which legal ramifications require getting some or all of the wording exact in order to avoid law suits, liability, or unwanted contractual obligations. Finally, the presentation may be intended for printing and distribution exactly as delivered. The preparation of speech manuscripts is a central aspect of speech writing and is, therefore, considered in some detail in Chapter 15.

The fourth choice, a memorized presentation, is a special case of the manuscript speech. There may be reasons to memorize the text in order to avoid reading from a script during the presentation. The availability of modern technology such as teleprompters and graphics for script preparation reduce the need for memorization.

For our purposes here, we assume that the decision has been to deliver an extemporaneous presentation.

Characteristics of Delivery

Speakers exhibiting effective extemporaneous delivery have the following characteristics: They sound conversational; they establish rapport with the audience; and they are dynamic. We will explain each of these characteristics in a little more detail.

Conversational Style.   Many presentations are delivered before small groups or meetings, for which a formal platform style would be inappropriate. Even in platform settings, people respond positively to a speaker who seems to be conversing with them rather than speaking at them. One reason for avoiding a script or memorized presentation is that it is very hard to sound or appear conversational under the restrictions of a completely "canned" performance. Many speakers will seem rather formal during a prepared presentation and then relax and loosen up when answering questions from the audience. The relaxed, conversational mode of the question period should be used throughout the prepared remarks.

Rapport with the Audience.   Speakers with an effective conversational style usually develop a pleasant, friendly rapport with the audience members. Too much familiarity can be a problem, of course, should the speaker appear to presume on a relationship that is not really all that close or when there are important status differences between speaker and audience members. (Audience members are sensitive to the distinctions.) There may also be cultural differences that must be taken into account, as when too much American friendliness can be seen as a lack of seriousness. Nonetheless, the speaker should always give the impression of speaking directly to the people in the audience, rather than to the walls, an overhead projector, a script, or a chart. Look at people, establish and keep up eye contact, and talk directly to the people present.

Dynamism.   In most cases, audience members respond well to speakers who exhibit liveliness or enthusiasm, given the caveats already introduced regarding

▶ *Gestures indicate a natural and conversational style.*

status or cultural differences. Vitality and movement help to attract and hold listeners' attention. We have all experienced the problem of paying attention to a speaker who drones on with minimal movement, few gestures, and little to excite or kindle our enthusiasm. Enthusiasm, of course, can be overdone; the speaker should always be prepared to adapt to the audience and the setting. Appropriateness is the most important watchword in this matter. Cues that indicate enthusiasm to a typical American audience include conversational variation in vocal pitch and tone, spontaneous and conversational gestures and movement, and expressive face and eyes that are in tune with what is being said.

Techniques for Achieving Effective Delivery

Effective delivery involves the use of voice and action. This section briefly reviews the basic techniques for the employment of voice and bodily action to achieve the conversational, audience-centered, dynamic quality desired.

Vocal Delivery.   Audiences expect and want speaking voices to be clear, distinct, and fairly definite; that is, audiences expect speakers to give the clear impression that they know what they are talking about. In short, the speaker has two obligations: to be understandable and to be interesting.

Comprehensibility.   The first obligation is the more important: that is, to be comprehensible is the most important requirement for vocal delivery. It is important for you to bear in mind, therefore, the factors that determine your distinctness or understandability:

- Volume
- Articulation
- Rate
- Pronunciation

First, concerning volume, people must be able to hear you before anything else can occur. With small groups in a small room, this should be no problem. With larger groups and rooms, you may need some kind of equipment to amplify your voice. You may also ask someone in the group to give you a signal whenever your voice begins to drop off so that you can be sure of maintaining the proper volume.

It is possible to speak too loudly for a given setting and, thereby, to wear down your audience. In the rehearsal time before your actual presentation, you could work with some friends or associates to help you adjust your volume to the conditions.

Second, once you are sure that everyone can hear you, you need to remember that speaking before a group requires clear and distinct articulation. Articulation is the enunciation of the actual speech sounds, that is, how clearly you form the sounds of your words. Articulation is different from pronunciation, since you can very clearly articulate a mispronunciation. The problem usually is that when you are some distance from your listeners, typical in a public presentation, you need to be more careful about your articulation than in normal, everyday conversation. Another consideration is familiarity. People who know you well and work with you become accustomed to your manner of speaking. When you speak before others, perhaps strangers, you must be more careful in your articulation. Try writing a note to yourself as a reminder to work harder than normal on articulating your speech sounds.

Third, your rate of speech can affect how people understand what you are saying. Obviously, if you rush through your presentation, people will not concentrate enough to catch everything you say. On the other hand, some people have difficulty concentrating when a speaker goes too slowly, thereby allowing the listeners' thoughts to drift. Most inexperienced speakers, if they are feeling any stage fright at all, will tend to rush. Again, make a note to yourself to slow down, especially at the start of the presentation.

Fourth, pronunciation can affect audience comprehension; people make judgments about your competence or credibility when they hear obvious mispronunciations in your delivery. Check with others or with a dictionary to ensure that your pronunciations are standard.

To meet your first obligation—to be understood—you need to give attention to the factors of volume, rate, articulation, and pronunciation.

Maintaining Audience Interest. The second obligation you have as a speaker is to be interesting, because that helps you to hold the audience's attention. Interest is communicated by voice mainly through vocal variety or flexibility. When we are in an animated conversation, we automatically vary our volume, rate, and pitch to emphasize what we are saying. You should strive for the conversational sound referred to earlier as a characteristic of effective delivery.

Vocal variety is natural to most people when they are speaking to a group of friends in a relaxed atmosphere about something that interests them and about which they are fairly knowledgeable. Establishing good rapport with your audience during the presentation is crucial to maintaining this type of conversational sound. Look at people and talk to individuals directly in order to develop this kind of interchange with them so that you can naturally fall into a conversational pattern of delivery.

Second, being well acquainted with your subject and being interested in what you have to say contributes to the dynamism or enthusiasm you will convey in your voice. Effective delivery relies upon previous effective preparation. In fact, achieving good vocal interest depends more on your preparation, audience rapport, and enthusiasm for your subject than on specific techniques.

Physical Action. The presentation is not only heard but is also seen by most of your audience. The manner in which you present yourself and your material can affect how they receive your material. As with vocal delivery, your attitude and approach to the speaking situation is more important than memorizing specific techniques. The principles for effective visual presentation include the following:

- Present a professional appearance.
- Establish and maintain rapport with your audience.
- Be aware of feedback from individuals in your audience.
- Maintain appropriate eye contact with your audience.

First, a professional appearance, or image, is important to establishing your credibility. Depending upon the setting or occupation, dress may be significant in setting the proper tone in your appearance. While clothes do not make the person, they provide an immediate basis for judgment for many people. Your audience analysis should give some thought to the audience members' expectations about speakers' attire. The key point to remember is that you wish to indicate proper respect for them and to maintain an appearance that suggests competence and professionalism as well as poise. This does not always mean formal or office attire, but clothing that indicates your awareness of your audience's norms and expectations.

Second, establishing and maintaining good rapport with audience members is critical to success. People like to feel that you are talking to them individually.

▶ *People judge how well you have "dressed for success."*

Diversity in the Workplace

Gestures May Not Travel Well

Americans usually respond well to speakers who use natural, conversational gestures as they speak. Using such gestures communicates your enthusiasm and can help you work off nervous tension as well as reinforce your points. Remember, though, that nonverbal symbols vary from culture to culture as much as languages. Emblems, gestures that have specific meaning (recall the classification in Chapter 6), can be a particular problem in making cross-cultural presentations.

The "thumbs-up" sign, used by Americans to mean "everything's fine," or "well-done," has vulgar or obscene meanings in countries such as Iran and in parts of Africa. Pointing at people or the audience is considered rude in many places in southern Europe and Africa. In some countries, like Bulgaria, shaking the head and nodding mean "yes" and "no," respectively, exactly the opposite of the meanings in the United States.

Of course, it isn't possible to memorize all the potential differences in meanings of gestures from culture to culture. Still, it is possible to speak with people familiar with the gesture language of your prospective audience. They can at least recommend some things to avoid. If you are an especially vigorous gesturer when giving presentations, you may wish to practice toning down a little before attempting a cross-cultural performance.

For an early systematic discussion of the culture-bound nature of emblems, see P. Ekman (1976). Movements with precise meanings. *Journal of Communication* 26, 14–26.

They usually do not appreciate being read to, especially if they feel that you should know enough about your material to just talk about it. You should therefore probably stay away from complete manuscripts of these presentations, because your tendency will be to read directly from the script, perhaps without looking up hardly at all. You can have too many notes for the presentation, as well, so that you become wrapped up with the notes, losing direct contact with your audience. Another danger is to become engrossed in overhead projections, slides, or other visual aids to the extent that you direct more of your attention to those things, rather than to your listeners.

Third, concentrate on the feedback that you are getting from the audience. Be aware of individuals and what kind of response they are giving you. This principle is to keep focused on the purpose of the presentation—communicating some information to individuals—rather than focusing too much on what kind of job you think you are doing.

Fourth, to help to achieve this necessary rapport with your audience, concentrate on maintaining as much eye contact as you can with audience members. Sometimes, inexperienced speakers fear looking directly at people in the audience, because they worry they will forget what they were going to say or they will be too self-conscious. Actually, speakers tend to be reassured by the faces of other people, especially if you can pick out someone who is responsive and friendly or seems to be listening carefully. You can concentrate on these people and, fairly soon, you are engrossed in your subject rather than giving a speech.

Using Visual Aids.   Be sure to integrate your visual materials as you make your presentation. Review the principles for presenting visual aids from the Chapter 10. Maximize visibility for all the people in the audience. This means that all charts, drawings, and the like must be large enough to be seen by everyone in the room; 3 feet by 3 feet is a good size. Keep charts as simple as possible for instant clarity. Use solid lines and contrasting colors for easy visibility. Present only one major idea or table per each visual aid. Don't scrimp on the chart paper or transparencies by crowding too much information on each chart.

Explain the visual aid as you present it to listeners. For example, what do the scales mean? What is the source for the information? How was the material collected? In order to maintain eye contact with the audience, be sure that you are familiar with the visual aid or chart, so that you can talk about it without losing direct contact with your audience.

Also, review the considerations discussed in Chapter 10 regarding the use of projected images, film, and videotape during a presentation.

Building Confidence in Delivery

Following these principles for delivering the presentation should also help you to build your confidence. This can be an important topic regarding the delivery of presentations. There is no doubt that many people avoid giving oral presentations mainly because of a fear of speaking in public.

Any instruction in giving speeches or presentations can help to reduce this apprehension, so by reading this book or taking this course, you are already beginning to build your confidence. But there are some other techniques for making you more confident about these situations, as well.

• *Good preparation.* First, there is probably no substitute for preparation in reducing any anxiety that you may feel about your performance. When you have laid out and followed a systematic approach to preparing for your presentation, your confidence level naturally goes up. One of the reasons that we stress such a methodical approach to audience analysis, organization, and preparation for delivery is because having a system enhances most speakers' feeling of confidence.

● *Audience contact.* Second, involving and maintaining contact with the audience, emphasized so much in the previous section, allows speakers to forget their own self-consciousness and to give attention instead to the subject and the problems of communicating. It may be helpful to find ways to get the audiences actively involved in the presentation by having them respond to questions, suggest alternatives, or otherwise participate. Such audience participation helps to establish the feeling of audience contact that reduces anxiety.

● *Visual materials.* Third, the use of visual material along with verbal material can help to redirect your attention away from over-concern about yourself and the state of your nerves. One reason that we advocate the use of visual materials is precisely this extra benefit; not only do people remember better things they have seen as well as heard, but it is likely to reduce the speaker's fears as well.

● *Speaker's activity.* Fourth, movement during the presentation has the effect of working off some of the excess nervous energy that you may be experiencing. The key idea here is to work, physically, at what you are doing. Some nervousness results from your own awareness of the excess energy created because of the anticipation of speaking in public. If you do not provide for working off this energy, you could get caught in a vicious circle of experiencing the energy as tension, which makes you more nervous, leading to the experience of more tension, and so on.

● *Realistic expectations.* Fifth, it is important to have realistic expectations about the situation. Sometimes we put too much pressure on ourselves and blow out of proportion the importance that others may be attaching to our performance. Building confidence and overcoming stage fright requires giving attention to the main purpose of the presentation: communicating some information. The tension that we experience as stage fright can be reduced by concentrating on the audience, the message, and visual aids. Work at communicating so that you can work off some of the excess energy that builds up whenever you feel you may be on the spot.

▶ ### Rehearsal and Preparation of Notes

There should be a close relationship between the next stage of preparation—practicing for the actual delivery of the presentation—and the preparation of speaker's notes. When rehearsing the presentation, you will probably find places where you need to use notes and where you need specific kinds of information readily available.

Use of Speaker's Notes.   Some consultants recommend preparing only drawings in place of written notes to remind the speaker of points to be covered. These drawings supposedly lead speakers away from overreliance on exact or memorized wordings of ideas and thereby make them more flexible and spontaneous in the presentation. The drawings can then be adapted for use as visual aids for making the presentation.

It isn't necessary to recommend any one system of this sort for notes to be used in a presentation. People vary too much in their style of thinking and speaking. Most inexperienced presenters prepare far more notes than they actually need. As a result, these speakers become too dependent on notes and very concerned with keeping them in proper order and reading from them during the presentation. The important principle to remember is that you want to talk to people about your subject and show them that you really understand the topic and are not dependent on reading from notes.

If your preparation has been thorough to this point, you should have enough familiarity with the topic to allow you to prepare for delivery without too much difficulty. There are some important guidelines to bear in mind regarding your speaking notes.

- *Clarity*. Your speaking notes must be simple and easy to read. Your notes should have immediate meaning to you. During your rehearsal, check that all your notes meet this simple test. Typing or printing of the notes should be highly visible and easily readable. Remember that you may be under stress or operating under less than ideal lighting conditions when giving the actual presentation. Be sure the notes are legible (that is, writing is large enough and dark enough for clarity).

- *Ease of use*. You must be able to handle and manipulate the notes easily and accurately during the presentation. One of the main reasons that speech coaches recommend the use of stiff note cards is that they are handled much more easily than full sheets of paper. You are also more likely to keep your notes brief if you restrict yourself to what will fit on a 3 × 5 or 4 × 6 file card for each idea or point.

- *Sufficiency*. The notes should provide you with a reminder of the overall organization of the presentation (for example, a card can be used for the preview and another for the summary of the main points). Notes should remind you about special points to make, such as a quotation for the attention step, as well as specific facts that you want to be sure to give accurately, such as statistics, regulations, and the like. Remember that much of this material can be placed on visual aids to enhance audience retention and take the place of notes.

Rehearsal for the Presentation.   Although the presentation will be extemporaneous and not memorized, it is extremely important to rehearse, out loud, the delivery of the presentation as often as feasible. Coworkers or team members should provide good support for these practice sessions; ask for their feedback and suggestions.

Practice in front of a videotape recorder if possible so that you can critique your own performance. An audiotape recorder works nearly as well if VCR equipment is not readily available. The rehearsal sessions in front of friends or recorders should be for polishing delivery and increasing your confidence that you are well prepared.

A useful procedure for rehearsing is to begin speaking through the presentation before first writing out notes. The act of putting the outline in final written form should allow you to stand up and talk about the subject, at least for a brief time, without any script or notes. Try doing that first: Study the outline carefully, getting in mind the pattern of the ideas to be presented. Stand up and try to talk your way through the presentation without referring to the outline as you do so. This exercise may not go too well at first. The more you try talking through the presentation, however, the easier it should become. At that point—when you feel fairly sure about the general flow of the presentation—begin to make some notes that will provide good protection for your memory during the delivery.

▶ ### Evaluation

The final step in giving presentations is to seek out audience feedback and response. Methods for obtaining feedback can range from formal techniques, such as distributing surveys or questionnaires, to informal methods of conversation or just listening for unsolicited responses. Feedback may be immediate, in terms of a sale or a vote won or lost.

Question and Answer Periods.   Many presentations are followed by a question and answer period, which gives a speaker some indication of whether or not the message got across. This period is a continuation of the presentation, albeit in a more informal, give-and-take manner. Answering questions provides the presenter with the opportunity to clarify points and to reinforce parts of the case that may have seemed less convincing to listeners.

There are some specific guidelines that can help ensure an effective and useful question and answer period:

- *Repeat the question.* Except in small groups or settings, it is a good idea to repeat the question as you heard it. This gives you an opportunity to organize an answer, and it ensures that you understand the question that is being asked.

- *Divide complex questions.* In repeating the question, break it into parts that may be more easily answered: "What you have there, Evelyn, is really a two-part question, so let me answer first the one part and then the other." You may have noticed that politicians can often avoid a sticky part of a question by answering only the last part of a complex question.

- *Rephrase unclear parts of question.* You may have to ask the questioner to rephrase or explain some particularly complex questions. This technique also gives you more time to prepare a good answer. Try to get the questioner to use specifics, such as specific names, events, and situations. If there are alternative interpretations possible, ask the questioner to indicate what alternative is meant: "Do you mean full-time enrollment or full-time equivalent enrollment?" Make sure that you understand the question before attempting an answer.

●　*Address your answer to the whole group*. In general, you should try to frame your answer so that it is of general interest to the whole group. This technique can also prevent the setting up of a continuing dialogue between you and the questioner, leaving the rest of the audience out of the conversation.

●　*Postpone questions that are of individual or very special concern*. Some questions interest only one person present, the questioner, or may require an answer that should be presented only to that particular person: "Why was my bill $59.00 last month?" Suggest that the individual see you immediately after the formal question and answer period for a personal response.

●　*Say "I don't know" when that is the case*. It is usually not a good idea to try to bluff your way through answers when you are not sure. When you have to say that you do not have an answer, give a good reason why you don't and indicate how the questioner can obtain a satisfactory answer to that question. For example, you may point out that in your part of the operations you don't deal with the relevant subject area: "Well, Mr. Jones, I am in the marketing area, so I don't really get involved in production. I know who can answer your question, however, and I'll see that she gets in touch with you."

Formal Evaluation Techniques.　　Many firms that send out speakers, such as on a speakers' bureau, distribute questionnaires to the whole audience or to program planners after a presentation. Such formal procedures usually are effective for providing specific kinds of observable information, such as, was the speaker on time? Did he or she speak on the topic you expected? For the expected amount of time? Such instruments can also provide information on how much the group felt they learned, or how much they changed position on the topic. While these tools work well for external, more formal presentations, they are less likely to be useful for internal, or in-house, presentations; informal feedback may be more typical for in-house presentations.

SUMMARY

This chapter covered the principles of organizing and delivering your presentation. First, we emphasized that patterned (organized) material is more easily learned and more easily retained by audiences. Being well organized can be a crucial determinant of your success. We presented several useful methods for organizing presentational material. The organizational template is intended to provide a guide for organizing your material.

Second, we addressed the principles and techniques for preparing yourself for the actual vocal and physical presentation of your material. We stressed extemporaneous speaking in this section; Chapter 15 deals more specifically with preparing manuscripts. We also indicated some ways to prepare notes and to rehearse for your presentation; we recognize that overcoming stage fright can be an important consideration, as well. Finally, we suggested ways to obtain feedback from your presentation audience.

EXERCISES

1. Prepare a presentation with the following guidelines:
   Title: "Thought Piece"
   Time: 10 to 15 minutes.
   Speaker: Political figure from the Republican or Democratic party, for example a Congressman from the Midwest.
   Occasion: Newspaper editors' conference, Chicago, Illinois. Afternoon session entitled "Focus on the Issues."
   Topic: Select a significant problem or significant area of political concern.
   Special conditions: A draft version on videotape due one week before the final presentation is to be given.

2. Prepare a persuasive presentation following the guidelines given:
   Purpose: You have to persuade the audience to take one of the following actions.
   1. Volunteer to support a specific charitable organization or activity.
   2. Take specific steps to learn about a certain career.
   3. Motivate high school students to attend your university or alma mater.
   4. Motivate graduating seniors to support actively your university alumni association.

3. Team presentation:
   Each team will consist of four members to research, prepare, organize, and develop supporting materials. Roles are to be assigned by the team.
   Written materials (to be submitted at the time of presentation):
   1. Complete analysis of the audience.
   2. Complete outline for the presentation showing problem and solution.
   3. Report on the team meetings, division of labor, and work contributed by each member. This report should date each meeting and describe the activities of each team member thoroughly.

4. All research reports, including interviews, with dates, bibliography or other materials used or consulted.

Time for presentation: 10 minutes.

Evaluation: Professionalism, expertise in handling materials, oral presentation, delivery skills, and thoroughness of written materials. Evidence of problem solving, effective group organizing, and teamwork taken into consideration.

SELECTED SOURCES
FOR FURTHER READING

Adler, M. J. (1983). *How to speak, how to listen*. New York: Macmillan.

Arnold, W. E., & McClure, L. (1989). *Communication training & development*. New York: Harper & Row.

Damerest, W. A., & Bell, A. H. (1990). *Clear technical communication: A process approach* (3rd ed.). San Diego: Harcourt Brace Jovanovich.

Morrisey, G. L. (1982). *Effective business and technical presentations* (2nd ed.). Reading, MA: Addison-Wesley.

Munter, M. (1982). *Guide to managerial communication*. Englewood Cliffs, NJ: Prentice-Hall.

Reference

1. *Wall Street Journal*. (1987, December 29). p. 15.

Media and Mediated Communication Systems

●

12

CHAPTER

After studying this chapter you should be able to:

1. Understand the characteristics of various types of media used in organizations.

2. Choose among the various types of presentational media, including slides and videotape.

3. Understand the characteristics of interactive media, including the telephone and the computer-mediated systems such as E-mail.

4. Understand potential uses and effects of media.

Overview

The premise of this chapter is that the medium or channel of communication is an important and evolving element in the organizational communication process. The importance of the channel of communication has been a subject of inquiry for several decades.

The old media include face-to-face communication such as conferences and meetings, mail, internal memos, and the telegraph and telephone. Each of these media have been incorporated into the organizational communications network. The new technologies include video, the facsimile or fax machine, and, especially, the computer. Computer enhanced communication or CMCS (computer-mediated communication systems) include electronic mail (E-mail) for internal communication, and interactive video for training.

One view is that the new technology is really just an extension of the old, more familiar technologies. For example, Frederick Williams writes in *The New Communications*,"When you think of these technologies as extensions of old, you may begin to sense that the new communications technologies are not in and of themselves as radical as popular writers often make them out to be."[1]

The other view of the technology sees the new media as revolutionary. According to this, the new media will transform the way that individuals communicate and, consequently, how we live and work. James Chesebro, writing in the June

1984 issue of *Critical Studies in Mass Communication*, sets forth the belief that the electronic media, including the integration of computer technology with such media, are having a significant effect upon the culture and the way that we communicate within that culture. Chesebro points out, as we are no doubt aware, that Americans live in a "media environment," surrounded by televisions, telephones, radios, records, films, and video games. These technologies are themselves undergoing tremendous change thanks to cable television, home computers, audio disks, and video casette recording systems. Further, the media are getting smaller and more portable. The Walkman, the Watchman (TV equivalent of the portable radio), and the laptop computer are widely marketed examples of the new portability. Chesebro suggests that the result will be greater dependence on media: "All indications are that in the future more and more of our daily activities will be centered in front of display screens which integrate an increasing number of media." The effect, according to Chesebro, is ". . . that the media exert an independent and profound influence upon the nature of reality apprehended by human beings."[2]

This chapter takes the second position: that media transforms the message. Marshall McLuhan in his exploration of the world of popular culture and mass media coined or, at least popularized, the phrase that the "medium is the massage."[3] The puns on the word *massage* illustrate how McLuhan views the new world. The medium is the message or the massage (the message washes over, kneading our senses). Are we living in the age of mass or the age of mess? McLuhan's basic thesis is that the channel of communication transforms the content of the message.

Take something very personal and simple, the wristwatch. If you are older than 30, you remember watches with numbers, 1 through 12. In these analog watches, time was described in relation to 12: quarter after the hour; quarter of (to) the hour; and half-past the hour. Today, there are digital watches. Time is precise; the readout is 11:47 A.M. exactly. In addition, the digital watch is more than a watch: It is a calculator; it has alarms. The digital watch is a new medium, and our language changes to accommodate the new medium.

Additionally, the digital watch is symbolic. Ten years ago, the digital watch said, "I am up-to-date, modern, at the cutting edge!" On closer inspection, however, the mass-produced digital watch is and may look cheap. To avoid the one-in-a-crowd, mass-production look, now, our watches are more elaborate and more expensive or just different. In fact, the analog watch is making a comeback. Some have cartoon character faces (to indicate playfulness?); some have precise mechanisms (the quartz watch); and some have elaborate functions (such as those for scuba divers). Media and the messages of media change and change constantly.

The watch is a starting point and a simple example. The development of relatively inexpensive electronic media can affect directly how an organization conducts its business. Given a cellular car phone, a portable computer, and a facsimile machine (fax), for example, sales personnel are not tied to the office. The personal computer and the modem mean that the office as a physical entity could become a thing of the past. Of course, there may be other reasons for keeping an office and an office schedule. For example, creativity and sociability are enhanced by face-to-face interaction in the work place. However that may be, time and space are no longer barriers to an office detached from the headquarters. Modem, fax, and computer could allow you to stay at home and still be a productive member of the team. If the vice president gets an idea at 3 A.M., for example, she could communicate that immediately.

Although we speculate about the future of media, most of our emphasis is on using media in presentations and in the organization today. Specifically, this chapter encompasses the following topics:

- Characteristics of communication media
- Types of media: Presentational and interactive
- The future of media in business and professional communication

CHARACTERISTICS OF COMMUNICATION MEDIA

Different media exhibit dissimilar characteristics. In other words, in selecting media, one must remember that they are not all interchangeable in terms of the effects that they may have on the communication process. Some important variables to consider when analyzing media follow.

1. *Relation to audience*. Each medium has a specific and distinct relationship to the receiver(s) or audience(s). As the medium is changed, so is the relationship with the audience. For example, the audience can be actively or passively involved in the communication. Television presupposes a passive audience (the couch potato who sits in the home and watches until the eyes glaze over). Face-to-face conversation presupposes the active audience. As you talk, I do more than listen, even if I do not respond verbally. I may nod my head, grunt, or hum. I frown or smile. In the classroom, lecture presupposes a more passive audience, discussion a more active one.

Relationship to the audience is also a question of formality. Does the medium require a formal or an informal relationship among the participants? Cues indicating whether the relationship is formal or informal include frequency of interaction, ease of access and use, and environmental stimuli. A public presentation would be considered relatively formal if the speaker and the audience wore conservative business attire; if the speaker stood on a raised platform behind a podium; and if meetings were held infrequently. E-mail is more informal, especially if the network is used routinely for notes, announcements, and social and business patter.

2. *Organization*. Each medium presupposes its own processes of organization. Written communication is linear. Written English stresses the linearity by grammar and syntax: subject linked by a verb to an object: *A* is *B*; *A* equals *B*; *A* causes *B*. The traditional nineteenth century narrative or novel was designed to be read in a linear fashion from cover to cover. Each story in a newspaper is intended to be read in order. The headline and lead paragraph should contain all the important information. But a reader does not have to start with the first page. A reader can begin with the editorial or obituaries or the comics instead of the front page. Consequently, you would read a novel in one way and read a newspaper in another. Each medium presupposes a distinct and different way of organizing information.

3. *Audience control.* The active audience has more control of the situation. In face-to-face oral communication, the receiver can set the agenda by asking questions or introducing new topics. Contrast that with the reader. Although the content cannot be altered, at a minimum, the reader controls the pace or rate at which the story unfolds. A chapter can be read in subsequent nights or in one sitting. The reader can even control the organization by skipping to the finale, which is common in mysteries or suspense novels. In texts, control by the audience is enhanced by the table of contents and the index. Film unfolds its message in a different manner. The viewer sees one scene after another. The audience has little control over timing or pace. The modern video has increased the ability of the audience to control the pace somewhat. Due to the power of the computer, the VCR, compact disc (CD), and CD Rom (use of compact disc as a storage device for computer text and image) are now allowing more audience control. The user can access data in any order.

4. *Access.* Some media are cheap, physically available, easy to use, and encouraged by cultural norms. The telephone is an example of such a medium. We assume that most households and businesses can be reached by telephone. Access can be

▶ *The computer is the center of many new media networks.*

limited, however, by placing barriers between source and intended recipient. These barriers include gatekeepers, such as secretaries who screen incoming calls and answering machines that record messages. Modern systems such as voice-mail, which is basically a sophisticated phone answering machine, can act as gatekeepers. With voice-mail, decisions are made as to what choices are available to the caller. An open system allows access to anyone in the organization; a closed system restricts access. Of course, gatekeepers also increase availability by providing a destination when the intended recipient is unavailable.

As a medium, computers are becoming more accessible. Twenty years ago, the computer was a secret system. Only the computer guru knew the secret incantations and had access to the inner temple. Today, even programming languages are becoming simple enough for many people to use. Finally, availability has political implications. If the organization limits E-mail to a few upper-level managers, then E-mail is a source of status, power, and control. If the organization provides all individuals with access to E-mail, status and power may be of less importance.

5. *Setting.* Setting and medium interact to produce different effects. One example is the response of audiences before television and after television. Before television, cinema audiences tended to react as though they were at a play or a concert. When television was introduced into the home, the immediate effect was to make the living room more like a movie theater. Individuals would sit and watch television without talking. Initially, television stifled conversation. Audiences were reluctant to laugh unless the cues for a response were fairly obvious. Anyone who talked during a performance was considered rude. Certainly, there was considerable social pressure and therefore strong inhibitions against talking in a theater. With the advent of television, however, audiences changed. Since you could talk in your own living room, the inhibition against talking in the theater lessened.

6. *Senses affected.* Is one picture worth a thousand words? Each medium stresses different receiver senses or combinations of senses. Despite attempts to use a process called "sensaround" that involved vibrating chairs for the movie *Earthquake* and experimental use of odors, usually touch and smell are not part of the film experience. Cinema depends on the audience's eye and ear. Like film, television stresses the ear and eye. The need for a strong visual image to avoid the "talking head" leads to a stress on images or pictures. With strong, compelling pictures, a story will more likely be featured on the six o'clock news; without those strong images, the story is less likely to be aired. Moreover, the medium can strongly affect the verbal content. In the first of their 1960 presidential debates, John F. Kennedy reportedly made a much stronger showing than Richard Nixon for those who watched on television. For those who listened on radio, Nixon seemed to win the debate. The receptors or the senses affected by the medium can alter the nature and meaning of the communicated message.[4]

7. *Permanence.* Oral communication is transient. The spoken word is uttered and quickly gone. If the conversation is face to face, the listener can ask to have the message repeated. If the media is radio or television, complex meaning may be harder to convey or discover because of the lack of immediate feedback and the absence of a permanent record. A frequent question in the movie theater is, "What did she say?" Some media, such as books, provide a permanent record.

8. *Relationship with other media.* Both audiences and creators are influenced by their perception of the relationship between one medium and another. For the creator, evolution of the medium and professional or technical training is vital. Evolution refers to the elements of the old media that influenced the new media; spoken language preceded written language. In the earliest recorded epics of most cultures, consequently, oral elements are preserved in written form. Homer's *Iliad* and *Odyssey* preserve many elements of orality such as predictable meter and memory devices. Even today, poets and novelists who recite their works for audiences have a different concept of language than those who write but do not recite

---

Example of Motion Pictures

The development of the American motion picture illustrates how media are related to one another. American film, a legacy of other media, took its early form from three sources: (1) the Victorian novel with its expressive verbal descriptions and sentimentality, (2) the late nineteenth-century melodrama characterized by attempts to recreate natural disaster such as forest fires on stage, and (3) the American newspaper color-comic strip, especially the work of the American cartoonist Winsor McCay characterized by creative camera angle.[5] In its infancy, any new medium is treated as an extension of some older medium and reflects those influences.

As a medium such as film develops, a second generation of creators develops; they then build on the work of the pioneers. A Steven Spielberg builds on the pioneering work of an Orson Welles who builds on the work of a John Ford. Additionally, the filmmaker looks to other media for new ideas of how to present material. In his 1941 work *Citizen Kane*, Welles pays homage to the work of the comic artist. *Citizen Kane* influences Alain Resnais's *L'Anee Derniere a Marienbad* and *Muriel* and Jean-Luc Godard or Francois Truffaut.[6] Of course, the more immediate plot and character examples of *Superman*, *Dick Tracy*, and *Batman* illustrate the influence of comics on cinema. Each medium influences the other.

their works. The American poet Walt Whitman exemplifies the latter trend; reportedly, Whitman lopped off lines of his poetry in *Leaves of Grass* so that the published poem would "look better" on the page. Lewis Carroll's poem, "The Mouse's Tail," or e.e. cummings's work illustrates how visual elements are a part of the poet's technique.

9. *Time and space.* Until relatively recently, communication was severely limited by time and space. The modern communication revolution began with the telegraph. Before then, human communication was limited by the loudness of a voice, the line of sight, and the speed with which a messenger could travel. With the invention of the electronic telegraph, time and space become less important barriers. Communication could travel faster than a human. President Abraham Lincoln could sit in the White House and receive the news of victory and defeat for the Union Armies hundreds of miles away almost instantaneously, unless the wires were down.

The telephone allowed more nearly instantaneous feedback and added a non-verbal element to the message because pitch, rate, and vocal variation are communicated as part of the telephone message. With the invention of wireless or radio, limitations of pole and wire became less important.

10. *Degree of audience acceptance.* As communication technology advances, people will differ in their level of comfort with the new media.[7] Some individuals become proponents of the new media, whereas others resist. Within any modern organization, there are individuals who advocate a particular technology or variation. Given different computer operating systems, for example, the potential for political battles is great: IBM versus Apple, or Macintosh Excel versus Lotus 123. Some argue for efficiency through standardization, since efficiency is increased when everyone is trained to use the same equipment. Others respond for selection of hardware and software based on need and function. In 5 years or less, standardization may allow quick movement between systems and programs; for now, however, the question posed by compatibility remains open.

If individual computer choices are allowed within the organization, for example, some individuals will pick one brand or operating system and others will pick another. Among the individuals who use a particular system, some will learn how to do the minimum and continue to do that; others will test and develop their skills further. Consequently, individuals will differ in their ability to use a medium efficiently and effectively.

Highlights of Characteristics of Communication Media

Media are important in the modern organization. The variety of media that can be utilized has increased rapidly in the last three decades. With more choices of media comes the problem of decision. Which medium should be used for the best effect? To make an informed choice, communicators need to understand the nature

Diversity in the Workplace

Telecommuting

Computers linked with modems and video screens could mean the
end of the dichotomy between home and office, at least for some
people. Consider, for example, a media-relations manager for
AT&T Bell Laboratories in Short Hills, New Jersey. After
breakfast, she gets ready for work, goes downstairs and steps
directly into her office without leaving her home near Burlington,
Vermont. The development of low-cost but powerful personal
computers together with voice-mail and fax machines allows this
manager to telecommute from home to office.

Still, today this situation is relatively rare, because many
managers like to have their people readily available for face-to-face
consultation and supervision. Other companies that have tried
telecommuting for some employees report an increase in
productivity, however. This gain probably results from people using
the time normally spent commuting actually on the job in home
offices. In addition, the telecommuters may be less physically and
emotionally drained from fighting traffic. Also, people working at
home on their personal computers are less likely to be clock-
watchers and are more likely to devote more time and attention to
particular projects.

There are predictions that the move toward telecommuting will
grow in the decade of the 1990s. One example obvious to the
authors is the use of telecommuting in the book publishing industry.
In producing this book, authors and editors worked in different
cities, linked by telephone, fax, and personal computers with each
other and with the publishing company's headquarters in yet a
different city. As a result, work is no longer time-bound (9 to 5) or
space-bound.

See M. Alexander (1990). Travel-free commuting. *Nation's business*,
78, 33–37.

of media because each has its own unique characteristics. The important ones
discussed in this section include: relationship with the audience; organization; audience control; access; setting; senses affected; permanence; relationship with other
media; time and space; and degree of audience acceptance.

TYPES OF MEDIA: PRESENTATIONAL AND INTERACTIVE

This discussion treats media in the organizational setting according to two types: presentational media (or media that emphasizes one-way communication, such as any projected image), and media that emphasizes interaction. The functions of presentational media are mainly to provide visual support for business and professional presentations. The first section, therefore, considers the uses of media for this purpose. The second section looks at the ramifications of new technologies, such as computer mediated communication systems (CMCS) for communication uses.

Presentational Media

Presentational media in organizational settings includes projected images, as well as broadcast media, cable, and video. Characteristically, these projected two-dimensional images have been used as visual aids. Even if these media constitute the entire message, feedback is delayed and/or limited. Presentational projected images include overheads, slides, and video. We discuss the first two under the category of still images, and then cover the more complicated medium, video, at greater length.

Overhead Projectors. Use of projectors with acetate rollers allows the speaker to draw, diagram, or summarize key words or concepts as the talk proceeds. In

▶ *The overhead projector has many advantages for visual presentations.*

essence, this machine replaces the blackboard in that the speaker draws or prints and the material is magnified by the projector. The process is relatively quick and easy. The overhead works best when large bodies of material are to be presented in one sitting, and there is inadequate time or money for a more sophisticated type of presentation.

In some ways, the overhead has advantages over the slide projector or other media. Certainly, modern reproduction services can provide excellent quality; moreover, the presenter can write on the transparency to make changes as necessary. For example, the speaker can circle an important point or change a number or label. Further, the speaker can place one transparency over another to create a multilayered visual.

The use of an overhead projector with prepared transparencies guarantees neater appearance and a more polished presentation. The prepared transparency can be a chart, diagram, or picture that is a simple line drawing or other black and white representation. The use of the projected image allows for the possibility of varying the distance from the projector to the screen. This varies the size of the image, allowing for its use with different numbers of people.

Even if the overhead transparency is drawn on the spot, the overhead has one chief advantage over the blackboard or flipchart. When using the overhead projector, the speaker is able to face the audience. In this way, the speaker can maintain eye contact and observe the audience feedback while talking about the visual aid.

Slide Projectors.   Slides are the most complex of the projected still images. Consequently, use of slides requires more planning than overhead or opaque projections do. The complexity of slides, on the other hand, allows more control over

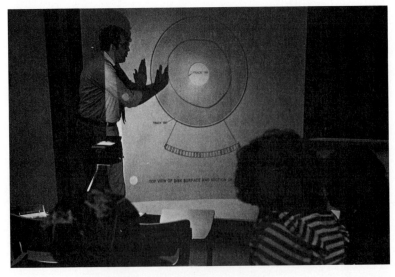

▶ *Slides can add professionalism to the presentation.*

the message that the audience receives. Through photo reproduction, slides (like the overhead transparency) can be reduplicated and used in different locations simultaneously. The increased sophistication that comes from the "reality" of a photograph can heighten the evocative power of the message. A reasonably talented amateur with a relatively inexpensive 35 mm. camera can produce clear, and even brilliant, images.

On the other hand, slides are rather inflexible. All the materials have to be planned weeks in advance: A script has to be prepared, pictures have to be shot and processed, and time must be allowed for redoing vital shots if necessary. Finally, the slide presentation minimizes audience feedback, audience involvement, and the speaker's adaptation to the audience. Once the program has been produced, last-minute adjustments are costly and unlikely.

Projected Moving Images: Film and Video. In the last 20 years, video has become an important medium of communication. For the purposes of this chapter, we are not making a distinction between the use of videotape and the use of internal television, or direct feeds. Instead, we are concerned with the communication effects of the televised image, whether presented by tape or from a direct feed.

Prior to 1970, a good case could be made for the use of film over the use of video. Before then, film had many advantages over video, including its sense of permanence. Any performance that was worth preserving was preserved on film; in addition, film was more effective on the large screen. Most videotape monitors served relatively few people who had to be near the screen to view the video. Even multiple monitors did not solve this problem completely. For audiences of more than 50 individuals or for conveying the same message to many audiences, film was the medium of choice.

Since 1970, however, video has become the medium of choice and could continue to be so into the immediate future. Although some viewers claim to see a difference in quality between film and video, technical advances, including high-definition video, have narrowed the gap between film and video. The cost and ease of in-house production make video increasingly attractive. Furthermore, video may benefit from the rapid development and availability of the personal computer. Video may be edited and integrated with text, picture, and sound in a sophisticated multimedia presentation. Of course, as the power of personal computers increases, video on laser disc may become an increasingly available technology.

Videotaping has some other unique advantages over film. The cost of a video recorder, camera, and monitor plus appropriate editing facilities is relatively low. Further, even a novice can operate a videotape system after a few minutes' instruction. As an instructional device, finally, the video presentation is extremely flexible because portions of a message or a presentation can be played, rewound in a few seconds, and played again.

By 1980, corporations were spending more than a billion dollars on in-house video. Specifically, they were using video for a variety of purposes, including training, orientation, new product demonstration, and communication of information (video newsletter) on health, safety, and benefits.[8] Video is used by organizations, then, for three broad purposes: training; employee communications; and public information or public relations.[9]

In regard to training, several points stand out. As an organization grows, has increasing need for retraining to stay competitive, and has greater audience expectation for sophisticated media presentations, video becomes more important. As a training medium, video is useful when movement is necessary to fully understand the situation. Human relations problems may best be understood through a dramatic story or role-playing situation. A process or method of operation may be understood through a narrative that combines verbal material, visual material, and sound cues.

Advantages of video media.   Whether the use is training or employee or public communication, video is an inexpensive and relatively permanent medium. Video allows the use of the exact same presentation before many different audiences, at many different times, and at many different locations. If we know of an expert or a great teacher, a skilled salesperson or a brilliant craftsman, we may want to preserve that person's efforts on film.

Video is one of the most versatile and pervasive multimedia aids. The pervasiveness of television in our society has transformed the habits of viewing into cultural norms. Audiences respond automatically to TV stimuli. Of course, the familiarity of your audience with video can be a problem. Years of exposure to, say, MTV and movies have created sophisticated and literate consumers of mass media. Consequently, you need to know what must be in a video in order to achieve your purpose. Video consists of images juxtaposed with other images (montage), sound effects, music, and dialogue or narrative. All of these elements interact to produce the desired effect. Even if you are not producing the video yourself, you are still responsible for it; the success or failure will rebound to your credit or discredit.

In addition, if you use video a polished presentation can be guaranteed. The tape can be edited to remove errors or, if the mistakes are major, the presentation can be rerecorded. In addition, various materials can be added, including sound effects, music, and narration. Moreover, video (and film) can incorporate other visual materials. Charts, graphs, models, and other visual devices can be recorded on videotape. This is especially valuable when manipulation would prove difficult or awkward during the live presentation.

Effective preparation and use of video in multimedia presentations.   In both film and video, the emphasis is on the visual and the dramatic. Although video and film both stress the visual, video is more informal, and its verbal style is more conversational.

The picture or scene has to move; there should be physical movement and dramatic action. Unlike in film, however, the narration in video should be conversational. Unless you are presenting dramatic action or dialogue, the verbal material should be very relaxed and less emotional than film, public, or any live presentation. Therefore, attempts to record speakers as they make presentations are never as effective as the original live performance.

Like all media, video has its own grammar and syntax, or principles for effective use. If you produce a video, try to get help from skilled technicians who can make a polished tape. On the other hand, you as producer should consider what you are doing and why. What is your purpose? How will the tape be used? Who will use it? Who is the intended audience? Of course, being aware of these principles should help you even if you are not doing the production yourself in that they will make you a more knowledgeable collaborator with the technical people.

The following general principles are a good guide to effective video presentations:

1. *Keep your purpose constantly in mind.* Usually, business and professional presentations must convey information precisely and accurately. Maintain your audience's sense of perspective. At all times, they should know what they are hearing, what they are seeing, and what that information means.

2. *Visual orientation.* Your audience must know what they are seeing. Provide them with as much information about objects as possible, including size, color, shape, uses, and construction.

Consider field of vision/camera angle. Show the object as a viewer of average height would see it. Have the camera at eye level or between 5 and 6 feet off the ground. If you are showing a large object, pan around it slowly at eye level. If you are watching someone perform a task, shoot over the person's shoulder. If you are showing a small object, turn it around slowly while keeping the camera in one spot.

Be careful of proportion and size. Inclusion of an object of known shape and size in the picture will alert the audience so that they can recognize or better understand. For general comparisons, use an average human or some part of the human anatomy such as a hand. For more precise comparisons, a scale ruler or a specially enlarged scale might be appropriate.

Finally, consider emphasis and exaggeration. Additional color, labels, arrows, and masks can emphasize what is important. Just as actors use make-up, so you might want to make up the objects that are being filmed. A supply of chalk dust or acrylic paint may be all that is needed to highlight an object.

3. *Verbal orientation.* As with any presentation, make sure that you tell them what you're going to say, tell them, and then tell them what you've said. The verbal description should precede the visual. For example, "Next you will see our projected retail outlets in Arizona as of June 1, 1999. These are represented by a blue star. Our present locations are indicated by a white dot." At this point, the audience will be looking at the map of Arizona. They should be seeing a carefully labeled diagram that includes a map key which repeats the same important information: "White dots = Present outlets. Blue stars = outlets as of June 1, 1999."

4. *Sound orientation.* Sound effects add realism to the situation and, in some cases, may be essential. Certain terminal cues are associated with certain correct actions, such as applause at the end of a brilliant speech or the click of a metal part sliding into place in a machine.

5. *Test your video presentation.* Even if your video is professionally made, you may want to increase your chance of success and minimize potential problems by careful tryouts with audiences that are similar to the target audience. The more you know about the audience, the easier it is to create a test audience. Try to match essential characteristics of the real or target audience with characteristics in the test audience. Present the film as many times as possible, keeping in mind the limitations of time and money.

6. *Present the video.* Be sure to tell the audience what's in the video so that they know why they are seeing and hearing the information. The presentation itself should include the following points:

- Reveal the overall point or theme of the video.
- Tell the audience what specific points are important.
- Tell them what they should do with the new information that they are about to receive.
- At the end of the video, be sure to summarize and conclude.

Computer Projection.   Recently, computers have been used alone or combined with overhead projectors and with videotape to produce more polished and sophis-

▶ *The computer permits orchestration of visual materials.*

ticated presentations. In some cases, the computer is used as a blackboard or flip chart would have been used in the past. For example, the computer is hooked to an overhead projector. The presenter types on the computer keyboard, and the material is projected onto a large screen. In this way, changes can be made instantaneously and presented clearly and concisely to a large audience.

Computer projection has replaced the slide show in many cases. The images, charts, or illustrations are scanned into the computer, enhanced and edited with various software programs and combined into a computer slide show. With the use of other computer software programs called presentation software, elaborate color graphics including titles, photographs and drawings, charts, and graphs can be created and displayed.

Finally, computers can be used in combination with video presentations, which can be very useful for demonstrating a process or training. Either the video can be displayed on a separate screen, or the video is displayed on the computer monitor. Even split-screen effects can be used. One portion of the screen can be used for the video display with other visual material, such as charts and graphs.

Highlights of Presentational Media.   Presently, the most common corporate medium is video. Contemporary audiences are prepared for this sophisticated type of communication; moreover, the inexpensive yet permanent nature of video makes it an attractive medium. Conversely, video is source-centered, which means that feedback is delayed and audience adaptation is relatively difficult.

The previous section discussed traditional media including overhead projectors, slide projectors, and video. The basic assumption is that these traditional media will be used as visual and aural (in the case of video) aids. The media production checklist at the end of the chapter takes you through important questions about media presentations. Now let's turn to interactive media.

Interactive Media

Interactive media attempt to overcome the problems of delayed feedback by allowing immediate interaction. For example, memos take a few days to be delivered, read, and responded to. Within the modern organization there is a growing demand for a freer exchange of information between executives and subordinates. Moreover, executives recognize that subordinates want more face-to-face, interactive communication.[10]

The common types of interactive systems are the telephone, computer-mediated communication, and teleconferencing. Computer-mediated communication systems (CMCS) include E-mail, computer conferencing, computer bulletin boards, and voice-mail, or messaging.

Telephone.   In the United States, the telephone is the most common interactive technology. The advantages are interaction over distances, immediate feedback, and the availability of both verbal and nonverbal communication. We hear the tone of voice as well as the message. The disadvantages are (1) lack of physical nonverbal feedback such as eye contact or gestures, (2) difficulty of creating a permanent record, and (3) the fact that written materials such as contracts must

▶ *Interactive media allow people to keep in touch regardless of time or distance.*

be conveyed by other means. Although conference calls are possible, group inter-action is even more frustrating. Furthermore, mobile or cellular phones are not private; the signals can be intercepted by anyone who has the proper equipment. As a result of its disadvantages, the telephone is supplemented by or attached to a variety of other media, including answering machines and voice-mail.

Computer-Meditated Communication Systems. The most modern of the inter-active systems are enhanced through computer software. Although impersonal, computers provide users with access to unparalleled amounts of information. Using a modem, the computer can receive information from a variety of on-line infor-mation services, including information of general interest, court cases, business information, popular periodicals, and scholarly journals. In addition, those with access to the network can exchange, edit, produce, and store new messages. Two or more people at distant locations could simultaneously work on the same doc-ument. Unlike the telephone, computer-mediated communication systems (CMCS) do not require that the two people follow the same schedule in order to commu-nicate, as the system will store messages until one or the other participant is ready to deal with them.

    The use of CMCS is proliferating at a dizzying rate. Once considered to be

Interactive Media and Film, or Is Anything New?

Interactive media or, at least, audience participation in film is not a new idea. Woody Allen's film, *Yellow Rose of Cairo*, is based on the premise that characters on film can step out of the screen and interact with their audience. *Rocky Horror Picture Show*, with its audience mimicking, responding to, and punning the action on the screen, is a recent example where the audience participates but the film characters do not respond.

An early example of interactive media involved Winsor McCay, the famous New York cartoonist who also pioneered the animated cartoon. His 1914 film *Gertie the Dinosaur* combined the animated dinosaur with McCay's own appearance on the vaudeville stage. As Gertie walked across the screen to center stage, the live McCay "commanded" the animated dinosaur to perform tricks, catch objects tossed to her, and even to tip McCay's hat.

mainly for hackers and computer programmers, it is now considered routine for many professionals and organizations. While experts are not yet certain what the long-run effects of this new type of mediated communication will be, certain characteristics are especially important. For example, computers stress content (data or information) rather than relationship, context, or process. For example, nonverbal cues are eliminated and role differentiation or the importance of a leader is diminished.[11] This point is developed further as we consider some of the most important kinds of CMCS used in organizations today.

E-Mail.   E-mail (electronic mail) is a computer-mediated or enhanced system of communication involving the sending of written messages from one workstation to one or more others. As the name implies, E-mail is analogous to the traditional internal memo which, in turn, is based on the analogy of nationwide mail service. E-mail is more than an electronic memo system. It gives the sender access to many individuals with one written message nearly instantaneously. Written information is distributed rapidly and efficiently. The network may be internal, within an existing organization, or national or international in scope. Such networks as Ethernet, CompuServe, and BitNet are examples of widely available E-mail networks that allow people located at widely separated locations to work together on projects.

E-mail has important advantages and disadvantages. To convey numbers and short messages, E-mail is efficient and effective. For longer private messages or

Problem-Solution

Memo: Writing an effective E-Mail Message
From: The authors of the text
To: All readers
Re: The effective use of E-Mail

Of course, an effective E-mail message reflects the principles of effective communication. Always keep the characteristics of E-mail in mind: It is quick, fast, informal communication.

   1. Analyze the audience and the organizational culture. What will be the effect of your message? What types of messages are acceptable? Birthday greetings and jokes? Only business? What language is appropriate? Slang? Jargon? Profanity?
   2. The message should be clear. Be sure the reader knows what is expected. The heading (see, for example, "Re" above) should, like the specific purpose statement, give the gist of the message in one line. Make it easy for the recipient to respond. Be sure to put your E-mail address on everything.
   3. The message should be short. E-mail is meant to save time. If the size of the screen is limited (9-inch, for example), the length of the message should fit within the screen.
   4. For longer messages, use attachments or enclosures, but sparingly. Attachments or enclosures are longer documents that are linked to the E-mail messages. The enclosures should be introduced and labeled clearly, including your E-mail address.
   5. All information should be as accurate as possible. In addition, spelling and grammar should be correct (especially if your company has just introduced E-mail). When E-mail becomes widespread, grammar, etc., will be less important.
   6. Carbon copies (CC) should be sent to all interested parties; but use this feature sparingly.

For a slightly different perspective, compare our suggestions with G. Kawasaki. E-Mail etiquette. (1991, November). *MacUser*. pp. 29–30.

---

complex messages, face-to-face communication is preferred.[12] Interestingly, E-mail's influence on interpersonal communication is both positive and negative. A skilled and sensitive communicator will use E-mail effectively; an unskilled communicator will not. When the interpersonal climate is poor, moreover, E-mail can be used for interpersonal withdrawal; when the climate is positive, E-mail can enhance the interpersonal communication.[13] Finally, the potential of E-mail remains. Users will be limited by the mail analogy for a time. Although E-mail can make printed memos redundant, many executives mistrust electronic storage and so continue to rely on the paper trail. Eventually, trial and error will allow users to discover how to use (and abuse) E-mail.

More importantly, E-mail has the potential to change how the executive communicates within the organization and, consequently, how the organization is structured. E-mail, with other channels of media, may have the potential for flattening the organization, for example. E-mail can convey the thoughts, ideas, and general or specific orders of the CEO instantaneously. The temptation for the chief executive to control the entire organization might be too great to resist.

Voice-Mail.   Voice-mail is a variation on E-mail, which stresses spoken rather than written communication. Analogous to the answering machine, voice-mail offers a variety of simple choices. An attempt to phone Ms. Rodriguiz, for example might produced the following conversation:

Voice-mail system: "Ms. Rodriguiz is away from her desk right now. Please press 1 on your telephone if you would like to leave a message. Please press 2 on your telephone if you would not."
[*You press 1.*]
Voice-mail system: "At the sound of the tone, please leave your name, phone number and message." [Date and time are recorded automatically.]
[*You record your message.*]
Voice-mail system: "If you wish to rerecord your message, please push 1. If your message is satisfactory, please push 2."
[*You push 2.]*
Voice-mail system: "If you wish to communicate with another member of this network, please push 1. If you wish to leave the network, please push 2."
[*You push 2 and the voice-mail system hangs up.]*

In this example of voice-mail, we used just two alternatives, 1 or 2. Some systems have as many as 10 options. Further, voice-mail can be tied to phones outside the building, for example, from home. Even the simplest answering machine has minimal elements of interaction. Voice-mail adds more elements, which allow simple choices to be made, including the opportunity to clarify or rerecord the message.

Computer Conferencing.   The use of E-mail and interactive networks allow for the establishment of work groups linked by the network rather than by face-to-face contact. Each person is linked directly to the others in the group through his or her computer terminal and modem. The advantages of such arrangements are that people can be brought together without the expense and time of travel to and from distant places. Presumably, therefore, more wide-ranging expertise can be brought to bear upon problems or tasks before the group.

The results of using computer conferencing indicate that there are disadvantages as well as advantages. The decision to use computer conferencing, therefore, should not be an automatic one, but one that considers the goal and realities of a given situation. A set of studies comparing face-to-face groups and computer-linked groups in performing tasks found that the computer groups generally took longer to arrive at a decision than the face-to-face groups, displayed more equally distributed participation, were less inhibited (more expletives, for example), and showed more "choice shift."[14] The term *choice shift* refers to the tendency for people in a group to change initial positions and to take more extreme positions than they might otherwise because of the stimulation of the group interaction.

Concerning the question of efficiency, other studies have suggested that as people become more experienced with computer conferencing, the time to complete task decreases (the first study did not look at people regularly involved in such computer-linked groups).[15] It also appears that computer conferences are not particularly efficient at managing or resolving conflict; perhaps the lack of nonverbal cues makes the handling of conflict more difficult. Another consideration in this regard derives from the finding that people are less inhibited using their keyboards than they are in face-to-face interactions. In fact, the term *flaming* has been coined by network users to denote the tendency toward stronger expressions on the network than one would use in person. This tendency could be related to the greater sense of impersonality or to frustration that others' responses could not be monitored directly: that is, the feeling that you may not really be getting through when you can't see the other person.[16] The sense of depersonalization and frustration may also account for the tendency of computer groups to take more extreme decisions: Each person feels less personal responsibility because of a sense of anonymity sitting at a keyboard. These factors need to be carefully weighed, therefore, in considering whether a task should be handled face to face or through computer communication.

Teleconferencing. In its most sophisticated form, the teleconference uses media in innovative ways to create an interactive environment. Specifically, Group A is located in Boston while, let's say, Group B is in Springfield. At either site is a media-equipped room that contains video for visual and aural communication, a fax machine for transferring documents, a computer, and a printer. For flexibility, a separate video screen could be used for displaying graphs, charts, etc. Note that this setup would require cable, satellite, or similar direct-feed capability for the video portion of the system. Some large organizations do have in-house television networks, which are sometimes referred to as corporate video. But it is possible, and often more economical, to rent facilities or transmission services from agencies that provide this service.

The advantages of such a system are significant. The use of all of the elements together allows the organization to overcome the disadvantages of each. Both verbal and nonverbal messages are transmitted. Feedback is instantaneous; more complete information is conveyed; and adjustments can be made as the teleconference proceeds. Contracts and documents or other hardcopy can be modified on the spot and transferred to the other location by fax.

If several cameras are used at each location, a variety of different groups or scenes can be shown. If there is a problem with an analogue lathe on the production floor, for example, the engineers at the plant can take part in the conference and a view of the lathe on the production floor can be shown. With a split screen, the engineers in the conference room and the lathe could be shown simultaneously. If the organization is large and complex with offices scattered across the country or around the world, more sites could be added to the network. The home office in Boston can teleconference with not only the Springfield in Massachusetts but also the Springfields in Vermont and Illinois. Teleconferencing is not the end of face-to-face communication. It will not eliminate business travel, but it can reduce the need for it.

The disadvantages of teleconferencing are initial cost, willingness of organizations to use the new technology, and the need to be on site. The disadvantages mirror the advantages of some of the other systems. The full teleconference as just described requires the presence of all the participants at the same time; the coordination of schedules and some travel will be required.

Highlights of Media

In the modern organization, a variety of new interactive communication technologies are being used to enhance the communication process. As exemplified by E-mail and teleconferencing, these new technologies do not replace older media of communication. Instead, they enhance and support the older media, and essentially, each saves time by linking individuals through space.

Changing technology produces changes in the organization and resistance to those changes. Examples of changes made possible by interactive communication systems involve attempts to elicit feedback from employees.[17] Such systems include E-mail or even telephone systems. Anonymously or publicly, employees ask questions and make statements about their concerns. The answer can be directed to employees in general, to specific employees through mail, or even in face-to-face communication. The basic premise is that employees need a forum for articulating their concerns.

As suggested, on the other hand, resistance to rapidly evolving new technology is apparent in any organizational setting. Changes in communication technology cause other major changes in relationships, power, status, and even sales. Fear of the new and unknown is based on the realization that change brings about unintended by-products that could have disastrous consequences for the individual and the organization: Change is risky. This leads to our last topic of concern: the future of media and communication.

THE FUTURE OF MEDIA

Given the rapidly changing nature of communication technology, speculation about the future of communication technology and its effects on our organizations and culture is useful. Individuals who understand and can use the new technologies will be at a relative advantage. As you approach new media, you can ask general questions about who benefits or how will it affect the organization and culture as well as specific questions about how it will affect you and your status in the organization.

Philosophers, sociologists, and others have been concerned about the nature of the effects that communication technology has on us, our organizations, and our culture. Jacques Ellul, formerly of the Faculty of Laws of the University of Bordeaux, has long studied the effects of technologies on their users. At least two of his works are well known in the United States: *The Technological Society* and *Propaganda: The Formation of Men's Attitudes*. The sociologist, Robert Merton, says concerning Ellul's idea of technology: ". . . it [technology] converts spontaneous and unreflective behavior into behavior that is deliberate and rationalized."[18] People come to focus their attention on what Ellul calls *technique*, losing sight of other considerations. They embark upon a quest for improved means for obtaining carelessly examined ends. Know-how becomes an ultimate value.

Ellul has written of technology as a "spiritual force," "a complex of attitudes, values, desires, and hopes," and "a new definition of what it means to live a human life."[19] He believes that there is a tendency for technology to make slaves of those who invented it: The computer, to use one of his examples, was created by a genius, but key-punching or the manufacture of microchips is drudgery or tedium. Ellul sees within people a tendency to worship human products (such as computer technology) for its purported efficiency, rationality, and contribution to "progress."[20] Once we have created a technology, we come to think of it as some sort of force external to ourselves, as something creating or affecting us. Similarly, Lewis Mumford has claimed, ". . . the machine tended increasingly to dictate the purpose to be served, and to exclude other more intimate human needs."[21]

The computer, integrated with the electronic media of communication, can and will affect our lives. There may be some danger in William's confidence as expressed on p. 361 that these new media will be merely a way of doing something more quickly or more easily.

What are some of the potential effects of the new technologies? Three areas seem prominent: effects on language, interaction, and ways of knowing or understanding the world.

Let's consider language first. William Exton, management consultant writing in *Communications and the Future*, suggests potential linguistic changes. Rapid developments in technology, of the sort we are experiencing, leads to popular interest in its applications, bringing additions to vocabulary (for example, input, interface, or "down" for out of order). The pervasiveness of such media can make new phrases, words, or symbol cliches virtually overnight. "The means of conveying language," according to Exton, "exerts its own effects upon the forms and usage of language."[22] Computerized media not only extend or disseminate messages in a particular language; their mechanisms feedback upon that language, reshaping it, changing it. In efforts to develop computer-produced language or speech (machines that can talk, such as Hal in *2001: A Space Odyssey*), the form of language may itself be changed.

Second, the nature of interactions can be altered. Computer networking, E-mail, and teleconferencing can potentially redefine communication interactions. A part of the changing nature of interactions is the changing nature of access to those interactions and to the information necessary for interactions. The April 1983 issue of the *UN Chronicle* was concerned with the following possible abuses. The creation of computerized personal data systems can lead to invasions of personal privacy, as well as extensive surveillance possibilities. Can we know who is taking part in the interaction? The "marriage of computers and communications through the process of remote access" can lead to information monopolies.[23] The control of information can be centralized; only those with the right computer access can use that information.

A more recent book lays out more thoroughly the dangers from electronic defense apparatus and high tech surveillance dangers. Its authors feel that Americans require an education not in computer literacy, which is acquired without much effort, but an education in so-called computer citizenship. Interestingly, the authors, feel that the skills of reasoning and communication will be the most important skills in such an education.[24]

In the organizational setting, interactive technology may alter the nature or the effects of cohesion, status, power, and credibility. As noted above, E-mail or any mediated system separates the message from the source of the message. In face-to-face communication, the status and prestige of the speaker are obvious. We are subject to all the subtle nonverbal cues of credibility such as clothing, voice, height, and eye contact. In the computer-mediated situation, the message is paramount.

According to Judith A. Perrolle, computer-mediated communication acts to reduce the effects of status and power especially in existing groups. E-mail and its relative, voice-mail, may undermine the power of existing social groups because we are no longer subject to the cues to face-to-face communication. Groups may experience inability to enforce rules of behavior. Ironically, this lack of familiar social cues may heighten our willingness to trust the stranger.[25] The stranger's message is judged on content rather than on face-to-face social cues. The reasons for the alteration of relations leads to the third major implication: How do we know what we know?

Third, Chesebro, in the article referred to in the beginning of this chapter, has shown that the electronic media, especially as updated by computerized technology, can provide a social reality for many people. In the preceding discussion, E-mail eliminates the nonverbal cues of credibility such as voice and eye contact. Faced with a lack of cues, we substitute other reasons for trust, such as good evidence. Those who fare well in face-to-face communication may not fare so well in computer-mediated communication. Obviously, what we know, or think that we know, about the world determines how we communicate with other people.

In the film *My Dinner With André*, Wallace Shawn tells André that he will not give up his electric blanket in order to experience a deeper reality. Life is hard enough, he argues, so why give up those things that protect us from the harshness of the cold? If an electric blanket can alter our experience of the world, how much more can the pervasive computerized technologies of today shape our speech and thoughts?

SUMMARY

The medium of communication changes and alters the nature of the message and how the modern organization structures itself. With the variety of media now available, the organizational communicator has both problems and opportunities.

Checklist for Producing a Media Presentation

Use of media should involve careful analysis of goals, message, audience, setting, and resources.

Goal of Media Presentation

What are the goals of your presentation? Inform (general) _____
Train __   Persuade __   Create goodwill __   Sell __

What should the audience understand or do? Be specific:
1. _____
2. _____
3. _____
4. _____

Message. What type of information is appropriate?

General __   Specific to your organization __   Specific to your field or industry __

Do media already exist to provide your message?
List: _____

What are the problems with using this media?
1. _____
2. _____
3. _____

How would other or new media improve the presentation?
1. _____
2. _____
3. _____

Audience and setting. Who is the intended audience(s)?
_____

Problems include choosing the most effective communication channels to convey messages and its effect on the cohesiveness of the organization. Opportunities include the possibility of conquering time and distance. Face-to-face communication is still important but other means, such as E-mail and teleconferencing, can offer effective means of communication.

At how many locations do they exist? _____
_____

What type of equipment is available at that location? _____
_____

Frequency of use? Once ___   Once a month ___   Several times a year ___

Life of media? This month ___   1–2 years ___   Indefinite ___

Schedule for demand? Regular ___   Predictable ___   NA ___

Copies needed? One ___   Several ___

Relation to other media? Stand alone ___   Other media used ___

Control over other media? None ___   Some ___   Complete ___

Will it be used with a presentation? ___ Yes ___ No

Will several individuals use it? ___ Yes ___ No

How will they be trained? _____

Resources.
Budget? Cost estimate $_____   What can you afford? $_____

Have you developed media before? Yes ___   No ___

In-house ___   Contracted out ___

What is the level of involvement? Script _   Deciding format _   Budget _
    Renting equipment _   Production location _   Postproduction (editing) _
    Talent ___   Crew ___
    Distribution and marketing (this also serves as a checklist for steps in
    producing complex media such as video). _____

Bottom line: Given limitations, what media will best meet my goals?
_____

EXERCISES

1. As discussed early in this chapter, different media have different characteristics. Using the diagram supplied below, compare and contrast two or more media. We have attempted to stimulate your thinking by using film as a starting point.

	Media	
Characteristics	*Film*	
Relationship with audience.	Passive and infrequent. Audience pays.	
Organization.	Linear (flashbacks are confusing).	
Audience control.	Little.	
Access.	Relatively cheap but videotapes are cheaper and easier to use.	
Setting.	Audience responds but discussion is frowned upon.	
Senses affected.	Ears (dialogue, sound effects, music) and eyes.	
Permanence.	Relatively permanent but easily damaged.	
Relationship with other media.	Video influences how film is made.	
Time and space.	Go to theater; need permanent and expensive facility.	
Degree of audience acceptance.	Widely accepted.	

2. Given the rapid development of communication technology, what will the office of the future look like? Describe what the modern office will be like in 10 years if technology is used effectively. Will offices as we know them exist? Why or why not?

3. What we expect is not always what happens.
   a. What barriers do you see to the diffusion and effective utilization of new technology?
   b. Many examples of what the world would be like appear in utopian novels and articles. Find an example of a prediction of how technology would transform our world. Did it occur? To what extent did the prediction come true?

4. With what types of communication media do you feel most comfortable? Why? Least comfortable? Why?

5. Literature, including film, abounds with examples of how technology can be used to control or stifle as well as liberate the human spirit. Can you find examples of each? Did the predictions come to pass?

SELECTED SOURCES FOR FURTHER READING

Allen, T. J., & Hauptman, O. (1987). The influence of communication technologies on organizational structure: A conceptual model for future research. *Communication Research*, *14*, 575–587.

Bush, J. M., & Douglas, P. (1981). *Private television communications: Into the eighties* (pp. 51–53). Berkeley Heights, NJ: International Television Association.

Chesebro, J. W. (1984, June). The media reality: Epistemological functions of media in cultural systems. *Critical Studies in Mass Communication*, *1*:2, 112.

Chesebro, J. W., & Bonsall, D. G. (1989). *Computer-mediated communication, human relationships in a computerized world*. Tuscaloosa: University of Alabama Press.

Chester, E. (1969). *Radio, television, and American politics* (p. 120). New York: Sheed and Ward.

DeWine, S., et al. (1986, May). Techno-sense: Making sense out of the technological impact on human communication. Paper presented at the International Communication Association Convention.

Ellul, J. (1967). *The technological society* (J. Wilkinson, Trans.). New York: Alfred A. Knopf.

Exton, W., Jr. (1982). The future of language: Basic tool of communication. In H. F. Didsbury, Jr., (Ed.), *Communications and the future*, (p. 23). Bethesda, MD: World Future Society.

Fell, J. (1974). *Film and the narrative tradition*. Berkeley: University of California Press.

Gayeski, D. M. (1983). *Corporate and instructional video, design and production.* Englewood Cliffs, NJ: Prentice-Hall.

Johnson, N. (1988). The semantics of computer communications. *Etc.*, *45*, 250–255.

Kiesler, S., Siegel, J., & McGuire, T. W. (1984). Social psychological aspects of computer-mediated communication. *American Psychologist, 39*, 1123–1134.

McCathrin, E. Z. (1989, July). Beyond employee publications making the personal connection. *Public Relations Journal.*

Mumford, L. (1967). *The myth of the machine: Technics and human development.* New York: Harcourt, Brace & World.

Perry, G., & Aldridge, A. (1967). *The Penguin book of comics.* Baltimore, MD: Penguin Books.

Rice, R. E. (1987, Autumn). Computer-mediated communication and organizational innovation. *Journal of Communication, 37*(4).

Scharr, J. H. (1983, May–June). The possibility of freedom in a technological society. *The Center Magazine, 16.*

Williams, F. (1984). *The new communications* (p. 161). Belmont, CA: Wadsworth.

▶

References

1. Williams, F. (1984). *The new communications* (p. 161). Belmont, CA: Wadsworth.
2. Chesebro, J. W. (1984, June). The media reality: Epistemological functions of media in cultural systems. *Critical Studies in Mass Communication, 1*:2, p. 112.
3. See for example, M. McLuhan, *Understanding media* (1964). New York: McGraw-Hill; and M. McLuhan & Q. Fiore, (1967). *The medium is the massage.* New York: Bantam.
4. Chester, E. W. (1969). *Radio, television, and American politics.* (p. 120). New York: Sheed and Ward.
5. Fell, J. (1974). *Film and the narrative tradition.* Berkeley: University of California.
6. Perry, G. & Aldridge, A. (1967). *The Penguin book of comics* (p. 236). Baltimore, MD: Penguin Books.
7. DeWine, S., et al. (1986, May). Techno-sense: Making sense out of the technological impact on human communication (p. 6). Paper presented at the International Communication Association Convention.
8. Bush, J. M., & Bush, D. P. (1981). *Private television communications: Into the eighties* (pp. 51–53). Berkeley Heights, NJ: International Television Association.
9. Gayeski, D. M. (1983). *Corporate and instructional video. Design and production* (pp. 3–6). Englewood Cliffs, NJ: Prentice-Hall.
10. McCathrin, E. Z. (1986, July). Beyond employee publications making the personal connection. *Public Relations Journal*, p. 16.
11. See J. W. Chesebro & D. G. Bonsall. (1989). *Computer-mediated communication, human relationships in a computerized world* (pp. 116–125). Tuscaloosa: University of Alabama Press, for a discussion of the social implications.
12. Rice, R. E. (1987, Autumn). Computer-mediated communication and organizational innovation. *Journal of Communication, 37*(4), pp. 78–80.
13. DeWine, S. et al. (pp. 12–13).
14. Kiesler, S., Siegel, J., & McGuire, T. W. (1984). Social psychological aspects of computer-mediated communication. *American Psychologist, 39*, 1128–1129.
15. Chesebro & Bonsall, p. 123.

16. These effects are discussed in more detail in Kiesler, Siegel, and McGuire, esp. pp. 1129–1131.
17. McCathrin, E. Z., (p. 20).
18. Ellul, J. (1967). *The technological society* (J. Wilkinson, Trans). New York: Alfred A. Knopf.
19. Scharr, J. H. (1983, May–June). The possibility of freedom in a technological society. *The Center Magazine, 16,* 52.
20. Scharr, J. H. *16,* 53–54.
21. Mumford, L. (1967). *The myth of the machine: Technics and human development* (p. 201). New York: Harcourt, Brace & World.
22. Exton, W., Jr. (1982). The future of language: Basic tool of communication. In H. F. Didsbury, Jr., (Ed.), *Communications and the future,* (p. 23). Bethesda, MD: World Future Society.
23. *UN Chronicle,* 20:40 (April 1983), Computers: The limits of use in democratic society. 30–32; Communications, 33–35.
24. Siegel, L., & Markoff, J. (1985). *The high cost of high tech* (p. 11). New York: Harper & Row.
25. Perrolle, J. A. (1991, Summer). Computer-mediated conversation (pp. 21–22). *National Forum, 21,* 21–22.

VIDEO CASE

Communication Breakdown: Dependence on Communication Technologies

This case returns to the breakdown in AT&T's long distance phone system in New York City on September 17, 1991, which led to the disruption of air travel in New York City and throughout the northeastern United States. Recall that this incident resulted in the cancellation of over 700 flights at three airports, with untold effects on the travel and business plans of thousands of people. Had the long distance service been interrupted during business hours, the resulting cost to business in the area could have been over $1 trillion a day.

The first segment of the video shows Congressman Scheuer, a member of the House Committee on Telecommunications and Finance. Congressman Scheuer feels that the technology problem represented by this communication breakdown is really, at base, a human problem. To understand the points he makes one needs to understand the two main federal agencies discussed.

The Federal Communication Commission (FCC) is responsible for overseeing the nation's communication systems, including the telephone companies, to ensure that they are operating in the best interest of the public. These companies, called long distance carriers, include AT&T, Sprint, and MCI. Because of the public's dependence on the services of these private corporations, they are required to operate under some governmental supervision.

The Federal Aviation Administration (FAA) is responsible for overseeing the nation's airline industry. One of the primary public interests in regard to this industry, of course, is public safety. The FAA carries out inspections and requires certain reports to ensure that the private airlines, such as TWA, United, USAir, and others, are meeting federal safety standards.

Note that analogy that Congressman Scheuer draws between the way that the FAA and the FCC operate. Recall that in this particular incident, generators that were to provide electrical power for the AT&T long-distance control center were out of order. Some alarms to alert technicians of the problem were actually turned off by telephone employees, and other alarms were ignored. Also, the generators were located in a part of the facility that was vacant during the critical six hours. Note also the function of nonverbal communication in leading to Scheuer's impression of the Chairman of the FCC when he testified before the Congressional committee. What were the cues that communicated this negative impression to the Congressman?

After viewing the video, discuss the solution that Congressman Scheuer suggests for problems of this sort. To what extent is the problem in this case a problem of human, interpersonal communication?

This case focuses on the information media and technology created and used by modern firms and institutions. One of the major points made is that innovations in communication technology, both in transmission and in the developing dependence on computer mediated communication systems (CMCS), lead to a heightened vulnerability resulting from the concentration of information. Because of an awareness of the dependence of the huge business community in New York on the telecommunications channels, a special task force was created to help coordinate ways to deal with a breakdown of the sort that occurred.

The second segment of the video involves a discussion with Thomas Dunleavy, Assistant Commissioner of Telecommunications Policy for New York City, and Mitchell Moss of the Mayor's Task Force on Telecommunications Network Reliability. Dunleavy reminds viewers that human beings are ultimately responsible for the uses that they make of the communication media and technologies. What are the solutions recommended by Dunleavy and Moss for problems of this sort? Note especially Moss's discussion of the importance of redundancy.

The discussion on the video indicates that it is usually difficult to determine ultimate blame or responsibility in cases involving large, interlocking media systems. Was the FCC at fault for failing to ensure that AT&T would not allow this sort of breakdown? Or, was AT&T to blame for not properly maintaining their system and making sure that their people would follow procedures? Or, was the FAA at fault for not having set up a separate telephone or other communication system not be subject to the breakdowns of electric utility companies or private long distance telephone carriers? Ultimately, is Congress responsible for failing to provide funding for separate communication media for the air traffic control system, as Moss suggests? In actuality, it was the General Services Administration, of the Executive Branch of the Federal Government, that denied the FAA's request for an independent phone system for air control: Was the GSA therefore ultimately responsible for the problem?

In your discussion of the issues raised in this video case, note the significance of the communication elements of channel, channel capacity and overload, and redundancy.

Special Applications in Business and Professional Communication

This part discusses several situations that arise in business and professional settings that call upon special skills of human communication.

Chapter 13 deals with the widespread phenomenon of conflict between and within organizations. The chapter focuses on the aspects of conflict that can be dealt with from the communication perspective we have been developing in this text.

Chapter 14 looks more specifically at the techniques of negotiation, bargaining, and mediation as forms of communication for dealing constructively with conflict.

Chapter 15 recognizes the importance of communication training within many organizations and the need for helping others put together speeches and presentations. We provide some general guidelines for communication training and for speech writing in organizations.

PART 4

Conflict Management

●

13

CHAPTER

After studying this chapter, you will be able to:

1. Describe the positive and negative effects of conflict.

2. Analyze the factors in conflict episodes.

3. Explain the typical conflict management styles.

4. Understand the factors in selecting conflict styles.

5. Describe the effects of different conflict styles.

Overview

Throughout this text, we have often followed a problem-solution format, so you might expect that we would begin this chapter with a discussion of the problem of conflict. In fact, conflict itself is not necessarily a problem.

Conflict in Organizations

Conflict can have positive as well as negative effects, as we will point out in a moment. Furthermore, conflict is built into some systems, where it is actually expected and seen as appropriate. The American legal system immediately comes to mind as a good example. The premise of our legal system is that from the clash of two opposing sides, the best arguments and evidence for both sides will be produced, leading to a decision based on the best possible information. The system, therefore, requires conflict.

Similarly, conflict is expected in political democracies. The premise underlying such political systems is, again, that in the competition between two or more political parties or candidates, the electorate will be presented with the best arguments from both sides. Whether this goal is always fulfilled or not in practice may be another question, but the idea of choice arising from conflict or from competition is central.

Other systems are based upon the desirability of conflict. Labor-management negotiations usually assume an adversarial relationship intended to bring about the best result for both the firm and for the employees; again, practice may not

▶ *Conflict is a fact of life in most organizations.*

square with the ideal. The budgeting method used in many organizations assumes some kind of conflict among various units as they compete for limited resources or budget lines.

Conflict may therefore be seen as a natural part of certain systems, to be expected and not to be eliminated or avoided. There are some estimates that managers spend over 20% of their time dealing with some kind of conflict.[1] Earlier theories of organizations, such as the classical theories discussed in Chapter 2, assumed that conflict was somehow unnatural or just did not occur in organizations. Organizations were conceived of as basically single-motive entities. Later theories of organizations, however, have stressed that organizations tend to be mixed-motive conglomerations.

For example, the case workers in a social service organization probably have a different view of the goals of their organization than the business manager may have. Teachers may have goals that are different from those of their school administrators. Engineers may see the goals of a manufacturing organization in terms of state-of-the-art design; the upper management may see it in terms of dividends or return on investment.

Conflict is undoubtedly a widespread feature of our organizational lives. The problem is not the existence of conflict but the difficulty that people or organizations have in managing conflict constructively. Conflict has the potential of becoming destructive if not channeled or controlled.

▶ ### Conflict and Culture

Expectations concerning conflict are influenced by the cultural context. Conflict, expected and even required in the American legal tradition, would seem inappropriate in some other cultures. The amount of overt conflict permitted varies from one political culture to another. The Finns, for example, although very democratic, are not comfortable with overt expressions of political conflict within their political system. They prefer that dissent be expressed in indirect or nonconfrontational ways. On the other hand, Italian or British parliamentarians revel in outward expressions of overt political conflict, with calls of "Shame! Shame!" occasionally punctuating political speeches in the British House of Commons.

In addition, one should bear in mind possible differences within various corporate cultures. You would expect more openly expressed conflict in so-called tough-guy, macho cultures than in process cultures. Certain accepted and sanctioned ways of dealing with conflict and negotiations develop that are specific to particular organizations, such as, "That's the way we handle things around here." National and corporate cultures may therefore partially determine how conflict is perceived and how to deal with it.

Methods of Conflict Management

Conflict can be managed or dealt with in several ways: litigation, arbitration, negotiation, bargaining, or mediation. The first two methods—litigation and arbitration—represent formal, procedural methods in which the outcome is intended to be a mandated or legally binding decision. These legal processes have their own technical rules and procedures that place such proceedings beyond the scope of this text. Often, they represent the most expensive and time-consuming solutions for conflicts; and legal proceedings often lead to ill-will between contending parties, thereby making future dealings among them tense, if not impossible. Occasionally, conflict is passed up to a higher level in the organization to allow someone to make an administrative decision. This situation is rather like internal arbitration, although the administrator may or may not be impartial and may or may not investigate the matter thoroughly before coming to a decision.

The discussion here concentrates on the less formal proceedings emphasizing the use of communication skills, such as negotiation, bargaining, and mediation, which are taken up in more detail in Chapter 14. In sum, the expression of and the managing of conflict involves communication and how effectively the conflict is dealt with usually is a function of the communication skills of the people involved.

As you read through this chapter and the next, you will notice some principles reinforced from earlier chapters.

Effective Listening.   One of the most significant examples of such reinforcement lies in the central importance that skills in good listening play in conflict management, negotiation, and mediation. We will refer several times to the listening skills, especially empathic listening skills, that we first discussed in Chapter 3.

Problem-Solving.   Second, we will also point out that problem-solving skills are at the heart of effective conflict management and negotiation. One of the most effective approaches to dealing with conflict involves defining the conflict or negotiation in terms of joint problem solving. The widely used approach of Fisher and

Ury, from *Getting to Yes*, for example, emphasizes the technique of redefining a conflict as a problem-solving situation.

We first discuss the nature and causes of conflict in professional or organizational settings. This discussion includes the ideas that conflict can have both positive and negative effects and that conflict can occur at various levels within an organization or between organizations. In the next chapter, we turn to the specific principles of negotiation and bargaining and then mediation, including discussions of the conditions under which these various conflict management strategies are in order.

THE NATURE AND CAUSES OF ORGANIZATIONAL CONFLICT

Positive and Negative Aspects of Conflict

We have already pointed out that conflict is sometimes structural, that is, built in to the system. Clearly, those who designed or developed such systems perceived conflict to have positive effects. There are several advantages that conflict can have for a group, organization, or society.

First, conflict brings attention to the existence of a problem that might otherwise be ignored or overlooked. Often we may be unaware that some problem exists until a conflict breaks out, virtually demanding our attention. In this way, conflict can be a prerequisite to bringing about needed change or to redressing grievances. Many would argue that the protests associated with the American Civil Rights movement, especially in the late 1950s and 1960s, brought an important conflict into the open in American society.

Second, conflict can unify a group, causing the members to set aside destructive or counterproductive wrangles while they attend to some perceived threat, that is, the new conflict. Not only are people drawn together as a result, but they also feel new energy and a renewed commitment to some shared goal that had been momentarily forgotten. Conflict, therefore, can be a motivating force for individuals and for groups and can bring about group cohesion and commitment.

Third, conflict can sharpen the issues of a problem situation. In fact, we may not actually realize exactly what our own needs and purposes are until we have to articulate and defend them as a result of some conflict. In having to defend our position, we find that we must study it, learn about it in more depth than we had before this sudden need to explain, and defend it. Conflict can hence be educational for ourselves as well as for others.

These functional benefits of conflict help to explain why the research on conflict management tends to favor the use of confrontation as the preferred method for dealing with conflict.[2] Confrontation in this sense is used in contrast with other strategies, such as avoidance (that is, ignoring the potential conflict, hoping it will go away), accommodation (that is, basically, giving in at the sign of conflict), forcing (that is, using authority or power to end the conflict), or compromising (that is, dividing the loaf, each side giving away something desired). Confrontation is a strategy that calls for bringing the conflict directly to the attention of everyone involved and out into the open for immediate discussion. Confronting the conflict generally has the benefits just listed: bringing needed attention to a problem, unifying and motivating people, and sharpening issues. One influential work on conflict resolution summarizes the potential benefits of conflict as follows: "It prevents stagnation, it stimulates interest and curiosity, it is the medium through which problems can be aired and solutions arrived at, it is the root of personal and social change."[3]

On the other hand, conflict can have negative effects, which is why it should be held to manageable proportions and dealt with constructively. Obviously, conflict can be threatening to individuals, who may become emotionally involved. Recall that relationship conflicts are usually counterproductive. Continual conflict can lead to people's withdrawing from participation in the organizational or group activities, thereby lowering productivity and satisfaction. Given the feeling that knowledge is power, there may be a tendency to withhold information from others and to avoid their using what we know to get an advantage. Some may manipulate group loyalties and feelings, leading to cynicism and a resultant lowered commitment and job satisfaction. Prolonged conflict can lead to people's avoiding one another or avoiding communication altogether. When conflict remains unresolved, people may automatically turn increasingly to authorities or power figures for administrative solutions, rather than working out their own solutions through a problem-solution format. If people continue to mull over the conflict in their minds, they tend to become more intransigent and less likely to cooperate.

Despite the positive effects of conflict, therefore, there are aspects of conflict that can be destabilizing or disruptive. The dysfunctional aspects of conflict are usually the result of ineffective attempts to deal with the conflict rather than the conflict per se. Unfortunately, as some dispute resolution experts have pointed out, ". . . the costs of disputing—lawyer's fees, lost wages and production, physical and emotional injuries—are often too high. In addition, the outcomes of disputes are generally unsatisfying: people do not get what they want or need, relationships are strained, agreements collapse, old disputes reemerge."[4] Ultimately, we may not know whether a conflict was productive or not until we have seen and evaluated the outcomes. If the outcome leaves people feeling defeated, frustrated, or dissatisfied, the conflict was not constructive; if at the end of the conflict, people feel

▶ **Table 13.1**

Positive effects of conflict	Negative effects of conflict
Identifies problems	Threatens individuals
Unifies people	Leads to avoidance behaviors
Sharpens and clarifies issues	Leads to withholding of information
Can be educational	Can cause cynicism and reduced communication

that all have been treated fairly and satisfied in some way, the conflict was, to that extent, positive.

▶ ### The Nature of Conflict

This section analyzes conflict as typically experienced within organizations. The purpose of this discussion is to develop a systematic way to look at such conflicts. Such a scheme enhances our understanding of how conflicts occur and provides a basis for understanding the causes for conflict. Conflicts can be analyzed in terms of the following:

- The level at which the conflict occurs.
- The substance of the conflict.
- Issues of personality.
- Depth: superficial versus fundamental conflicts.
- Metaconflict: conflict about how to handle conflict.

First, conflict can be experienced at the following levels: intrapersonal (that is, one feels some internal conflict), interpersonal (that is, between two people, usually in a continuing relationship within the same group or department), intragroup (that is, among people within a specified work group), intergroup (that is, among groups or departments or divisions within a larger organization), and interorganizational (that is, between one organization and another). In other words, conflict can be experienced at the individual, group, organizational, or wider, even societal, level, as shown in Figure 13-1. Most of our concern in this chapter focuses on communication principles that are relevant for interpersonal, intragroup, and intergroup conflict within an organization. Of course, there are personal ramifications to many conflicts and effects of some conflicts spill over into the larger society.

Second, conflict can be analyzed in terms of the substantive grounds for disagreement. For instance, people may have conflict over the facts of a case (that is, what really happened or will happen), over the values to be placed on the situation itself (that is, it is important versus trivial; it is an ethical issue or an issue in which ethics are irrelevant; and so on), and, finally, over the question of what to do about the situation (that is, matters of policy, the best solution to a problem, and so on). In addition, a conflict can be about the goals or purposes of the group or organization and the best methods for attaining those goals or purposes, the degree to which the goals are being achieved (and questions of how to measure or judge success), and methods for distributing rewards to those within the organization or group.[5] The substantive issues of a conflict usually involve some disagreement about facts, interpretation or value of facts, proposed actions, or ends or goals.

Third, conflict can be considered in terms of personality issues. We have all heard of someone having a so-called personality clash with someone else, such as a boss, a coworker, or a teacher. Presumably, when one has a personality conflict

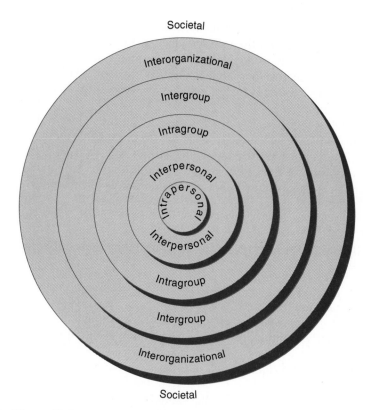

Societal
Interorganizational
Intergroup
Intragroup
Interpersonal
Intrapersonal
Interpersonal
Intragroup
Intergroup
Interorganizational
Societal

▶ **Figure 13-1**   *Levels of conflict.*

with another, the problem is not necessarily with any of the substantive matters, such as the goals, methods, facts, or what have you. Rather, one person feels that he or she simply cannot get along with another person; often, one finds that personality clashes may reinforce or in some way be tied up with substantive disagreement, as well. Such personal conflicts, or relationship conflicts, can result from the attributions concerning another's motives or circumstances, as will be discussed later. Of course, cultural differences can also account for such personal conflict. In short, conflict can involve socioemotional issues as well as task, or substantive, issues. Please note in referring to the task-oriented or factual conflicts as substantive, the authors do not intend to imply that personal conflicts are not serious; on the contrary, such personal clashes can be real and significant.

Fourth, conflicts can be analyzed in terms of whether they are fundamental or superficial, short-term or long-term. For example, we can imagine a conflict that is long-lasting or even permanent between two departments in an organization. Such a longstanding conflict resulting from, perhaps, a different view of what the goals of the organization are, will be more difficult to resolve than a minor disagreement concerning choosing methods to meet an agreed-upon goal. As noted already, the different objectives of labor and management mean that there will usually be something fundamental about their disagreements. Recall, though, that both labor and management may share goals such as economic viability for the organization concerned. In collective bargaining conflicts, school boards and teacher groups still share some important fundamental goals, such as quality education for students in the district.

Fifth, conflict can result when there is a disagreement about the nature of the conflict itself: How is the conflict to be handled? What are the permissible methods for resolving disputes? The conflict can be about the proper way to handle the conflict itself over the very rules of the game. We refer to this kind of problem as a metaconflict, since it is a conflict over a conflict, or how best to handle a conflict.

Analyzing the Causes of Conflict

One can begin an analysis of a conflict, therefore, by considering these different views of the conflict:

1. At what *level* does it occur?
2. What is the nature of the *substance* or factual topic of the conflict?
3. Is it primarily a substantive conflict, or is there also a relationship or *personality* clash?
4. Is the conflict based mainly on *fundamental* differences or more transitory or superficial issues?
5. Is there disagreement over the way the conflict should be dealt with (we could think of this as *metaconflict*, or conflict about conflict)?

We will now briefly show how, by considering each of these five elements in a conflict situation, one can begin to get at the causes for conflict.

The Level of the Conflict.   The first task is to determine the level at which the conflict appears: Is it between individuals, within a group or department, between groups or organizations? Interpersonal conflict is that which exists between two individuals. In the workplace, one of the most typical kinds of interpersonal conflict is that between a person and his or her immediate supervisor. The most frequent kind of such interpersonal conflict involves performance evaluations. Specifically, there is often very little agreement between supervisor and supervisee regarding the latter's evaluation.[6] This fundamental cause for conflict reminds us of the importance of the performance-appraisal interview, as discussed in Chapter 7.

A problem may first come to light as a conflict between two departments or work groups. Upon investigation, however, it may turn out that the conflict is actually the result of some sort of rivalry between two people, each a member of the two respective groups. The cause of the problem may reside, therefore, not in competition between groups, but between individuals. One must be alert to such possibilities in trying to locate the level at which the conflict is actually occurring: that is, between individuals or between groups. For example, what appears to be a dispute between two departments over control over a program may actually be based in a personal competition between the two department heads for status.

Of course, intergroup conflict is also real. Intergroup conflict may be a natural result of competing demands by various groups for resources or personnel within the larger organization. Such disputes may be of the built-in variety described earlier. The two most typical kinds of intergroup conflicts are those pitting one department against another (say, for control of resources or for allocation of funds) and those resulting from labor-management disputes.

The Substance of the Conflict. After locating the level at which the conflict occurs, one then determines the substance of the conflict. We have seen that disagreement could be over the facts of the matter, the value or meaning of the facts, or what to do about the facts. Consequently, it would be important first to find out whether there is agreement on facts and their meaning before taking up other matters. For example, there may be a conflict over whether to discontinue production of a particular item because of declining sales; but further discussion reveals disagreement about what the sales figures or potential actually is—a disagreement over the facts rather than values. In trying to discover the cause for conflict, then, one should find out whether the conflict is based on disagreements about facts, values, or proposed courses of action. It is possible, of course, that there is a disagreement on all three points. Not only do the two groups disagree on the facts of the matter, but also what the facts mean, and what should be done.

The substance of the conflict may in reality be a conflict over goals rather than facts or means. It would make some difference to know that the reason people disagree on a course of action could be that they do not agree on the direction the whole group should be going in the first place. Therefore, it is important to discover whether or not the two parties share the same interests or goals, because differences on those points could easily result in different interpretations of facts and appropriate courses of action.

The substance of dispute, therefore, can arise from disagreements over facts or data, the value or significance of the data, the course of action to take, and the goals or purposes of the group or organization.

Personal Elements in Conflict. Next are the questions of personal elements as potential causes of conflict. Is the conflict related to personality problems between conflicting parties? Is there some kind of personal rivalry or competition wrapped up in the conflict? While substantive conflicts are often productive, relationship conflicts of this sort are often not constructive. These kinds of personal conflicts can lead to defensiveness and counterproductive behavior.

Seriousness of Conflict. Another point in our analysis of the conflict is to determine the seriousness of the cause of the conflict. Conflicts over goals or ends are usually more significant than conflicts concerning practical means to achieve those ends. In other words, conflicts over principles are more difficult to resolve than conflicts over specific means. Substantive conflicts may be but are not always more serious than conflicts resulting from personality clashes. Still, if people feel that their self-esteem is at stake or is threatened, if they feel in danger of losing face,

Diversity in the Workplace

Personality or Cultural Clash?

Possibly some conflicts are more likely to arise between certain people because of the clash of preferences, styles, or even culture. Those who have studied the corporate cultures, likewise, point out that there may different cultural expectations regarding the handling of conflict from one part of a complex organization to another. As our organizations become more heterogeneous and multicultural, we should expect more "friction," more natural conflict as a result of that heterogeneity, which reflects the wider diversity found in the society at large. For example, studies have suggested that African-Americans and whites may assign different meanings to the same words or nonverbal signs in the workplace. Rules governing eye contact in conversation, for example, may differ enough to cause misunderstanding among coworkers or between a supervisor and supervisee.[7] In thinking about the causes of a conflict, therefore, it is a good idea to be alert to possible cultural differences, that could lead to so-called personality clashes.

the conflict may not be easily resolved. Personality clashes, therefore, can sometimes be difficult to resolve.

When we find groups within organizations in conflict, we may find that these groups represent different interest groups within the larger organization. The interests of such parties can vary from those that are objectively substantial to ones more highly subjective, such as matters of personal preference or taste. If the conflict is over the color of the brochure, it is not as serious as a conflict over the content of the brochure. The nature of the interest groups in conflict, therefore, can help us to decide how serious or fundamental the current conflict actually is.

It may be possible to determine, as a result of this analysis, that a conflict does not necessarily require much time or attention; it can be "satisfied" if it is not really serious and does not threaten to disrupt productive work. On the other hand, one should be aware that unresolved problems, which may seem small at first, can become serious irritants if not settled. One interesting study has pointed out that prolonged thinking about a dispute ("mulling" it over), without coming to a solution, can exacerbate the seriousness of the conflict between individuals, making it more rather than less difficult to deal with later on.[8]

Conflict over Conflict Management.   Finally, we should be aware that some causes of conflict are the result of a disagreement over how to deal with conflict in the first place. We have noted, for example, that Finns prefer the appearance of group consensus to an open conflict. We see here the possibilities for conflict resulting from different approaches to conflict management in an organization comprising Finnish and American managers. Japanese managers are said, also, to prefer a conflict-management strategy that avoids overt disputes. Second, there are differing preferences that people show for different approaches to dealing with conflict (confrontational versus accommodating, for example). We will go into more detail regarding these different strategies and preferences a bit later. Suffice it to say at this point, that one manager may prefer to use a coercive, or forcing, style to resolve a dispute, whereas a colleague may prefer to use a problem-solving, or integrative, approach. Clearly, they could find themselves in a conflict over the right way to approach that conflict.

Highlights of the Nature and Causes of Conflict.   Conflict can occur at several levels within an organization; determining the location of the conflict is a first step in analyzing and dealing with the conflict. Conflicts are usually over substantive matters involving different perceptions of data or the facts, different values placed on the facts, different interests or needs of the parties in conflict, or a perception of unequal distribution or control over desired resources. Relationship conflicts are those resulting from a clash between individuals due to different styles, preferences, values, or even cultural or gender differences. Such relationship clashes may or may not be related to substantive conflicts. Such personal clashes may be the result of misperceptions or stereotypes or the difficulties of communication in increasingly heterogeneous organizations. Conflicts can differ in their seriousness and therefore in the amount of effort required to deal with them. A final cause of conflict can be a difference over how to deal with conflict itself, a so-called meta-conflict.

Stages of Conflict Episodes

A final point concerning the nature of conflicts concerns the stages through which they characteristically move. An attempt at conflict management may depend upon recognizing how far along the parties are in a particular conflict. In general, conflicts seem to proceed through three major stages: latent conflict, emerging or felt conflict, and manifest or outright conflict, as shown in Figure 13-2.

Latent conflicts are characterized by the recognition of some underlying tensions. People have not felt the need to take sides yet; we may say that the conflict is not yet highly polarized. At this stage, some, but not all, of the participants begin to be aware of the coming conflict. Some authorities think a latent conflict should be brought out in the open, but it is being repressed or ignored. If that is

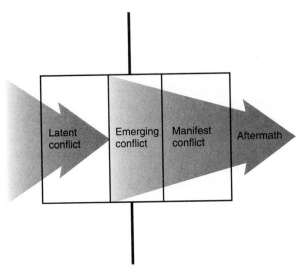

| Latent conflict | Emerging conflict | Manifest conflict | Aftermath |

▶ **Figure 13-2**   *Four stages of conflict.*

the case, a latent conflict should be moved forward into the emerging or manifest conflict stages, which are described next.[9]

Emerging conflict represents the situation when all parties involved acknowledge a disagreement or dispute exists. At this point, there is potential for the conflict to escalate. People sense that tension is building in all potential participants. In Chapter 8, we touched upon the conflict stage as a typical part of the life cycle of small groups. In their early stages of development, groups often experience emerging conflict before group norms, and roles are completely worked out. Once these roles and norms are established, the group often may not proceed on to the next stage of conflict, which is manifest conflict.

Manifest conflict is the stage of open, ongoing conflict. At this point, the people involved may have already begun to seek ways to resolve or deal with the conflict. Such efforts could include attempts to begin negotiation or bargaining or to seek mediation or intervention by third parties. At this point, the parties may feel that they are truly at an impasse, and no progress toward settlement is being made.

There will be some aftermath following the conclusion of the conflict episode. The parties will somehow resolve their differences, or one side will win and the other side lose, or relations will be broken off for good, making future cooperation among the parties difficult, if not impossible. The positive or negative aspects of this aftermath no doubt depend a great deal upon the strategies that participants or interveners use in managing the conflict. Effective conflict management begins with a systematic analysis of the conflict in question: its nature, its causes, and the stage in which it finds itself. This analysis should lead to an understanding of the conflict and, it is hoped, a constructive approach to the conflict based on that analysis.

STRATEGIES FOR CONFLICT MANAGEMENT

Conflict Management Styles

People differ in their orientation toward conflict and therefore in their preferred way of dealing with it. In real life situations, you have probably seen people who deal with conflict by pleading, arguing, threatening, withdrawing, going to higher-ups, joking or teasing about it, or complaining to others. Most of the research concerning conflict management acknowledges two basic approaches with variations in between: hard and soft.

A hard approach to conflict is represented by a tough stance, in which one emphasizes aggressively trying to win all the issues. Informally, this orientation is usually called a win-lose approach. This approach is also called a distributive approach, because it assumes that there is a fixed-pie that can be distributed in only so many ways. Economists and those involved in game theory often refer to this approach as assuming a zero-sum game, which means that whatever one side wins, the other side must lose, so that the gains and losses cancel each other out and always add up to zero.

A so-called soft approach is less aggressive and does not place so much emphasis on winning and losing. Sometimes this orientation is referred to as an integrative approach because the hope is to integrate the interests of the two sides to come to a solution of the problem causing the conflict. This integration of the interests of the two sides should lead to a win-win result, in which both sides can be said to win. But the soft approach can also be associated with lose-lose outcomes, such as avoiding any solution (an impasse, no one wins) or compromising (both sides give up something, no one wins completely). A hard approach, then, stresses competition, whereas a soft approach stresses cooperation.

Each of these orientations regarding how to behave in a conflict can be seen in the personal strategies individuals enact when they are involved in a conflict. Obviously, those who take the hard approach will be more aggressive and oriented to winning at any cost than those who take one of the softer approaches. A very useful way of categorizing people's characteristic responses to conflict in organizations has been derived from the grid theory of Blake and Mouton, discussed earlier in Chapter 2 dealing with organizational communication. This set of five categories has been widely used in the research literature of conflict management.

You may recall that Blake and Mouton characterized managers by their concern for production, on one hand, and their concern for people, on the other. A manager's concern for production could be very high or very low; likewise, her concern for people could be very high or very low; and there could be many possible combinations in between.

Managers who were high on production concern, but low on people concern, would probably respond to conflict in their departments or organizations by a forcing strategy: That is, they would try to force a resolution upon others. Managers who are low on both concern for production and concern for people would probably react by avoiding or ignoring the conflict. Those with a high concern for people but low concern for production would probably be accommodating, likely to give in to smooth over any conflict. The managers in the middle of the grid, with a moderate concern for both production and for people, would probably exhibit a compromising strategy during conflict episodes. Finally, the managers showing very high concern for both production and for people would respond to conflict by adopting a problem-solving strategy.

▶ ### Factors in Choosing Conflict Styles

The response that any one person may exhibit in the face of conflict depends upon several factors. First, we may assume that personality factors partly determine a person's favored way of responding to conflict. Some people tend to be more aggressive or competitive than others, who may prefer to avoid or smooth over conflicts. Still others may characteristically respond to conflicts by adopting more of a problem-solving approach.

Gender and Cultural Differences.   Researchers have wondered whether these personal differences are related to gender or cultural factors. Concerning gender differences, there has been some research support for the hypothesis that women tend to adopt the more cooperative-type strategies, whereas men select more forcing or coercive styles. However, more recent research has suggested that what appears to be a gender difference may be the result of power or status differences. Women have not in the past tended to occupy positions as high in authority as men; and those in authority show a tendency to choose the more coercive styles than those in lower managerial positions.[10]

It does appear likely that there are cultural factors that shape an individual's response to a conflict situation. Culture represents the accumulation of a people's beliefs, values, and world views. These beliefs and values are organized into systems characteristic of each human culture. It is to be expected that how to deal with conflict is an important subject in these cultural value systems, and that, consequently, different cultures will view conflict and conflict strategies or styles differently. A Japanese colleague, in other words, may have a perspective on conflict management at odds with that of his American colleague. The clash of styles could become part of the a larger, substantive conflict. The Japanese tend to prefer dealing with conflict in ways that emphasize group solidarity and consensus, while the Americans may take a more competitive, or hard, approach.

Responses of Other Parties.   There are other factors that could cause a person to respond to conflict in different ways. If one attempts to get compliance through one strategy, say, a cooperative strategy, and gets no results, one may switch to a different conflict style. This change results from the transactional nature of conflict communication. The conflict, like other communication episodes, is an unfolding process, with one's moves and strategies changing during the episode in response to moves and strategies by the other party. Conflict strategies, therefore, do not remain static, but may evolve during this unfolding process.

One study found that while initially managers predicted that they would use an integrative style for dealing with a subordinate who was reluctant to comply with

Problem-Solution

Dealing with Differences in Style: Gender and Conflict Management Style

Deborah Tannen discusses some characteristics of women managers, including their styles in meetings and negotiations. Her research suggests that women "use language to achieve rapport; they want to get their way, but they prefer to get their way by having everyone agree." According to this view, women are similar to many Asian businessmen, who prefer to conduct business negotiations only after they have gotten to know the other people involved and who also stress consensus in settling differences.

Tannen warns that women have different styles, just as do men; ethnic or national origins or other influences from one's upbringing can lead women to have aggressive and argumentative styles, as well. Her generalizations are just that, general observations that apply on average for American women.

Maureen Dowd, who covers the White House for the *New York Times*, agrees that women display many different approaches to power and confrontation. In general, Dowd believes that women leaders' style of wielding power and influence has affected corporate cultures, loosening up what she describes as formerly "the rigidly impersonal and competitive relationships" between men and women in the workplace.

See When a women speaks, does anybody listen? Interview of D. Tannen by L. A. Lusardi, *Working Woman*, July 1990, pp. 92–94 and M. Dowd, Power: Are women afraid of it—or beyond it? *Working Woman*, November 1991, pp. 948–999.

the directions of the manager, they would in fact change to more coercive strategies in the face of the subordinate's continued noncompliance. At first, people claim that they will try to be reasonable, but then the conflict may escalate if the matter is not resolved. There was a slight difference between female and male managers, in that the women tended to persist in the integrative or cooperative strategies longer than their male counterparts.[11] Such escalation during conflict episodes is typical. Katz and Kahn report, "One of the best-established findings about conflict interaction is the tendency toward similar or reciprocal behavior and the consequent escalation of the conflict process."[12] A sort of vicious cycle is set up with each side feeling that it is matching the other. Katz and Kahn also point out that the result of such escalation goes beyond just intensifying the current conflict; it spills over into other issues, making further cooperation difficult.

Shared Goals of Parties Involved.   A third factor that can determine one's choice of conflict style is the nature of the relationship with the other person involved. The important factors in the relationship appear to be a perception of shared goals, the long-term nature of the relationship, and the power or status differential in the relationship.

If person *A* believes that person *B* has the same goals and desires as *A*, *A* will likely be more cooperative in a conflict with *B*. If *A* believes that *B* does not share his or her goals, then *A* is likely to be more competitive or combative. Shared goals or interests, then, usually lead to more cooperative strategies. This point would suggest that where there are perceptions of major differences in goals, values, or life-style, there will be more resort to the competitive styles.

Nature of Relationship among Parties.   It appears that each party's view of the long-term nature of their relationship has an effect on the conflict style used. In those cases in which both parties believed that they would have to work together cooperatively in the future, there was usually a preference for the more cooperative or problem-solving styles of conflict management.

Of course, perceptions of power and status differences may be an important variable, too. One is more likely to use a softer approach with a boss or superior, regardless of one's approach in other situations.[13]

Setting and Audiences for Conflict.   Finally, the setting in which the manifest conflict occurs and the audience who may be observing the conflict may influence the type of conflict style that is employed. In a formal business meeting, an aggressive battler may tone down his or her normal conflict behaviors in order to impress

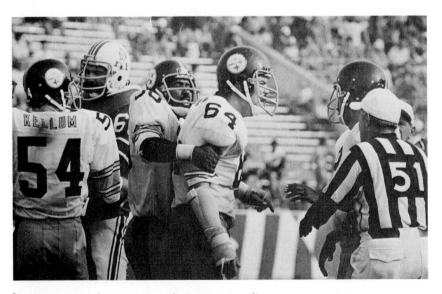

▶ *Many times disputants are playing to an audience.*

others. Or, one can imagine a person who would normally avoid a conflict becoming a battler because of others' expectations. If you have to go back to your own in-group and defend your actions, you may become more combative in order to show your friends that you really stood up for the group. In other words, a person responds as a member of a group instead of as an individual, and that group membership may change one's normal preferences.

For example, if a representative is sent to negotiate with the other group over a conflict, that representative may feel that he or she has a choice between being seen by the group as a hero (a winner) or a traitor (one who gives in to the other side). If both representatives see their choices in that way, they are probably going to choose tough conflict styles, and, as a result, resolution will be difficult.

Although we may say that most of the time George or Mary uses a forcing strategy, or an accommodating strategy, or whatever, we need to recognize that there will be circumstances in which each must use a different style. We can summarize these factors as follows:

- Gender and cultural differences.
- The response of the other party to initial efforts at resolving the dispute.
- Perception of shared goals.
- Perception that the relationship between parties involved in the dispute will be short- or long-term.
- Perceptions of differences in power or status between the parties.
- The setting or audiences for the conflict.

Strategies selected to deal with conflict are the result of several factors present in a given conflict situation. The conflict is a communication episode and therefore shows the process and transactional natures of any communication interaction. The styles and tactics used by people in conflict shift and change in response to their perceptions of these various factors. We should be aware, then, that we may have a certain preference for dealing with conflict, but that the history of the conflict, our view of the other parties and their interests, our relationship with the other parties or with outside audiences, and the setting or situation in which the conflict occurs can all influence the actual conflict style that we use.

Effects of Conflict Styles

Seeing that there may be many reasons to select various conflict styles, we consider each of the styles in more detail. We will consider conditions that are typically associated with each style and some of the effects to be expected from each.

Win-Lose, or Forcing Style. First, the win-lose approach of the forcing style assumes that there must be one winner and one loser. Whatever one side wins or gains, the other side must lose or give up. As mentioned earlier, this approach assumes a zero-sum game or a fixed pie. Generally, each side sees the conflict only from their own point of view. This style seems to be adopted under conditions in which future relationships between the two sides is not an important consideration (correctly or incorrectly). Of course, if the two parties are going to have to continue to work together for some time into the future, the damaging effects of the win-lose orientation become apparent. This approach is often found when one party clearly has more power than the other, or when one party is more aggressive than the other. A win-lose approach can result in an impasse, a situation in which the conflict is not resolved but continues, perhaps below the surface.

Lose-Lose, or Avoiding Style.   An impasse or failure to resolve the conflict can also result from the use of an avoiding style in conflict. Both sides may choose to ignore the conflict, perhaps because of a perception that the issues are not all that important or because of a perception that both sides are fairly weak and lack the power to force through a resolution. Avoiding may be a kind of lose-lose approach to a conflict. We may not win, but if we ignore the problem, maybe the other side can't win either. The avoiding strategy seems to be associated with situations in which there is a lack of trust among the parties involved. It should be no surprise that most people rate avoidance as the least favored style.[14]

Lose-Lose, or Compromising Style.   Another type of lose-lose approach to conflict is the compromising strategy. Although we often think of compromise as a good thing, it usually refers to outcomes in which both sides give up something, lose something that they had hoped to hang onto or to gain. Neither side is fully satisfied. Like a win-lose approach, the compromising style assumes that there is a fixed pie, a zero-sum game, but in this style the plusses and minuses are shared by both sides. Compromising, then, stems from the same kind of view of conflict as the forcing style. Because of a perception of a strong need to cooperate, or because of a perception of nearly equal power, the decision is made to share the pie rather than have the whole thing.

Lose-Win, or Accommodating Style.   We can think of the accommodating conflict style as representing a lose-win approach to a conflict. What we lose in order to accommodate the other side, they win. Accommodating often is an attempt to appease the other side. Perhaps we believe that they are too powerful. On the other hand, we may perceive the other party as being very attractive and we therefore do not wish to jeopardize our relationship by holding out in a conflict. We may accommodate the other side if we see some long-range benefit from the gains they might make: If they remain stable and in business as a result of our giving in one time, they may be in a position to become good customers later on, for example.

Win-Win, or Problem-Solving Style.   The fifth style, problem-solving, is associated with a win-win approach to conflict. The problem-solving or integrative strategy is usually found when future relationships and cooperation among the parties to the dispute is important. In this case, there is probably not a power struggle or personal clash between individuals involved on either side. Parties to the conflict probably see that their goals or interests are somehow interrelated or mutually dependent. Those taking a win-win approach do not assume that there is a fixed pie, nor that what one side wins the other side must lose. Rather, the approach assumes the conflict results from a problem that the two sides, working together, can solve. Problem solvers search for integrative solutions, that is, solutions that serve to integrate the needs and the interests of the parties involved. The intent is to find solutions, perhaps not thought of before the conflict, that allow both sides to win.

This win-win approach, as we shall see, is at the heart of the negotiation process in conflict management. The emphasis is more on cooperation rather than on competition. Although it may sound ideal, the problem-solving approach is not possible in all cases and would in fact be unrealistic under certain circumstances. (There really is a power struggle over very limited resources between parties with quite incompatible goals or styles.) A problem-solving strategy is often favored by parties who perceive each other to be similar in important ways: sharing the same values and goals, being part of the same in-group, culture, or coculture.

Highlights of Conflict Style. The way that conflict is handled, therefore, can be categorized by certain conflict styles, employed by the people involved in a dispute. While there may be personal preferences or tendencies toward certain styles, the actual circumstances of a conflict may determine the strategy selected. Because conflict represents a dynamic process of communication, strategies may change over time and in response to actions by other parties. The five basic strategies of forcing, avoiding, compromising, accommodating, and problem-solving are characterized by different views of the nature of conflict and the specific factors individuals perceive in a particular conflict situation. Clearly, the relationship (past and projected) plays an important role in people's decision to use a competitive or a cooperative approach.

SUMMARY

This chapter has been wide-ranging because conflict is a significant and probably inevitable part of our professional lives. Dealing constructively with conflict is an important skill. That conflict seems to occur often may not be a bad thing; we have indicated advantages but also disadvantages to conflicts.

We have attempted to show that approaching conflicts as problem-solving situations is usually the most constructive. An important point to bear in mind is that such communication strategies, as represented by integrative negotiation and mediation, have been shown to work the best in terms of maintaining productive and long-term relationships.

As always, it is important to remember that there may be cultural factors that interact with other circumstances to determine the kind of conflict resolution people may prefer. We noted that Confucian cultures generally prefer mediation and place a high value on a process that maintains group solidarity. African leaders were traditionally honored for an ability to settle disputes through listening and talking through issues thoroughly until everyone was satisfied. Within other more individualistic cultures, such as the American one, aggressive defense of one's rights may be seen as an important virtue in dealing with conflicts.

The increasingly multicultural nature of our organizations and society gives more attention to the need to be sensitive to interests of all parties in conflict. Effective listening and the capability to envision the perspective of the others involved will remain at the heart of the communication skills necessary to deal effectively with conflict.

EXERCISES

1. Describe a conflict that you have observed or participated in within your housing unit, fraternity, or sorority. Describe the conflict in terms of the level of conflict, the substance or objective reasons for the conflict, and the seriousness. To what extent were personality conflicts involved? What does your description suggest regarding an effective solution?

2. Do you have a characteristic style for dealing with conflict? Describe that style or styles. What things determine how you react when someone frustrates you or prevents your obtaining some desired object or goal?

3. You have been assigned to a group to complete a class term project; all five of you will share the same grade. Two people in the group are eager to get an A, and therefore begin doing most of the work and bossing the other three around. Two people feel that that's fine, but you feel that their monopolizing the group frustrates your ability to contribute meaningfully. You also feel that they assume that you couldn't do A work without their direction. Explain some different strategies for dealing with this conflict. Identify the interests of all involved in this situation.

SELECTED SOURCES FOR FURTHER READING

Blake, R. R., & Mouton, J. S. (1964). *The managerial grid*. Houston: Gulf Publishing Co.

Blake, R. R., Shepard, H. A., & Mouton, J. S. (1964). *Managing intergroup conflict in industry*. Houston: Gulf Publishing Co.

Blake, R. R., & Mouton, J. S. (1984). *Solving costly organizational conflict*. San Francisco: Jossey-Bass.

Deutsch, M. (1973). *The resolution of conflict*. New Haven: Yale University Press.

Fisher, R., & Ury, W. (1983). *Getting to yes: Negotiating agreement without giving in*. New York: Penguin Books.

Rahim, M. A. (Ed.) (1989). *Managing conflict: An interdisciplinary approach*. New York: Praeger.

Ury, W. L., Brett, J. M., & Goldberg, S. B. (1988). *Getting disputes resolved: Designing systems to cut the costs of conflict*. San Francisco: Jossey-Bass.

References ◀

1. Tjosvold, D. (1989). Introduction, in M. A. Rahim, (Ed.). *Managing conflict: An interdisciplinary approach*. New York: Praeger, p. 3.
2. Newell, S. K., & Stutman, R. W. (1991). The episodic nature of social confrontation (p. 361), in J. A. Anderson, (Ed.), *Communication yearbook*, 14. Newbury Park, CA: Sage.
3. Deutsch, M. (1973). *The resolution of conflict*. New Haven: Yale University Press, pp. 8–9.
4. Ury, W. L., Brett, J. M. & Goldberg, S. (1988). *Getting disputes resolved*. San Francisco: Jossey-Bass, p. xi.
5. Roloff, M. E. (1987). Communication and conflict, (p. 496), in C. E. Berger & S. H. Chafee, Eds. *Handbook of communication science*. Newbury Park, CA: Sage.
6. Roloff, p. 499.
7. Such difficulties are summarized by M. K. Asante & A. Davis (1989). Encounters in the interracial workplace, (pp. 374–391) in M. K. Asante & W. B. Gudykunst Eds. *Handbook of international and intercultural communication*. Newbury Park, CA: Sage.
8. Roloff, M. R. & Cloven, D. H. (1991). Sense-making activities and interpersonal conflict: Communicative cures for the mulling blues. *Western Journal of Speech Communication*, *55*, 134–158.
9. See Deutsch, p. 14.
10. Gayle, B. M. (1991). Sex equity in workplace management. *Journal of Applied Communication Research*, *19*, 154–169, supports this explanation with a study of 302 men and women managers in similar occupations and positions.
11. Conrad, C. (1991). Communication in conflict: Style-strategy relationships. *Communication Monographs*, *58*, 135–155.
12. Katz, D. & Kahn, R. L. (1978). *The social psychology of organizations*. (2nd ed.). New York: John Wiley, p. 634.
13. Support for this point is summarized by Putnam, L. L. & Poole, M. S. (1987). Conflict and negotiation, (p. 558), in F. M. Jablin, L. L. Putnam, K. H. Roberts & L. W. Porter, Eds. *Handbook of organizational communication*. Newbury Park, CA: Sage. They conclude that forcing is the preferred strategy of superiors, while avoiding, smoothing, or compromising is preferred by subordinates.
14. Putnam & Poole, p. 558.

Negotiation, Bargaining, and Mediation

•

14

CHAPTER

After studying this chapter, you should be able to:

1. Understand the differences between negotiation, bargaining, mediation, and arbitration.

2. Describe the conditions that should be present for effective negotiations and mediation.

3. Identify typical problems in negotiating.

4. Apply a problem-solving approach for successful negotiations.

5. Explain the main steps in preparing for and conducting mediation.

Overview

Negotiation is widespread in all kinds of organizations and is encountered daily in many professions. This statement may seem an exaggeration initially; after all, most of us are not diplomats nor are we involved daily in labor-management negotiations. Still, most people engage in some informal kind of negotiations nearly every day. It may be a trivial matter, such as deciding with a friend where to have lunch. It may be something that seems less trivial; perhaps you are planning with your supervisor goals and objectives for the next 3 months. In these cases, your friend and you, or your supervisor and you, probably negotiate in order to arrive at some final decision. Planning, choosing courses of action, or selecting resources are all things that we do jointly with others on the job and are often occasions for negotiating and bargaining.

We begin with some clarification of these various terms in order to indicate the directions that we will be taking in this chapter.

Negotiation refers to the process in which people share important goals, work together to solve problems or to make decisions, but do not begin with the same wishes in regard to making those decisions. A definition that we find especially useful is as follows: "When two or more parties within one or in different organizations jointly make decisions and do not have the same preferences, they are

▶ *Negotiations are an important part of organizational life.*

negotiating."[1] In their influential book on negotiating that grew out of the Harvard Negotiation Project, Roger Fisher and William Ury present the following meaning for negotiation: "It is back-and-forth communication designed to reach an agreement when you and the other side have some interests that are shared and others that are opposed."[2]

The term *bargaining* can be used interchangeably with negotiating, although the idea of bargaining suggests trading of some assets among the parties as the method used to solve problems or to make decisions. In the often-rerun TV series, "M*A*S*H," Radar was always making deals with other supply sergeants on the phone line to obtain various supplies for his unit; he was an astute bargainer. Negotiating, in other words, can be seen as a more inclusive term than bargaining, because negotiation can include methods other than exchanging assets in order to reach an acceptable resolution.

Mediation refers to the situation in which a neutral third party is introduced into a conflict to work with the two parties to help them arrive at a solution. The mediator, then, becomes the person facilitating the negotiating or bargaining between the parties involved. Arbitration differs from mediation in that the arbitrator, the third party, has the authority to make a decision on his or her own that may be binding on all parties to the dispute. Arbitration is therefore more like adjudication or litigation, more of a legal process, as indicated before. In mediation, then, the people involved in the dispute work out their own solution; in arbitration, an impartial third party makes a decision for them.

▶ *Bargaining is practiced by everyone at one time or another.*

NEGOTIATION

Although we have defined negotiation as joint decision making, further clarification is necessary. If two people have exactly the same objectives and agree on the same course of action, they are engaged in joint decision making, but not negotiation; there is really nothing to negotiate. Negotiation implies starting with different preferences in regard to the final decision. If two people have nothing in common and do not see the need to come to a joint decision, they go off on their own; that's not negotiation either. For negotiation to occur, there must be a felt need to cooperate; people must share some interests and needs if real negotiation is to take place. Negotiation involves more than one party, who have potentially different interest or desires but also some in common.

Negotiation is essentially a process of communication, for it is by communicating with one another that two parties arrive at some decision. Often, the final decision is something different from what either party started out to obtain. Negotiated decisions tend to evolve and to develop as an outcome of the process of communication. If a forcing conflict style is used, the outcome is what one party intended from the first; this is true when an accommodating style is employed as well. When a compromising style is used, the result is usually not a new solution, but half what one side initially wanted and half of what the other side wanted. A negotiated settlement, in contrast, is often something new, possibly something that neither side had envisioned when the process of negotiation began.

At first, the difference between compromising and negotiating or bargaining may not be clear. When making a compromise, the two sides both agree to give up something that each had wanted; each side gets half the loaf. The outcome of bargaining or negotiating, however, could result in one side getting the whole loaf and the other side getting something else in compensation. Or negotiating could result in one side getting all of the crust of the loaf and the other side getting all the interior bread for sandwiches. By compromising, or simply splitting the loaf, one side gets only half the crust wanted and the other side, only half the interior bread. Compromising is a process for distributing resources or benefits that are seen as fixed or limited. Negotiating, on the other hand, is more a process of finding new solutions, intended to find new or creative answers to the problems that divide the contending parties.

▶ ### Conditions for Negotiation

Some situations lend themselves better to a negotiation approach than others. We have already noted that certain factors, such as the relationship between the parties involved, determine the likely conflict-management style adopted by the people involved.

Two conditions are particularly important when deciding whether negotiation is an appropriate strategy: (1) when both sides need to cooperate for best results; and (2) when both sides have some power of the other. Let's look at these two conditions in a little more detail.

Cooperation.   Negotiations seem to work best when both sides perceive some kind of interdependence with each other. A recurring type of conflict reported in businesses is that between sales and manufacturing. Conflict between these two areas often results from production feeling that the salespeople make unrealistic promises in order to obtain customers and orders. Salespeople, on the other hand, feel that production people tend to be unreasonable and inflexible in meeting schedules that salespeople believe is necessary to beat the competition. These two departments obviously must depend upon each other, however. Without sales, the manufactured goods sit in the warehouse; without manufacturing, the salespeople have no product. Such interdependence suggests that negotiations between these two groups is probably a good strategy for dealing with this kind of conflict.

Of course, interdependence is often likely when the contending parties come from within the same organizations, but interdependence also is present in many conflicts between different organizations. Interdependence characterizes the relationship between service providers and clients of a service such as health care, for example. Each group needs the other. If there is some conflict concerning the schedule or manner of care-giving, representatives of the two groups could be convened to negotiate these issues. Customer complaints can be handled this way as well. A type of interdependence results from the hope the business has for repeat business or for good recommendations. There is motivation, then, to work out an amicable settlement through negotiation.

Conflict arises when two parties perceive they have incompatible interests. As a strategy for dealing with such conflict, negotiation requires that the parties also have some important interests in common.

Power.   In order for negotiation to be a viable strategy and to have a chance of working, each side must have some power relative to the other. If one side has all the power in a situation, then that side can simply dictate the solution; the other side must have some access to leverage or control over some resources to prevent such an outcome. It is therefore important to be clear about the kinds of power available in most organizational contexts.

The early classical management theories, like the ones discussed in Chapter 2, assumed that the power always lay with the management. Theories of bureaucracy assumed that the position of one in a hierarchy conferred the necessary power on the person occupying that position. The history of labor-management relations in the United States, however, made it clear that power was not unilateral within business or other bureaucratic organizations. In other words, there are different kinds of power within organizations, which make negotiation possible, even between superiors and subordinates.

Because the notion of power is so important in understanding the conditions in which negotiations take place, we will discuss the types of power at this point.

The influential set of categories developed by R. P. French and B. Raven highlights the fact that people may have power that at first may be overlooked by a simple perusal of an organization chart.[3] First, there is coercive power, such as the police have to enforce compliance with community laws. Second, there is legitimate power, which derives from one's position in a hierarchy. A supervisor can direct a subordinate to perform some job-related task. Third, there is reward power, based on the ability of one person to buy the compliance of another. Reward power is based upon one's access to or control over resources such as information; it is the same as remunerative power. As a result, people, such as salespeople, who have access to information from outside an organization may have a certain power within that organization. A fourth type of power, termed *expert power*, is based upon some person's expertise, an ability to do something that another person cannot do. The mechanic who knows how to fix your car has some power over you, in other words. The scientists who work for a research and development firm have more power over their employers than less technical workers in the firm have. The fifth kind of power is referent power, or attraction power. If you wish to be identified with another person, if their acceptance is very important to you, then that person has referent or attraction power over you. People who are well liked and attractive therefore have some power, regardless of their location in a hierarchy.

The types of power can be summed up as follows:

- Coercive power, or the use of force.
- Legitimate power, or the use of authority.
- Reward power, or the use of payments of some kind.
- Expert power, or the use of technical skill or knowledge.
- Referent power, or the use of personal attraction or group norms.

Diversity in the Workplace

The Components of Power in Different Cultures

The components of power, as presented in the familiar Raven and French scheme presented in this chapter, may vary from culture to culture. In some cultures, one's power is partly determined by perceptions of connections with other important or high-status people, such as marriage or family relationships with such people.[4]

People in Eastern, Confucian cultures tend to associate age or seniority with power. Traditionally, African cultures tended to accord power to age, as well, although this tendency has been weakened by the association of youth with so-called modern education and technical expertise.

One of the authors, while observing an election campaign in the East African nation of Kenya, noted an instance of the conflict between old and new definitions of power. One candidate for a parliamentary seat was a venerable politician from pre-independence days, who criticized his opponents as unripe or green youths, who thought all they needed were *madigrii* (Swahili for college degrees). The younger opponents, on the other hand, criticized the older candidate as out of touch with the modern needs of Kenya. In a different constituency, one candidate appeared at meetings wearing his cap and gown to emphasize his educational qualifications.

The upshot of this discussion is that bosses or executives may have one type of power, legitimate or reward power, but subordinates may have other kinds, such as expert power or referent power.

Highlights of Conditions for Negotiation.   In short, negotiation depends upon the two parties recognizing that each has some power in relationship to the other. That power is not necessarily based upon one's obvious position such as boss, or supervisor, or director. The other person may have some kind of power that allows for the give-and-take leading to successful negotiation and bargaining.

The conditions for negotiation, therefore, remind us that there is a past and a future for most conflicts. There is a need to consider past and future relationships between the parties in the conflict, as these relationships can indicate the conditions of interdependence and power sharing necessary for a viable negotiation climate.

Problems in Negotiation

In order to make negotiating work, you should be aware of typical problems that could derail the process. This section is intended to alert you to such potential problems.

Emphasis on Winning.   In their influential book on negotiation, Fisher and Ury refer to this orientation as "positional bargaining," in which one or both sides are committed to a particular position. Why is this a problem? First, they maintain, "When negotiators bargain over positions, they tend to lock themselves into those positions." The more people defend a position, the more committed they feel; egos become identified with holding that ground. Second, as more attention is paid to position, less attention is given to the underlying needs or concerns of the parties, their true interests. Arguing over positions becomes a contest of wills, which can damage the ongoing relationship between the people involved.[5] As a result, an emphasis on winning can often lead to decisions that are less than satisfactory for all concerned.

Refusal to Negotiate.   One party may simply refuse to participate in negotiation. They may believe that they have all the cards or sufficient power to force through the kind of solution that they desire.

In many labor-management relations, there is a legally mandated "duty to bargain." This mandate is based on the National Labor Relations Act, which grew out of the Wagner Act of 1935, the Taft-Hartley Act of 1947, and the Landrum-Griffin Act of 1959, among other landmarks. Not only do these acts establish a duty to bargain when labor-management issues are involved, they establish a legal obligation to bargain "in good faith." It has been held at law that a party who enters negotiation with no intention of arriving at an agreement or with the intention of obstructing the process in some way is guilty of bargaining in bad faith. In situations covered by collective bargaining or union-type contracts, therefore, this problem may become a legal matter.

In other kinds of conflicts in which one side refuses to negotiate, such refusal may occur because of a misperception of the real conditions. It may be necessary to make the reluctant party aware of the interdependence or the shared-power conditions referred to in the previous section. Instead of banging your head against a wall, try to explore with the other side the reasons behind their stand.[6]

Should the other side remain adamant in refusing to negotiate, it may be necessary to consider a third-party method of resolution, such as taking the problem to a mediator, arbitration, or even litigation.

Overconfidence in One's Own Judgment.   Overconfidence may lead to the problem of refusing to negotiate. Psychological research has indicated that people usually are overconfident regarding their ability to judge or predict various kinds of outcomes. Negotiators often show too much confidence in their belief that a neutral third party (an arbitrator or judge) will agree wholly with their position. Such overconfidence can cause negotiators to "hang tough" with their positions in the belief that the other side will eventually come around.[7]

Lack of Perspective-Taking.   This problem occurs when people have difficulty putting themselves into the other person's shoes. One of the goals of negotiation is to bring both sides to understand the needs and goals of the other side. Effective negotiation requires the ability to see how the other side sees things. You may recall from the discussion of interpersonal communication that such communication depends upon the ability and willingness of people to take on the role of the other person. One possible tactic when faced with this problem is to try some of the active listening exercises mentioned in Chapter 3. For example, you could try the exercise in which each discussant must first paraphrase what the last speaker said to that speaker's satisfaction before adding to the discussion. Or you could try role-playing in which participants take on the role of others (such as superiors, observers, journalists) and then verbalize the other points of view.

Escalation: Commitment in Public.   Once a public commitment has been made, some people fear the loss of face or status if they change that position. People may see more than one audience for the messages they send during a negotiation process. Internal or institutional politics could affect how negotiators think that they should behave. Peoples' remarks may be directed to some outside audience or constituency rather than to the other negotiators. Remember, as well, that reciprocity is one of the strongest findings of the research about communication conflict episodes. People will usually respond to others' actions in kind, especially if they feel that their esteem or standing is somehow being threatened. Be aware of your own tendencies when negotiating in this regard. Do you find yourself involved in escalation, taking tougher and tougher stands because you are concerned about what others will think of your performance?

Misleading Framing of Alternatives.   One result of a win-lose approach to negotiating is to frame the alternatives in terms of winning and losing. To frame an alternative means to place it a particular context, or to phrase the possibilities in a certain way. A typical kind of problem of framing is the mythical fixed-pie. People assume that there is a definite and finite amount of resources to divide up. What one person gets, another person does not get. One of the keys to successful negotiating is to find ways to avoid framing the alternatives in such an either-or way. Later sections discuss methods to expand alternatives and thereby to expand the size of the pie, or to find additional pies. Some of the problem may stem from the emphasis on competition and sports metaphors, especially in the business world. When the issues or alternatives are framed based on a metaphor from, say, football or baseball, be alert to those things that are excluded from such a metaphor, such as cooperation of the two parties in inventing new ways for both sides to win.

Another framing problem can be wording alternatives in such ways as to seem particularly threatening to one side or the other. If one begins a session by saying, for example, "Well, we are here to discuss the possible discontinuation of your department or organization . . .," the negotiations may already be off track. The people in that department or organization are going to hear everything else in terms of that threat to their continued employment. While one may feel that one ought to be up-front and direct, such an approach can also suggest that a decision has already been made.

Listening Problems.   As explained in Chapter 3, when we speak of listening problems, we are not thinking of hearing problems. Rather, we are concerned with problems of understanding, interpretation, and evaluation. If both sides remain committed to their positions and concentrate on their own messages, then little true listening will occur. As said repeatedly, people listen, and respond, from their own points of view.

Problems of listening can be related to other problems already discussed. If one is playing to another audience or if one is unable to take the perspective of the other side, barriers to effective listening will probably result. One useful solution may be to get negotiators to articulate the other side's interests or needs. Another approach is to bring out into the open the points of view, attitudes, and beliefs that may be interfering with people's listening to each other.

Emotions can be a significant barrier to listening during negotiations. Negotiators need to be aware of emotional responses and to acknowledge them. Trying to ignore the feelings of the other side may only inflame emotions. It may be necessary to allow time for venting emotions. Still, one should avoid reacting in like fashion to other's emotional outbursts, since that could likely exacerbate the communication problems. So-called contentious behavior, such as suddenly appearing stubborn or obdurate, accompanied by emotional expressions, could have some positive results, however. Such behavior lets the other side know where your important interests lie and could force people to face issues they had been avoiding. Usually, however, emotional behavior during negotiations can derail the proceedings by interfering with effective listening on both sides.

Lying and Deception.   We left this problem for last because it can be particularly important in negotiation and bargaining. Therefore the issues related to this problem will be developed a little more fully.

The problem of deception in negotiation derives from a dilemma often felt in negotiating: the dilemma of openness versus giving too much information away. For negotiations to work, both sides need to trust the other side to a certain extent; negotiators have to believe that their counterparts will do what they say they will do. Similarly, you, as a negotiator, need to win the other side's trust by being somewhat open and candid; yet you may fear that if you allow the other side too much knowledge of your actual needs and situation, they will take advantage of you. Some deception may actually be an accepted part of many bargaining processes. Still, too much deception can lead to deterioration of the relationship and, in the long run, unsatisfactory outcomes. Obviously, if you believe that the other side habitually lies and cannot be trusted, there is no point in going forward with negotiation at all.

Deception during negotiation can take several forms. First, people can misrepresent their actual position, such as indicating a lower price than would be acceptable. Second, bluffing is the practice of falsely indicating an intention to take some action, such as threatening something that one does not intend to carry out. Third, one can simply present false data or information, which is close to outright lying. Finally, one could misrepresent one's interests or constituencies: Consider the salesperson who claims that he or she would allow a certain price but that some mysterious "they" would not permit such a thing. A similar tactic involves deception about one's authority to make an agreement; in this instance, after you have made your concessions to the other bargainer, it suddenly appears that he or she must now clear the deal with someone else.

Of course, there may be circumstances when some of these tactics may be seen as legitimate, say, when negotiating with terrorists or kidnappers. The point is that one negotiator feels that an important advantage can be gained over the other party by the use of deception. The intent is to provide the other side with distorted information: to prevent their having the best information regarding alternatives, interests, needs, costs, and so on.

Factors Influencing the Use of Deception.   The research on lying and deception in negotiation has suggested some situations that tend to be particularly associated with these tactics.[8] Attempts to discover personality variables, or personal attributes, that might predict a tendency to use deception or lying have not been very successful. Arguments about one's morals or moral development have tended to be circular: "We know the people who have higher morals, they cheated less—and they cheated less because they have higher morals." There have been attempts, as well, to look for factors such as "Machiavellianism," leading to the labelling of people as having "High Mach" and "Low Mach" scores. Those with a High Mach score were thought to be prone to aggressive and deceptive tactics, and thus more successful in their deceptions.

Factors specific to given situations and the relationships between the parties involved seem to provide better explanations, however, than personality differences. The factors described next have been found to influence the use of deception and lying.

- *The size of the prize.* The more valuable the reward, the more tendency there appears for shady actions. When there is a high level of competitiveness and much stress on winning, there is more temptation to deceive. If the costs for being caught are not great, there is even more such tendency. The operation of big-time athletics is a case in point. The alleged use of performance-enhancing drugs in Olympic and international competition, for example, come to mind as illustrations of these kinds of temptations. Although these athletic cases may not involve negotiations, they indicate the kind of circumstances under which lying and deception may be more likely.

- *The relationship between the parties involved.* Most people consider it more unacceptable to lie to a friend than to a casual acquaintance, or someone else who is not well known. Perceived similarity is part of this equation. It seems somehow more acceptable to be deceptive with people different from oneself, such as, a different sex, ethnicity, national background, or culture. The expected length of relationship is involved as well. If the two parties will have to cooperate and work together in the future, deception is less likely. The power or status dimension in the relationship can be important also. Those in high-power positions show a tendency to bluff and use other deceptive tactics when dealing with people of lower status or power. These findings may be distressing, but they are factors nevertheless.

- *Norms or organizational culture.* Different groups, occupations, or organizations may have different expectations regarding what are considered deceptive practices. Some occupational cultures allow for more bluffing and misrepresentation than others. Again, recall the distinction between the tough-guy, macho culture and the process-oriented culture. In the first, in which individual toughness and winning is valued, one can expect more deceptive tactics in negotiation, and such things may be accepted as part of the game. In the process culture, on the other hand, one can expect more attention to proper form and teamwork and, consequently, less reliance on deceptive tactics.

The consequences of lying and deceptive practices in negotiating and bargaining are usually negative. Again, the research on lying in organizational contexts suggest that liars tend to overestimate the likelihood of their escaping detection.[9] Over the long run, liars suffer losses in their credibility, which leads to a diminution of their power, whether it is seen as expert power or attraction power or both. These consequences are most significant for ongoing, especially work, relationships.

The tendency to overestimate one's ability to get away with it may be explained by cognitive dissonance, when people feel the need to justify to themselves their own deceptive behavior. People explain away their own questionable behavior by claiming that external circumstances forced them to do it. The use of deception and lying in negotiation reduces the likelihood of both parties finding high-quality solutions—ones that meet the needs and interests of all parties involved.

The detail regarding this last problem in negotiation was warranted because of its significance and widespread fear of its use. One may note that the problem of deception, as well as many of the others, can be attributed to an overemphasis on winning and losing. One can begin to deal with many of these problems, then, by changing the view that people take toward conflict and toward negotiations and moving from a competitive to a cooperative point of view.

Highlights of Problems in Negotiation. Typical problems that often make negotiating difficult include an overemphasis on winning, or positional bargaining, in which winning takes precedence over discovering actual needs and interests. Other problems can include one party's outright refusal to negotiate, overconfidence in one's own judgment, and a lack of perspective-taking. Making a public commitment can result in escalation, in which the parties retaliate against one another. A typical win-lose orientation can lead to the perception of the mythical fixed-pie, the belief that what one side gains the other side must lose. There can be problems of listening; emotions are a particular listening barrier. Finally, the use of lying or deception can seriously damage the negotiating process.

The Process of Successful Negotiation

Successful negotiation as a conflict management strategy requires that two sides feel the need to cooperate and that both sides perceive that each has some power in relationship to the other. Effective negotiations are conducted as a process of mutual problem solving rather than competition. Negotiation requires skill in communication, especially skills in perspective-taking, listening, and the framing of alternatives.

Effective negotiation outcomes are integrative solutions, or solutions that integrate the needs and interests of all sides. Such integrative solutions tend to be more durable because each side feels some ownership in the solution. Such agreements should have the effect of improving, or at least not harming, the relationships among the various parties. Good solutions, then, are those that are lasting and seen as satisfactory by most people involved and by the community at large.

Achieving good outcomes from negotiations involves being aware of the potential pitfalls or problems of negotiation, as outlined in the preceding section. Obviously, the major way to avoid such pitfalls is to avoid the win-lose, fixed-pie orientation as much as possible. The approach favored by most negotiation experts is to make the negotiation process into a problem-solving process. To do so, people must begin with an analysis of the problem at the root of the conflict.

Finding the Real Problems.   Positional bargaining occurs when two sides successively take different positions until either a stalemate or a compromise comes about. For example, the union demands a 5% increase in wages plus a 90% con-

▶ *Successful negotiations result in mutual satisfaction.*

▶ *Ineffective negotiations can escalate into open conflict.*

tribution to group health insurance; management offers a 2% increase and no change in the health insurance package. The two sides make counteroffers until an agreement is reached, probably somewhere in the middle, or a strike is called.

The Harvard Negotiation Project, in contrast, favors a focus on "interests" rather than "positions." Instead of beginning with positions (5% increase versus a 2% increase), negotiators should begin by exploring what the real interests of the two sides are. In a later work, Ury defined interests as "needs, desires, concerns, fears—the things one cares about or wants. They underlie people's positions—the tangible items they *say* they want."[10] One of the major interests of the union may be to avoid giving the impression of selling out their constituents, for example. Increased competition from a new producer of the same product may be behind management's real interests. Negotiators should try to find ways to meet the real needs, or interests, of the two sides while coming up with a wage and benefits package that takes those interests into account. Instead of compromising in the middle on the two positions, it may work out that the health insurance contribution is much more important to workers than the wage increase because of the fear of spiraling health costs. A change in work rules or vacations may also be in the interest of workers, allowing for more give on the wage issue. Merely trading position statements might not allow the negotiators to get at these other potential solutions; in other words, by not discovering the real problems, they don't discover the real solutions.

Blake and Mouton suggest a process that they call the Interface Conflict Model, which focuses on examining real interests while getting away from concentrating on "who's right and who's wrong."[11] As the name of the model suggests, these researchers are especially concerned with intergroup conflicts, at the interface between the functioning of one group and another.

Often attempts to resolve such interface conflicts are ineffective, Blake and Mouton believe, for many of the same reasons that have been discussed already. In sum, there is a pride in membership in one's own group, which makes it difficult to see the problem from the other group's point of view, that is, lack of perspective taking. Second, group solidarity creates a feeling of us versus them, leading to a win-lose orientation. The representative of the group, sent to negotiate with the other group, risks being seen as either a hero or a traitor, making it difficult for the representative to make any concessions at all, for then he or she will be seen as a traitor by other group members.

The interface model calls for a so-called critical mass of people from each group, which is defined as all those who are needed to commit their whole group to any agreement. Also needed is the support of the highest level of administration and the presence of neutral observers to facilitate the discussions.

First, the groups of representatives, meeting separately, develop solutions for the problems that have been occurring between the operations of the two groups. Then the two groups go through the same exercise in a joint meeting. In the third step, the groups meet separately to describe the actual relationship between the two work groups and then do the same in a second joint meeting to work out a consolidated description of their interface. The purpose of these four exercises is to break away from stereotyped images the two sides may have maintained in the past and, instead, to look at their common interest in solving organizational problems. The two groups then jointly develop a plan for implementing changes in the relationship to bring about the solutions suggested in the earlier meetings. The last step is to plan followup joint meetings to monitor the success of their plans for change.

The key to the Interface Conflict Model is to get the two sides away from their everyday environments. They then look at the nature of the problems they are experiencing and jointly come up with solutions. This model is a specific blueprint for applying the problem-solution format.

For example, there was a problem meshing the work of maintenance staff, on one side, with production workers, on the other, in a manufacturing facility. One of the interests that was not being met, from the point of view of maintenance people, was their right to respect from the other workers. The perceived lack of respect, therefore, was underlying the real problem in this case. Until that interest was brought out into the open, there was little progress in the negotiations between the two sides to develop better methods for working together.

Effective negotiation begins with an effort to understand the actual needs of the other side in order to discover the real problem. Also, finding and stressing the interests that both sides have in common is important. In a case of intergroup conflict, within the same organization, presumably there are plenty of common interests based on both sides' need for the larger organization to be successful.

Finding Creative Solutions.   A second defect with positional bargaining is that the two sides are already locked into their proposed solutions for the problem. An element in successful negotiations is to get away from preconceived solutions or position and to try to generate as many new solutions or alternatives as possible. The need is to invent new solutions. The obstacle in the way of inventing new solutions is perhaps our way of envisioning the bargaining process. We tend to stick with the first workable solution that comes along; satisficing, in other words. We also may tend to narrow the range of options in order to avoid the confusion of having to deal with too many alternatives. In addition, people assume that the parameters with which they started, before analyzing each sides real interests, remain fixed for all time.

If the two sides arguing over the loaf of bread never find out that one needs the crust (for croutons) and the other the inside (for finger sandwiches), they will not think of the solution of separating the crust from the rest of the bread; instead, they will probably end up splitting the loaf in the middle, giving each side half of what it wanted. Such results are more likely if the two sides stick to a competitive approach—us versus them—unwilling to investigate the real needs of the other.

Some ways to invent creative solutions include the techniques that follow.

- *Expand the pie.* It may be possible to come up with more resources than at first thought possible. Investigate why the pie seems to be fixed. Are there ways to acquire new resources through new fund-raising techniques, applying for grants from outside agencies, foundations, or governmental bodies, or by finding new markets? The pie may appear to be fixed because someone has made a budget based on certain projections and figures. Keep in mind that budgets can take on a life of their own.

- *Replace the pie with cake or other commodities.* Perhaps the interests of one side can be met by some type of compensation not immediately related to the resources in dispute. This technique is based on finding some nonspecific compensation for one side's giving up part of the original pie. In sports, one often hears of deals based on a player or players to be named later. The other side, in other words, may be satisfied with some kind of benefit not originally part of the discussion. It may be possible to reduce the costs that one side perceives in giving up something if they can be compensated for such costs in some other way.

Both of these techniques attempt to avoid the framing problem of the mythical fixed-pie.

- *Try "logrolling."* In some cases, there are several points in dispute between the two sides in a negotiation. In fact, often the negotiators are looking at a complex mix of needs and positions. An analysis of the priorities of the two sides may indicate that the two sides do not value these different points in the same way. International diplomacy offers many such cases because of the often-complicated nature of international disputes. When President Bush was trying to appeal to Arab negotiators in the Middle East by holding up some aid for housing to the State of Israel, for example, he attempted to get the United Nations to repeal a resolution that equated Zionism with racism as compensation for Israel in this matter. The point of logrolling, then, is to suggest that we will give up this if you give up that, and so on. Note that such an approach does require a situation in which there are several competing demands and needs.[12]

● *Try joint brainstorming.* Recall the techniques for brainstorming suggested in Chapter 9 for dealing with small group communication. The intention of brainstorming is to come up with as many ideas as possible as quickly as possible. No evaluation of these ideas is to be allowed until the group feels that it has exhausted the possibilities.

Fisher and Ury suggest a specific style of brainstorming for conflict management[13]: Their approach requires dividing the process into three parts: preparation, active brainstorming, and aftermath. For preparation, they recommend that few participants be selected from each side, where there are several people on each side. Change the environment; take the group out of the setting in which an impasse may have occurred. Select a facilitator with some experience with brainstorming methods.

For active brainstorming, they recommend that the participants be seated side by side to emphasize the cooperative nature of the exercise. Remind participants that no criticism is to be permitted of any ideas suggested during the brainstorming. Each idea should be recorded on a chalkboard or sheet of paper in full view of all participants. After the completion of the active brainstorming, the group should "star" the most promising ideas and begin to work on those proposals. At the end, they should have an improved list of alternatives to take back into the negotiation setting.

▶ *Brainstorming is an effective method for creating new solutions to problems.*

• *Try "bridging."* Bridging implies coming up with new solutions that are intended to meet the interests of both sides. The intention is to dovetail the different kinds of preferences that both sides may have. For instance, one side may be interested in the short-run solution to the immediate problem, whereas the other side is concerned about setting a precedent for future cases. If there is a way to stipulate that the solution to this problem is to be a one-time expedient and not to be considered a precedent for future decisions, both sides may find their interests met. One side may be interested in security rather than immediate gain. In that case, one side may accept less in profit or reward in return for guarantees of security. The union may accept a lower wage settlement, for example, if there are guarantees of job protection, for instance.

• *Try the "other experts approach."* Negotiators try to look at the problem before them through the eyes of different specialists. How would an economist, a minister, a teacher, a parent, or a law enforcement official look at the problem of high school students congregating at a local mall after school hours? The different points of view may suggest new or alternate solutions that might not immediately occur to the store owners and school administrators who may have been originally negotiating this case.

The second step in effective negotiations, therefore, is for the two sides to work together to come up with creative or new solutions. The hope is to discover solutions that succeed in meeting the real needs of both parties.

Getting Agreement for the Solution.   Once a solution has been selected by the two sides, the need is to implement the solution. Both sides must agree that they will carry out the provisions of the plan. Remember that one of the steps in the Interface Conflict Model of Blake and Mouton was planning for subsequent meetings to check on progress in implementing agreed-upon changes. It is a good idea to develop some mechanism for jointly monitoring the solutions that have been worked out.

The last stages of negotiation, therefore, often involve negotiating the standards or the criteria to be used to determine that both sides have upheld their end of the bargain. Measurable and observable standards are needed that can be applied by anyone, including fair market value as printed, and replacement value.

In addition, the negotiators need to develop fair procedures for implementing the solutions. The authors always liked the friend who settled disputes over who gets the biggest piece of cake among her children in the following way: One child cuts the slices, and the other chooses which slice he wants. Needless to say, the slicer is very careful to make the pieces as equal as possible.

A negotiator should approach the discussion of determining standards for implementing agreements exactly as the solution was itself arrived at, as mutual problem solving. Ask the other side for recommendations of standards or criteria or procedures for carrying out the solution. Avoid the trap of "Don't you trust us?". Remember that the goal is to come up with fair and wise solutions that can be recognized as such. Someone other than the original negotiators may eventually be involved in overseeing or implementing part of the solution; therefore, procedures that can be explained and justified in a rational manner, such as market value, prevailing standards, and so on, to a potential third party should be developed.

Successful negotiations, then, result from approaching the conflict as an opportunity for joint problem solving. Both sides should see themselves working together to solve a problem, rather than against each other. Such negotiations require that there be need for cooperation and that there be mutual power sharing between the parties involved in the conflict.

▶ **Highlights of Negotiation**

Successful negotiations require that both sides have some need to cooperate and that both sides have some power in relationship to the other. Recall that there are several kinds of power beyond obvious authority or position in a hierarchy.

Typical problems affecting the negotiation process include an emphasis on the win-lose orientation, a refusal by one side to negotiate, overconfidence in one's own judgment (the belief that objective outsiders will agree with your position), a lack of ability in taking the perspective of the other side (seeing how they might see the problem), escalation with public commitment, and framing misleading alternatives (such as the mythical fixed-pie, problems of listening, and the use of lying and deception). Regarding the last problem, the use of deceptive tactics depends upon factors such as the size of the prize involved, the relationship between the parties (especially whether or not the two parties will have to work together in the future), and the norms of the organizational culture.

Successful negotiation involves three steps. The first step is to concentrate on discovering the real problem that separates the two sides and articulating the important interests of each side. The second step is to develop new alternative solutions. An important key is the ability to find creative solutions that serve the interests of both parties, that is, win-win solutions. Possible tactics for finding such solutions include expanding the pie, replacing the pie with cake (satisfying one side with some reward other than the one being contested), logrolling, joint brainstorming, bridging the differences, or using the other-experts approach. The final step is to work out systems for monitoring and ensuring fair implementation of the solution.

◀▶ **MEDIATION**

Sometimes the conditions for successful negotiation are not present. An impasse is reached, and it appears there is no immediate prospect for a settlement. At such a point, the parties in the conflict may decide to submit their dispute to a third party. In some cases, this third party, a judge or an arbitrator, may be given the

▶ *Many people need to seek the help of mediators.*

power to come up with a solution on his or her own. In other cases, the third party is called in to help the two parties arrive at their own solution; such a third party is a mediator. Managers, administrators, or coworkers may often find themselves thrust into this role of mediator, dealing with intragroup or intergroup conflict.

Mediation can be defined as "the process by which the participants, together with the assistance of a neutral person or persons, systematically isolate disputed issues in order to develop options, consider alternatives, and reach a consensual settlement that will accommodate their needs."[14] Mediation is an "extension and elaboration" of the negotiation process with the intervention of "an acceptable, impartial, and neutral third party" to help complete the negotiations. Mediation, therefore, logically follows negotiation when the negotiations do not result in satisfactory solutions.[15] In other words, "Mediation is essentially negotiation that includes a third party who is knowledgeable in effective negotiation procedures . . ."[16]

Conditions for Mediation

Positive Conditions. These definitions of mediation suggest the conditions that must be present for mediation to be an effective strategy for conflict management.

Problem-Solution

> ### *Availability of Mediation Services*
>
> While there may be conditions under which mediation is not the best strategy, it has been growing in popularity as an informal and relatively inexpensive manner for handling conflicts. Since the Federal Mediation and Conciliation Service (FMCS) was established in 1947 to help resolve labor and industry disputes, other agencies have been formed to enhance mediation as a conflict strategy. In 1964, the Community Relations Service of the Department of Justice was established by the Civil Rights Act of that year to aid in settling interracial and similar community problems. The American Arbitration Association operates to further the use of mediation for disputes at all levels, as well as a professional society: the Society of Professionals in Dispute Resolution (SPIDR). These associations can help individuals or organizations find competent mediators. The Dispute Resolution Act of 1980 was intended to have the Department of Justice administer alternative conflict resolution programs in order to help reduce the overloading of the American courts. More recently, conservation and environmental groups have been involved in forming organizations to help mediate disputes involving pollution or environmental problems.

First, the parties to the conflict should recognize that they maintain control and authority in the process. The outcome is still to be a solution mutually agreed upon by the two sides. The mediator does not impose his or her own solution; that would be the function of an arbitrator.

Second, the mediator selected should be acceptable to both sides: that is, someone with the requisite ethos to be seen as a potential helper in this situation. In addition, the mediator is seen as impartial, which means that the mediator lacks a preference regarding the outcome or solution. Neutrality, the other attribute of the mediator, refers to the mediator's behaviors during the sessions with the parties. Also, the mediator should have experience or understanding of the negotiation process and be concerned with a fair process rather than a particular outcome.

Third, the goal of mediation is to help develop options and to explore alternatives. This process involves the isolation of the real issues and interests in the dispute. The process is probably short term and will be conducted more informally than a formal court or adjudication procedure. Presumably, the two parties have already been trying to reach an outcome in prior negotiations but have not succeeded.

In the event of an impasse in attempts to resolve the conflict, mediation is probably a good idea when both sides want to settle the matter fairly quickly and without the cost in time and money of taking the matter to litigation. If the parties are to have a continuing, cooperative relationship, as the discussion of negotiation showed, the informal process of mediation is preferable to arbitration or litigation.

In short, then, positive conditions for entering mediation include the recognition by both parties of the purposes and advantages of mediation, and the availability of a mediator with the requisite expertise, lack of bias, neutrality, and acceptability. It can be a good idea when both sides prefer a fairly quick and informal resolution and will continue to work together in the future.

Negative Conditions.   On the other hand, there are conditions that argue against the use of mediation in the resolution of the impasse. It may be desirable to lay down a precedent on the case at hand. Upper-level administration may be called upon to arbitrate a decision in order to establish that precedent for future cases; or there may be cases that require a quick resolution because of outside demands or conditions. In such situations, an administrator or judge may be called in to make a quick and definite decision. Or there may be times when one or both parties do not wish to go to mediation. Perhaps one side does not feel that the available mediators meet the criteria of impartiality, neutrality, or skill in negotiations. There may also be legal ramifications to the case that could result in later litigation or jeopardy for the organization or potential mediators. Universities, for example, have faced such dilemmas in attempting to deal with allegations of sexual harassment or misconduct. Such legal issues should be understood prior to the initiation of mediation procedures.

Many communities have groups or individuals that may be available to assist an organization that wishes to try mediation. An organization could decide to seek the services of an expert mediator (that is, a consultant from outside the organization), or a peer mediator (that is, one from inside the organization). If the decision is to use internal mediators, outside organizations, such as those listed in the Problem-Solution Box, may be available to help with information or training materials.

The Process of Mediation

As noted earlier, there are professional mediators and other professionals skilled in the mediation process. It is not our intention to provide the kind of detailed instruction that would give you the skill of one of these experienced professionals. It may be useful for you to be aware that such professionals exist and may be available. It is our assumption that in a business or professional setting, you may need to apply some of the informal communication techniques of the mediator, and that is what we hope to provide here.

There are several aspects involved in conducting a process of mediation: the roles of the mediator; planning for the mediation; and conducting sessions.

Roles of the Mediator.   The mediator takes on several roles in attempting to bring both parties to agree to a fair settlement. First, the mediator is there to open channels of communication. Presumably, the two sides have reached a point at which they are no longer listening to each other. The mediator, therefore, needs to reestablish listening between the two sides. Such a function may involve ensuring that all parties accept the legitimacy of each other and the rights of all to their own points of view.

The mediator functions, second, as a process expert. The mediator understands a set procedure that has been used in other cases to help two sides negotiate a settlement.

Third, the mediator should function as an educator or trainer, in that it is his or her objective to educate the two parties so that they will be able to resolve their own disputes in the future.

▶ *A room set up for mediation sessions.*

Planning.   In preparing for mediation, one should take the following points into consideration.

1. *Analyze the setting.* Neutral sites are usually preferable for sessions, rather than the turf of either party or on the grounds of the larger organization to which both groups might belong. The obvious advantages to a neutral site are that distractions can be controlled or kept to a minimum, and participants will have more control over their time and use of space. When people remain at their job sites, it is too easy for coworkers, secretaries, and others to interrupt. Disadvantages could be that there may not be ready access to information or other parties that might be needed. Of course, finding a neutral site may be too time-consuming or costly, as well.

The physical arrangement is an important element of the setting for the sessions. Some mediators prefer simply to use chairs without tables, perhaps with the chairs arranged in a circle. Recall that in brainstorming, participants should be seated side by side rather than facing one another. There may be disadvantages to such arrangements, however. The table space may be useful in providing reticent participants with the feeling of some control over space; and tables may provide psychological barriers to prevent escalation. Many mediators prefer a roundtable because it does not clearly set one side against another, while allowing for working space and territorial control.[17]

Another important consideration regarding the setting is the provision for additional space for caucuses and group meetings. One technique often used in mediation is for the mediator to meet separately with the two sides in order to allow for discussion of items that either side may wish to conduct outside the view of the other. It is a good idea, therefore, to have planned for some additional rooms to which the parties can go for such caucuses, without having to send away the other side. One may also consider the need for extra space for eating or relaxing away from the conference room itself.

2. *An opening session should be carefully planned.* At the beginning of the mediation process, the mediator makes an opening presentation and sets forth some of the plans and ground rules for conducting the mediation. Such an opening presentation should begin with an explanation of what mediation is and how the mediator sees his or her role. The mediator should explain that the process is voluntary and that any decision will be mutually agreed upon by the participants, rather than imposed by the mediator. In other words, all should understand that the authority and responsibility for settling the conflict still rest with the parties themselves.

In addition to planning the opening of a presentation, the mediator will probably work out in advance details such as speaking order and similar rules. The mediator may even want to explain how disagreements over information will be handled, the possible use of witnesses or other observers, the use of private meetings or caucuses, and the like. There also may be discussion concerning the tone of the meetings: that is, the emphasis on cooperative behavior and the discouragement of personal attacks or interruptions. The mediator may also wish to set forth some agenda for the meeting or meetings, if there are to be several sessions.

Conducting Sessions.   Once the sides have agreed to mediation and the mediator has prepared for the first meeting, the process can go forward. The first meeting begins with the mediator welcoming the parties and arranging the seating. Informal greetings or offers of coffee, tea, or the like are in order at this time. The ideal is to present a feeling of comfort and some informality in which all present can work together for mutual benefit.

The mediator should then give the prepared opening presentation. The intention in the early stages is to establish an atmosphere of trust and cooperation. The mediator may wish to explain the difference between positional bargaining and integrative negotiation that was developed in the previous section.

A useful first step in the mediation process is to get each party to begin to articulate their own interests and those of the other side. Following the completion of the opening statement, the mediator may ask each person in turn to explain what he or she hopes to achieve as a result of participating in the mediation. During this period, it may be useful to have each person articulate, as well, an understanding of how the mediation will be conducted in order to clarify related problems or questions.

The next step in the process is to arrive at an understanding of the real needs or interests of each side. The mediator must grasp the nature of the interests of the two sides. One side, for example, may be concerned about substantive conditions (such as control over money, time, and resources) whereas the other side may be mainly concerning about following proper procedure or psychological needs (such as emotional, expressive needs, respect, and the like.)[18] The earlier discussion of negotiation alerted you to the possibility of different kinds of needs and interests on the two sides. To be successful in negotiating, avoid believing in the mythical fixed pie.

During this early stage in the process, then, the mediator should focus on long-term interests rather than specific positions. The mediator should discourage either party's making speeches advocating a particular position at this time. In other words, the mediator should lead the participants through the steps of the negotiation process outlined earlier: (1) Find the real problem; (2) find creative solutions; and (3) find fair ways to implement the solution. As in the negotiation process, the mediator should try to keep the parties on track by insisting that they follow the steps in order: First analyze the problem, then create alternative solutions, and so on. Note that the Interface Conflict Model or the brainstorming techniques can be useful for facilitating these steps.

Occasionally, the mediator will want to caucus with the two sides individually. A caucus is a meeting between the mediator and one side without the presence of the other side. Normally, to maintain impartiality, the mediator will want to caucus with both sides whenever any caucuses are conducted. Caucuses may allow one side to explore alternatives or ideas that they may be reluctant to present in front of the other side. They might be afraid that the other side would perceive them as weak or backing down if they made certain suggestions in open session. That is, they may fear suggesting some concession to the other side without talking it out with the mediator first. In front of the mediator, they may feel freer to air or explore such ideas.

The mediator may initiate the caucus when he or she feels that something needs to be said in private to one or both sides. For example, the mediator may want to tell one party that they are being unrealistic or unfair but fears that to do so in front of the other side would cause that party to lose face or be weakened in the negotiations. Of course, such a caucus also protects the neutrality of the mediator if he or she is not seen as reprimanding one side or the other. The caucus then allows for the mediator to facilitate communication by serving in a role that is probably unavailable to either of the interested parties.

During the open sessions themselves, the mediator should play the role of the active listener, using techniques such as those described in Chapter 3. The mediator should attempt to ask for clarification and explanation when claims are made. "When you say that these people do not provide you with enough information on clients, could you give some examples of where that has been a problem?" In other words, the mediator asks for details, examples, illustrations, in order to clarify the meaning of various claims.

Occasionally, the mediator should paraphrase and summarize what the participants have said or agreed to at a certain point. If there is difficulty getting either side to explore a particular issue, the mediator may have to pose some open-ended questions to get things going, such as, "What do you see as the background to this current situation?" or "What would you see as a fair distribution of workload?"

At some point, the mediator will wish to begin recording on paper or chalkboard the points made by the two sides. For example, such a list could include the interests or needs that the two sides have in common, to remind them of the interest both have in coming to a workable solution. When the session comes to the point of inventing options and working on a plan of action, of course, the mediator should begin to get these things down on paper. One approach to developing solutions, as suggested both by Blake and Mouton in their Interface Conflict Model and by Fisher and Ury, is the single document technique. Both sides are to write a joint draft of the agreements and solutions that they have arrived at, at a given point. The idea is to emphasize the working together on a joint project in writing such a draft.

Highlights of Mediation

The mediation process should be seen as a continuation of the negotiation process but with the addition of a third party to help direct and facilitate the negotiations. The mediator, therefore, should be familiar with the techniques of successful negotiation, especially problem solving and active listening.

Conditions for mediation include the following:

- The parties maintain their control and authority.
- The mediator is acceptable to both sides.
- The goal is to develop options.

There may be conditions present that argue against the use of mediation, such as the need to establish a precedent; the need for a quick decision; and the need to maintain legal standing or to avoid legal jeopardy.

The process of mediation generally involves an understanding of the following areas:

- The roles of the mediator.
- Planning the setting, location, opening session, and rules of procedure.
- Conducting sessions, including joint sessions and caucuses.

The mediation process, given the presence of the third party, allows for the use of caucuses to explore alternatives and new ideas or even to let off steam. Caucuses allow the mediator to serve as a go-between and sounding-board, roles that are not usually found in the straight negotiation setting. Mediation can therefore be a good strategy when regular negotiation has reached an impasse.

SUMMARY

Systematic methods for dealing with conflicts in business and professional settings include negotiation, bargaining, and mediation. Negotiation and bargaining represent a process that two or more parties voluntarily undertake to work out their differences face to face. For there to be successful negotiations, the parties involved should be interdependent and each should have some power in relationship to the other. Problems interfering with effective negotiations often revolve around a competitive view of negotiations, which leads to a win-lose orientation and the assumption of a fixed-pie. The parties are usually most successful when they approach the negotiation process as joint problem solving.

When the contending parties are unable to work out their differences through negotiation and bargaining, it may be time for third-party intervention. Mediation involves the use of a third party who serves as a facilitator, helping the two sides work out a mutually acceptable solution. The mediator needs to be able to help the two sides work through a problem-solution approach to their conflict, employing effective listening techniques and the principles of good negotiation.

Both processes require an ability to identify the authentic needs and interests of people involved in a conflict and to help them find creative solutions.

EXERCISES

1. Explain the conditions that are conducive to negotiation and to mediation. What kind of conditions could exist that suggest that negotiation or mediation may not be the best strategy? Describe situations you have been in that might have been settled by negotiation or mediation. What would have prevented the use of these methods of conflict management?

2. Why is compromise not always the best way to deal with conflicts? Describe situations in which compromising may result in less than satisfactory outcomes. On the other hand, describe circumstances in which compromise may be a wise solution.

3. What is meant by a fixed-pie, or a zero-sum game? What tactics can be used to get away from these ways of framing conflict situations?

4. Ralph noticed that several women in his computer-programming teams regularly missed the early morning meetings of his team because of problems with child care. It seemed that there was constant turnover in sitters and care centers, meaning that they were always, it seemed, missing time to seek out new care alternatives. Suggest some approaches for resolving this latent conflict.

SELECTED SOURCES FOR FURTHER READING

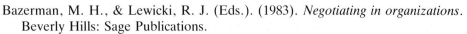

Bazerman, M. H., & Lewicki, R. J. (Eds.). (1983). *Negotiating in organizations.* Beverly Hills: Sage Publications.

Blake, R. R., & Mouton, J. S. (1964). *The managerial grid.* Houston: Gulf Publishing Co.

Blake, R. R., & Mouton, J. S. (1984). *Solving costly organizational conflict.* San Francisco: Jossey-Bass.

Blake, R. R., Shepard, H. A., & Mouton, J. S. (1964). *Managing intergroup conflict in industry.* Houston: Gulf Publishing Co.

Bok, S. (1968). *Lying: Moral choice in public and private life.* New York: Pantheon.

Deutsch, M. (1973). *The resolution of conflict*. New Haven: Yale University Press.

Etzioni, A. (1961). *A comparative analysis of complex organizations*. New York: The Free Press.

Fisher, R. & Ury, W. (1983). *Getting to yes: Negotiating agreement without giving in*. New York: Penguin Books.

Folberg, J. & Taylor, A. (1984). *Mediation: A comprehensive guide to resolving conflicts without litigation*. San Francisco: Jossey-Bass.

French, R. P., & Raven, B. (1959). The bases of social power, in D. Cartwright, Ed. *Studies in social power* (pp. 150–167). Ann Arbor: Institute for Social Research.

Griffin, T. J., & Daggatt, W. R. (1990). *The global negotiator*. New York: Harper Business.

Moore, C. A. (1986). *The mediation process*. San Francisco: Jossey-Bass.

Rahim, M. A. (Ed.). (1989). *Managing conflict: An interdisciplinary approach*. New York: Praeger.

Ury, W. L., Brett, J. M., & Goldberg, S. B. (1988). *Getting disputes resolved: Designing systems to cut the costs of conflict*. San Francisco: Jossey-Bass.

Zimmerman, M. (1985). *How to do business with the Japanese*. New York: Random House.

►

References

1. Bazerman, M. H., & Lewicki, R. J. (Eds.). (1983). Preface. *Negotiating in organizations* (p. 7). Beverly Hills: Sage Publications.

2. Fisher, R., & Ury, W. (1981). *Getting to yes: Negotiating agreement without giving in* (p. xi). Boston: Houghton Mifflin.

3. French, R. P., & Raven, B. (1959). The bases of social power (pp. 150–167). In D. Cartwright, Ed. *Studies in social power*. Ann Arbor: Institute for Social Research.

4. See L. B. Nadler, M. K. Nadler, & B. J. Broome, (1985). Culture and the management of conflict situations. In W. B. Gudykunst, L. P. Stewart & S. Ting-Toomey, Eds. *Communication, culture, and organizational processes*. Beverly Hills, CA: Sage.

5. Fisher and Ury, pp. 5–8.

6. Fisher and Ury, pp. 113–118.

7. Bazerman, M. H., & Neale, M. A. Heuristics in negotiation. (1983) In M. H. Bazerman & R. J. Lewicki (Eds.). *Negotiating in organizations*. Beverly Hills, CA: Sage, pp. 58–59.

8. For an excellent summary of these points, see R. J. Lewicki, Lying and deception: A behavioral model (pp. 68–90). In M. H. Bazerman & R. J. Lewicki (Eds.). *Negotiating in organizations*. Beverly Hills, CA: Sage. Fisher and Ury also discuss these deceptive practices, and a good general treatment is S. Bok. (1968). *Lying: Moral choice in public and private life*. New York: Pantheon.

9. These findings are supported in the summary by Lewicki (1983).

10. Ury, W. L., Brett J. M., & Goldberg, S. B. (1988). *Getting disputes resolved: Designing systems to cut the costs of conflict*. San Francisco: Jossey-Bass.

11. Blake, R. R., & Mouton, J. S. (1984). *Solving costly organizational conflict*. San Francisco: Jossey-Bass.

12. These first three ideas are further developed by D. G. Pruitt, (1983) Achieving integrative solutions (pp. 35–44). In M. H. Bazerman & R. J. Lewicki (Eds.). *Negotiating in organizations*. Beverly Hills, CA: Sage.

13. Fisher and Ury, pp. 63–65.

14. Folberg, J., & Taylor, A. (1984). *Mediation: A comprehensive guide to resolving conflicts without litigation* (p. 7). San Francisco: Jossey-bass.

15. Moore, C. W. (1986). *The mediation process* (p. 6). San Francisco: Jossey-Bass.

16. Moore, p. 7; see also Ury, Brett, and Goldberg (1988), Mediation is negotiation assisted by a third party, p. 49.

17. See Moore, pp. 113–115.

18. See Moore, p. 37.

  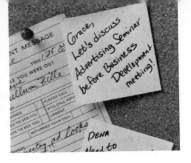

Communication Training
and Speechwriting

●

15
CHAPTER

After studying this chapter, you will be able to:

1. Understand the importance of communication training in organizations.

2. Explain the principles of effective training.

3. Describe useful techniques for communication training, such as role-playing.

4. Understand the nature of speechwriting in organizations.

5. Describe the process of speechwriting.

6. Be aware of the pitfalls of speechwriting, such as ethical problems.

Overview

As the Preface to this text indicates, numerous studies show the need that business and professional people have for various communication skills. Many organizations provide such skill training to their employees. As the authors' own survey discovered, corporations typically plan to provide their own communication training. At the same time, many organizations try to coordinate the public messages they disseminate. Such coordination often involves not only training but also preparation of scripts or at least outlines for public presentations.

This chapter considers these two special applications of business and professional communication in the work place: communication training and speechwriting. Communication training and speechwriting can be directly related. For example, the director of an organization's speakers' bureau may be responsible for both communication training and the writing of speeches. Speechwriters are often involved in training to the extent that they coach their speakers on the delivery of prepared speeches. Communication training will be discussed first, followed by speechwriting.

▶ *Training begins as soon as one enters an organization.*

COMMUNICATION TRAINING

Nature of Communication Training

A major reason for looking at training is its pervasiveness in modern organizations. Corporations are constantly involved in education and training. Rapid developments in technology, refinements in personnel and managerial techniques, and new government regulations are just a few of the reasons for corporate interest in training.

Some of the training is in-house, such as when large organizations with special needs develop their own training departments. In many cases, in-house training is justified by the need to protect trade secrets or specialized operations. Large training departments are costly, however. Costs of personnel and time and of developing special training devices and materials put the cost of corporate training into the billions of dollars. As Chapter 12 mentioned briefly, much of the costly new media technologies are intended for training programs. For example, the cost of developing an interactive computer program can be in the six figures. As a result, many organizations turn to external trainers or consultants.

External consultants can be very specialized; for example, a company called Communispond specializes in training corporate executives in public speaking.[1] Although consultants such as Communispond are specifically in the business of training, other corporations may find themselves involved in providing corporate trainers as a side line. Several large corporations such as Florida Power & Light have been willing to provide educational services and training for other corporations.[2]

In many cases, you will participate in such training as a trainee, rather than as a trainer. In our professional lives, most of us expect to be trainees. We attend seminars to keep up with innovation and development. Some of us need or want to be certified by professional associations; workshops, seminars, and classroom work prepare us to achieve this. When a new product or process is introduced in our work place, employees might attend special meetings or workshops to learn the basics about the new product. New government regulations on sexual harassment or equal employment opportunity may necessitate special training as well.

On the other hand, your professional life will involve many situations that place you in the trainer's role, even though you are not a training professional. As a manager, a coworker, or a subordinate, you will be an informal trainer. When you instruct your superior in how to use a new computer software program, you are involved in training, for example. Although most such training is informal, the principles of effective training apply. The steps that a professional follows to develop a successful training program are the same ones that you use to instruct a subordinate in a new process or to give directions to others.

The next section proceeds to discuss the nature of corporate communication training, including principles and problems of communication training.

Preparation for Training

Training is much like any situation requiring effective communication. Effective communication needs to be ongoing and two-way, allowing for immediate feedback and evaluation. Good training has these same characteristics; moreover, effective training involves careful audience analysis. Communication begins with getting someone's attention: People must be aware of the need for and the opportunities for training before a program can be effectively implemented. Then good planning, involving steps similar to analysis of the audience and occasion, is essential. Preparing for effective training programs also requires setting and communicating worthwhile goals and motivating people to participate and to learn. Each of these preparatory steps will be discussed in turn.

● *Need for awareness of training.* The basic question for the employee is, what training programs are available? In an audit of training for a local utility, one of the authors discovered that many members of a corporation were unaware of ongoing programs of corporate training.[3] Most individuals know only about specific training programs when they are invited to participate in them. Otherwise, they seem to have only limited awareness of the full range of a training department's activities, scope, or objectives. Moreover, they may be unaware of when various programs might be offered in the future or of mechanisms for getting themselves or subordinates involved in future training programs. In addition, many employees may be unaware of how people are selected for the various training programs or even whether there is a system for selection.

In some cases, managers may fail to pass along the training calendar or a list of available programs except when they feel that certain employees need to know about them. The practice is understandable and even defensible, but as a result, the training department will have a low profile among employees. The existence or functions of the training program may not be brought to the attention of employees on a regular basis. The practice may also prevent employees from initiating their own involvement in training. When employees are unaware of the schedule, they will not think of a related training program unless the supervisor initiates the involvement.

A number of steps can be taken to enhance the ability of a training department to perform its mission. Suggestions include a widely circulated calender of training programs for the year. The target audience would have to be informed of all changes and updates in the calendar. In addition, the trainer could use a newsletter or other medium to keep individuals in the field informed regularly about training activities.

• *Planning*. Planning requires an analysis of the potential audience and the situation. In the same way that a speaker analyzes an audience and the occasion to prepare for a presentation, the communication trainer analyzes the potential trainees and the situation. Planning involves asking several questions:

1. *Who?* The primary question refers to which specific individuals should receive the training. Problems can arise if you choose the wrong people or if you try to work with too many people. When the training is essential for performing a person's task, the answer is simple. For example, an executive secretary has developed an office routine that depends on a specific word-processing program. He acquires an assistant who is not familiar with that program, and training is likely to be needed.

If the training is less specific and involves executive development, such as training in management-employee relations or problem solving, then the selection of trainees is not as clear-cut. Those chosen should be likely to benefit from the training, but the selection should avoid the appearance of favoritism. Be aware that exclusion of an employee from training might be seen as discriminatory.

2. *Motivation?* In any training or learning situation, motivation is important. All learning is, in a way, self-learning; consequently, volunteers are likely to be more motivated than people required to attend. In either case, training is effective if the reason for the training is made explicit to the trainees. The emphasis should be on the benefits of the training for both the organization and the individual. If the employee has some sense of reward, then the employee has a vested interest in the task at hand.

3. *Timing?* In most organizations, timing of the training is important. For a busy individual or department, training could conceivably be scheduled for the wrong time. Training may provide long-term development and increase productivity in the future, but it may disrupt a department schedule and decrease productivity in the short term. Supervisors and employees may see training as taking time away from what they consider more important functions. In that sense, there are times when it is best to delay training.

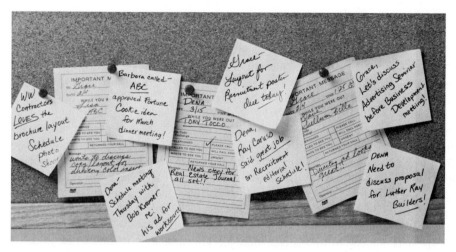

▶ *Training information can easily get lost in the clutter.*

Time of day for the proposed training session is a related consideration. Many people tire as the day proceeds; after lunch, for example. If possible, try to present complex material when trainees are well rested, alert, and attentive.

4. *Facilities and accommodations?* Just as a meeting coordinator or a speaker should consider the setting, the arrangement of the room, lighting, temperature, and so on, so should the trainer consider such factors. The well-fed or tired person for example, may have trouble learning.

5. *Materials?* The trainee should have necessary materials. The trainer should have materials prepared ahead of time and should arrange for reasonable backups. Many things can go wrong with electronic media, for instance; bulbs burn out, slides stick, and computers turn sullen and cranky. In addition, materials, such as films, may be out of date; some films are dated because the information is passe, and others because the actors are dressed in old-fashioned clothes. When giving directions, make sure that all the materials that a subordinate needs are available and current.

• *Communicating goals.* Communicate the objectives of the training program to all members of the organization, including supervisors and management. Everyone needs to be clear about what programs are being planned or are presently available. Besides uncertainty about programs, many employees seem to be unsure of the functions of the training staff.

Supervisors need to know the objectives of training programs and of the need to provide followup or reinforcement of the training back home. Otherwise, local supervisors and managers may not always reinforce the training, partly because they may not think that is one of their functions. The press of time and day-to-day problems can make followup or support of training by field managers difficult. In addition, the role of local managers in reinforcing training may not have been clearly communicated to them. Consequently, supervisors should be encouraged to review the skills or material covered in training periodically with returning trainees.

● *Motivating associates and trainees.* Motivation is an essential step in teaching, and it is therefore necessary to find ways to increase trainees' motivation. Employees need incentives that will make training more attractive and more credible. Other factors can also enhance the attractiveness of training. For example, someone in a remote local office may welcome the opportunity to interact and to learn how things are being done in other locations.

People may feel motivated to learn and to apply new skills, but in the long run there may appear to be no real change. This situation results when trainees are sent back to an unchanged environment in which there is little incentive to enact their newly learned behaviors. Motivation, therefore, must be sustained by followup. Initially, trainers should prepare trainees' supervisors to ensure that learned skills be applied and reinforced regularly. Trainers should also follow the training with reinforcement such as written reminders and periodic review sessions. Such reinforcement should start within about three weeks of the original training.

Conducting Training Sessions

Certain communication techniques are important to provide effective, credible training during the sessions. Trainers should build upon existing skills and know-how—the usual—rather than rushing into new, unknown fields too quickly.

Trainers should make the training both job and situation specific. The trainees need to be able to see immediate and specific application for the new skills in real-life situations. Field observations can be carried out by the training staff to discover ways to bring this kind of specificity to their training. If outside consultants are used, the outside trainers should spend time in the field as well in order to find examples and techniques that the trainees will see as relevant and current. Such direct field observations permit trainers to adapt programs more obviously to organizational environments. A concern for using relevant, current examples will enhance trainers' credibility.

The use of peer tutors also enhances the relevance and specificity of training sessions. Some organizations train and assign peers as mentors to newly hired or transferred employees, as described in the discussion of superior-subordinate communication in Chapter 5. Another technique is to use former trainees from earlier sessions to show how they have applied the training back on their jobs.

As noted in the sections on presentations in Chapter 10, credibility is created by the perception of an audience that the speaker has expertise and has the best interest of the audience in mind. A trainer needs to show this expertise by using current and relevant examples. The reliance on field observations, peer trainers, and former trainees can add to the currency and relevance of sessions.

Diversity in the Workplace

Mentoring as Training in Multicultural Organizations

The emergence of the multicultural corporation is one reason for the rapid development of formal mentoring programs for training in many organizations. The Security Pacific Corporation, for example, with the assistance of outside consultants, has instituted a formal training program that includes a minority officers' network and a mentor-trainer program. Many other firms have also initiated mentoring-training programs for new minority and women associates because of mentoring's advantages in providing coaching, role models, and support within a diverse and unfamiliar environment.

Many interpersonal communication skills can be learned quickly and naturally within a mentoring relationship. As a member of a team with the mentor, the trainee can learn while participating in presentations, negotiating sessions, or interviews. Such training has been found to be especially beneficial for teaching sales and customer-relations skills. The hands-on learning has the relevance and immediacy that provides for realistic feedback and excellent motivation.[4]

The business literature has many articles dealing with mentor programs as training for minorities and women; see, for example, J. A. Wilson and N. S. Elman (1989), Organizational benefits of mentoring. *Academy of Management Journal, 4,* 88–94; C. A. McKeen, R. J. Burke (1989) Mentor relationships in organizations: Issues, strategies and prospects for women. *Journal of Management Development, 8,* 33–42.

Special Training Techniques: Role-Playing

Trainers use a variety of methods, often in combination. Much training can be accomplished through self-paced media such as interactive video. More traditional methods of training include lectures, use of case studies, and a variety of film, video, and slide components. An especially useful training method, mentioned before, is role-playing. As the name implies, in this method, trainees are asked to play various roles and act out behaviors advanced in the training.

Role-playing is useful for sessions dealing with conflict management, group problem solving, interviewing, and negotiation and bargaining. For example, one person could pretend to be a subordinate who is taking a complaint to a role-played supervisor. The role-players could try to act out typical problems that they have seen or heard about. Other trainees could then discuss how best to deal with problems portrayed in the exercise. Role-playing could also be used for training in intercultural communication, especially if trainees or others present have had some intercultural experience to bring to their role enactments. Also, role-playing is often a part of public speaking training in which trainees, while listening to others speaking, role-play a particular audience and give feedback and ask the kind of questions that the speaker could expect from a real-life audience.

There are several advantages to the use of role-playing exercises. First, new or novel situations can be created for the trainees, thereby keeping up interest. Second, role-playing provides for the active participation of people in their learning, which is a proven educational technique. Third, by actively taking the role of another, people should be enabled to develop new kinds of awareness and, thus, new interpersonal skills. Fourth, role-playing can be adapted to specific audiences and problems; trainees develop their own role-playing situations based on actual experiences they have had on the job. Finally, people can analyze a communication problem from another person's viewpoint, which is a key element in facilitating more effective communication.

To set up role-playing exercises, follow some simple steps, as outlined here:

1. *Define the problem.* The problem must be specific and clear. If possible, deal with factual, personal, and real human relations problems. Of course, use dramatic license.

2. *Define the situation.* Background information and other relevant detail should be provided. Participants should receive detailed descriptions of the character and motivation of the roles that they are required to play. You might want to keep some specifics of the situation from your participants, to simulate real-life situations.

3. *Plan the roles or characters.* In role-playing, four or five characters are usually enough. Generally, roles should not be assigned to individuals. Finally, individuals should volunteer.

4. *Prepare the participants.* Participants should be reminded that they are playing roles that need to be interpreted, that is, they have some freedom to enact the role based upon their own experiences and observations. Each participant should interpret the role but avoid creating a tight script.

5. *Analyze and discuss the outcomes.* After the situation is played in front of others, discuss and analyze what happened. Remember that your focus is on the role played and not the participants' acting ability. The analysis should include a discussion of specific roles and the specific problem.

6. *In some cases, the situation could be played again.* A replay could allow participants to use new approaches or apply new insights.

Role-playing, then, is a useful device for getting people involved in a training session. As the individuals act out the roles, they begin to identify with the various parts that they are playing. This aids the participants to empathize with situations and ideas other than their own or to put themselves in another person's shoes. Although time consuming, role-playing adds a sense of identification and commitment not often found in studying real or hypothetical cases.

Interactive Video and Training. Interactive communication devices can be adapted to a variety of training functions. Interactive computer software allows individuals to make choices about what they learn, the order in which they learn, the pace at which they learn, and when and where they learn. When learning a simple process, such as running a machine, the trainee can start at the beginning or in the middle, depending on previous experience, knowledge, and time. The trainee can rewind or review, answer prompts from the software, and so on.

Feedback and Evaluation of Trainees. For communication training, immediate and objective feedback is important. This means allowing the trainee to see the performance as others would see it as soon after the performance as possible. Videotape, therefore, is very useful. The trainee makes a presentation, which is taped. After the presentation and any critique or discussion at the end of the performance, the trainee immediately replays the presentation. If the trainer can view the tape with the speaker to point out strengths and areas that need improvement, learning is enhanced. Taped performances have an impact that written or

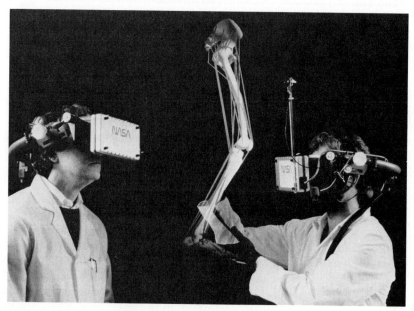

▶ *Equipment used for virtual training.*

Problem-Solution

Virtual Reality

A typical problem in training is the need to make the sessions both realistic and interesting. One recently developed technique uses interactive devices to create so-called virtual reality.

When combined with promising new technologies such as virtual reality, training can be exciting. Virtual reality places the trainee within what seems to be the actual environment but without the risks. Prior to computer-created reality, trainers used models and mockups (such as flight simulators for pilots) or even games (war games for generals and international simulations for political scientists). Limitations such as lack of reality, time, and cost inhibited widespread use of these methods. Computers now allow control of the trainees senses more thoroughly and cheaply. Through goggles, the trainee receives broadcast images and interacts with the simulated environment through a sense of touch conveyed by a pressure-sensitive glove. For example, the airplane pilot trainee can see the cockpit and the runway, sense the "stick" and even feel the plane respond. The trainee can see an object and can touch and manipulate that object while seeing the results.

spoken critiques often lack. Trainees see exactly what others have seen; often, they are surprised to learn that they did better than they thought, so this technique can be helpful in building a feeling of confidence.

Negative feedback should be balanced by positive feedback as much as possible. If, as in most cases, the performance of the trainee is somewhat erratic, the trainer stresses that part of the performance that contains the correct or positive behaviors. Positive reinforcement can be emphasized with videotape. Negative aspects of the performance are usually clearly seen on the tape and can be discussed away from the rest of the group, where it can be less threatening.

Evaluation of Training Programs

Those who receive training may not know how to provide input for planning future training, nor how to provide suggestions or ideas for new training programs. The tendency in large, dispersed organizations to view the general headquarters as being out of touch with the front lines can exacerbate this lack of feedback. Of course, the belief can become a self-fulfilling prophecy: "Well, they won't listen to us in the field, so we won't tell them anything." In this case, even when people at headquarters are eager for feedback from the field, none is forthcoming.

As a result, feedback should be a primary concern for anyone who conducts training. Consider as many types of feedback as possible to assess the process of training as well as the results of the training. Self-reports from trainees immediately after the training session can measure so-called consumer satisfaction. For example, was the training tied to day-to-day tasks? Could it be used on the job? Objective studies of the effect of training over time are also important in assessing effect. These studies could depend upon observations and reports from supervisors or consultants. The important point is that there should be ongoing efforts at obtaining feedback. In a way, the discussion has come full circle from the planning stages for training. Recall that planning should include field observations to determine precisely what kinds of programs are needed. The feedback from one training program can become the field observations for planning the next.

Highlights of Principles for Communication Training

Many corporations and other organizations recognize the need for training and development, especially in various communication skills. Good training follows the same guidelines as effective communication: Know your goals, analyze your audience and the setting, and present your material in ways that are relevant and motivating to that audience. Some specific principles follow:

- Involve local managers and supervisors in active support of training sessions. Clear attempts to reinforce the material learned at a session are important. Without followup and reinforcement by supervisors, training soon wears off.
- Initiate direct, face-to-face communication between training staff and employees in the field, such as regularly planned field visits to determine future needs and to assess past training programs.
- Provide opportunities for employees in the field to participate in the planning of specific training programs and classes.

The following outline represents an example of a plan for a public speaking training workshop. This particular workshop is limited to one day. It assumes that the participants want general principles and tips for improving their presentational skills. This means that all important topics will be covered, but not in depth. Perhaps the audience has done some presentational speaking and the workshop is intended to be a refresher course. The day ends with the preparation, delivery, and critique of a presentation by each trainee.

PUBLIC SPEAKING WORKSHOP

	(One-day format)
8:00–9:00	Registration: Coffee, sweet rolls
8:30–9:00	Introduction. Introductory exercises. Uses of public speaking. Preview and goals of the workshop

Informal Training: Giving Directions

Communication training, as stressed, is formal and structured. Managers and supervisors are trainers in many everyday interactions. Sometimes the training is explicit, as when the manager instructs an employee to use a new process and leads the employee through its steps. At other times, the training is less obvious, such as when the manager or supervisor communicates orders or gives simple directions.

The giving of directions has much in common with the more formal training. Supervisors giving orders or directions should go through the same process that trainers go through to plan a formal training session.

1. Planning must take place. The supervisor needs to consider what should be done, analyze the capabilities and interests of the trainee, and then select the best techniques for giving the direction or order.

2. Motivation is necessary. The supervisor should clarify what is to be done and why. Incentives and rewards are a part of learning. The supervisor should be explicit about what rewards are possible.

3. Communicating the directions should take account of the principles of good verbal and nonverbal communication. Positive nonverbal communication may be essential in creating a positive tone and environment.

4. Feedback and evaluation are essential. Feedback from the trainee is the only way to determine if your communication has been successful. The trainer needs to provide feedback, of course, concerning how well the other person has completed the assigned task or enacted the new skill. Obviously, action and reaction continue as the skill is refined.

5. Reinforcement is necessary. As with formal training, learning becomes routine through reinforcement. That is why we have stressed the importance of reinforcement of new skills, which continue after the training has been completed.

9:00–10:00	The communication process
	Preparing content, including audience analysis
	Determining your specific purpose:
	Informative purposes
	Persuasive purposes
10:00–10:15	Break
10:15–11:00	Organization and outlining
	Patterns for organizing presentations
	Introductions and conclusions
	Internal transitions
11:00–12:00	Principles of delivery
	Verbal delivery
	Nonverbal delivery
	Handling speech apprehension
	Dealing with questions and answers
12:00–1:00	Lunch break
1:00–2:00	Outlining practice presentations
	Discussion of outlines
2:00–2:30	Practice presentations and critiques
2:30–2:45	Break
2:45–4:45	Practice presentations and critiques
4:45–5:00	Summary and wrapup

SPEECHWRITING

Speechwriting can be considered a very specialized form of communication training. Speechwriters produce speeches for individuals or groups who have neither the time nor the experience and training to produce a presentation or speech on their own. In many cases, speechwriting involves coaching the individual speaker to improve delivery or to overcome mild stage fright.

Speechwriting falls into two categories: political speechwriting and corporate speechwriting. Of the two, political speechwriting has received the most attention in the press, and, as a result, we know more about it.

In this country, political speechwriters have toiled, for the most part, anonymously. Most presidents, including Washington and Lincoln, received help in composing their speeches from cabinet members, secretaries, and other staff members. Warren Harding was the first president to employ a full-time speechwriter; most others employed at least one speechwriter. Richard Nixon used at least three. Since then, the speechwriting staffs have grown. Yet, presidents were reluctant to admit that the words the audience heard were not their own.

The anonymity of speechwriters and the reluctance of politicians to admit that they used them brings up the related question of ethics. Is speechwriting ethical? Students are not allowed to purchase speeches (or term papers) and present the speech or paper as their own. Politicians and chief executives, on the other hand,

▶ *Peggy Noonan, speechwriter for Presidents Reagan and Bush.*

do it all the time. If it is not acceptable for a student, should it be acceptable for a politician or a corporate executive to use speechwriters? The issue of ethics will be discussed at more length under the pitfalls of speechwriting.

At any rate, speechwriting and political speechwriters have become an open secret. In part, the realization that the president employs others to write speeches may partly explain the increasing prominence of the White House staff. The public realizes that the presidency is too complex to be run by one individual who writes all his own speeches. During the Nixon Presidency, the names of his speechwriters were known, and they have since published accounts of their work. Since the publication of Peggy Noonan's *What I Saw at the Revolution*,[5] with detailed accounts of her and the staff's involvement in creating President Reagan's speeches, politicians are less reluctant to admit that the words they speak are not their own. Now, all presidents and presidential candidates, and many, if not most, politicians have staff members who compose and polish speeches.

Similarly, organizational executives may be too busy to write all their own presentations. In addition, they also may lack the experience or talent to produce effective presentations. Furthermore, some fear speaking in public and so hire the speechwriter to train and rehearse them in delivery as well as to produce the manuscript itself. Consequently, executives, like politicians, turn to staff members or external consultants to produce their presentations and speeches.

Since you or any member of the staff in your company could potentially be called upon to produce speeches, the study of speechwriting deserves attention here. We could simply suggest that you go back and reread Chapters 10 and 11, since they detail the steps in preparing speeches or presentations. Of course, those chapters do provide information basic for preparing a good presentation, whether for yourself or for someone else. This section adds a discussion of the factors that are particular to the speechwriting situation.

The Special Nature of Speechwriting

Although many organizations produce extensive guides for their executive speech makers and speechwriters, others do not. If you are called upon to write a speech, the first step is to review the principles of good presentations. Then you have to consider the unique aspects of producing a presentation for someone else to deliver. An explanation of this unique aspect falls under three issues: (1) your relationship with the speaker; (2) your role as a speechwriter; and (3) the importance of oral style.

Relationship with the Speaker. If possible, the speaker and speechwriter should have a close working relationship. The writer should know and understand the intended speaker well enough to have a feel for how she thinks about certain issues and how she typically expresses herself. The writer is trying to reproduce that style in the presentation. Also, the speech will probably be a better product, and more reflective of the thinking of the speaker, when the speaker has been involved at various stages in the production of the manuscript itself. The best situation is probably one in which speaker and writer work as a team in producing the speech. Of course, if the speechwriter is lower in the hierarchy than the speaker, this kind of working relationship may not be possible or welcomed.

More important than interaction is the trust of the speaker in the writer. Techniques and strategies involve choices. The speaker has to trust the speech-writer's ability to make choices that will produce effective communication. Even though your day-to-day relationship to the speaker is that of subordinate to superior, the relationship is different as writer to speaker. In this sense, the relationship is more that of a consultant (the speechwriter) to client (the speaker). You, the speechwriter, are providing a needed service; you have the expert power in this case. The speaker, even if he or she is your boss, has to trust your judgment in crafting an effective message.

Roles of a Speechwriter. Often, the role of the speechwriter is simply to take down the ideas of the speaker and add a couple of anecdotes here or a summary and a transition there. Speechwriters, however, can have a significant role in organizational policy-making, if the speaker allows it. This means, first, that the writer often takes what may begin as a vague idea and makes it meaningful by fleshing it out. The CEO sends you a message saying that he has to make a 20-minute acceptance speech and wants to stress three topics. You job is to add substance to the executive's ideas and make them clear and memorable. In so doing, you may be making new company policy on those three topics by the way you phrase the arguments.

Beyond shaping vague policies, the speechwriter can play an even more decisive role in formulating policy. The trusted staff member may have the opportunity to create rather than simply edit the speaker's idea. For example, the writer may know that a specific occasion is coming up: The boss has to speak to the Chicago Council on Foreign Relations in 3 months' time. The writer can proactively research and develop a topic and then suggest it to the boss. In other words, the speechwriter has actually initiated the topic and policy decision. This role is probably played only by very high-level associates of the person in charge, however. Another situation in which a speechwriter may develop new policy is when a coordinator has to develop talks for a speaker's bureau. The coordinator or the communications department may find it necessary to develop policy in working up the talks.

Speechwriters, when functioning in a policy-making or policy-shaping role, will probably find that a major restriction on their creativity is the approval process. As the text is worked out, you find that it must be approved by top management, then by the legal department to ensure there is no danger of liability, by the marketing department to ensure that the speech promotes the products appropriately (or won't hurt sales), by the public relations department, and perhaps by many others. Peggy Noonan and other presidential speechwriters have some fascinating stories about the labyrinthine approval processes, or gauntlets, their speeches had to run through. Once, Ms. Noonan found that the president's daughter was in a position to edit or rewrite presidential speeches, for example.

Importance of Oral Style.   A major difficulty with writing a speech is that we fall into the trap of *writing* it in writing. The written language and the oral language are not the same; the written form of English (or German, or French, or whatever) is derived from the spoken form. It is an abstract form of the oral language. Most of us can tell when someone is reading "writing" instead of talking. The sentence, with a nice clear subject, predicate, and object, is not as sacred in oral language as it appears to be in writing, for example. We speak in phrases more than in the regular sentences of writing.

When trying to write a speech, therefore, you must overcome the tendency to make it sound like writing instead of talking. One simple way to do that is to talk through the ideas into a tape recorder and then play it back; listen to the phrasing and the rhythm, and try to write it that way. Oral language, then, is more informal than writing. You can use more direct references to the audience and to the speaker than would seem appropriate in writing. The sentences are shorter or more like phrases than sentences. Listen to the sounds as you put them down on paper. Read them out loud, again into a tape recorder. How do they sound? Do your words sound conversational, or do they sound like writing?

Humor often comes up as a stylistic question that speechwriters must face. Many speakers believe that they ought to be funny. Writing humor, though, may be a real problem for the speechwriter. For example, the client wants to begin with a joke, but, unfortunately, the speaker knows few jokes that serve the purpose of focusing attention on the topic. What can the speechwriter do if the client insists on using humor? A number of speechwriters offer simple advice about good humor. Criteria for effective use of humor involve a few straightforward tests. Humor, like any other supporting material, should be relevant to the goals of the speech. Also, humor should be in good taste and relatively new (that is, not an old joke) or adapted to new circumstances.[6]

The Process of Speechwriting

Sorting out your relationship with the speaker goes on during and complicates the process of speechwriting. Ideally, you will have nearly unlimited access to the speaker and can thoroughly discuss with him or her the intended ideas. In less than ideal circumstances, you may be able to arrange only one or two conferences, perhaps by E-mail or phone.

At the minimum, the writer should be able to arrange a first conference for roughing out the ideas, and one or two followup conferences as the drafts of the speech are written. After the final draft has been approved, it is good practice, though not always possible, to arrange for rehearsal and final revision sessions. We will look at each of these steps in the process in a little more detail.

First Conference. The first conference should set the main goals and purposes of the message. The speechwriter needs to know what the purpose of the presen-

▶ *The best outcomes result from collaboration between speaker and speechwriter.*

tation is and what specific topics or material should be included. A face-to-face conference is the most useful, but a phone call or an E-mail message will serve in a pinch. Remember that this is an information-gathering interview, so be sure to do your homework in advance. For example, read or listen to any previous speeches by your speaker, if possible. The techniques of good information-gathering interviews should be used at the conference iself.

Be prepared at the first conference to take the lead. You might have to suggest topics or themes. Try to select material that is familiar to your client, since this produces comfort. The speaker will probably do a better job speaking on familiar terrain. Also, be sure to gather information about the intended audience for this speech; begin to develop an audience analysis following the steps in Chapter 10. Try to select material that will be vital and interesting to the potential audience.

Followup Conferences.   After you have gathered the material for the speech, you should produce an outline before writing the first draft of the presentation. It is preferable to share this outline with the speaker before proceeding, although that is not always possible. Certainly, the client needs to see and approve a first draft.

After the speaker has had time to read the first draft, another conference should follow. At each conference, the speechwriter concentrates on the ideas and content as well as on the style and language of the speaker. Interviewing techniques such as probes (discussed earlier in the text) are useful to get the speaker to expand on and to clarify ideas. Your purpose is to understand as fully as possible what the speaker wants. Be sure to listen for the speaker's style as he or she speaks; phrases, word choices, examples, and figures of speech are all important. Does the speaker use a lot of comparisons or analogies to explain points? Does the speaker seem to use long, complex sentences, or shorter sentences? Does the speaker seem to be comfortable with humor? With story-telling? If the speaker is not comfortable telling jokes, don't use them in the text.

Rehearsal and Revision.   Conferences should take place as each new draft is produced and analyzed. If time permits, an oral run-through of the completed speech is a good idea. If you are going to be called upon to help with delivery, this will be a natural part of the process. Remember to review the techniques of rehearsal in Chapter 11, as well as techniques of effective delivery. If possible, record the speaker and review strengths and weakness before taping again, if time permits. All of this depends upon the importance of the speech and the time available, of course. If this presentation is fairly routine, obviously you would not go through all these steps.

After you have produced the manuscript, you might want to do something else, especially if you will be writing other presentations for this individual: Try to observe the presentation or try to get a recording. Hearing the individual in a live situation will provide information about the speaker's abilities and style. For one thing, you might observe whether or not the speaker seemed comfortable with your text. Then after you have reviewed the result, you can start creating files of potential topics for future presentations.

The Pitfalls of Speechwriting

The process may go smoothly at some times but not so well at others. Writing speeches for other people to deliver can be a tricky business, so some pitfalls and dangers to watch for follow.

Ethical Questions. As mentioned earlier, the question of ethics has loomed large in the discussion of speechwriting over the years. The opponents of speechwriting argue that a speaker's style is important in determining the speaker's competence. If the style is really a speechwriter's, then we are being misled about the speaker's competence and even ideas.

Those who feel that speechwriting can be ethical counter with the argument that the speech of an organizational executive is a corporate effort. Just as members of a speaker's bureau represent the organization rather than themselves, the executive does not represent himself or herself but, rather, the organization or corporation. The speech is understood to be the product of an organization, written and presented as an extension of the corporate voice. In other words, it resembles corporate advertising or public relations.

A related issue is the problem of speechwriters being asked to defend a position that conflicts with their own beliefs. Again, the proponents counter that the individual is not the corporation, and that the individual can maintain his or her own values. Frequently, an analogy is to an attorney in our judicial system; the attorney makes the best possible case for clients, regardless of the attorney's own belief. In the same way, the speechwriter makes the best case possible for the corporate position. You can argue for your position within the firm, but you may not convince the whole organization. Of course, if you believe that the policy being put forth is unethical or illegal, then you have a more serious problem. In some jurisdictions, recall that professionals, such as physicians, engineers, or accountants, are required to "blow the whistle" on dangerous or illegal practices. At the least, you may find that you have to turn down the assignment if it seems unethical or dangerous.

Access to the Speaker. Another obvious problem in speechwriting is access to the client-speaker. If the justification for employing a speechwriter is time, then the speaker may not have the time for extensive conferences or consultation. Speeches are produced in relative isolation, especially if the speechwriter lacks samples of the client's style. In political speechwriting, for example, speechwriters frequently lack direct access to the president, or whoever the client is. The result is a speech style that may not be comfortable for the speaker or a speech that has passed through so many hands that every ounce of spark and creativity is gone.

Anonymity. A third problem for the speechwriter is anonymity. Until recently, speechwriters were so far behind the scenes that they were called "ghostwriters." Even now, however, most speechwriters do not receive credit for what they produce. The absence of recognition and, by implication, the absence of reward, produce a certain amount of frustration. Moreover, all of the attention will go to the executive who delivers the presentation. On the other hand, the speechwriter may get some satisfaction from being known to the top members of the organization.

Burnout on Speech Topics.   Another problem with speechwriting is the subjects themselves. Certain topics or repeated topics could produce boredom for the writer. Although a major policy address by the CEO is a stimulating challenge, the fifth or sixth similar presentation may not be as exciting. Further, you might find yourself producing presentations where the need to provide information in a limited time removes any creativity from the process. In effect, you just start spewing out the information as it comes from marketing, or wherever.

Highlights of Speechwriting Pitfalls.   Speechwriting is an old practice; it involves serious, unresolved questions for many speechwriters. The pitfalls listed range from the philosophical, such as the ethics of speechwriting, to the practical, such as the burnout from writing the same speech repeatedly. We have not attempted to do more than suggest the basic pitfalls and problems here. Obviously, the questions

[SMILE]   1

"Thank you—Bill.
And greetings!
The last time we met—**you**
had a tough job to do—
introduce and establish a
totally new line with superb
styling and performance—
but with higher prices. And
you had to rekindle dealer
interest in a product most
dealers had forgotten.

SLIDE ONE
SALES CHART

Well, **you** did both!

▶ *Manuscript layout on the page.*

of ethics previewed here deserve much more serious consideration for a potential speechwriter or a speaker who uses speechwriters.

Developing a Manuscript for a Speech

The basic rule is simple: Make the manuscript as easy to use and to read as possible. The manuscript should be so unobtrusive that the speaker will not appear to be reading. For an effective manuscript, follow these guidelines:

- Use heavy paper (20 lb or more).
- Use just one side of the paper.
- Use wide margins so the speaker sees one line at a glance.
- Make finished copy dark and easy to read.
- Use a large font; use clear fonts or typefaces such as Helvetica, Geneva, Orator, etc.
- Use triple spaces between lines.
- Paragraphing: *Never* carry a sentence or paragraph from one page to the next. Also, use small paragraphs. Use only the top two-thirds of paper. Indicate media or visual aids in margin.
- Avoid staples or paperclips since they are hard to work with.
- Number pages clearly at the top, upper-right.
- Indicate pauses with leaders . . . or dashes —.
- Avoid abbreviations; spell it out.
- Keep statistics or word combinations together.
- For emphasis, underline or **boldface** words.

SUMMARY

This chapter considered two special situations involving helping others with communication needs: communication training and speechwriting.

The principles for good training are basically the same for effective communication: setting goals, analyzing the audience and the occasion, planning, implementing training sessions, and evaluating the effects or feedback. We have provided a sample outline for conducting a public speaking workshop and some guidelines for techniques such as role-playing.

Corporate speechwriting is a widespread practice. The speechwriter needs to adapt the principles and techniques for preparing good presentations to the special situation of writing for another speaker. Important considerations include the relationship between the writer and the speaker, the roles that the writer fulfills, and the need to write in an oral style. We have suggested steps to follow in speechwriting and have discussed some typical pitfalls of speechwriting, particularly ethical questions.

EXERCISES

1. Design and use a role-playing situation to illustrate some interpersonal conflict among students in a university housing unit.

2. Consider the following: Is speechwriting ethical? For politicians? For executives?

3. Prepare a short outline for a 2- to 3-minute presentation. Record the presentation while speaking from the outline. Make a transcription or a manuscript of the presentation. What elements of oral style do you find in the transcription? Now have another student deliver and record the same presentation from your outline. Make a transcription of the second presentation. What differences in style do you find between the two manuscripts?

SELECTED SOURCES FOR FURTHER READING ON TRAINING

Arnold, W. E., & McClure, L. (1989). *Communication training and development*. New York: Harper & Row.

Meiser, J., & Reinsch, N. L. (1978). Communication training in manufacturing firms. *Communication Education*, 27:3, 235–244.

SELECTED SOURCES FOR FURTHER READING ON SPEECHWRITING

Einhorn, L. J. (1981, April). *The ghosts unmasked, a review of literature on speechwriting*. Central States Speech Association Convention, Chicago.

Harte, T. B., Keefe, C., & Derryberry, B. R. (1988). *The complete book of speechwriting* (2nd ed.). Edina, MN: Bellwether Press.

Noonan, P. (1990). *What I saw at the revolution, a political life in the Reagan Era*. New York: Random House.

Tarver, J. (1987). *The corporate speech writer's handbook*. Westport, CT: Greenwood Press.

References

1. Bragg, A. (1989). Is a mentor program in your future? *Sales and Marketing Management*, 141, 54–63; Mendleson, J. L., Barnes, A. K., & Horn, G. (1989). The guiding light to corporate culture. *Personnel Administrator*, 34, 70–72.
2. Meyer, H. E. (1977, August). A $900 lesson in podium power (pp. 196–204). *Fortune*.
3. Deutsch, C. H. (1991, October 27). How is it done? For a small fee . . . (p. F.25). *New York Times*.
4. Neher, W. (1982, September). Audit of consumer services training. Report submitted to Public Service of Indiana.
5. Noonan, P. (1990). *What I saw at the revolution, a political life in the Reagan Era*. New York: Random House.
6. Tarver, J. (1974, February). How to put "good" humor in your next speech (pp. 15–17). *Public Relations Journal*.

CREDITS

INDEX